MAX LERNER

Portrait of Max Lerner as a young man (early 1930s). Courtesy of Edna Albers Lerner.

Max Lerner

*Pilgrim
in the
Promised
Land*

Sanford Lakoff

The University of Chicago Press
Chicago & London

SANFORD LAKOFF is professor of political science (emeritus) at the University of California, where he served as founding chair of his department and continues to teach. Among his books is *Democracy: History, Theory, Practice* (1996). He has held fellowships at the Woodrow Wilson Center for Scholars and the National Humanities Center.

The University of Chicago Press, Chicago 60637
The University of Chicago Press, Ltd., London
© 1998 by The University of Chicago
All rights reserved. Published 1998
Printed in the United States of America
07 06 05 04 03 02 01 00 99 98   1 2 3 4 5

ISBN: 0-226-46831-3 (cloth)

Library of Congress Cataloging-in-Publication Data

Lakoff, Sanford A.
    Max Lerner : pilgrim in the promised land / Sanford Lakoff.
        p.   cm.
    Includes bibliographical references (p.   ) and index.
    ISBN 0-226-46831-3
    1. Lerner, Max, 1902–1992.   2. Political scientists—United States—
Biography.   I. Title.
JC251.L44L35   1998
320.5′092—dc21
    [B]   97-52640
                                                                     CIP

♾ The paper used in this publication meets the minimum requirements of the American National Standard for Information Sciences—Permanence of Paper for Printed Library Materials, ANSI Z39.48-1992.

What then is the American, this new man? . . . Here individuals of all nations are melted into a new race of men, whose labors and posterity will one day cause great changes in the world. Americans are the western pilgrims, who are carrying along with them that great mass of arts, sciences, vigor, and industry which began long since in the east; they will finish the great circle.

—J. Hector St. John Crèvecoeur, *Letters of an American Farmer* (1782)

Contents

"Who is this Max Lerner?"

During a New York newspaper strike in 1963, when only the *Post* continued to be published, the cartoonist imagines the grim reaction of conservative commuters forced to read a liberal columnist. Drawing by F. B. Modell; ©1963 The New Yorker Magazine, Inc. (p. 43).

From the early 1930s through the 1960s, and to a gradually diminishing extent until his death at the age of eighty-nine in 1992, Max Lerner was a prominent writer, teacher, and political commentator. His life history and the course of his thinking chart many of the changing tides of American experience over the century. During the Great Depression he was a militant advocate of democratic socialism. After Pearl Harbor, he helped rally support for a "people's war" to be followed by a "people's peace." By the late 1940s, he became a centrist liberal in favor of containment abroad and continued reform at home. In the 1950s, he experienced what *Time* magazine described as a "crush on America." [1] In later decades he became a cultural and political maverick, endorsing some aspects of the erotic revolution of the 1960s and 1970s and of the conservative politics of the 1980s. Throughout, he saw himself as an earnest seeker after truth and civic engagement guided by the motto he took from Justice Oliver Wendell Holmes, Jr.: "As life is action and passion, it is required of a man that he should share the passion and action of his time at peril of being judged not to have lived." [2]

During his lifetime, his writings attracted a devoted following, and many of his books and essays continue to be read with enjoyment and appreciation. His essays have been reprinted in dozens of anthologies. His first book, a tract for the times brashly entitled *It Is Later than You Think*, appeared in 1938, was reissued in 1943, and republished in 1989. "Those of us who read it at the time," the political scientist and historian James MacGregor Burns has recalled, "may still remember the bracing effect it had on our minds, our hearts, and our hopes."[3] In the 1940s came several compilations and editions with typically vivid titles: *Ideas Are Weapons, Ideas for the Ice Age, The Mind and Faith of Justice Holmes, Public Journal,* and *Actions and Passions.* His magnum opus, *America as a Civilization,* appeared in 1957 after a decade of writing and revision; it was hailed by eminent reviewers as a rich synthesis worthy of comparison with the classic studies of Tocqueville and Bryce. Over 100,000 copies were sold in English and in translation, and it was reissued thirty years later in an anniversary edition. In the following two decades he published another compilation of his columns, *The Unfinished Country,* as well as *Tocqueville and American Civilization,* originally written as an introduction to an edition of *Democracy in America; The Age of Overkill,* a study of world politics in the shadow of nuclear weapons; two short books on education, *Education and a Radical Humanism* and *Values and Education;* and *Ted and the Kennedy Legend.* Even in his last, illness-wracked years he managed to work on *Nine Scorpions in a Bottle,* a compilation of his judicial essays edited by Richard Cummings, and to publish *Wrestling with the Angel,* an account of his struggle with cancer and aging.

Posthumously have come his *Thomas Jefferson: America's Philosopher-King* and *Wounded Titans: American Presidents and the Perils of Power,* a collection of essays, both brought to light and ably edited by Professor Robert Schmuhl of the University of Notre Dame. Also widely read were his gem-like introductions to the Viking Portable edition of Veblen, an edition of the writings of John Stuart Mill, the Modern Library editions of Aristotle's *Politics,* Machiavelli's *Prince* and *Discourses,* and Adam Smith's *The Wealth of Nations,* lately assembled by Professor Schmuhl in a single volume entitled *Magisterial Imagination.*

In addition to books, Lerner's published writings include many essays and reviews and a strcam of newspaper columns written over almost fifty years. It can safely be said that no American writer in the century wrote for as many different audiences. His earliest academic work appeared in the *Encyclopaedia of the Social Sciences,* of which he was appointed managing editor in 1927, right out of graduate school, and then in the *Dictionary of American Biography*. His articles and reviews, along with unsigned editorials, appeared first in *The Nation*, when he was its political editor in 1938, then also in *The New Republic*, to which he was a contributing editor. He wrote for journals like *The Atlantic Monthly*, *The Saturday Review of Literature*, *The American Scholar*, and *Foreign Affairs*, for several Ivy League law reviews, and for such mass circulation magazines as *The Ladies' Home Journal* and *Playboy*. His newspaper columns (some 7,000 in all) were followed most closely in New York, first by readers of the short-lived but innovative *PM*, then in the *New York Post*, and in later years by a broader national and international audience. During the peak of his influence, his column was syndicated in more than seventy newspapers, reaching readers in most of the major cities of this country and some overseas.

While doing all this writing, and traveling far and wide to interview foreign leaders, he had what amounted to a second career as a teacher and lecturer. Although he treasured the introspective solitude that writing requires, he thrived on the give and take of the classroom and lecture hall, especially the classroom because it kept him in touch with the young and reinforced his determination to remain youthful in spirit. He held teaching appointments at Sarah Lawrence, Williams, Harvard, Brandeis (for the longest period), and in later years at United States International University in southern California and at Notre Dame. In 1959–1960, he was a Ford Foundation professor circuit riding the Indian subcontinent from a base at the School of International Studies in New Delhi. During several summers he took part in the American-sponsored Salzburg Seminar in Austria. He was often on radio and television, beginning with such popular public affairs programs in the 1940s as "Invitation to Learning," "Town Meeting of the Air," the "Chicago Round Table," and his own fifteen-minute Sunday New York radio program. He continued into the television era as a panelist on such programs as "The David Susskind Show," "The Open Mind," and "Meet the Press," and as the host of a Public Broadcasting System series of his own, "The Age of Overkill," based on his book. He was especially popular with the liberal New Yorkers who loyally enrolled in the adult education course he offered each year in the fall at the New School for Social Research in Manhattan.

A frequent speaker on university and college campuses and in lecture halls all across the country, he spoke to college presidents for the American Council on Education and to countless gatherings of teachers. For several years he was invited by the State Department to talk to foreign service officers and by the Army War College to lecture to high-ranking officers. He relished invitations to appear in debates, seeing himself as a pint-sized Anteus who would prove his own strength by taking on all comers. Again, it is safe to say that no one in his time made so many public appearances before so many different audiences. The archive cartons housing his papers in the Sterling Library at Yale University are fairly bursting with letters thanking him for his talks and praising his eloquence—including one from Justice Hugo Black, who wrote in 1943, after listening to Lerner over the radio, "Few men have the gift you possess to think profoundly and speak simply." [4]

Lerner's way with words brought him to my notice while I was still in high school in Bayonne, New Jersey, a medium-sized city in the New York metropolitan area that proclaimed itself "the peninsula of industry." By coincidence, the Lerner family had lived there for several years shortly after arriving in America, though his memories of a Bayonne boyhood were not as fond as my own. Lerner was then the chief editorial writer for the newspaper *PM*, and I found his work captivating, especially as I was then a budding journalist. Many others also found his "opinion pieces" in *PM* inspiring and even electrifying. In the best-seller *Inside USA* (1947), the journalist John Gunther took humorous note of Lerner's growing celebrity. A "Bourbon friend," he claimed, had remarked that the most powerful influence over the United States was being exerted from—of all places—the Russian city of Minsk. Why Minsk? "Because Minsk is the birthplace of Max Lerner . . . Lerner runs *PM*. *PM* runs the American Labor Party. The American Labor Party runs New York City. New York City runs New York State. And New York State runs the country." [5]

When *PM* went under in 1948 and was replaced briefly by the *New York Star* (whose one moment of glory came when it was the only one of the city's papers to support Harry Truman in 1948), Lerner wrote a column just before the election announcing he would "throw his vote away" on Norman Thomas, the perennial Socialist candidate, because it had become obvious that Truman could not win.* Shortly after Truman's upset victory over Governor

---

*Many years later he revealed to his readers in the *New York Post* that when he entered the voting booth he changed his mind and voted for Truman.

Thomas Dewey, Lerner came to Bayonne to give a public lecture in the auditorium of my grammar school. I took a seat in the first row of the balcony and could hardly wait for him to finish his talk so I could ask him how he could have made such a blunder. "I was wrong," I remember him saying frankly, explaining that he had failed to appreciate how much working people who were worried about pocketbook issues trusted Truman more than the "do-nothing" Republicans.

He was as appealing in person as in print. Although comparatively short, at under five feet, seven inches, and not handsome by the usual standard, he had a striking stage presence and an expressive face that could be serious and pensive one minute and the next brightened by an irresistibly warm and winning smile and twinkling brown eyes. His voice was deep and distinctive, remarkably free of any regional accent, his diction impeccable, and his intonations rich in emotional range. Like Chaucer's Friar, "he lisped a little, out of wantonness, to make his English soft upon his tongue." He could have become an actor in youth, somewhat after the manner and appearance of John Garfield or, later, Edward G. Robinson; even more certainly a great trial lawyer like his friend Louis Nizer.

An adolescent with my upbringing and fascination with the written and spoken word could hardly have found a more satisfying role model. Sometime in 1949, I listened to a trans-Atlantic "Town Meeting of the Air" radio broadcast debating the question of economic planning—a major theme of postwar contention in Friedrich Hayek's *The Road to Serfdom*, and Barbara Wootton's response, *Freedom under Planning*. Lerner and his friend and British counterpart Harold J. Laski were paired against an American businessman and a British Tory. Lerner and Laski were in top form, Laski especially, and it seemed to me (though I was predisposed to them) that they had the best of the argument. I remember only the rhetorical flourishes, not the arguments. Laski deftly deflected one verbal firecracker. "I'm a student of Professor Laski's at the London School of Economics," one hostile questioner observed, "and I should like to ask him how he proposes to introduce socialism to this country without relying on the guns and barbed wire of the Soviet Union." After the mixture of applause and boos had died down, the crowd waited hushed and expectant. Laski answered, in a gently ironic tone, "I should venture to suggest that the young man has taken too many courses with Professor Lionel Robbins [a champion of free market economics at the LSE] and not enough of my own." * When the American businessman warned that socialism would crush all personal initiative, Lerner rose to the challenge and answered proudly that when the Tennessee Valley Authority was created during the New Deal, "the valley blossomed like a rose," bringing widespread prosperity to the entire region. Laski's performance sent me to my favorite haunt, Bayonne's splendid Public Library—ironically, the contribution of that arch capitalist, Andrew Carnegie—where I read everything available by him. Laski became my foreign idol, Lerner my household god, though I reserved a niche for the moral iconoclast Philip Wylie, a kind of popular Nietzschean, whose *A Generation of Vipers* excited my youthful skepticism toward the unreasoning conventions of organized religion and the hypocrisies of middle-class morality.

In the summer of 1949, on being accepted for admission to Columbia, Brandeis, and Rutgers, I chose Brandeis because it was new, farthest from home, and offered a tuition scholarship. When the newspapers reported that Lerner would teach there, I felt sure I had made the right choice. His first class met in a large lecture hall on the ground floor of "the Castle," then the major building on campus. It was open only to "seniors" (as those in the first class, then actually sophomores, were called), so I stood outside the open door and listened. I think I took every course he gave, slaving over term papers for him. On one of them, he wrote a comment I have smarted over ever since. Unsure how to end the paper, I resorted to a time-honored evasion by writing, "How this will turn out, time alone will tell." He gave the paper an "A" and commented, in his thick black newspaperman's copy pencil, that it had "one of those 'lap of the gods' endings." I have tried never again to be quite so equivocal.

My adulation soon became obvious and made me the butt of jokes. Lerner had a barely noticeable flesh-colored mole on one side of his nose. When a much more repellent wart suddenly sprang up on a middle finger of mine, some of my classmates claimed it was psychosomatic and that I was rubbing it against my own nose in the hope I would get to look more like him. Sophomoric humor

---

*Lerner credited Laski with another classic put-down which seems too good not to have a more venerable pedigree. Heckled once by a listener who claimed he was deviating from Marx's thinking, Laski is said to have replied, as if intending to mollify the heckler: "My dear comrade, we both follow the same master, you in your way, I in his."

aside, he was entitled to some hero worship because he was in many ways an exemplary teacher. Occasionally, he lectured in formal style, but he preferred a Socratic give-and-take, whatever the size of the class. Because he was also a working journalist, he often brought the real world into the ivory tower. One day in 1949, a bleary-eyed Lerner opened his introductory politics course by saying, "I was up all night with John L. Lewis" (the United Mine Workers of America leader favored by cartoonists for his great bushy eyebrows), and he proceeded to give us a blow-by-blow account of their exchange on the situation of labor in the postwar world. The course he created on American civilization was famous for its informal style. Draft chapters of the book on which he was at work were distributed in blue-typed offset versions, and we were expected to read them and to be prepared to discuss them in class. He would sit on the lip of the stage flanked by two younger assistants, dubbed the "bookends," and lead the discussion.

In the early years, one of the bookends was Leonard W. Levy, who subsequently won a Pulitzer Prize and has become a canonical authority on American constitutional history. Another was Merrill D. Peterson, who was to be appointed the Jefferson Professor at the University of Virginia and won the coveted Bancroft Prize for his study of the Jefferson image. They were not there by accident. Lerner did his best to hire bright young assistants and also to help recruit the best middle-rank and senior faculty available. He wanted us to have the chance to study with gifted teachers, and it didn't bother him in the least that we might find some of them more learned or inspiring than he was. Thanks in no small part to him and to Frank E. Manuel, another superb teacher, the campus attracted an outstanding faculty in the history of social thought and social theory, including, in the early years, Lewis Coser, Philip Rieff, Herbert Marcuse, and such visiting faculty as the historians E. H. Carr and Henry Steele Commager and the sociologists C. Wright Mills and Hans Gerth. A British political scientist who taught there remarked with good reason that Brandeis was "a kind of Oxford of the mind."

As a teacher, Lerner was keenly concerned for his students and generous toward them. When I called his attention to a minor error in one of the draft chapters, he not only sent a note of thanks but accompanied it with the present of a book. He inspired students like me, who would become academics, Martin Peretz, who was to follow in his footsteps by becoming both an academic and editor-in-chief

of *The New Republic,* and Stephen Solarz, who was to serve im-
pressively in Congress. Lerner also set a standard for aspiring journalists of an analytical bent who knew him only from his work, like
the radio and television reporter Sander Vanocur. He was fun to be
with, in or out of class. He could be deadly serious one minute and
the next pass on some old wheeze like, "Everything I know I learned
at my mother's knee—and at other low joints." He loved to quote
clever sayings and well-turned phrases and was self-critical enough
to cite the well-known satirical rhyme about journalists: "You cannot bribe, thank God, or twist / the British journalist / But seeing
what unbribed he'll do / There really is no need to." At a time when
most teachers were especially careful to be straight-laced with students *(in loco parentis),* he was utterly uninhibited in a way that I
for one found as refreshingly honest as it was surprising.

He also had the artful teacher's way of turning a student's poorly
worded question into a smooth and pointed inquiry. "I think what
the young man is trying to say," he would begin, and proceed to
make a silk purse out of a sow's ear of a question. The "young man"
would usually think for a moment and say, "Yeah, that's what I had
in mind." But much as we liked it when he performed this rhetorical alchemy, we resented the paternalism that seemed to lurk behind
it. We were therefore delighted when one evening he got his come-
uppance. He had initiated a course eventually called "General Education S" (for seniors) in which notable people would present intellectual autobiographies, emphasizing their crises and turning
points. The visitor for that class was Alexander Meiklejohn, an
older man famous as an educational innovator. At one point, Lerner arose to help clarify something Meiklejohn had said and made
the mistake of treating him as though he were one of his students.
"I think what Mr. Meiklejohn is trying to say," he began in his
usual fashion, whereupon Meiklejohn interjected, with some heat,
"Goddam it, Max, when I want to say something, I will; I don't need
you to interpret for me." We cheered lustily, feeling what I might
now be tempted to describe as a *frisson* of *Schadenfreude.*

In my senior year I was fortunate to receive several fellowship
offers for graduate study in political science. At the time I was naive
enough to suppose they were all awarded in recognition of my own
irresistible qualities, but in retrospect I feel sure they were due
rather more to the letters of recommendation Lerner must have
written on my behalf. When I went on to graduate school at Harvard, my earlier journalistic impulse having been nipped in the bud

by exposure to the social sciences, I kept in touch with him for the next few years, but thereafter saw him only rarely. At Harvard I came under the spell of two renowned teachers of political theory, Carl J. Friedrich and Louis Hartz. As will become evident, Hartz's interpretation of American political thought colors my understanding of the shifts in Lerner's thinking.

Lerner's writings and his career as a teacher and lecturer put him in touch with some of the leading figures of his time. These included Laski and several Supreme Court justices. (The Max Lerner Papers at Yale include approximately 350 letters to and from Felix Frankfurter, dating from both before and after he was appointed to the high court.) He had warm and thoughtful exchanges with many prominent political liberals, including Chester Bowles, Arthur Goldberg, Vice President Hubert H. Humphrey (who thanked him for being "a wonderful friend")[6] and Eleanor Roosevelt; with such foreign leaders as U Nu of Burma, Michael Manley of Jamaica, and the Israeli prime ministers David Ben-Gurion and Moshe Sharett; and with the historians Carl Lotus Becker, Arthur Schlesinger, Jr., and Commager. His columns on the work of writers, artists, dramatists, and film makers, including Edward Albee, Robert Ardrey, James Baldwin, Albert Camus, Marc Chagall, Charlie Chaplin, Dore Schary, Robert Frost, Hugh Hefner, Langston Hughes, Louis Malle, André Malraux, Irwin Shaw, Lillian Smith, Thomas Wolfe, and Tennessee Williams, evoked appreciative responses from them and often led to warm friendships.

Many who read and heard him swore by, others at, his provocative opinions. In the '30s and early '40s, he championed a social goal he described as "democratic collectivism." From the late '40s through the '70s, he became a leading spokesman for those who came to be called liberals, in the modern American sense of the term. He opposed efforts to overturn New Deal regulatory and welfare programs. He was a consistent and outspoken critic of all forms of bigotry and discrimination* and a strong supporter of civil lib-

---

*In 1943, when irrefutable evidence was received confirming reports of the Nazis' systematic campaign to eradicate the Jews of Europe, Lerner spared no effort to rouse public awareness and end the indifference to their plight at the highest levels of government. In an editorial for *PM* the same year supporting fair employment laws and an end to the "Jim Crow" law in the armed forces, he wrote: "What have we done to ease the daily crucifixion of the Negro in our midst, which leaves him with nothing but smoldering bitterness?" (June 23, 1943). He was proud that his first honorary degree was conferred by Wilberforce University,

erties. In foreign policy, he supported both containment of communism and diplomatic efforts to achieve arms control. In the '80s, he adopted a more "centrist" position in sympathy with efforts by conservatives to promote economic growth and curtail the size of government.

During the McCarthy years, so-called superpatriots tried, sometimes successfully, to prevent him from speaking in public. They cited House Un-American Activities Committee reports listing his membership in what were described, using the loosest criteria, as Communist-front organizations, though he had never been a Communist and by then was staunchly anti-Communist. In 1949 a teacher in a Buffalo, New York, high school was fired for posting a notice of a lecture by Lerner, and was restored to his job only after the case went to the state Supreme Court. In the 1960s, *America as a Civilization* was removed from a reading list in a town in Illinois for citing Alfred Kinsey's findings on sexual behavior.

Other adversaries, to their credit, were more tolerant and even admiring. Barry Goldwater publicly praised him for his steadfast liberalism; Ronald Reagan once told Richard Nixon that he always read Lerner's column;[7] even the once notorious isolationist, Senator Burton K. Wheeler, wrote to agree with one of his columns in 1969 and confided, "I read your column rather religiously."[8] When Richard Nixon retired to New Jersey, a decade after he had included Lerner on his "enemies list" in the early 1970s, he invited Lerner to dinner and they enjoyed each other's company, the more so because Lerner had by then become outspokenly critical of many liberal pieties. To younger, self-confident conservatives, like William F. Buckley, Jr., who addressed him as *"mon vieux,"* he was a worthy model and foe. The *Cleveland Plain Dealer,* which ran both their columns, advertised the rivalry gleefully: "Buckley's got a lightning right, but just watch Lerner's left . . ."[9]

---

the nation's oldest black-sponsored campus, in recognition of his ardent support of the struggle for civil rights. During the same period, he denounced the wartime relocation of Japanese-Americans as "the most glaring instance of military injustice to civilians in our whole history" (April 6, 1944). Other commentators were not as outspoken in defense of human rights. Walter Lippmann, for one, kept silent about the Nazi persecution of the Jews and the American government's indifference to their plight, as well as about racial segregation of blacks and the wartime relocation of Japanese-Americans. (For Lippmann's views see Ronald Steel, *Walter Lippmann and the American Century* [Boston: Little, Brown, 1980], pp. 373–374, 394, 550.)

Lerner used his newspaper column as his bully pulpit. Although he sometimes wrote on whatever struck his fancy—including the joys of fatherhood, the latest plays and books, championship boxing matches, and sensational murder cases—most of the columns dealt with politics, domestic and international. Unlike other political reporters and pundits, he did not confine his commentaries to the analysis of the day's events, but often tried to set these events into some broader context, drawing upon the latest historical studies and psychological theories.

He did not hesitate to speak his mind on burning issues or to change it when he realized he had been mistaken. Describing himself as a "secular Jew," he never wavered in his passionate support for Israel's independence and security, agreeing with Henry Kissinger, whose diplomatic efforts he greatly admired, that "Israel has a special moral claim on the world's conscience." Yet, at the young state's moment of greatest triumph, at the end of the Six-Day War in 1967, he urged the people of Israel to seek peaceful coexistence with their Arab neighbors and to help resolve the plight of Arab refugees. Several years later, he supported consideration of a plan under which, in exchange for Arab recognition, Israel would return its territorial conquests and agree to the internationalization of Jerusalem. He championed the right of all peoples to self-determination and freedom from colonialism—especially the Burmese, for whom he had a particular fondness. Although drawn to Henry Wallace's visionary belief in "the era of the common man" in the early 1940s, he refused to support Wallace's campaign for the presidency in 1948 when he saw that Wallace had naively allowed Communists to infiltrate the party and failed to appreciate the real threat of Soviet expansionism. When Whittaker Chambers accused Alger Hiss of espionage, Lerner was at first skeptical of the charge and, like many a defensive liberal, more inclined to take the word of a New Dealer (and Frankfurter protégé) than that of an admitted ex-Communist. But when Chambers produced the "pumpkin papers" and laid out his case in compelling detail in *Witness,* Lerner recanted and praised the book as one of the most important of the era. He denounced the Communists for trying to manipulate Jewish feelings over the atomic espionage prosecution of Julius and Ethel Rosenberg, and argued that the death penalty pronounced upon them was understandable in view of the harm their spying had done. But when expert scientists testified that the Rosenbergs' espionage had been of comparatively little importance, he urged that the sentence be commuted to life imprisonment. In the 1950s, he was among the first to publicize the Kinsey Report's findings about sexual behavior, praising it for breaking the taboo on the discussion of sexual behavior while criticizing its reductionist avoidance of related psychological and emotional dimensions. He won the deep appreciation of homosexuals, some of whom wrote anonymously to thank him, for writing objectively and sympathetically about what was known about the sources of their sexual preference and about their plight as social outcasts.

In the 1960s, he wrestled with the problem of the Vietnam War—as much a moral and political quagmire for liberals like Lerner as it was a military quagmire for the American armed forces. At first he defended the Vietnam policy of the Kennedy and Johnson administrations, out of a belief that American military involvement was vital for the defense of freedom and the containment of communism. This put him at odds with his own two draft-age sons and many others of their generation, until in 1966 he began to express deep misgivings both about the depth of the American involvement and what was at stake. He continued to disagree with those who called for a unilateral American pull-out. Throughout, he urged that the war be kept limited, in the hope that it would lead to a settlement after the precedent of Korea.

In 1993, after Lerner's death, I was invited to contribute a paper to a memorial symposium at Brandeis organized by Professor Lawrence Fuchs at the suggestion of Peretz. The paper was published the following year in the journal *Social Research*.[10] I am grateful to the editors for allowing use of passages from it here. Renewed interest, coupled with nostalgic feelings heightened by the passage of time, led me to want to do this biography. As I began to gather materials, Lerner's eldest daughter, Connie Lerner Russell, called my attention to a videotape of an interview he did in 1990 with her daughter Daria. His son Steve kindly let me make use of an uncompleted memoir his father had begun too late to finish. Because there is practically no documentation for these early years and because Lerner himself gives so enthralling an account of them, I begin with an edited version in his own words drawn from both sources. Otherwise unattributed references and quotations in later chapters are also drawn from the memoir. Although newspaper journalism is notoriously perishable, many of Lerner's writings remain very much worth reading, for style as well as substance—as the recent reissue of most of his books goes to show. But they must stand the test of time on their own. My aim, above all else, is to re-trace his life and thought for what it reveals about his encounter with "American civilization." In so doing, I will pay particular attention to the major book in which he developed his view on that subject as well as to the evolution of his political and cultural views in other writings and comments, both published and unpublished. In dealing with Lerner's personal life, I have kept in mind his own comments on the writing of biographies. "Some day," he quoted Walt Whitman admonishing a friend, "you will be writing about me: be sure to write honest; whatever you do, do not prettify me: include all the hells and damns." In a newspaper column, Lerner praised Irving Fineman's biography of the Zionist leader Henrietta Szold for being truthful about her love life:

> The author has dared to break the tradition that a biography of a great and respected person must never tear away the veil hiding the inner life, especially where *Eros* is involved. The result of the tradition has usually been stuffy and stilted biographies, even when the life behind them has been covered with scar tissue. I take my hat off to Fineman for using the private papers, letters and diaries of Miss Szold as sensitively but as forthrightly as he has done.[11]

To the best of my ability, I will follow his injunction and try to present him sensitively and honesty—including some of the scar tissue.

Sanford Lakoff
La Jolla, California

From Minsk to Manhood
A Memoir by Max Lerner

*I was delivered by a midwife some-
time in December 1902 shortly after my mother and I both had a narrow
escape from death by drowning. She was in the late stages of pregnancy
with me when labor pains made her swoon in the* mikva, *the Jewish ritual
bath. After being rescued and revived, she was taken home, where she
soon gave birth to me. Otto Rank says that the birth of the hero is always
accompanied by omens. The circumstances of mine may at least account
for a life-long terror of swimming.*

*Years later I thought of my mother's account of our mutual deliverance
when I encountered Dryden's observation on love:*

*Love still has something of the sea
From which his Mother came.*

We lived in a shtetl *or little town called Iveniz in the district around
the White Russian city of Minsk, on the border of Poland. The peasants
there spoke Polish, not Russian, because control over the land tended to
rotate between the two countries. I remember some things about my childhood. I can recall sitting on a stoop when I was four with a little girl
named Hannah—*Channele *in Yiddish—holding hands and spooning
with her. This was very early, but I remember my sentimental feelings*

about her. And I remember a few other things, like the big gray brick ovens in my mother's and grandparents' house.

I have no way of knowing how far back the family goes. Physically, I belong to the Russian branch of the Jews, the branch that has broad Slavic faces and squashed pug noses like mine rather than the narrow faces and sharp noses thought of as Levantine or Semitic. There must have been a fair amount of intermingling between my Jewish ancestors and ethnic Russians over the centuries—perhaps, as has been speculated, with the Khazzars who are said to have converted to Judaism in medieval times and then dispersed throughout the region. My grandfather's name was Duvid *or David and my grandmother's* Gita Reza, Reza *meaning "redhead" like Gorbachev's Raissa. My grandfather died in his seventies. My grandmother lived to be a hundred. She died of fright when the Nazi soldiers invaded her village during World War II.*

My father Benyumin (Benjamin) *was one of two children. He adopted the name Lerner. Our family name had been Ranes, but he took a new name in order to avoid military service. He was one of two children, but if you appeared on the records as an only child you could escape being taken off by the Czar's recruiting officers. In Yiddish a* lerner *is someone who cares about learning. The name must have been chosen deliberately, because my father was a* Yeshiva bocher, *a kind of Talmudic graduate student, a religiously learned young man who read the* Torah, *the sacred writings, and moved around to spread the light. He had no money but would circulate through the Jewish villages in the area and board with different families who felt honored to have such a guest.*

My mameh, *or mother, whose name was* Basha (Bessie) Podberesky, *came from a relatively more affluent family in a different* shtetl *near Vilna. Her father had owned a livery and transport service and an inn where the peasant drivers drank and congregated. A distant younger cousin, later to become a leader of the Labor Party in Israel, adopted a more Hebrew-sounding name and became known as Shimon Peres.*

Their marriage was arranged by a shadchen, *a marriage broker. He was twenty-four, she twenty, and they seemed to like each other. She was a black-eyed, raven-haired beauty who was a barmaid at the inn as early as sixteen. Years later, in school, when I read Walter de la Mare's poem,* The Highwayman, *I recognized her in "Bess the black-eyed daughter of the innkeeper." She was twenty-eight when she gave birth to me. I was her fourth child, really her sixth because she had twins who did not survive. She was a passionate woman, who loved strongly and was very independent. She was the dominant parent.* Tateh, *my father, was gentle, handsome—with a broad nose, though, like mine. They were not an ideal couple. My father was not strong enough for my mother, and for all I know he may not have been romantic enough. As was often the case in Jewish families in which the husband was preoccupied with teaching and learning, she had to assume the burden of leading the family, becoming the aggressive one, the active one. My father was always very gentle, very learned, not good at business or at daily life, though he worked very hard. Later in life, long after my own Oedipal phase, when I discovered Freud's views on the role of the father in the family and on the parricidal reaction to that role, I thought that they applied much more to the conjectural early history of the race than to the Russian-Jewish culture, with its lovable dreamlike fathers of gentle learning and its strong-willed mothers.*

When my maternal grandfather was suddenly found dead near his abandoned horse and wagon, probably the victim of foul play, the young couple moved to Iveniz where they set up a general store. In 1902, while my mother was pregnant with me, my father decided to go to America, leaving the store in her care. She went on running it by herself for four years before we were able to follow him. The children—two sisters and a brother and then I, the youngest—remained with my mother until he was able to send for us in the summer of 1907.

We left because of persecution. The pogroms became frequent just around the time I was born and a little later. Our store had a small bar where drinks were sold to the peasants, who would sometimes brawl at night. I remember the fear my parents had that there might be some ugly incidents. I don't have any personal memories of pogroms, but I remember them worrying that the peasants might at some point get drunk and start savaging us. Tateh set forth as an outrider to reconnoiter the new world. Not long after he left came the Kishinev pogrom on Easter Sunday in 1903, when a mob rampaged through a Jewish community, murdering, raping, wounding, and pillaging, and then razed 1,500 homes while the police stood by.

Finally, he had saved enough money to bring us to America. I remember little about our trip to Bremerhaven but a good deal about the voyage from there, above all the anxiety we had about this fateful decision, which drew us from our home in our familiar shtetl and cast us into the cold world outside, amidst alien people and languages. Why had we left the big warm room I had loved in our combination of store and house, and the stone fireplace that could prop you up at night, and where the family could keep a glesele tée, a little glass of tea, hot on the hearth? This was a question beyond a child's capacity to answer. But I have since then often wondered what physical or metaphysical passion drove millions of families like ours across the ocean in that first decade of the new century when

Jewish emigration from Eastern Europe to America was at its height. For hundreds of years the Jews had endured so many uprootings, crossings, resettlements, that constant wandering, dispersal or "diaspora" seemed a perpetual fate. But this convulsive movement was different. It embodied a single-purpose, tenacious will to get to the goldene medineh, *the golden land, and settle there for good.*

We crossed the ocean in an old hulk of a ship of the sort that was used in those days to ferry great numbers of immigrants. We were in steerage, a gaping Black Hole which offered none of the luxuries of beds or mattresses or blankets or even food. You brought what you could of your own, bedded down as you could, survived on the food you had carried on board. During the day we went on deck to escape into the sun, to talk and mend clothes. The tossing made life in the hold intolerable, so mameh *decided we should take our belongings out on deck and sleep there. I had constant nose bleeds, and she fed me syrupy stewed prunes, which I loved, to help me over them. The ship was slow-moving and the voyage took sixteen or eighteen days. A few days out, we had a collision at sea with a little Portuguese fishing boat and we all rushed to see what had happened. Fortunately the fishermen were saved and our ship did not sustain the damage we feared.*

At last we approached land, and excitement grew as we passed the raised torch of Liberty, standing there as a protecting as well as a welcoming goddess. But when we came ashore on Ellis Island, we felt a new fear— fear that we might be prevented from entering the country because of some sort of illness or infirmity. The stories had circulated aboard ship. They would inspect everything: your scalp, your teeth, your ears, your eyes—especially your eyes! I worried about my right ear, which had been running ever since it had become infected from scarlet fever and pneumonia in infancy. But to our great relief we all passed the tests and were allowed in.

I remember seeing our relatives standing around outside, waiting to receive the "greenhorns" and show us the ropes. One of my more vivid memories is what happened when we first came out. There was my father, of course, standing with seven or eight other family members and then running toward us and I running toward him. This was my first embrace of my father, his first embrace of me.

Then the four children were lined up by age. The question of names was important because we had only Yiddish names. Together, we ran down the list of forenames. My aunt and uncle would ask, what is this one called? "Chaya Elke?" No, she must be Ida. This one was "Sorke" (Sarah)—so she became Sadie. (She never liked the name Sadie; she changed it to Sylvia later on.) And then came my brother. What is this one? "Chaim." *So he became Hyman. Then they came to me:* "Who is the little one?" *The little one, we said, is* "Mikhail." "Mikhail," *they said questioningly.* "Oh, that's 'Michael,' but you can't call a Jewish boy 'Michael'—it's an Irish name"—*so instead of Michael I became Max.*

Ida was petite and dark; Sylvia started as dark but rapidly learned as she grew up that hair could be dyed; she lived the rest of her life as a blonde. Both were beautiful, each in her own way. Hyman was very talented, a brilliant boy, two-and-a-half years older than me. I lived in their shadow, of course, particularly Hyman's. He was my older brother and I looked up to him. I was the one who tagged along after them.

We had a warm, cohesive family life, even though we were always on the rim of danger. We never knew where the next meal was coming from. Father's lodgings had been the garment loft where he worked for four years; he had not rented a room for himself because he only earned six or seven dollars a week and wanted to save it all in order to bring over the family. When his pay increased to ten dollars a week, he became a "boarder," with a room in someone's flat, and kitchen privileges. By the time he had enough to send for us, he was earning twelve dollars a week. When we did come over, he gave up his job sewing clothes and did what he knew best to make a living, which was to give Hebrew lessons, by which he earned a little more. From his garment work he had somehow saved up not only enough to bring us all over but seven hundred dollars extra. One of my earliest memories after getting off the boat was standing with my father on line at the bank. This was during the panic of 1907, and there was a run on the bank. His seven hundred dollars was all that he had—all that stood between us and starvation—and he was scared to death of losing it all. So we stood for hours in line as they tried to slow down the panic. Finally we got to the cashier where the teller examined tateh's savings passbook carefully and just as carefully counted out the money. He was given the savings in silver dollars, so it took a long time to count out. I remember his relief and exaltation when the counting was over and he had his precious treasure back.

From that time on, my mother never trusted banks. She put whatever money we had in a little cloth bag which she tied around her neck and wore day and night. I recall once waking up in the middle of the night hearing her scream because the cloth bag was missing. We all wept with her. What had happened? She was sure it had been stolen. We would be destitute, she cried, completely without money. We searched frantically all over. At last, with a feeling of enormous relief, she discovered the little cloth bag under the bed. The string holding it around her neck had been

*worn down so much by her sweat that it had come apart during the night
and the bag had fallen off. At that near-miraculous discovery, of course,
our weeping turned to joy. Our entire family future had turned on a rot-
ting piece of cord, but when the unlikely amulet it held around her neck
was restored, it was as if its magic was working for us again.*

    *Our daily life had many moments of happiness and warmth, but like
the folk culture in which it had been shaped, it was pervaded by a fear
that all happiness would somehow end in sorrow. I remember a sentimental Yiddish song we sang about the king and queen and the little bird that
expressed this mixture of joy and melancholy. It tells of a king who had a
queen who had a palace and a vineyard. In the vineyard there was a tree
and on the tree a branch, and on the branch a little nest, and in the nest a
little bird. But suddenly all is ruined. The king dies, the queen is desolate,
the branch is broken, the bird gone from the nest. And then the mythic
veil is lifted and the comparison with our own lives is drawn overtly:*

    *Ach, feygele, vos kukst du mir un
    Das ich kenn sich kein rihr nit tun?
    Az och un veh zu unsere yuren
    Vos fun uns beide iz gevoren!*

*"Little bird, why do you look at me, / when I cannot even make a move? /
Woe to our years / to think of what has become of us both."**

    *But against all our doubt and skepticism we also lived with the hope
that by hard work and perseverance we could somehow elude the fury of
fate—a hope that was all too often dashed by misfortune. The first misfortune was cultural. Our new life in America began in New York where
my father taught Hebrew to children. But we had to be Americanized,
and the sooner the better, so Hyman and I were taught only enough Hebrew to get through our bar mitzvahs. For the children, English was the
language to learn and use, not Hebrew, not even Yiddish. The need to
change language cut us off from our past, but it was harmful in a different
way to our parents. Because they had no command over this new language, they lost a measure of parental authority over us. They became
outsiders in this new culture, "greenhorns" and second-class citizens,
while we children became their ambassadors and mediators rather than
offspring who would learn from them and follow in their footsteps. As we
played and ran about and learned our new language in the wonderful*

---

    *The song is entitled *A Mol Iz Geven a Mayse.* See Eleanor Gordon Mlotek,
ed., *Mir Trogen a Gezang: Favorite Yiddish Songs of Our Generation* (New York:
Education Department of the Workmen's Circle, 1972). The last stanza is not included in this version.

school of the streets, tateh *read his books in Hebrew,* mameh *read Tolstoy and other authors in Yiddish, and both read a Yiddish newspaper and saw plays given in Yiddish on Grand Street featuring the actors Jacob Adler and Boris Tomashevsky. The alienating effect of the double language was even greater, I think, than the loss of religious belief and ritual we experienced in emigrating. We children were always in danger of seeing our parents through the eyes of the "Americans," as strangers and aliens, and thus shrinking and belittling them. The worm eating inside us was the sense that because our parents couldn't speak the language all around us, their experience could no longer be our only trusted guide. It was a small thing but we even stopped calling them* tateh *and* mameh. Tateh *became Father and Dad and Daddy.* Mameh, *with the characteristic downward fall of the last syllable, became momma and mother.*

How ironic that with all our insecurity and hunger for acceptance, we immigrants were seen as such a menacing shadow by the masters of the culture we were so desperate to acquire. Around the time we arrived, the novelist Henry James returned to New York after a long stay in Europe, and went slumming to see the lower East Side of Manhattan for himself. Rutgers Street, he wrote, was "an outpost of Israel." It is not beyond imagining that I was part of the dense hurly-burly of humanity that dazed and revolted the great novelist that day. "There is no swarming like that of Israel," he wrote, "when once Israel has got a start," and there was no escaping "the whole hard glitter of Israel." What dismayed him most—as he sat in one of the little Jewish cafes, listening to the alien intonations— was the fear that they would destroy his English language: "It was in the light of our language, as literature has hitherto known it, that one stared at this all unconscious impudence of the agency of future ravage."* One day I would come to understand that the language he revered was mine to cherish and create with, as much as it was his. But my parents, alas, could never make it theirs.

Our first venture out of New York was to Bayonne, New Jersey, an oil storage and refinery town on a peninsula south of Jersey City with a lovely French name but an air of unremitting desolation hanging heavy over it. Much later when I read William Blake's line about the "dark Satanic mills," it recalled Bayonne. My parents drew on their savings to buy a place with a few bleak rooms, a stable with some twenty defeated- looking cows, a horse, a delivery wagon, an assortment of milk cans, and a delivery route. Father, mother, and sometimes one of my sisters milked

---

*Henry James, *The American Scene,* ed. Leon Edel (Bloomington: Indiana University Press, 1968), pp. 131–138.

the cows as late as possible in the evening to cut down the souring, the cans were loaded onto the wagon, and then overnight my father delivered it in quarts, half-gallons, and gallons at the assigned doors. Hyman got sick from the work; he developed a rheumatic heart and died of it later.

My brother and sisters went to the nearest school but I didn't. I was old enough but small and sickly, and my face was broken out in blotchy pimples due to a violent case of eczema. When I presented myself at the school, a nurse there sent me back home, and my parents—too frightened of the authorities to present them with a problem—decided to wait. So I watched and listened while the older children did their homework.

I did some street learning too. I became, as so many youngest children do, a secret little boy, watching everyone covertly, listening, consuming their words. There were also hidden things that the secret words named. Once I came upon my brother and some friends of my sisters, huddled away from the rain under the porch, clumsily enacting the forbidden. I was scared and tried to run away, but they pulled me toward them, laughing, and swore me by the deadliest oaths to secrecy—and went on with their giggling and contriving. I had little notion of how "it" was done or even what it was about, but I sensed that I was witnessing something momentous for my life.

Much of what happened during those Bayonne years is shrouded in memory by the shapes of a sunless, stifling dream. In that shadowy dream is our horse. For Aeschylus, the horse was the crowning pride of the rich man's luxury. For our little family he was the sheerest necessity. He had no name. He was only dos pferd, *the horse. But we treasured him, wiped off his sweat when he came back from the delivery route, combed out the tangles of his matted hair, and washed him after he rolled in manure.*

One day someone left the manure pit partly uncovered, and the horse slipped in and couldn't get out. I was in the house, heard my mother's agonizing cry, and rushed out to see the horse struggling in vain. We called for help, and pulled him out with a length of rope, but he lay there with his sad, imploring eyes, his leg broken, trying to get up, falling back helplessly. One of the men got a gun and shot him through the head, while our entire family stood around in the raw, unheeding rain, weeping hopelessly.

Were our hearts broken because of affection for him? Yes, but for something else as well—the reality principle. The horse was our biggest investment. Without him we had no enterprise, no way of earning and saving for the next venture. In the end we were able to replace him, although we could not overcome the sense of loss. But the bitter thing was the feeling that fate, poised as an adversary, had dealt us an unjust blow. We were to feel it a number of times in those bleak early years as immigrants. Much later, when I was a Latin teacher at the Roxbury School, in New Haven, tutoring rich girls and boys with improbable exam passages in Virgil, I came across his "Sunt lacrymae rerum"—these are the tears of things— and remembered that first time our family stood huddled in the rain and shed the tears of things.

We seemed always to be skirting tragedy, but the warmth of the family and the intensity with which we held together was wonderful. The trage-dies and near-tragedies made us even more cohesive. "Whatever doesn't destroy you strengthens you," it is said. This didn't destroy us so it strengthened us.

Months after that sad event came another that brought great joy, to me as well as to the family. An autumn sun was shining over the grimy city when I presented myself again at school. My heart fluttered as I neared the sacred portal. Would it open for me this time? It was September 1910; I was seven and well into my eighth year. No truant officer brought me. "Readiness is all," the learning theorists have said. There I was, bursting with readiness. Mother had washed and dressed me up, scrubbed my hair against telltale lice, given me a handkerchief for my too often misbehav-ing nose. I was sturdier, less runty than the year before, and my face was less splotchy and serrated. Surely this time they would take me.

They did. They more than welcomed me; they embraced me. I recall a middle-aged teacher who quizzed me at first, and myself being stern-faced, then radiantly disbelieving as she showed me off to a wondering ar-ray of fellow-teachers who clustered around me. In whatever circle of Dante's Paradise she may now be, I invoke all the blessings on her for opening the gates of wonder to me.

I have only a blurred recollection of what happened that morning but one thing stands out with cameo clarity—the memory of having been taken by my teacher guide from one classroom to another, staying for a time at each, raising my hand eagerly, reading, reciting, answering ques-tions, then being escorted to another classroom while my heart thumped with wild triumph. We stayed for a while in the first grade but that was absurd, then in the second which was almost as absurd, then in the third—a much longer stay because there were some things I hadn't yet encountered on my own outside school. But then we moved on from there too, and I settled down in the fourth grade room. And that was it.

Miracle of miracles! In a single morning, in that all but forgotten drab little schoolhouse on the Jersey flats, I had begun to be drawn out of the shadow world, like one of the prisoners in Plato's cave, into the sunlight of learning, led through the first stage of paideia, *in the American version of the core curriculum meant for the making of civic character. I had been touched with the sword's tip that would in time usher me into the only knighthood America has had, Jefferson's schooled "aristocracy of virtue and talent," Emerson's "chivalry of man thinking."*

These imaginings were all of course beyond even my bursting little brain at the time. What I remember is the heady excitement of having crashed through the first big entrance exam into the America of our dreams. My family felt it too. When I recounted my triumph to them, my father beamed proudly, my mother's eyes filled with tears, my brother and sister pointed out that I couldn't have done it without the help they gave me by doing their lessons. Theirs was the true verdict. The public school system had not yet done anything for me except to tolerate my perverse early years of absence and set me where I belonged when I entered. The real achievement of my preschool years was the family's—the home environment, the importance of which has only recently begun to be appreciated. My father, with his years of Talmudic concept formation, had been my Jean Piaget, while my mother was a Jungian Great Mother archetype. Our weeks of voyaging, with our memories of life aboard ship and arrival in a strange land, had been my wanderings of Odysseus, and the fears of pogroms, coupled with our stubborn loyalty to our traditions, had shaped my unconscious mind. The little boy who presented himself to the startled teacher at the school in the raw and grimy city was—for all his quivering infirmities and insecurities—the deposit of thousands of years of wanderings and rememberings. What his Bayonne teachers could do for him was minimal compared with what his family and forebears had already done.

I did miss something important—manual skills, physical development, play and games. Home education, à la Swiss Family Robinson, doesn't work unless the children are involved with each other in physical rough-and-tumble as well as mind play, and unless the parents have enough leisure to interact with them regularly. That wasn't true of us. We were too involved with the daily struggle for sheer survival to leave much scope for play or body-contact sports. Missing them in those early years, I missed them all my life because they have to start early, just as mechanical skills must be acquired early if they are to flower to later. Much later, when I watched my own children grow up, I came to understand how utterly premechanical and preindustrial I am, and how starkly an anachronism in this age of advanced technology.

My father had always dreamt of being a farmer. He had the Zionist and Tolstoyan belief in returning to the land. His dream was to have a farm of his own and cultivate the earth. From a distant uncle, he learned of a farm that was for sale in the Catskill Mountains in the town then *called Centerville, near the bigger town of Ellenville, and bought it sight unseen. He put down most of our savings, $2,000 in cash which mother had extracted from her cloth bag, and took out a mortgage for the $6,500 balance. The uncle pocketed an agent's fee. The farmstead turned out to be a far cry from Tolstoy's idyllic Yasnaya Polyana. The uncle did not tell him that most of the sixty acres of land was so full of rocks it could not be farmed. When we got there and saw it for the first time, we all wept. For years afterward, when the family gathered around the Passover table, pouring out the wine in memory of the ten plagues inflicted on Pharaoh, we children would add imprecations upon the dastardly betrayer of an uncle who had sold us out.*

But there we were; what could we do? Father tried clearing the rocks but only ended up with a hernia that afflicted him for the rest of his life. Mother came up with a different plan. We would turn the very big thirty-room house that came with the farm into a boarding house for summer guests. Once we earned enough, we would abandon the farm and the mortgage and start afresh somewhere else. My aunt Fanny, who was a great cook, came during the summer and would turn out the meals for the guests. The rest of us waited on tables, cleaned the rooms, helped with other chores. The other children and I were enrolled in a nearby four-room schoolhouse. I recall the tang of the wind as we walked to school, often through snowdrifts, and the cheery clutter of clothes we shed. Again there were streaks of sheer joy. There were the horses to hitch to the buggy or the dray wagon, and the cows to milk and the chickens' eggs to gather, and the kitchen we kept supplied and in which we took our meals. I have fond memories of tapping the maple trees in the winter, cutting huge blocks of ice from a frozen lake and stowing them in the ice barn below ground, and going off for hay rides.

During our second winter, tragedy struck. Hyman, who was only twelve and who had worked so hard for all the years of his youth, died during the middle of a very cold winter. The house was not heated. We had only a small wood stove in the center of the huge living room. He caught a cold which turned into pneumonia and his heart was too weak. I remember the doctor being called and bringing oxygen tanks and for days and nights we clustered around that stove while Hyman struggled and died. When it was over, we all wept. The memory of that night was to remain with me all my life.

We buried him on a wretched rainy day in an alien cemetery. It was my first death. Dylan Thomas wrote, rightly perhaps, that "after the first death, there is no other." This became for me the paradigm death—of someone unjustly taken, at an untimely age, from a life of high promise.

*When my daughter Pamela—vivid, talented, bewitching—died of cancer
at twenty-eight I retraversed the earlier ground of the paradigm death
and got no better answer than I did as a boy of nine, standing at the grave
with each hand clasped in the hand of a sister. I thought of Hyman's death
again many years later when I had my own bout with serious illness. I
didn't want to die because I felt I still had a lot of possibilities ahead, even
in my eighties.*

*In a curious way, Hyman's death released me. For a while I felt guilty
about it but I learned not to. The truth is that I had been in Hyman's
shadow, loved but ignored. Now I became the only child and as such "the
messiah" of the family. Every Jewish family doted on its eldest son. Because Hyman was the messiah, I wasn't; because he was the brilliant one,
I wasn't; because he was the handsome one, I wasn't. I was all right but I
wasn't Hyman. At the funeral, I felt a surge of love passing from my sisters' hands to mine symbolizing that the hopes of the family now rested
with me. And I began to flower. I'm sorry to say it, but it's true: life feeds
on death. From that point on I became the darling, the one everyone focused on, the one who would achieve great things. This messianic fixation,
this hope that the eldest son will achieve success and somehow bring salvation to the family or even to his entire people, is an age-old Jewish longing.*

*There was another kind of promise that we all felt. On the ship people
talked of the new world in miraculous terms, as though even the paving
stones were made of gold. It wasn't so, of course; life in America was very
hard for immigrants. Our family life was often very tragic. My father in-
jured himself in hard manual labor. My mother worked all her life. So
have my sisters, both of them. My brother Hyman died because of the harsh
conditions we had to endure. Our life was full of such hardships. And yet
the promise was still there. It had driven us across the ocean, as it had earlier driven the Jews across the desert out of Egypt into the land of Zion.
America became the Promised Land for the Jews of Russia. We believed
in the old world/new world myth that has been so central to the whole
American experience, the idea that by leaving the old world for the new
we could start life over and remake ourselves. And there was a kernel of
truth in the myth, because here you did have the chance you never had in
the old world, the chance to make something else of yourself by your hard
work. We did that. The new land was not golden in any sense, however,
but very hard, even heart-breaking.*

*Soon afterward we sold the livestock, auctioned whatever the neighbors
would buy, and abandoned the farm. With the money rescued, we moved
to New Haven and bought a milk delivery route. This time we didn't keep
cows but drove out to a farm six miles outside New Haven to pick up the*

milk, in forty-quart cans, then bottled and delivered it. I took Hyman's place, washing the couple of hundred quart and pint bottles by hand after school, and rising at perhaps three or four in the morning (by which time mother and father had bottled the milk, by machine, loaded the wagons, and harnessed the horses), and went off to deliver the milk.

On Friday nights, father would return home, after making collections, his pockets bulging with dollar bills and coins, and mother would sit him down and have him empty his pockets on the table before she lit the candles. She would count it out to see if there would be anything left over after we paid our debts, and find out from whom he had not collected and why.

Sometimes I witnessed, sometimes missed, the trauma attendant on the random visits of the Inspector. He remains to haunt my dreams, a nightmare Kafkaesque figure who would suddenly descend on our enterprise to confiscate the bottles carrying the stamp of the other dealers, levying a dollar fine for each. Twenty-five bottles could wipe out several days of family toil. My father couldn't afford his own stamp, and used either unmarked bottles or the contraband of the established companies which employed the Inspector as a policing instrument to keep men like my father out of the business. We never knew when the Inspector, like some drunken Czarist officer, would pounce on us, and we lived always on the anguished margin of danger. This didn't keep me, I must add, from furtively picking up illegal or unmarked bottles when I spied them on my delivery rounds. There was no other way to survive.

Every night for several years, I and Napoleon—the horse—patrolled our route on the streets of New Haven. Napoleon was more than my horse. He was my confidant, my faithful ally, my Rosinante, my love. He was milk white (appropriately), a bit spare, short of wind, and blind in one eye, yet he saw as truly as he needed to with the one that remained. He knew every stop I needed to make, paused long enough for me to jump off, and met me at the next stop when I returned with empties.

I told Napoleon everything—my dreams, defeats, loves, triumphs. He was also the audience for the declamations I rehearsed while washing bottles—Poe's Bells and The Raven, Lincoln's Gettysburg Address, Spartacus's speech to the Roman gladiators, Patrick Henry's "Give me liberty or give me death." Because of his missing eye, Napoleon had a way of cocking his head, the better to see, which gave him the look of a constant and attentive listener. He absorbed everything I recited, I feel certain, and became the most learned horse in New Haven.

Some of what filled my head came from formal schooling, but much more came from voracious reading on my own. In the Catskills the man who had sold us the farm, a Mr. Logan, had showed us through the big *house and took me up into the attic where he had old books. Before the boarders came, I would sit up there day after day reading the trashy novels he had stored there. I just ate them up. They inflamed my imagination. I was not a very attractive teenager, yet much of my reading in those years of growing up was romantic. From the money she earned as a shopgirl in New Haven, Ida bought me sets of books. Thanks to her, I read the Waverly edition of Sir Walter Scott, the* Marguerite de Valois *series of Alexandre Dumas, and James Fenimore Cooper's* Leatherstocking Tales.

My lifelong romanticism must have had its start in my reading. There was love between my parents but it was scarcely romantic. There was little room for romance in the Jewish tradition into which I was born. Because of Yale, New Haven had a number of booksellers who put the debris of their overflow in the outside stalls for a dime or even a nickel a book. They consumed all my spare money. I could launch on a book-buying expedition with a dollar and return like a pirate ship laden with delight— Emerson's Essays *and his* Representative Men, *Hawthorne's* Tanglewood Tales *and* House of Seven Gables, *Thoreau's* Walden, *Izaak Walton's* Compleat Angler, *Edmund Burke's* Speeches, *Bulfinch's* Age of Fable, Poor Richard's Almanac, *a volume of Burns's or Byron's poems, and— greatest prize of all—whatever novel I could pick up by Horatio Alger. I knew the difference between Hawthorne and Alger but I devoured both. I read* Pluck and Luck, Paul the Peddler, *and* Phil, the Fiddler *to absorb the strive-and-succeed ethic, as I read Burns and Byron for my romantic self-image and Hawthorne and Emerson to learn the intellectual map of the world conquerors to whose country I had come.*

I also roamed the New Haven streets with my peers. My best friend was a Jewish boy whose mother was suspected of having made her money as the madam of a bordello. A little band of us located dog-eared copies of cheap little "dirty books," taught each other forbidden ballads about the sex act, and exchanged "how to" information gleaned from the older boys. Since my brother was gone and my father was stone silent on sex, this street lore was, I fear, the sole source of my erotic education.

Somewhere toward my eleventh year I fell in love, even more intensely than I had with Channele *back in Iveniz. She was Marion—long-haired, almond-eyed, lovely, and ten years old. We sat on her porch evenings, holding hands, star-gazing, talking endlessly. Our paths diverged and nothing came of it, but the memory retains the mystic quality of the unfulfilled dream.*

Apart from that fleeting affair, I was a lonely boy. When I later read Rousseau's Confessions, *with its account of his adolescent loneliness and his insistent sexuality, I felt the shock of recognition. Puberty came early,*

*about the time I entered high school, and I tossed about in bed and mas-
turbated often and with profuse guilt, not so much over the act itself as
over the desolating fact that I had to be solitary in my sexuality, acting
out my fantasies because I had no girlfriends.*

*I prowled the streets a good deal, expecting to meet I know not whom—
which never happened. It wasn't sex I needed but intimacy. During my
high school years, I haunted the movie houses. I saw the early silents—
Mary Pickford in* Tess of the Storm Country, *Theda Bara, Gloria Swan-
son, and the* Perils of Pauline *series. Norma Shearer became a Jungian
anima for me—the archetypal figure of all the women I dreamt of. Many
years later, when I read Scott Fitzgerald's* The Last Tycoon, *based on the
life of Shearer's husband, Irving Thalberg, I understood the hero's passion
for this woman, glimpsed fleetingly in the crowd, who possessed him as
she had possessed me at Poli's Theater in New Haven.*

My anima *kept reemerging in different guises. At one point she was
George Meredith's Diana of the Crossways, talkative and imperious, at
another she was Tennyson's Maude, scarcely seventeen, yet "tall and
stately," just entering her garden where I waited for her alone at the gate.
What ran through all my fantasies of girls was my lonely desire for them.
The reality was depressingly different. I had few dates and none that was
successful sexually. I wasn't invited to kissing parties or dances. When the
Senior Prom approached I asked a pretty girl whose father owned a bak-
ery near us. She put me off for a time, probably to see whether she could
do better, then accepted. She was shy, I was awkward in my ill-fitting
rented tuxedo, we danced but had little to say to each other, I saw her
home, and that was the end of it.*

*These should have been halcyon years for me, but they weren't. They
were my fledgling years and intellectually I was learning to spread my
wings and fly high, but emotionally my wings were tied and I couldn't
get off the ground. I wanted to be an insider and succeeded only in being
an unhappy outsider. I was not alone in this. It was the melting pot tragedy and it was true for many of my Jewish immigrant generation. In our
eagerness for assimilation we ran the danger of uprooting ourselves without being able to succeed in putting down new roots.*

*Actually, I was luckier than most because our family stayed cohesive
throughout all the assimilation. We children grew up in love and felt that
there was love between our parents. I loved my father very much though
I somehow sensed that he was not the strong one, that my mother was the
strong one. But rather than distorting my sense of who I was and whom
I should emulate, I was endowed with the best that each of them had to offer—my father's gentleness and intellectualism and my mother's strength.*

Was I my mother's child or my father's? I have the sense that I am something of both.

My father was learned and had the traditional longing for Zion, but he was not deeply religious. Every Friday, my mother lit the candles. After the benchen *or blessing of the candles, we sat down to a Sabbath meal of* gefillte fish, knaidlach *(dumplings) in broth, and an overcooked chicken. It was orderly and festive and it made us feel that all was well with our world. On Saturday, they both attended services at the synagogue. I went on the high holidays, sitting downstairs with my father while my mother and sisters sat upstairs in the segregated section for women. At the Passover seders, I stumbled through the asking of the four questions in an indifferent Hebrew, with an intonation I used to rehearse in my mind for hours before the family gathered, to get it exactly right. And then after the questions my father recited the matchless opening of the story of the enslavement and the Exodus.* Avodim hayenu, *slaves were we unto Pharaoh in the land of Egypt . . . It was like the release of a mountain freshet, which came cascading down, growing in volume and speed as it wound through the familiar landscape. Sometimes I would drowse a bit in the less dramatic passages, only to wake again and be reassured that the stream was flowing, the story was moving, and all was well. I would lose myself in those pictures of Moses and the Angel of the Lord, and the Red Sea cleaving before the fleeing Jews and closing again upon Pharaoh's host. Years later, in the time of the Nazis, I used to ache for the succor of that sea and puzzle over the finalities of legendry which are so much more comforting than the enigmas of history. On Yom Kippur they would all observe the fast, but little Max was allowed not to fast because I was too little or too precious or something.*

When, many years later, in his ninetieth year, my father became ill with a fatal cancer, they sent him home to die. I had been traveling and, when I heard he was approaching death, I hurried back and found this very gentle man, who had worked so hard, delivering milk, teaching Hebrew, in a coma. It was very sad, and I sat there hoping he would awaken. And he did. He opened his eyes, the first time he had done so for days, and saw me. He said, "Maxele." "Little Max" had always been my name because I was the youngest. He stretched out his hand and I took it. He seemed very content. We sat there for several hours and then he looked at me and said, "Zay rufen fun Tzion"—they are calling from Zion—and he died.

Like my father, I care about the Jews as a historical community, an old and creative civilization with a wonderful past, though I am not myself religious in the sense of being a synagogue goer. One of the things I am

sorry about is that I never followed up learning Hebrew after my bar
mitzvah *even though my father was a Hebrew teacher. But I am deeply
Jewish in the sense of identifying with the whole of Jewish history, and
with the Jewish emigration to America. I find a strength in these immigrant Jews that I find nowhere else. And I find that I am never as happy
as I am when I am among them, even though I don't care for some of their
values, particularly when they are pecuniary concerns that I don't share.
But there's so much more to being Jewish than that. Any people with such
a long tradition of persecution is bound to be anxious about security and
well-being. What is more remarkable about the Jewish people is its love of
learning and law, its striving for achievement and betterment, its tenacious
stress on the ties of kinship and community. These Jewish values, incul-
cated in childhood, were and remain a source of pride and identity for me.*

    *I was very much aware that I carried the family's love of learning and
hope for the future when in the fall of 1915 I entered Hillhouse High
School. Because of the presence of Yale in New Haven, it was one of the
nation's crack high schools. It didn't have quite the standards or rigor of
the French lycée but it was the better for being more adaptive, and I was
lucky to benefit from its excellence.*

    *These were the years of Progressivism, and Woodrow Wilson became
the first president I really experienced. I debated German autocracy and
American neutrality, committed to memory Wilson's war speech to Congress, and drilled with a junior ROTC unit on the school's front lawn.
I swallowed Wilson's moral idealism whole and believed that this was
a war to "make the world safe for democracy" as well as a "war to end
war." Wilson became not only my political hero but my literary hero as
well, and I fear that his rhetorical style, with its long rolling periods and
mounting climaxes, corrupted me even more than his overly simplistic
thought did. Inspired by him, I even dared to run for class president. I
drew few votes; I had the wrong face, build, and name to become "popular" or a political leader.*

    *But I did become a debater. I haunted the courtrooms where a mar-
velous hunchback Irish lawyer named Fitzgerald held the juries and me
in his spell. One day, in the high school debate team competition, I used
Patrick Henry's classic lines as my peroration: "I have but one lamp by
which my feet are lighted, and that is the lamp of experience. I know but
one way of judging the future and that is by the past." This was greeted
by a burst of laughter which I understood only much later when I recalled that in speaking of the lamp I had pointed to my feet, and in speaking of the future and the past I had pointed forward and backward. I won
the competition but gave up gesticulation forever.*

My strong subjects were Latin, English, and history, my fatal ones math, shop, gym, and labs of any kind. Caesar's Gallic Wars *and Cicero's orations against Catiline ("How long, O Catiline, will you continue to abuse our patience?") were the start of an amateur's lifetime of delight in Latin.*

In my last year at Hillhouse, I found my talents gaining some recognition. In the American history class, my teacher asked me to stay behind for a moment after class. "I can't have you here any more," she said, trying to look severe. "You'll have to leave the class." My heart quavered. "Why?" I asked. "Because you know too much history for the class. You may even know too much for me. When I ask a question, your hand is up and you have the answer before the others can raise their hands. Everyone else feels shut out. I can't have it," she said, her face breaking out into a broad reassuring smile. I was relieved to realize that everything was all right. Her plan was that I should leave the class and work independently. From the school library, she gave me Wilson's six-volume History of the American People. *I was to take it home, read it for the rest of the semester, and write a paper on it for her.*

By the end of the year a succession of minor triumphs had piled up. I won a citywide contest for the best essay on democracy. At graduation, I was class salutatorian, which gave me a chance to display my oratorical flourishes. Best of all, I received a four-year scholarship to Yale, awarded annually by the college to a Hillhouse (male) student who showed merit and need. My parents and sisters, sitting in array, beamed their joy. It was I, in Hyman's place, who had become their proxy on the long march to the gleaming city that was success in America.

TWO

The Education of a Social Critic

Eli, Eli—"The Pale at Yale"

Maxwell Alan Lerner—as he styled himself until he began to write for publication a decade later—became a freshman at Yale in September 1919, three months before he turned seventeen December 20th having been arbitrarily chosen as his birth date in the absence of any record. Both forenames were also adopted. To an adolescent's ear, "Maxwell" seemed more elegant than mere Max, and "Alan" was a name he found and liked in a story by Robert Louis Stevenson—very likely *Kidnapped*, in which the hero's name is Alan Breck.

The university he entered had much the same goals as it had when it was chartered in 1701 by the General Court of Connecticut to rear young men "fitted for Publick employment both in Church & civil State."[1] Denominationally affiliated with the Congregational Church, Yale stressed the building of character even more than the pursuit of learning. In keeping with the preferred self-image of all the Ivy League schools, its aim was to turn its students into "well-rounded" citizens rather than aesthetes or intellectuals. The perceptive observation of the young Harvard philosopher George Santayana about Yale in 1892 was still generally accepted: "The solution of the greatest problems is not sought; it is regarded as already discovered. The work of education is to instil these revealed principles and to form habits congruous with them. Everything is arranged to produce a certain type of man." [2] As in the leading English universities upon which it was modeled, Yale's teaching faculty was strongest in the humanities, less than adequate for the time in the natural sciences, and "deplorably backward" in the social sciences, as the distinguished psychologist James Rowland Angell admitted at his presidential inauguration in 1921. [3]

The mission of the undergraduate college—Yale's "vital, central heart" [4]—was thought to be the rearing of a cohesive, competitively self-reliant but civic-minded elite devoted to "public service." The "collegiate ideal" was that students "should eat, sleep, study, play and worship together, make friends, compete against each other and learn to stand on their own feet, in loyalty to the larger community." [5] In practice, this ideal amounted to the socialization of a select caste of young men, genteel and gentile, to take their places among the spiritual, business, and political leaders of their generation. From earliest times, however, Yale's guiding spirits had been of two minds about just how exclusive it should be. Although anxious to attract the sons of the wealthy and socially prominent, the university made a conscientious effort to remove financial barriers to the less fortunate. Because tuition was kept low throughout the nineteenth century and into the twentieth, the college became known as "the poor boy's Harvard." [6] But the social environment was not congenial for students of modest means, especially those who came from immigrant families and lacked the polish and the reassuring circle of friendships with which preparatory schooling endowed their more privileged classmates.

A Yale education was thought to require a grounding in the classics and in well-established modern forms of knowledge, but not in subjects that were considered too experimental or relied on findings not yet fully accepted. For all the enterprise and energy of the times, its authoritative chronicler has observed, Yale remained a chilly place for the strange or the unconventional: "Originality of ideas was suspect and, outside of a tolerated range, eccentricity of dress or conduct was frowned on." [7] Rumblings of discontent were confined to a minority of outspoken and youthful members of the university. In 1922, a student leader in Lerner's class, Russell Davenport, who would become a successful writer (and a major supporter of Wendell Willkie in the presidential election of 1940), complained in the *Alumni News* that "education at Yale, due mostly to the extra-curriculum, is primarily a development of character. What remains obscure is the other half of the definition—the acquisition of knowledge—the intellect." F. O. Matthiessen, a youthful rebel who would go on to write *American Renaissance,* a highly regarded book on early American art and literature, gave a thundering DeForest Prize Oration in 1923 entitled "Servants of the Devil." The Satanic disciples he had in mind were those in charge of the university. Yale's government, he said, was "an autocracy, ruled by a Corporation out of touch with college life and allied with big business." [8]

Even in the 1920s, Yale alumni were justly proud of the college's reputation for teaching, whatever merit there was to the added claim that the school put a stamp on its graduates markedly different from those inscribed by its fraternal Ivy League institutions. But the movement to make the university the home of research, open to all with talent, had made little headway. In the 1930s, the college went through a considerable academic upheaval, during which more power was gradually ceded to the faculty. Departmental majors were established and an honors degree created as an incentive to students to excel. Not until the 1950s and 1960s, under the bold leadership of President A. Whitney Griswold, did Yale's trustees and administrators decide once and for all to make the reforms that would set the university on its modern course to academic greatness. They realized that its clubby exclusiveness and its reluctance to put primary emphasis on scholarship had become an embarrassing anachronism and a threat to its academic reputation. Until then, the university had been a house divided, struggling to maintain its traditional devotion to *"lux et veritas"* in the face of the stubborn insistence of most of its alumni and undergraduates that it remain a finishing school for gentlemen, not an educational greenhouse for budding scholars and scientists. Along with the other Ivy League schools, Yale then began to remake itself by opening its doors to applicants of all backgrounds and both genders, and removing any doubt about the centrality of academic excellence to its educational mission.

These momentous changes came too late to benefit Lerner. The Yale he encountered was the unreformed Yale of the 1920s, even then a formidable institution. Its faculty revered the classics of the Western tradition and set high standards for itself and its students, but it was a campus whose undergraduates varied greatly in what they expected to get out of their college years. Most thought of the experience as a chance to achieve a treasured identity and prepare for successful careers. A Yale degree, they believed, would identify them as "old Blue" and connect them to a network that would help them in later life. Lerner was among those admitted to Yale who could not share these expectations, though he was exceptionally well fitted to benefit from a Yale education. The academic program at Hillhouse High was tailored to Yale's design. The university's admission requirements included Latin at a time when most American public schools, especially outside the East, either did not require or offer it. In this respect as in others of an academic character, Lerner's schooling prepared him well for Yale.

Otherwise, from the beginning he felt that the gates that had been opened to him would allow entry only into a new constricting enclosure. On his very first day at the college, an orientation event was held for nonresident students at Dwight Hall, a center for them and also for the Yale Christian Association. The affair had what Lerner described later as a "be-kind-to-the-heathen" atmosphere, as if the off-campus students were to be treated like the Chinese peasants to whom the school sent its overseas missionaries. The upper-class hosts were all casually but well dressed, the newcomers awkwardly arrayed and ill at ease. The chaplain offered words of welcome and explained that an upper-class member of the Yale Christian Association had been assigned to serve each of them as a guide. Lerner's "cicerone," grave, gentle, and ironic, turned out to be Thornton Wilder, whom he would not see again but whose thoughtful and beautifully crafted plays he would come to admire. In their absorption with time and tradition, Lerner would remark, Wilder's classic American works—*The Bridge of San Luis Rey, Our Town, The Skin of Our Teeth*—represented the very best of Yale.

But from that first day until the day of his graduation, Lerner was made painfully aware that Yale had a worst as well as a best, and that the worst was the obverse of its devotion to tradition and self-replication. There were two Yales, he thought, the Yale of the WASP and the wealthy, and the other, a cramped and constrained Yale he had grudgingly been allowed to enter. It was as if having escaped the pale of settlement in Eastern Europe to which Jews were restricted, he now found himself in "the Pale at Yale." This sense of constriction was all the more frustrating because of the high hopes admission to Yale had aroused in him. The tuition scholarship he had won in high school tantalized him with the hope of fulfilling

the yearnings of his boyhood. He desperately wanted to pursue the
life of the mind, to make a mark for himself in the world of letters,
to enter more fully into the culture of his adopted country, and to
meet and be accepted by the attractive young women of his fantasies. He was to achieve the first two goals, though not in the way
that he originally had in mind, but the others proved more elusive.
Yale, he discovered, was so obsessed with its past that it made students like him constantly aware of being outsiders:

> When you stepped into it, you stepped back 150 years. It was a gentle-
> man's college, stressing lineage and character-building. Many of the
> students had fathers, grandfathers, uncles, cousins who were Yale
> men. Many had Jr. and IIIrd at the end of their names. They looked
> on us—the off-campus boys   as newcomers and barbarians. I could
> have told them that I came of a lineage older than theirs, older than
> Yale or America. I could have told them—but I didn't.

Measured by his academic performance, these "bright college
years" were nevertheless an unqualified success. Like many Yale
undergraduates, he chose to major in English literature, the most
popular major between the two world wars. Even though it was the
most competitive, he excelled in it. At the end of his sophomore
year he won the Donald Annis Prize by compiling the best record
in combined English and German courses for the first two years.
He was among the select "junior 16"—those third-year students
given early admission to Phi Beta Kappa. By graduation, he had also
won the C. Wyllys Betts Prize for excellence in English composition, the Parker Dickson Buck Prize for the best essay on patriotism,
and the Scott Prize for the best examination in German drama. Yale,
like the country itself, held out these prizes to those who would strive
to earn them, and Lerner took full advantage of the opportunity.

But in the other respects then so important to becoming a "Yale
man," he was hardly as successful. He was not active in extracurricular activities except for the Debating Squad, continuing the interest he had developed in high school. He would not have been able
to devote much time to extracurricular activities in any case because
all through college he worked at various jobs to support himself.
He was a driver for a dairy, a waiter during the summers, a violin-
ist in a movie theater (a job that did not outlast his first performance), a translator for a firm doing business with German companies, a clerk, and a factory worker.

Worse yet, Lerner's life at Yale was dogged by the anti-Semitic phobia rife in the country, stimulated by increased Jewish immigration from Eastern Europe. At Yale, the visible and invisible walls separating all student "townies" from the proper Elis stood even higher for Jews, and only somewhat lower for Roman Catholics. In various ways, religious parochialism turned insensitivity and dislike into outright discrimination. Yale had been founded by devout Congregationalists with a deep sense of spiritual vocation. While members of other faiths, including Jews, had been admitted from early times, non-Protestants had been a small minority and were treated as guests without coequal religious status. Until 1926, when the requirement was dropped in response to faculty and student petitions, daily attendance at the college chapel was made compulsory for all students, except for those who worked as waiters or lived more than a mile from campus. Sunday church attendance was also required, although those affiliated with other denominations as well as Jews could be exempted by proving that they were attending Sabbath services elsewhere. How dramatically Yale was to change in this respect became clear in the 1950s, when an iconoclastic Roman Catholic who had just graduated from the college, William F. Buckley, Jr., gained celebrity by attacking the university, in *God and Man at Yale,* for allegedly inculcating secularism and materialism.

Although the Protestants who founded Yale and the other Ivy League colleges felt a strong affinity with the Hebrew lawgivers and prophets, their descendants often readily absorbed anti-Semitic stereotypes and conspiracy theories. In May 1920, Henry Ford's newspaper, *The Dearborn Independent,* whose circulation in 1924 reached 700,000, featured an article drawn from the forged *Protocols of the Elders of Zion* entitled "The International Jew: the World's Problem." [9] Similar sentiments pervaded the university campuses. In the nation as a whole, fewer than a hundred Jews held positions at the time on liberal arts and sciences faculties. No Jew held a faculty position at Yale College until World War II, although a few were appointed earlier to the graduate school faculties. [10] Letters of recommendation for the few who stood a chance of appointment routinely carried the assurance that the candidate had none of the obnoxious characteristics assumed to be typical of his race.*

---

*As one letter said, the candidate "is a Jew, though not of the kind to which one takes exception" (Jacob Dinnerstein, *Anti-Semitism in America* [New York: Oxford University Press, 1994]), 88.

With respect to students, no explicit limitations on admission had previously been adopted, although the requirement of daily chapel was seen by some as a deliberate effort to discourage applications from Catholics and Jews. But in the 1920s a need was felt to do much more. The waves of Jewish immigration from the 1890s to the mid-1920s greatly increased the numbers of Jewish young men anxious and qualified to go to college. Jewish families put a premium on learning and saw higher education as the sure path to prosperity and professional careers for their progeny. Parents scrimped and sacrificed so that their children could attend college. Unlike American Catholics, who built their own universities, Jews were without any alternative except for seminaries which did not provide an adequate secular education.

The result was that young Jews like Lerner began to flood the colleges and universities most accessible to their places of settlement. By 1918 Jewish students comprised almost 80 percent of those enrolled at the City College of New York, causing it to be stigmatized as "the Jewish University of America." New York University's Jewish enrollment was approaching 50 percent; Columbia's had hit a peak of 40 percent until a deliberate effort was made to scale it back. The "Jewish problem" was acute in Connecticut, Massachusetts, New York, and Rhode Island, where in 1927 Jews made up 13 percent of the population, in contrast to the rest of the country where they were under 2 percent.[11]

The most notorious effort to deal with the upsurge by imposing a quota was made by President A. Lawrence Lowell of Harvard. In 1922 Lowell confirmed a news leak to the effect that the university had decided to limit admission of Jewish students, after the number had tripled from 6 percent in 1908 to 22 percent. He believed that only a Christian could be a true American, and that a Harvard with too many Jewish students would lose "its character as a democratic, national university, drawing from all classes of the community and promoting a sympathetic understanding among them." *[12]

---

*Lowell was hardly alone in wanting to restrict Jewish admission. "Imagine," wrote an undergraduate, "having alumni so strongly Jewish that they could elect their own president and officers!" (ibid., pp. 84–85). Walter Lippmann, an alumnus of Jewish parentage, though he disapproved of the use of a specific quota, endorsed the aim of the policy, saying that he was "heartily in accord with the premise of those at Harvard who desire to effect a more even dispersion of the Jews, and of any other minority that brings with it some striking cultural peculiarity" (Ronald Steel, *Walter Lippmann and the American Century*, p. 194).

When Lowell's frankly stated policy aroused public criticism, he retracted the proposed quota and passed the issue over to a faculty committee whose membership included Jews. In 1923 the committee released a statement unanimously opposing any racial discrimination in admissions. Although the announcement aroused euphoric hopes among Jews that it would sound the death knell for discriminatory policies everywhere, its most immediate effect was only to persuade college administrators to impose restrictions informally so as to avoid bad publicity of the sort Lowell's announcement had generated.[13]

When Harvard took the lead in disguising its restrictive policy, others followed. Columbia, Princeton, Yale, Duke, Barnard, Cornell, Johns Hopkins, the Naval Academy, and many other less prestigious institutions adopted undeclared quotas for Jews. Application forms were revised to include questions on "strict Sunday observance," religious affiliation, parents' place of birth, mother's maiden name, father's occupation, and whether the applicant or his parents had ever been known by another name. Harvard introduced the criterion of "geographic diversity," on the assumption that few Jews would apply from areas outside the major cities of the East and Midwest. Virtually all colleges and universities kept admission of Jews to between 3 and 16 percent of the entering class.* [14]

Restrictions on admission posed the initial hurdles, but there were still others to be surmounted. Once admitted, the only way a student with any of the various social handicaps could win a real measure of acceptance among his peers was by excelling in athletics. At Yale, as on other Ivy League campuses, athletic achievement won an undergraduate an adulation that mere scholastic attainments could never earn him. The man who made the varsity team was lionized; the "greasy grind" was made the butt of jokes.

Lerner did not fit the mold of *Dink Stover at Yale*, try as he might. He went out for cross-country but finished last in his trial heat and did not qualify for the track team. He "heeled" for the *Daily News*

---

*Beginning in 1923, the year of Lerner's graduation, Yale put into effect a "Limitation of Numbers Policy" under which "discrimination against Jews would be a cornerstone of Yale undergraduate admissions for the next four decades" (Daniel Oren, *Joining the Club* [New Haven: Yale University Press, 1985]), pp. 54–55. The informality of the process by which Jewish candidates were screened out produced a wry joke among undergraduates. If an applicant could read the Hebrew letters on the university's seal, it was said, he was sure to be rejected.

but was rejected. The clubs, student offices, and fraternities were all closed to him. He yearned in vain to be accepted, especially by the WASP young women who seemed the special preserve of his classmates. He was very attracted to these women but too shy to approach them, fearing rejection, and therefore confined his ardor to fantasies. He felt as if he were still restricted to some ancestral ghetto:

> No one was deliberately cruel or openly anti-Semitic. But the flaming sword was undeniably there, and the anti-Jewish feeling was none the less strong for being tacit. The class officer posts, the honor societies, the secret societies, the literary clubs, the magazine editorships—they were all closed to us. We went to the football games but never to the parties before or after them. If any of us ventured to take a girl to one of the class dances we both had a wretched time of it. My classmates and I would exchange polite "hellos" on passing each other on the campus but not one of them ever spoke intimately to me about his home or girl or family or plans for the future. Nor did any of the faculty. Everything was done correctly and coldly. It was as if a quarantine had been thrown around us as a disease-stricken quarter. There were two colleges, not one at Yale. It was a we-they separation, but we were the *they* to their *we*, and we yearned to become part of them.

On "Tap Day," the climax of the period of fraternity "rushing," when students waited in their dormitories to learn whether they had been chosen for admission to Skull and Bones, Scroll and Key, and the other select societies, Lerner would sit on the Quad fence and watch the lucky ones being pounded on the back, disconsolately aware that he could not hope to be among the chosen. He would gaze longingly at the girls who came to New Haven from their boarding schools and colleges to attend class and fraternity dances, envying the laughter and familiarity between them and their dates.

At the start of his senior year, he was asked to join Phi Alpha, the national Jewish fraternity that had been opened in response to the refusal of the established fraternities to admit Jews. Although reluctant to join, because he did not like the idea of a self imposed ghetto any more than the one he felt had been imposed upon him, he finally accepted the offer. But the experience was hardly satisfying. He would hang around the frat house and take part in "the nasty politics of picking and rejecting our 'brothers.'" He attended the fraternity's Friday night dances, to which town girls, mostly Jewish, were invited, and met one, working as a secretary, whom he found somewhat seductive and accommodating. But he did not fall in love with her, and after a scare caused by her report that she was pregnant, which to his great relief turned out to be false, they stopped dating. Although the fraternity and its social life provided some consolation, he continued to yearn for assimilation, perhaps because it seemed so impossible. "What was it that made those on the other side of the fateful dividing-line so attractive to me?" he would ask himself. The answer seemed all too obvious: "Doubtless it was exactly the fact that they were unattainable."

His course work was far more gratifying, in part because it enabled him to forget his frustrations and devote his lively imagination to reading and writing. The Yale faculty, he discovered, was at its very best teaching literature, his favorite subject. In Freshman English, his instructor chose to assign Thomas Carlyle's *Heroes and Hero Worship* and selections from the essayist John Ruskin. Carlyle made him aware that he too carried a "fire in his belly," a burning ambition characteristic of the heroes Carlyle celebrated. The instructor read Lerner's paper on Carlyle to the class, and Lerner was pleased that even though the extravagance of his language evoked laughter the instructor approved of his enthusiasm.

As a sophomore, he took a survey course in which he was captivated by Chaucer's earthiness, by the sensuousness of Spenser's *Prothalamion* and *Epithalamion,* by the elegiac "dying falls" of Milton's lament at the death of his young friend *Lycidas,* and by the image of the stricken and damned but somehow triumphant Prince of Evil in *Paradise Lost.* With Yale's greatest faculty celebrity of the time, William Lyon ("Billy") Phelps, Lampson Professor of English Literature, a gracious and facile lecturer, he studied the formal verse of the sixteenth century and the Restoration and, like the other students, wrote required verses of his own. In other classes, he read the history of the Elizabethans, Pope and Dryden, and the nineteenth-century Romantic poets. Throughout his life, Lerner was to be enthralled by poetry. He needed only the gentlest prodding to recite from memory the whole of Poe's "The Raven" and long passages from Wordsworth, Arnold, and others, and he wrote poems himself, a few of which were published in magazines.

His two favorite teachers were Robert Dudley French, then an assistant professor, a Chaucer specialist who introduced him to the eighteenth-century novelists—Fielding, Richardson, Smollett, and Sterne—and his senior honors instructor, Stanley Williams, with whom he read the books most important to him: Charles Kingsley's *Yeast,* Cardinal Newman's *Apologia Pro Vita Sua,* and Matthew Arnold's *Latter-Day Pamphlets.* He found the Victorian tracts particularly engaging for a reason that was to point in the direction his own work would take. They were, he recalled, "great political prose" which cut to the heart of the social struggles of their time.

Other course work proved much less stimulating and altogether too isolated from new intellectual trends and the surrounding social reality. Lerner was inept in the natural sciences, and the social science courses he was offered were behind the times. Anthropology still relied on the teachings of Yale's own William Graham Sumner, the author of the pioneering *Folkways* (1907) and also the leading American champion of Social Darwinism as the foundation of political economy.* Yale's anthropologists had not yet caught up with the work of Franz Boas and Alfred Kroeber, who taught elsewhere. The economics course took F. W. Taussig's *Principles* as its bible and ignored the more critical perspectives of such economists as Thorstein Veblen and John R. Commons. A psychology instructor did assign E. B. Holt's *The Freudian Wish,* but that was as close as Freud came to being included in the Yale curriculum. The course in European history still recounted the dreary record of wars and dynasties a decade after Charles Beard and James Harvey Robinson sparked a virtual revolution in the study of history at Columbia by investigating social and economic history. Apart from literature, he came to realize only later, Yale was still purveying the bloodless conventional wisdom of the day when there was great intellectual ferment elsewhere. The college ambiance was also provincial in the sense that the great events of the outside world rarely reached the Yale Quad, then the center of student life. The year 1919 was the year of the Versailles conference and of radicalism and repression in America, the year John Dos Passos took as the theme of one of his novels, but little of this touched the cloistered life of the campus.

As graduation approached, Lerner came to feel that he had done so well in his studies that he should continue them in graduate school. But in a talk with Professor French, the first personal chat he had ever had with a faculty member, he was stunned to find that he

---

*"What do social classes owe to each other?" Sumner asked rhetorically in a book by that title. To him the answer was obvious: "Nothing. The state gives each man leave to run and promises him nothing."

was utterly naive about his real prospects. French asked what he planned to do after graduation. Lerner replied that he wanted to teach literature and write books of criticism. Where would he expect to get a position, French pressed him. "Wherever I can get a college post," Lerner answered. French ended the conversation bluntly: "I hate to tell you this, but you ought to know that, as a Jew, you'll never get a teaching post in literature in any Ivy League college. There is one Jew, Jacob Zeitlin, teaching at Northwestern, but that's all."

This keen disappointment, along with the general frustration he felt at Yale, may well have reinforced the ambivalent feelings Lerner had begun to have about his adopted country and his prospects in it. On the one hand, the difficulties only made him yearn all the more to enter the glamorous world he glimpsed at Yale and to resolve that if necessary he would somehow force his way in. On the other, he was being prepared psychologically, perhaps even subconsciously, to be receptive to critiques of the prevailing social structure and the pretensions of its upper class. Fortunately for him, Yale not only gave him a rigorous education in literature, much of it steeped in social protest and commentary, but also nurtured the writing skills he was to use so effectively to criticize the social order. Yale's education may have temporarily blocked his ambition to assimilate, but it gave him a personal reason to become a social critic and helped him learn how to express himself as forcefully as the Victorians on whose polemical prose he cut his teeth. Many years later, at the sixty-fifth reunion of Lerner's surviving classmates, he rose to give after dinner remarks, intending to recall the slights he had endured, but thought better of it:

> They were in their latter eighties (I was, at eighty-five, the class youngest). I had a few notes for the talk, including some memories of social exclusion in our student years. But standing there, seeing the little cluster of my classmates who had coped with life's scarrings and braved infirmities very much like my own to get there, that segment of my talk seemed suddenly irrelevant. Aging, like combat in war, is a great simplifier and equalizer. It brings a long perspective, abbreviating the less important, leaving only life's essentials.[15]

"To Reform the World": Becoming a Veblenian

Dismayed to learn that he could not make a career out of his love of literature, Lerner turned in the direction he had begun to explore in the debating clubs in high school and college by applying for admission to the Yale Law School. If he could not be a great literary critic, he would be another great jurist like the first two Jewish Supreme Court justices, Louis Dembitz Brandeis and Benjamin Nathan Cardozo. But his heart was not in it. Law school was for him a second-best option, pursued because he had become convinced that he could not make a career out of his love for literature. A life in the law seemed to offer a sensible alternative, if not the one he would have preferred. He had shown a talent for courtroom oratory, and he learned how to read carefully and write persuasively. By turning his joy in reading and skills at writing into a capacity for legal research and brief writing, he hoped to have a career that would make his parents proud. He was accepted and attended class for half the academic year before deciding that the life of a lawyer was simply not what he wanted. He was to make remarkably good use of this brief exposure to law school, however, not long afterward when he taught and wrote about constitutional law.

Before entering law school, Lerner experienced an exhilarating interlude that gave him a glimpse of another possible career. He spent the summer at the idyllic art colony town of Woodstock, New York, that would become better known more than four decades later as a symbol of the counterculture. After noticing an announcement on a bulletin board at Yale of an intercollegiate forum for the discussion of contemporary issues sponsored by the National Student Forum, he had applied and been accepted. The workshop proved beneficial in several ways. It was a relief for him, after the provincialism of Yale, to meet recent graduates of other colleges who shared his progressive views and accepted him as an equal. The forum gave him a chance to display his talents for argument. And for the first time, he met attractive young women who were drawn to him by his charm and intellect.

The student delegates lived together in a house that served both as a dormitory and a schoolhouse. Joining them that summer was a delegation of young Germans in their early twenties, all idealistic, democratic populists imbued with the values of the youth culture of the Weimar Republic. They told of the romantic organization known as the *Wandervögel,* whose members camped out in the open and sought to renew their sense of oneness with the soil and with those who tilled it. Their intellectual idol was Max Weber, the Heidelberg professor whose work on the sociology of religion was to produce the influential thesis that the "Protestant ethic" was the spiritual force behind Western capitalism.

One of the young Germans was Carl Joachim Friedrich, who, a decade later, would begin an illustrious career teaching political theory at Harvard, a post from which he exerted a great influence over American political science. One day in the course of an argument Lerner tossed a book to the ground. Friedrich picked it up tenderly, smoothed it out, and berated him for lacking reverence for things so sacred. It struck Lerner that given the rampant inflation in Germany, students must have thought of books as luxuries to be treated with care. He too treasured his books but as objects to be made use of, even marginally annotated, not to be treated as sacred items meant to be preserved in libraries or museums. But Friedrich's gesture moved him, and he was to remember it, with a twinge of guilt over his own behavior. He would collect and cherish books all his life.

And at this summer gathering, he also discovered that his intellectual talents could serve as appealing lures for attracting women. To his delight, the young women from such schools as Vassar, Smith, Wellesley, and Mt. Holyoke did not all find him repulsive, despite his fears that his earlier failures with women would be repeated. One of them, the daughter of a poet, spent hours talking with him, and said to him at one point, after he had shared some flight of fancy with her, "Where did you come from? You are incredible." After so many years of unrequited longing for that sort of feminine appreciation, he was thrilled to elicit her reaction and remembered it for years as a great turning point in his life.

With another young woman just out of Vassar, pretty and vivacious, he found himself love-struck. She invited him to the family's summer home in Connecticut. He arrived in a greenish suit too tight for him, carrying a cardboard satchel. The specter he presented prompted a quizzical aside from the girl's mother: "You *do* invite the *most interesting* people." The couple spent time together and saw each other a few times more, but the affair died out because, he thought, the social distance between them was simply unbridgeable.

After so idyllic a summer interlude, Lerner was especially disappointed to find his law school classes even drier and more conventional than most of those at college. The dreariness of the work was reinforced by the setting, a gloomy old building on College Street. The curriculum emphasized the case method introduced a decade earlier by Christopher Columbus Langdell at Harvard Law School. Every instructor assigned a massive casebook. His favorite teacher was Arthur Corbin, who would later publish a treatise on contracts described by one especially enthusiastic reviewer as the greatest law book ever written. But even "Corbin on contracts" ultimately left him cold. Other faculty members were knowledgeable and sharp-tongued, but none was inspiring. The great figure there at the time was Wesley Hohfeld, who had sought to define juridical terminology rigorously in a table of relationships cutting across the cases. Lerner was intrigued by Hohfeld's table for a time, but he came to feel that the case method tore the law from its social context and that efforts to synthesize the cases by abstracting principles only drained whatever lifeblood the case method extracted from the living human beings whose struggles for advantage and for justice were what the law was really about. Although the case method had the virtue of emphasizing the concrete and the factual, he thought, it led to a mechanistic fixation with precedent and with a lifeless logic divorced from history and philosophy as well as from the psychology and sociology of behavior. In time he would discover and embrace the pragmatic view of Oliver Wendell Holmes, Jr., that "the life of the law is not logic but experience," and the law schools would greatly broaden the scope of their inquiry.

Had the approach taken by "legal realists" like Roscoe Pound been used to balance the case method, Lerner later reflected, he might have found his legal studies more worthwhile. As things stood, the character of the curriculum made him feel uneasy about the prospect of becoming a lawyer. Was he to spend his life scrabbling for clients and fighting with other attorneys over wills and degrees of negligence? The opportunity to become a courtroom advocate was considerably more inviting, but not enough to outweigh the distasteful side of the adversary process. In practice, he came to feel, the ordinary "life of the law" was a constant commitment to cynicism and opportunism. What case work boiled down to, he thought, like many another perhaps too easily disillusioned law student, was that whatever a lawyer could find in the law to help a client was acceptable, so long as he could get away with it.

Lerner's grades at law school were good enough to put him into the competition for *Law Journal,* and he was at work on one of the Case Notes on which candidates were judged when he experienced a life-changing event. Around Christmas he fell ill, and his mother took him to recuperate to the Connecticut town of Danielson where she had a relative. In the town library he found Veblen's *The Theory of the Leisure Class.* This was Veblen's archly iconoclastic first book. Published in 1899, it became famous for satirizing the upper class and its acquisitive pursuit of trophies of "conspicuous consumption." Veblen affected to observe this behavior in the manner of an anthropologist surveying the development of contemporary society, couching his reports in his own original language. Economic competition, he declared, defying the Spencerian gospel of evolutionary individualism, was merely an "atavistic survival" of a primitive barbarian culture. With all the satirical power at his command, Veblen lampooned the follies of the latter-day predators and possessors, their pursuit of symbols of success with which to impress their neighbors, and the "pecuniary values" with which they "contaminated" religion and "the higher learning" in universities.

Lerner saw that Veblen was not just a satirical anthropologist but a deadly serious social theorist determined to show that capitalism, which he called the "pecuniary culture," was no better and in some ways worse than the hunting societies of the distant past. Lerner devoured the book and decided then and there to leave law school, to devote himself to the study of Veblen's ideas, and to follow in his intellectual footsteps. For some years, he was to remain convinced that Veblen was, as he would write in 1931, "the most considerable and creative mind America has yet produced." [16] Veblen supplied Lerner with exactly what he was missing in law school: the sense that law could not easily be separated from life, that it evolved with society and economic relationships, and that legal codes and prescriptions embodied changing values and responded to conflicting interests. Veblen showed that institutions such as the family, property, and contract, which the case method took for granted, embodied changing interactions between basic human drives (which he referred to as instincts or "bents") with the force of circumstance as well as the opportunities opened up by human ingenuity, itself the by-product of the "instinct of workmanship" and scientific speculation. He sought to show in detail that these relationships were neither static nor timeless and that they differed greatly from one era to another. It was therefore ridiculous to suppose, as the case method seemed to, that "whatever is, is right."

Veblen was no outright revolutionary. He did not suppose like the Marxists that the poor would rise up to overthrow capitalism and ring in the socialist utopia. He lamented the sheepishness of the downtrodden, consumed as they were with "pecuniary emulation" of the rich, and hinted darkly at the chaos to come if the social and economic order were not reformed. Even though it was hardly a manifesto for revolution, *The Theory of the Leisure Class,* as Lerner would later write, "was a savage attack upon the business class and their pecuniary values, half concealed behind an elaborate screenwork of irony, mystification, and polysyllabic learning." [17] Somewhat after the manner of Rousseau, who claimed that his radical critique of inequality was intended only as a panegyric on his contemporaries' ancestors, Veblen's critique of the status quo was clearly intended to promote a reformist if not a revolutionary sensibility.

Not surprisingly, the change of direction that his encounter with Veblen inspired Lerner to take seemed the most logical thing in the world: "Veblen completed what Kingsley and Ruskin, Arnold and Newman, had started for me and what the international workshop had continued—the heightening of consciousness and idealism. I was going to reform the economic and social system and the world."

Salvation in St. Louis

But how and where? Again a bulletin board at Yale came to the rescue. A poster announced graduate fellowships in economics at Washington University in St. Louis. The fellowships were endowed by a local industrialist, Robert Brookings, who had made his first fortune manufacturing and selling woodenware—clothespins, bowls, kitchen utensils, and rolling pins, along with other grocery items—and still another by building and leasing a freight terminal, all before the turn of the century. He became president of the institution at first called Washington College in 1895 and was later the prime mover in the creation of the Robert Brookings Graduate School of Economics and Government in Washington. Brookings's overall purpose in setting up the two related programs was to train young men and women for government service. Students who obtained their M.A. at Washington University could apply to the graduate center in Washington and, if accepted, earn their doctorate. He had originally intended to build the entire program in St. Louis but ran afoul of the Missouri laws governing nonprofit corporations. As a result, the graduate program had to be reincorporated in the District of Columbia in 1924.[18]

Lerner applied for admission to the M.A. program, inwardly intending to major in Veblen, whatever the curriculum. Among his strongest qualities he cited "a keen sense of the joy of life and work," among his shortcomings a tendency to be impatient with "what I think is sterile or unoriginal work" and a "tendency to grow polemical in my reports when I should be impartial." [19] He gave several of his undergraduate instructors as references. The one who knew him best, Robert French, wrote the strongest letter of recommendation. Although by later standards his reference to Lerner's physical appearance and ethnic background may seem gratuitous and even to indicate prejudice, judged in terms of prevailing preconceptions it shows an admirable humanity:

> Mr. Lerner worked with me in an Honors Course in English literature two years ago. This is a special type of course, limited to a few exceptionally bright young men, and the work is conducted by means of individual conferences between pupil and teacher. In the intimacy of this sort of work, I grew to know Mr. Lerner very well, and I have very great respect for the quality of his mind. He has extraordinary powers of penetration, and a natural ability in presenting material. Even as a Junior in College, he was doing a great deal of original thinking, and his ideas were always presented in a forceful and logical manner, which indicated genuine effort. Working with him in a field with which I am greatly familiar, I found myself constantly stimulated by the freshness and force of his ideas. I never gave him a piece of work to do which he did not perform with diligence, and most of his work was marked with genuine brilliance.
>
> He does not make a favorable impression at a first meeting. He is rather short and not in the least good-looking. He is a Jew, born in a family that has little means, and he came to college quite lacking in background. In spite of this handicap, he made himself respected both by the Faculty and by his classmates while an undergraduate, and everyone who worked with him intimately discovered a fineness of feeling in him which his appearance hardly promises. I myself developed a genuine affection for him; and if he had decided to do his graduate study in English, as he at first intended, I should have felt no hesitation in urging his appointment as an instructor in our own department upon the completion of his studies.[20]

When a letter awarding him a fellowship arrived from St. Louis, Lerner was ecstatic. His parents were a good deal less than thrilled, but his mind was made up and they had no choice but to resign themselves to his decision. He did not inform the law school, thinking his grounds for leaving too personal to be shared with school officials. He merely emptied his locker, said good-bye to his friends (who thought he had gone mad), sold his law books, and worked at a tutoring school to earn spending money. In 1924, at twenty-one, he felt that he was taking charge of his own life. Perhaps, he reflected later, the sexual and social confidence he had gained at Woodstock had spilled over into his thinking and emboldened him to embark on this change of course.

Washington University was modeled after the Ivy League universities of the east but lacked both their prestige and their snobbery. The students were mostly from lower-middle- and middle-middle-class homes, and Lerner felt more at ease among them than he had felt at Yale. Most were commuters from St. Louis and its suburbs. The school had only one dormitory, and he was able to get a room there and live on campus. The campus was attractive enough and spacious, but even in physical terms it lacked the sense of tradition that the Yale Quad had represented. Still, there was a cloistered isolation to it, which Lerner was prompted to protest in a short essay he sent to *The New Republic*, contending that universities should be built in city centers, on the margin of the slums. He was elated when the magazine published it as a letter—the first time anything he had written appeared in print.

Although well read in literature, Lerner was poorly prepared for the specific course of studies on which he embarked. At Yale he had taken only two economics courses—the basic course on economic principles and another on the financial history of the United States. He had read only two major works in the field, the text by Taussig and the one book he happened on by Veblen. He had never read the classics by writers like Adam Smith and Alfred Marshall, or anything on money, banking, international trade, corporations, or trade unions. His general point of view about the economy was that of a critical moralist, inspired by Carlyle's fulminations against laissez-faire and the "cash nexus," John Ruskin's view that wealth was "illth," and the utopian socialism of William Morris's *News from Nowhere*.

Fortunately for him, the program at Washington University made no presuppositions about a student's preparedness. He took five serious and well-designed courses, three of them seminars. In one, with Professor Isaac Lippincott, he was guided through the early history of economic theory. In others he studied transportation and monetary theory. With the historian Roland Usher, a specialist on the conflict between church and state in Tudor and Stuart England, he learned enough about English constitutional history to become sensitive to the differences between the common law tradition and its American offshoot. Usher was to complain that Lerner treated the course in a perfunctory manner because he did not take full and complete notes,[21] but Lerner showed later that the course helped prepare him to do excellent work on judicial history. In the remaining class, on the history of the American frontier, he found himself in almost constant disagreement with the instructor. It may have been due to a clash of personalities, but more likely, Lerner thought, it reflected the fact that he was coming to hold his own views and chafed at being expected to swallow interpretations with which he could not agree.

For Lerner, the centerpiece of his year at Washington University was his 111-page master's thesis on "The Economic Theories of Thorstein Veblen." The advent of the Great Depression later on would enhance Veblen's reputation for having identified a conflict between "business" and "industry," or between capitalism as a system of finance and ownership and the capacities for production, and perhaps even more for pointing to the growing separation of ownership and control. At the time Lerner first wrote about him, however, Veblen was apt to be dismissed as a clever eccentric rather than recognized as a major economic theorist. Most mainstream economists considered him too speculative and too given to peculiar usages and portentous language. Even those who had some appreciation of his work thought of him as more of a psychologist or a sociologist of the foibles of the leisure class than a serious economist. As the social sciences were fragmenting into specialized fields of inquiry, Veblen's eclecticism seemed out of date, even though in his breadth of interests he was following the precedent of Adam Smith, John Stuart Mill, and Karl Marx. Some of the more orthodox economists were at least discomfited by his strictures against the classical and neoclassical writers, but to most he was still not quite respectable.

Veblen did not exactly court the acceptance of his mainstream colleagues. He addressed many complaints to them, some quite trenchant. Their static image of exchange, he pointed out, governed as it was by a supposedly timeless interplay among land, labor, and capital, ignored the impact of technological change and the evolution of institutions. Indeed, it was the total neglect of institutions in modern economics that Veblen attacked most of all. The neoclassical economists assumed that economic actors were individuals, blithely neglecting the rise of the corporation, the trust, and the labor union. Then they compounded their analytical error by reading their theological beliefs into economics, insisting that free exchange and the right of property were somehow "natural," even though these notions were in no way part of a deterministic order of things. The "marginal utility" school was little better, even though it purported to be more emancipated. The adherents of this school simply read a different set of values, the hedonistic assumptions of Utilitarianism, into economic activity.

To some degree, Veblen may have appealed to Lerner because he was so original and so much of an iconoclast with respect to the conventional wisdom of the social and intellectual establishment. Veblen too was the child of poor immigrants and had an outsider's wry perspective on American society. In one of his essays Veblen attributed "the intellectual pre-eminence of Jews in Europe" to their social marginality. Lerner was to observe that Veblen might as well have been thinking of himself as the child of Norwegian immigrants to America; but the essay applied even more directly to Lerner as the child of Jewish immigrants. Veblen's unorthodoxy, moreover, was flaunted from within the economics establishment. At least some of his work was published in the standard economics journals, and he managed to find teaching jobs—though only after much struggle and painful isolation and hardship—at such prestigious institutions as the University of Chicago and Stanford University. Yet he persisted in thumbing his nose at virtually all established schools of economic thinking, even the historical school to which his own thinking was closest. He also vented his wrath at the very universities—lampooning them as citadels of the "higher learning" beholden to the vested interests—that gave him his livelihood. In his private life, too, Veblen flouted convention with studied abandon. He was dismissed from Chicago because of sexual indiscretions. At Stanford, the street where Veblen lived came to be known as "Sin Hollow." When reproached for taking up with the wife of a faculty colleague, Veblen is said to have shrugged and asked rhetorically, "What can one do if the woman moves in on you?" On all these counts, Lerner could well have felt Veblen to be a kindred spirit.

But it was not simply Veblen's cantankerous originality and rebelliousness that made him so interesting and important to Lerner. It was even more that Veblen had striven to understand social behavior, including economic behavior, with the comprehensiveness Lerner thought was necessary to the subject but altogether missing in the truncated, case-oriented approach he had encountered at law school. And although Veblen was by no means an advocate of wholesale revolution, or even an optimist about the prospects for reform, contenting himself with wry, even cynical observations about human folly, there was a moral edge to his analysis which strongly suggested that there was something wrong, even rotten, in the contrast between the wasteful life of the rich and the degradation suffered by the poor.

For the radically minded youth of Lerner's generation, Veblen served as a contemporary guide to the bedeviled. The movement for economic "nationalism" sparked by the extraordinary popularity of Edward Bellamy's 1887 novel *Looking Backward* had served an earlier generation as the equivalent of the utopian socialism of Charles Fourier and Henri Saint-Simon in France and of William Morris and Samuel Butler in England. Veblen did for this generation of Americans what the twentieth-century followers of Marx were doing to raise the socialist consciousness of Europeans. Strangely, given Lerner's voracious reading habits, there is no indication either in his accounts of college, in the record of his graduate courses, or in his notes and diaries that he had yet encountered the work of Karl Marx or of his followers. It was Veblen, rather than Marx, who shaped his radicalism, very likely because Veblen was an American and the upshot of his analysis was directed squarely at the American conditions with which Lerner was most directly familiar.

In preparing his thesis, Lerner read all of Veblen's published work and much of the critical literature it had evoked. He did not present a textual exegesis but a critical interpretation of Veblen's claims and arguments, sometimes in a declamatory style harking back to his early days as a debater. Over the next several decades he would present other accounts of Veblen, more mature and detached, and stylistically quite different: less argumentative, more analytical, and more sensitive to the cultural setting of Veblen's work.

Already in the thesis, however, Lerner achieved a certain degree of critical distance. He balances an appreciation of Veblen's insights with an acknowledgment of his shortcomings, points out certain logical fallacies and finds fault with the sketchiness of Veblen's solutions. In particular, he criticizes the supposition that "business" is completely inimical to technological progress, even a parasitic enemy of "industry." The relationship, Lerner argued, is more one of interdependence, because "business aims and business methods exercise some sort of selective surveillance over technical advance. If a technical change is really an advance, it must be susceptible of being translated into terms of pecuniary profits." [22] In the end, however, he salutes Veblen for his breadth of vision and for his insight, hailing him as the greatest economist since Mill: "Keenness of intellect, comprehensiveness of outlook, courage, and literary charm have combined to make him a figure almost unique in economic theory." [23]

Others inspired by Veblen, notably the writer Howard Scott, were to seize upon his diagnosis of the pathologics of the pecuniary culture, especially his ironic designation of the "engineers" as the potentially revolutionary rivals of the "Captains of Finance," to launch the movement known as Technocracy. Lerner knew better what Veblen had in mind. He was, as Lerner was to point out later, only a tongue-in-cheek agitator, more Mencken than Lenin, who knew all too well that the engineers were "harmless and docile," "well fed on the whole," content with the full dinner pail graciously allotted to them by the "vested interests." The engineers, Veblen observed, were as safe and sane, as commercial in their values, as the Captains of Industry and Finance who had made them their lieutenants. The owners had therefore nothing to fear—"just yet," he added ominously but ambiguously. For Lerner, Veblen's work was important not because it showed the way to revolution or technocracy but rather because it stimulated him to think carefully and imaginatively about the links between economic practices and human nature, and to ground his radical views on an understanding of that relationship. To that extent, he became a Veblenian. Only later did he turn to Marx, and even then his previous exposure to Veblen kept him from embracing the oversimplifications and economic determinism of orthodox Marxism. But he became much more aware in the 1930s than he had been in the previous decade of the similarities between Veblen's and Marx's diagnosis of capitalism. Veblen, he suggested in 1935, "was writing in the midst of a red scare." To avoid even more trouble than he had getting and keeping academic positions, "even when his thought was closest to the Marxian categories he chose to clothe them in other terms." [24] At the time he first immersed himself in Veblen's writings, however, Lerner himself gave no hint that he thought it safer to be a Veblenian than a Marxian. By 1948, in his luminous introduction to the *Portable Veblen,* he was to come to a more nuanced comparison of the two: *

> The thinking of both Marx and Veblen was cast in the image of the nineteenth century, with its notion of life and history as process. But while in Marx's case the idea of process was derived from Hegel, in Veblen's case it was derived from Darwin. Veblen did not regard Marx as a scientist, and pointed out that the Marxian system was completed before the Darwinian influence was felt. For Marx, as a Hegelian, history unfolded irresistibly toward a foreordained goal, through the class struggle toward a classless society. For Veblen there was no foreordained goals: only a ceaseless Darwinian process of continual adaptation, continual and cumulative change.
>
> Having pointed out these differences I must also point out the large area of common ground between the two systems of thought. Both of them contain a basic emphasis on the economic factors in history; both stress the relation between technology, class relations, power and ideas; both are anti-capitalist in animus while they lay claim to scientific validity; both look forward to a revolutionary overturn of one form or another—in Marx's case proletarian, in Veblen's vaguely syndicalist.[25]

At Home among the Veblenians: The Robert Brookings Graduate School

Warnings in letters from the instructors Lerner had offended might have cost him the chance to gain admission to the doctoral program in Washington, but a strong endorsement from Lippincott, his thesis adviser, more than offset the caveats. Lerner, wrote Lippincott, had "fine mental qualities and unusual power of expression." Describing him as "the most capable graduate student I have had," he added: "He has his work so well in hand that he can stand on the floor before the seminar for two hours and deliver his report with only brief notes, and he is able to word his expressions,

---

*When the *Portable Veblen* appeared in June 1948, the historian Daniel Aaron, who was working on his own *Men of Good Hope,* a book about American social critics, wrote to Lerner to say that he had devoured the lengthy introduction at one sitting and found it "a fine essay—discriminating, compact, informative—full of insight and extraordinarily readable. I think I prefer it to all of your other essays that I have read except the Brandeis essay, and it is a model of what an introduction ought to be" (Yale Manuscripts and Archives [YMA], I, 10, 495). Aaron did not exaggerate; it remains one of Lerner's finest pieces of writing.

not in stock phrases, but in good attractive English." Dismissing the contretemps with Usher as due to the fact that Lerner was already somewhat familiar with the material of the class, he raised only one reservation, of the sort he could expect would be taken as praise: "[T]here is a little 'cracked suredness' about Lerner but I can readily forgive this, because the man is of a quick and keen intellectual temperament and is a little bit impatient with those whose minds do not quite work as rapidly as his." [26]

On the application form, Lerner listed as "the strong qualities which you could bring to graduate studies:"

> 1) A very extensive reading. 2) Enthusiasm. 3) A love for "putting my words somewhat prettily together." 4) A penchant for close reasoning and clear exposition. 5) A horror of pedantry and of research possessing no significance or originality. 6) A prejudice for delving beneath the surface and also for viewing a problem in its larger aspects. 7) Some knowledge of law.

He added an apology for making the list so long, noting that he had tried to be honest at the risk of appearing vain, and an outline of his proposed program of study emphasizing American political and economic history and the development of economic doctrines and social theory more broadly. As career objectives he listed writing, teaching, and, if possible, government service. [27]

Government service was extremely important to the vision of Robert Brookings. He was one of many leading American industrialists who had come to fear that the government was not getting the expert direction it needed to frame economic policy, because political bosses and their urban machines were manipulating masses of ignorant voters to benefit themselves and the business promoters with whom they were in league. Graham Wallas, a British political theorist, reinforced this fear when he warned against "the rational fallacy in politics"—the assumption that most people could be expected to vote out of rational self-interest. In politics, he suggested, they were more likely to indulge their emotions by responding to irrational symbolic appeals. Wallas's disciple, Walter Lippmann, buttressed the point by showing the importance in the First World War of propaganda relying on stereotypes of the enemy. He followed up this study in *The Phantom Public* by proposing what would be called "democratic elitism"—the restriction of the function of the mass electorate to the choosing of leaders who would take on the actual burden of policy making. Industrialists like

Brookings were made particularly aware of the problems of relying on amateurs in government by their experience in Washington in World War I. Appalled by the sheer ignorance of officials charged with the making of economic decisions for a nation at war, they resolved to try to depoliticize government by taking administrative power out of the hands of politicians and turning it over to well-trained experts. They were not aiming to weaken the power of the state vis-à-vis private enterprise in order to allow market forces to determine all outcomes. Their view was rather that the failings of the economy were the result of poor management, both in the private sector and in the public, but especially in the public, because there market forces could impose no punitive sanctions for inefficiency.[28] The same general sentiment in favor of business-like government expressed itself before and after the First World War on the local level, beginning with the campaign for the commission system and culminating in the city manager movement. An even more influential result was the increasing use of "special districts," a technique that enabled an ambitious civil servant like Robert Moses to use the Port Authority of New York as a substitute for metropolitan government he could run without political interference.

Another outcome of this movement for nonpartisan managerialism was the founding or reorganization of graduate schools in public administration. Henceforth, these were dedicated to the training of the nonpartisan experts who could be counted on at least to moderate the harmful effects of partisan politics and at best to substitute their own neutral and objective judgment, relying on the "inner check" of professional responsibility. Brookings himself had served on the War Industries Board. He came away from this experience convinced that the government needed well-trained economists to collect and analyze information. To serve this need, he envisioned the creation of a nonpartisan economic research institute allied to a graduate school. He had earlier been involved in the Washington-based Institute for Government Research, which had lobbied for an executive budget system. Now he called for a tripartite arrangement in which the IGR would be joined by an Institute of Economics and a graduate school. He contributed enough of an endowment to assure the school an annual income of between $40,000 and $50,000. His wife-to-be, Isabel Vallé January, gave $350,000, and George Eastman of Eastman Kodak pledged $50,000 a year for seven years. With additional support from the Carnegie and Rockefeller Foundations, both new entities were established.

The Robert Brookings Graduate School of Economics and Government opened in 1924 in a converted old stone residence at 1725 I Street. The school and the IGR were each given a board of trustees, the positions filled by successful businessmen and other prestigious figures. A number of candidates for the presidency of the institution as a whole were considered, ranging from the president of Yale (who declined) to Wesley Clair Mitchell, the eminent economist then at work on a major study of the business cycle (who was ruled out as too much of a specialist). Finally, the job was offered to Harold G. Moulton, an economist at the University of Chicago known for his work on the role of money in a market economy. A Midwesterner, he had a reputation as an independent, empirically minded economist. After gaining assurance that he would have no interference from the trustees, who might seek to impose a partisan, business view, Moulton accepted the job of director of the Institute of Economics and as the first president of the Brookings Institution. He was to serve as president for thirty years.[29]

Once in office, Moulton recruited a group of twelve economists to direct the graduate program. Three of them, the agricultural economist Edwin Nourse, a Russian-born economist named Leo Pasvolsky, and Walton Hamilton, were to exert the largest influence over the direction of the graduate school. They agreed that past economic doctrines did not adequately explain what was wrong with the economic system. Alone among the three, Hamilton thought that Veblen's institutional economics set the ground rules for what was needed. A colleague described Hamilton as "the most extreme and articulate exponent of Veblen's institutional economics."[30] Fortuitously for Lerner, Hamilton was named dean of the school when it opened, a year before Lerner was to be admitted. Lippincott's recommendation offset the negatives, but what the reviewers at the graduate school probably liked most about Lerner was that he was a budding Veblenian, for a number of them were themselves acolytes of the same master.

At the new graduate school, the institutional approach meant that the focus would be on the historical development and interrelationships of property relations and such major entities as corporations and government agencies, rather than on abstract functional considerations such as monetary flows or production and consumption functions. Economic reform would require a knowledge of how the institutions evolved and worked and how they might be changed to become more effective in terms of the public interest. Hamilton's own courses sought to untangle the relations between economics on the one hand and government, laws, and institutions on the other. His aim was to identify a "way of order" that would represent common ground between managers, investors, workers, consumers, and the public. Intellectual history was valuable because it revealed the master ideas, such as those of property, equality, justice, and the public interest, used in struggles to advance competing claims. (It was to be a short step to Lerner's later adoption of the phrase "ideas are weapons" as the provocative title for a collection of essays.) Similarly, the study of constitutional law was valuable because it showed how these struggles were played out behind the facade of constitutional principles.

Lerner found this approach much more satisfying intellectually than the case method used in the Yale Law School. Indeed, it was just the sort of freewheeling, unconventional environment in which Lerner would flourish. A conventional graduate school might have proven a disaster for him, as one of his Brookings teachers, W. J. Shepard, observed perceptively in 1928, after Lerner had been graduated. In a letter to Professor Frederick A. Ogg of the University of Wisconsin Professor Shepard wrote about Lerner:

> He is the kind of person who probably would never have taken a degree where there was much prescribed work or definite requirements. He is too much a free lance to be contented to follow any course laid down by a graduate faculty. We let him do pretty much what he chose and it turned out he did more and better work in a variety of fields than any student we have ever graduated.[31]

Hamilton—affectionately known as "Hammy"—became Lerner's inspiration, model, and mentor. Originally trained as a medieval historian at Vanderbilt and then at Texas under Alvin Johnson, who persuaded him to turn to economics, Hamilton was appointed to the faculty at Amherst College. There, with Alexander Meiklejohn's encouragement, he developed a flair for educational innovation, establishing an interdisciplinary program for adult workers combining economics with philosophy, history, and the practical study of government. This background disposed him to require that the Brookings graduate program offer students an education in the other social sciences and the liberal arts as well as in technical economics, a prescription that suited Lerner to a tee.

Witty and irreverent, with a mischievous sense of humor, Hamilton was determined to make the school a lively place. He believed that teaching and learning happened best through informal Socratic dialogue among students and teachers living together. Lerner later remembered few formal classes but many a conversation around the lunch table with Hamilton at the center of it. He invited an exciting array of speakers to lecture, including Laski, Felix Frankfurter, and Roscoe Pound. Lerner arrived too late to meet Veblen himself and to hear him confirm his reputation as a wretched and indifferent lecturer. But he enjoyed listening to Bronislaw Malinowski, the Polish anthropologist who had written about the sexual life of savages, and Lewis Mumford, who discussed cities, technology, and architecture. Wallas, who had worked with the leading lights of Fabian socialism in Britain, made a deep impression upon him. Wallas had already made a disciple of Lippmann, and Lerner was flattered when Wallas asked him to accompany him back to England as his assistant—an invitation he politely declined.

The graduate school boasted a remarkable galaxy of permanent staff and visiting faculty. Charles A. Beard, famous for the radical critique of his *Economic Origins of the American Constitution,* lectured on American history, as did Carl Lotus Becker, who made a profound mark on a generation of historians of ideas with his *Heavenly City of the Eighteenth Century Philosophers* and *The Declaration of Independence.* Lerner was to correspond with Becker for many years. Philosophy courses were presented by Morris R. Cohen, a legendary teacher at the City College of New York, by Meiklejohn, and by Clarence Ayers, who was later to write about Veblen and other economic theorists. The anthropologist Franz Boas lectured on culture and society. The radical economists John R. Commons, J. A. Hobson, and Paul Douglas (later a Democratic senator from Illinois) presented their views on economics. William E. Dodd, a courtly Virginian, lectured on the history of the region.[32]

The seriousness of the curriculum did not rule out occasional levity. Lerner and a classmate concocted and sent a formal notice to Professor Leverett S. Lyon, an official of the graduate school, informing him of their intention to stage a handball tournament. Deliberately couched in the most egregiously pedantic style, the notice began by asserting that "a functional approach to any problem should not neglect the purposes of life," solemnly supported by a footnote to an article by Lyon himself ("A Functional Approach to Socio-Economic Data") in the *Journal of Political Economy.* It then went on for two pages (learnedly sprinkling *ergos* and *ceteris paribuses* along the way) merrily citing Veblen for the view that human beings should not be inert playthings of nature, Aristotle for the proposition that "man is a purposive animal," Herbert Spencer for the belief in the survival of the fittest, and, for good measure, the tennis star Bill Tilden and the humorist Will Rogers for the value of athletics.[33]

With Moulton, however, Lerner found himself decidedly uncomfortable. He saw in Moulton nothing but an arid technician, and Moulton saw in him a brash, immature radical. When Lerner took Moulton's course on the uses of statistics, he insisted on raising questions that went beyond the immediate application of the statistical method to challenge the positivistic philosophy behind them—the philosophy that took for granted the institutions and practices that presented themselves as data. Moulton did not like the line of questioning and made his displeasure so patent that Lerner dropped the class.

Because the school was in Washington, Lerner enjoyed a bonus in the form of the proximity of two Supreme Court justices he came to admire. One was Holmes, already bent with age, who lived in a house adjoining the building that housed the school. Every day, promptly at noon, the legendary "Great Dissenter" emerged for his constitutional. The other was Brandeis, the first Jew ever appointed to the high court, who would invite several of the younger students to his home Sunday afternoons. What stood out in Lerner's memory of these encounters was the passion with which Brandeis talked of his ideal of the small community, as exemplified in Periclean Athens, in Jeffersonian America, and in the new communities being built by Zionist settlers in Palestine. These were his three models of society as it ought to be, uncontaminated by concentrated power and what he called "the curse of bigness." Brandeis's son-in-law, Jacob Gilbert, tried to interest Lerner in Zionism, but Lerner was by then too distant from his Jewish origins to respond; it was only when the Holocaust forced his attention to the question of a Jewish homeland in Palestine that his sympathies were aroused for the Zionist cause.

Academically and socially, the Robert Brookings Graduate School deliberately sought to break with convention. Hamilton insisted that women should be among the students because their inclusion would raise the level of quality and assure better morale. Only reluctantly did he agree that the school should award the Ph.D., thinking of it as a concession to the peculiar ways of American higher education. He wanted the school to encourage a broadly humanistic approach to the social sciences rather than a dry and technical one. True to his ideas of how a doctoral program should be run, Hamilton decided that Lerner had earned a doctorate on the strength of the papers he had written, and that he would not be required to do a dissertation. Lerner had completed nine papers, including two on jurisprudence, one on the marketing of wool, another comparing English biographies of businessmen with American ones in an essay entitled "The Life of the Titan," and had also done a substantial amount of writing on the history of American railroads. All of the essays were well researched and written with exceptional verve. By the time he was graduated, he had also published a dozen book reviews.

The essay on the lives of the business "titans" displayed Lerner's critical and literary gifts, his sense of what was important in history, and his fascination with men of power. He began by comparing British and American biography, pointing out that until Samuel Smiles challenged convention by writing moralistic testimonials about the lives and virtues of entrepreneurs, British biography had reflected an aristocratic disdain for men of trade in favor of men of letters, the epitome being Boswell's life of Johnson. Despite Britain's role as the pioneer of the industrial revolution, "there is not in English literature a single capital biography of a great business-man or leader in industry. Carlyle, in 1840, lecturing on Heroes, does not include the *Hero as Businessman.*" American biography had at first followed suit. Few businessmen were included in the *Library of American Biography* edited by Jared Sparks in 1834. As it became more and more obvious that America's national genius was for business enterprise, "captains of industry" like Eli Whitney, Carnegie, and Rockefeller came to be lionized. Smiles's homilies were pirated by American publishers and widely read, and American imitators began to chronicle the deeds of "eminent mechanics" and financiers, at first, like Smiles, glossing over misdeeds to concentrate on accomplishments and philanthropy. Then had come the muckrakers, like Ida Tarbell, writing about Rockefeller and Elbridge Gary, and Gustavus Myers, writing his *History of the Great American Fortunes,* along with the realist novelists, who either attacked them as Frank Norris and Jack London did or wrote of them with pity like Dreiser. The biographers of businessmen had a rich opportunity to deal with "uniquely American experience"—the "native credo of success, approved motives, sterling American qualities," but judged in literary terms, their work, with the partial exception of Tarbell's, was of middling or mediocre quality. Even Tarbell's *Life of Gary* "reads like Bishop Butler's *Analogy*—a system of Christian apologetic." Most of the accounts are "variations upon the theme: here was a very good man; he has made his money because of his fine qualities; these qualities he displayed since early boyhood; he never cheated, and his watchword was Service; his wealth was justified by the service he rendered to the community while amassing it, and his generosity in parting with it." The biographers failed, even though they might have profited from the muckrakers, because they did not recognize that it was not because the Harrimans and Rockefellers were often unprincipled scoundrels or given to acts of piety and philanthropy that they are so fascinating and important:

> Their other qualities—daring, cunning, ruthless pursuit of purpose, large sweep of action—are the attractive qualities, and, in their field of activity, the great qualities; even though they may happen to be on the wrong side of the ledger in a Christian account-book. Benvenuto Cellini is not the less interesting because he was a braggart. Walt Whitman, too, knew that his fame would stand or fall upon the force with which he saw and expressed the simple human emotions, and not upon the presence of a few trivial personal qualities.[34]

Hamilton was delighted with both the quality and quantity of Lerner's work, even though it had not included a standard doctoral dissertation. By Hamilton's standards, all that remained for Lerner to qualify for a doctorate was the formality of an oral exam, and here too Hamilton decided on an unorthodox approach. One morning he casually sat down with Lerner at breakfast, chatted with him about his work, and suggested that he drop by the office afterward to continue the conversation. There, unshaven and in his undershirt, Lerner was surprised but still unsuspecting when several other faculty members also "dropped in" and joined in the discussion. He was asked a series of wide-ranging questions which went well beyond the discipline of economics. Along with such standard questions about economic theory as "What do you think of Wesley Mitchell? Is his place in economics a creative one?" and "Is Veblen a social scientist? Is he an economist? Or is he a literary artist?" came others inviting him to discuss his interests in literature, such as:

> Discuss Puritanism in the development of the English novel. In this connection where do you place Richardson, Fielding *(Tom Jones)*, Smollett, Scott, Thackeray? What about *Moll Flanders?* Was Defoe

a novelist? How have historians of literature selected a starting point for the history of the novel? Would a person without much knowledge of the history of the English novel but with a very good knowledge of the history of English morals be able to trace the development of the novel?[35]

After a couple of hours of this sort of wide-ranging repartee, Hamilton asked Lerner to leave the room. In a few minutes Hamilton emerged with a smile to tell him that he had just passed his Ph.D. oral exam. The informality of the process and the range of the questioning were as much an indication of the experimental character of the school as they were a recognition of Lerner's breadth and talent. In the letter to Ogg already referred to, Professor Shepard was to observe that "there is no question that it is the general opinion of the faculty and students at the Brookings School that Lerner is the most brilliant student we have had." And he made sure to add:

> He won't impress you at first, because he is rather unprepossessing in appearance—a little Jew who doesn't perhaps amount to much. But when you get acquainted with him, you will find that he is about two laps ahead of you on any question which you raise and that he possesses a critical ability and power of appraisal that is very keen indeed.[36]

Inevitably perhaps, the breadth of vision and informality that Hamilton inspired provoked opposition from the more conservative academic economists in the IGR, led by the former professor and government administrator W. F. Willoughby. Willoughby was supervising a gigantic project to produce fifty monographs on different government agencies. When after several years the graduate school turned out only one dissertation on a government agency, Willoughby concluded that its students were more interested in theory and politics than in what he called "applied government."[37] He complained to Brookings, who was having second thoughts of his own about producing professors rather than government administrators, and Brookings instituted a process leading to the creation of a committee that recommended integration of the three components and the elimination of the graduate school in 1929. Only Hamilton dissented from the report.

In defense of the program, Hamilton pointed with pride to the 120 students who had gone through it. They included a number who had already made a name for themselves, in addition to Lerner:

Isador Lubin, an economist who had studied with Veblen and was to become an important figure in the New Deal; the economic historian John U. Nef; Paul Thomas Homan, who was to write about Veblen and the other leading American economic thinkers; Frank Tannenbaum, who became a student of labor history at Columbia; Carl Brent Swisher, a student of constitutional law who was to teach at Johns Hopkins; and Mordecai Ezekiel, an innovative economic statistician.[38]

Hamilton also argued, in vain, that a principle was at stake. Would the Brookings Institution address larger questions of politics and policy or would it confine itself only to technical questions of economics and public administration? A case in point involving Hamilton himself had arisen a year earlier, in 1928, when he was preparing for publication a study coauthored with his colleague Helen Wright entitled *The Way of Order in the Bituminous Coal Industry.* Because they urged the creation of a federal board to regulate the industry, the mine operators tried to exert pressure on the institution to order them to change their recommendations, attacking the book as radical and socialistic. Hamilton believed that the industry needed to be regulated in the public interest and refused to back down. In effect, he was a New Dealer slightly ahead of his time, who paid a price for being out of step with everyone else.[39]

When the students got wind of the recommendation, they mounted a protest, arguing that it represented interference with academic freedom. As Donald Critchlow has pointed out, however, the real issue was not so much academic freedom as the proper direction of nonpartisan research. The historian Charles Beard volunteered to investigate the students' charges, but when Moulton supplied him with the relevant documents he came to the conclusion that the students' charge was unwarranted. The school was therefore allowed to die. Under Moulton's leadership, the Brookings Institution developed a narrower focus on economic studies and the promulgation of the economic truths that Moulton was convinced stood above partisan debate, such as the need for a permanently balanced budget—Keynes notwithstanding.[40] Relocated to Massachusetts Avenue, off Dupont Circle, it became what it is now, a university without students, whose fellows produce policy-oriented research in the social sciences, though in recent years in a rather less conservative vein than Moulton had envisioned.[41]

Short-lived as it was, however, the school was a remarkably successful experiment, and Lerner felt immensely lucky to have been part of it. The informal and innovative approach to teaching and the educational environment that was to characterize his own career was in the spirit he had imbibed from Hamilton and indirectly from Meiklejohn. Like them, he saw no contradiction at all between learning and liveliness or between a serious commitment to social reform and a readiness to poke fun at human folly. At Lerner's graduation in 1927, with his parents proudly in attendance, the doctoral candidates joined in offering an appropriate spoof, in the form of the "Brookings song," the lyrics of which had been dashed off by an anonymous and typically irreverent classmate:

> On the economic frontier, far from Smith and Mill,
> Stands our old RBGSEG, would it had a hill!
> Hail to Brookings, Alma Mater, Almus Pater too.
> World's foundations in the balance, Gosh what *shall* we do?

A Double Life

After receiving his doctorate, Lerner embarked on a lifelong dual career as both an academic working in the social sciences and a political journalist. When forced to choose between the two, he opted for the *vita activa* of political journalism, but he preferred to enjoy the best of both worlds. In his sexual relationships, he also pursued a double life, entering a first marriage he found unsatisfying and engaging in extramarital affairs. He was beginning to display an intensity and level of energy that was to characterize his career and his personal life as well. His public activities brought him considerable recognition, and his absorption with work and public affairs, along with his affection for his children, kept his marriage intact for thirteen years. During the years of Franklin Roosevelt's New Deal, he became an incisive critic of the Supreme Court for its opposition to Roosevelt's reforms and began to formulate his own more radical program of reform.

An Apprenticeship in the Social Sciences

Lerner's first job amounted to a six-year postdoctoral fellowship, beginning in 1927, as managing editor of a project to publish an ambitious *Encyclopaedia of the Social Sciences*. The manner in which he landed the post and his early teaching jobs afterward is a telling commentary on how barriers against Jews were beginning to fall, at least in postgraduate careers in the social sciences and in institutional channels controlled by cosmopolitan Progressives. Lerner was one of the relatively small cohort of American Jews to succeed in establishing intellectual careers in the 1920s and early 1930s. Soon, the Nazi persecution would bring a sizable trans-Atlantic exodus of refugee Jewish scientists and scholars. Both groups were the forerunners of a much larger native generation which, from the 1950s onward, would become a prominent contributor to American cultural life and higher education. Some in both earlier streams remained alienated from the country's cultural and political mainstream and helped nurture the "adversary culture" that emerged full-blown in the 1960s—in a few instances through their biological progeny. Others, like Lerner, found themselves drawn ever closer to the core values and institutions of the society and did not resist their pull. The deep sense of identification Lerner was to acquire with "America as a civilization" was undoubtedly nourished by the encouragement he met in this critical first phase of his career as well as by a growing appreciation for all that Herbert Croly had summed up as "the promise of American life."

Lerner landed his *Encyclopaedia* job thanks to a recommendation from Hamilton to his own former mentor, Alvin S. Johnson, another economist of Progressive leanings and director of the recently established New School for Social Research in Manhattan. Just as Lerner was receiving his doctorate in 1927, Johnson was appointed associate editor of the encyclopedia project. He wrote to Hamilton to ask if he knew of a talented young man who could assist him. Hamilton replied that he had just the man for the job and recounted Lerner's unusual range of interests and talents. When Lerner showed up for an interview, Johnson was immediately taken with him, despite his appearance: "He was of a slight, brief figure, so deeply enveloped in a coonskin coat one hardly saw anything but eyes of brilliant intelligence." [1] Johnson hired him on the spot. Afterward, Johnson's recommendations helped Lerner land other jobs. He was to receive his first teaching invitation from Constance Warren at Sarah Lawrence, his next from Carl J. Friedrich and William Yandell Elliott at Harvard, and another from James Phinney Baxter III when Baxter became president of Williams College. It was thanks to help from these well-established gentiles, who were not only free of prejudice but positively disposed to encourage members of minorities,* that Jews like Lerner were given opportunities still denied their coreligionists in other countries. Having endured anti-Semitism in his college years, he had now ironically become a beneficiary of what might almost be described as an "old *goy* network."

The apprenticeship proved very profitable for Lerner. He became acquainted with a very broad range of ideas and people, and he learned a great deal from those in charge of the project. Johnson, he observed, "was the last man who knew everything, and he carried it so lightly you were never aware that you were walking and living in the shadow of what you learned from him." Johnson decided that the best technique for compiling the encyclopedia was to farm out most of the entries to internationally recognized specialists to divide among themselves. The staff drew up lists of possible contributors and sent them solicitations, along with an outline of what had to be covered. Lerner drafted the section of the list dealing with contemporary developments in the social sciences. The editor-in-chief, the Columbia economist Erwin R. A. Seligman, told a wry story reflecting skepticism about such efforts to encompass all social knowledge. A reformer, he said, had once proposed to the aldermen of Chicago that Lake Michigan be beautified by the purchase of twenty gondolas. One of the less sophisticated of the politicians responded by suggesting that a less costly alternative would be to buy two gondolas, a male and female, and let nature take its course. Johnson too was dubious about the value of trying to integrate all perspectives; sometimes, he would say, "cross-fertilization only leads to cross-sterilization."

Lerner made friends with several of his colleagues. Two were hard-core Marxists, the anthropologist Bernard Stern and the political writer Lewis Corey. Stern had written a book on the American anthropologist Lewis H. Morgan, whose discussion of primitive

---

*In his autobiography, *Pioneer's Progress* (New York: Viking Press, 1952), p. 11, Johnson wrote that he prided himself on the "prosemitism" he had acquired from his father, a Danish immigrant. Johnson's benevolent attitude toward Jews also expressed the growing cosmopolitanism among American Progressive intellectuals of his generation, as David A. Hollinger has noted in his *In the American Province* (Bloomington: Indiana University Press, 1985), pp. 56–73. In 1930, after the *Encyclopaedia* began to be published, Johnson returned full-time to his post at the New School. A few years later he came up with the idea of inviting European scholars proscribed by the Nazis to join a "University in Exile" under its aegis.

communism had been used by Marx's collaborator, Friedrich Engels. Stern would later serve as long-time editor of *Science and Society*, the foremost American Marxist quarterly. Corey, who had changed his name from Lewis Fraina, had been one of the founders of the American Communist Party, along with the legendary journalist John Reed. Unlike Reed, Corey had subsequently broken with Lenin after concluding that the Bolsheviks were betraying the ideals of socialism, though he remained a militant Marxist. Lerner was impressed with Corey's intelligence and later helped him get a teaching position at Antioch College. Lerner's closest friend on the staff was Edwin Mims, Jr., with whom he collaborated on a lengthy and learned entry for the encyclopedia on "literature." In it they argued that fictional writing was continually influenced and renovated by interaction with new and varied regions of experience.*

Wooing the Daughters of the Conquerors

Lerner himself was also exploring varied regions of experience. Graduate school and the promising career it opened to him brought an exhilarating sense of liberation—erotic no less than intellectual. For young Bohemian intellectuals, the "Roaring '20s" may not have been as thoroughly dissolute as they were for the idle rich, but they were just as much an invitation to throw off traditional middle-class constraints. Erotic emancipation introduced Lerner to sexual pleasures he had previously only imagined, but with a paradoxical result. Rather than liberate him, the passions enslaved him to a quest for sensual enjoyment that could not be satisfied in a single relationship. More out of inertia than love, he drifted into a first marriage he came to think had been a colossal mistake and during which he pursued affairs with other women. He finally broke free of the marriage after experiencing a great romantic passion for the woman who would became his cherished partner for the rest of his life. He could have her, however, only by abandoning his first wife, to whom he had been wed for twelve years, leaving her to raise three daughters he adored. Even after remarriage, which brought him three sons he also doted on and a rewarding family life, he remained

---

*Mims would later write a book, *The Majority of the People*, in which, like Lerner, he advocated a democratized liberalism. His promising career was cut short tragically when his second marriage failed later in the decade and he committed suicide by jumping from a bridge.

intent upon sexual conquest and adventure. The result was that he led a double life, sometimes discreetly, sometimes not, causing hurt and embarrassment to those who cared for him most. "The winged god *Eros* draws blood," he was to remark, with good reason.

The constant frustration Lerner had felt as an adolescent and during his college years was a result, he had come to feel, both of physical unattractiveness and of being trapped between two cultural forces, unable to free himself from one and rebuffed by the other. On one side was the traditional Jewish way of life into which he was born and which he was ready to ignore if not repudiate, but which he was unable to escape completely. On the other was the even more formidable pressure of what he thought of as the "the culture of the conquerors." He saw himself as a supplicant, a would-be suitor "knocking for permission to meet their daughters at gates that wouldn't open for me." He wanted desperately to gain entry into the forbidden mansions and to win the favor of the fabled princesses waiting within. In his fantasies, he would escape the real dilemma altogether. He imagined himself sauntering up to his dream girl's home, dressed in white flannels, swinging his tennis racquet, as she emerged to greet him in lovely white shorts and cashmere sweater, holding her own racquet jauntily over her shoulder and gazing at him with a smile on her crimson lips. It was the same blissful image most teenage boys of the time absorbed from seeing magazine advertisements for Coca Cola, Packard roadsters, and Chesterfield cigarettes.

Except for the fashionable outfits and the tennis racquets, the fantasizing acquired a semblance of reality once he entered graduate school. Fulfilling erotic desires became easier still when he became a college teacher, a well-regarded writer, and a celebrity. All the barriers he had faced in New Haven melted away. He was to compensate for his adolescent frustration by wooing the "daughters of the conquerors" with unflagging zeal for the rest of his life.

In St. Louis Lerner had the first of a series of amorous successes. The earliest was with a library assistant who looked "like a cameo figure out of a Dutch painting—startlingly pretty, round-faced, with an appealing waif look that made everyone want to pick her up and hug her." He did exactly that and they became constant companions. They were able to spend a good deal of time in each other's company because Lerner was as ardent a bibliophile as he was a suitor. He practically ransacked the university library, reading the classics of economic literature as well as all the works of Veblen for his M.A. thesis, while continuing to devour novels, poetry, and literary criticism. The affair made for a blissfully convenient arrangement: when the library was open, he would read and take notes; when it closed for the day, he would check out the librarian. They roamed the parks, went to concerts, and poured out their life stories to each other. Eventually the relationship fizzled when they realized that (apart from a common interest in libraries) they had no enduring affinity. Next came a relationship with a fellow graduate student, who was much more his intellectual equal. She was writing a thesis on literary criticism, and her knowledge of literature made for a closeness he could not feel with the library assistant. They fell in love "hard," and went through a period of passionate attachment, the first he had ever experienced. The romance lapsed when he left for Brookings, but it was to be resumed later in New York.

At Brookings, social life was warm, informal, and intimate, in all the ways the liberated atmosphere of the '20s inspired. The students often slept with each other, "openly enough to get the reflected glow of it from the knowledge that others knew, discreetly enough not to cause too much scandal." Lerner had a fling with Martha Dodd, the daughter of a professor on the faculty. She was a not very innocent seventeen-year-old whose demure Virginia bearing hid volcanic sexual passions. When her father became ambassador to Germany during Hitler's rise to power, she was to have fiery affairs, well publicized in memoirs and novels, with prominent German admirers ranging from Nazis to Communists. Before then, she and Lerner enjoyed another series of trysts while both lived in New York.

During his second year at Brookings, he became more seriously involved with another student, Anita Marburg. She had auburn hair, very pretty features, and early American ancestors. Although these ancestors on her mother's side were Huguenots who had fled religious persecution not unlike the pogroms that drove Lerner's own family to America, to him they qualified as "conquerors" because they had come so much earlier and were thought of as one of the "first families of Virginia." Anita was to complain ruefully in later years, perhaps unfairly, that Lerner may have liked her more for her collateral descent from George Washington than for herself. She did not realize this, she recalled, until one day they were stopped by a traffic patrolman and, to her astonishment, Lerner brought up her family background, evidently hoping to avoid getting a ticket by impressing the policeman with her social standing.[2]

Anita's family was put off by Lerner's background, but she herself felt very close to him because of their absorption in the same social and political causes and in the same graduate school program. Her mother, a descendant of the Moncures of Virginia and a member of the Daughters of the American Revolution, "was a social snob," she would recall, "not rich but a Virginian; my professional father, an intellectual snob whose father had migrated comfortably from Germany." [3] The youngest of four children, she was three years older than Lerner. Before they met, she had gone to Vassar on a scholarship, where she became part of a generation of youthful idealists yearning to identify with revolutionary causes, very much in the manner of the radical journalists John Reed and Louise Bryant, who became romantic idols of youthful leftists in the 1920s. Anita went to Poland in 1921 with a Quaker relief organization and returned feeling a warm glow about the Bolshevik Revolution. Her radicalism was reinforced by a summer teaching working girls at the Bryn Mawr Summer School for trade unionists. She decided to study economics because the prospects for social reform seemed to hinge on an alteration of the market system. Although she was even less well prepared than Lerner in economics, she took a master's degree at the University of Cincinnati and came to Brookings a year after he did and earned a Ph.D. with a thesis on the coal strike of 1919, written under Walton Hamilton.

Lerner called her "Pixie" because of her somewhat eccentric charm. They took tea together, talked in her room in the women's dormitory across the street, and went on hikes with other students. By the time he left Brookings in 1926 (when she had another year to go) they had become so inseparable that their friends assumed they would marry. From New York, where Lerner was at work on the *Encyclopaedia*, he kept up a correspondence with her, though he did not propose marriage. In his spare time, he mooned about, went to dance halls, tried to pick up women, and was invited by friends to meet likely prospects, but none of these efforts panned out. At one point, a friend arranged a date for him with the anthropologist Margaret Mead. They had a pleasant evening, but whether it was for reasons of sex or temperament he was not destined to become one of her several husbands.

Soon, Lerner heard to his surprise and dismay that Anita's friends had given her an engagement shower. He felt that he was entrapped in a process that was not in his personal control but rather in that of the group mores in which he had become ensnared. They had slept together several times, and the shower and party seemed somehow to require that their relationship lead to marriage. How could he break off something all their friends at Brookings assumed would reach fruition? He was not really in love, but he felt powerless—too young and inexperienced—to stop events from taking their course. He was, he came to realize, a brash young man ready to pronounce on everything around him over which he had no control, but too immature to be decisive about his own life and therefore constantly overtaken by events.

Anita was in love with Lerner and determined to marry him. When she obtained her degree, she informed her family that they were engaged. Her mother expressed strong opposition, warning that she would be marrying beneath her and, with a mother's insight, that her intended was not the sort likely to prove a faithful husband. Lerner informed his own parents that he would be marrying Anita, though he hinted that he was not altogether enthusiastic about the match. His parents were too much in awe of his Americanized understanding to challenge his decision, though his mother offered an apt aphorism of Yiddish folk wisdom: *"Vi men makht di bett, azoi shlufft men"* ("As we make our bed, so we sleep").

The opposition of Anita's family only strengthened her resolve to go through with her announced intention. The result was that early one spring morning in 1927 Anita left Washington on an overnight Pullman and arrived at the 125th Street Station in New York City, where Lerner met her. As he caught sight of her walking down the platform to meet him, wearing "the wrong dress, wrong shoes, wrong hat (especially the wrong hat)," his insides went hollow and a voice inside him said, "No, no." But it was too late to back down. She had given up her home, broken with her family, and had no job and no place else to go. They embraced, had an early breakfast, collected two friends to serve as witnesses, and got a marriage license. The next day they were married in a civil ceremony and found a furnished apartment on Riverside Drive overlooking the Hudson River.

In emotional terms, it was scarcely a promising beginning, though both of them tried to make the best of the misalliance. She was twenty-eight, he twenty-five. She wanted the security of marriage, was happy to have a husband of such great promise who shared her social beliefs, and looked forward to sharing the adventurous life he seemed to have in store. He entered the marriage with a sense that it was simply what fate had decreed for him. Once they set up a home and began to build a family, he became a dutiful father, and Anita tried to be a good wife and mother. He was casual about money and paying taxes on time, which she put down to his being a genius. It was clear to her that he wanted very much to succeed and to overcome the handicaps of his childhood. She loved and admired him and wanted to be his helpmate.

On the surface, their home life was active and companionable. Anita liked to sing and had a rich repertory of revivalist hymns as well as Russian and labor songs—which she performed with an intensity that expressed her dreamy revolutionary romanticism. They attended radical rallies and took the children to the May Day parades. Their firstborn, Connie, who was named after Constance Warren, the president of Sarah Lawrence College, where Anita had gotten a teaching job, recalled a secure childhood but one that made her feel somehow different from her schoolmates. Her parents never gave her a pet name, she complained, and they never told her how cute she was (an unlikely memory, since her father bragged about her beauty for years). Her mother instructed her about the Russian Revolution and the state of the American economy but never bothered to read her bedtime stories. She remembered leafing through a picture book in the living room that included a photo of Lenin's brother being hanged as a revolutionary. From her mother she learned the words to the "Internationale" as well as to the "Star Spangled Banner."

When she was born, the family moved to a bigger apartment on Claremont Avenue, opposite the Riverside Church. When Pamela was born two years later, her proud father would wheel her carriage on Broadway on the weekends. In 1932, needing more space, they moved to Tuckahoe, New York, so that Anita could be closer to Sarah Lawrence in nearby Bronxville. (When Anita had inquired about property in Bronxville, she had been told as politely as possible that it was out of bounds for Jews.) Afterward, they moved to Yonkers.

Lerner encouraged Anita's teaching career and entered one of the most productive periods of his own life, but the marriage was unhappy for him from the start, and perhaps for her as well, because she may have sensed his unhappiness. When she assigned some working-class novels to her class, it struck him that she would do better at teaching literature. She made the change and devoted the rest of her academic life to teaching and studying Russian literature. But she was away most of the week, and Lerner felt unhappy and trapped in the relationship. When a mangy lost dog showed up near their doorstep one night, they took it in and called it "Perdita." Although they got its sex wrong, the name was, he thought, a fitting symbol for their marriage; both of them felt as lost as the dog.

Lerner's infidelities undermined the marriage from the start. "Never resist an adequate temptation," he would say, and mean it. According to Anita, he even had the gall to ask her not to mention her pregnancy to a woman he was seeing.[4] Lerner soon found solace with the literary "St. Louis woman" with whom he had been romantically involved and who had also gotten a job in Manhattan. Before long, he found himself locked again in a passionate and tortured romance with her. But she was attractive to other men as well and finally married one of them. For Lerner, it had been a mixed experience: "I had learned both the sweetness and the agony of an illicit relationship, and I was to taste both a number of times."

This would be only the first in a pattern of extramarital affairs that was to continue into his second marriage. Especially during this early stage of manhood, Lerner felt he was undergoing a curious reversal of his misfortunes at Yale. "The very same elements of my persona—Jewish, intense, liberal, voluble, of immigrant stock, romantic, overdramatic—which had been held against me at Yale in the early 1920's were now working for me in the changed cultural ethos of the 1930's." He exploited these advantages without the least compunction. In sexual matters, what he later wrote of Theodore Dreiser might just as well have described himself: "He used to call himself a 'varietist,' yet he had the talent to make each of the women feel that he was deeply involved with her, that a secret chemistry pulled them to each other, and that he saw the world through her eyes."[5] Lerner too had a warm admiration for the women he pursued that some of them found not only endearing but irresistible. As one of them explained, "Max loved the company of women." He often said that he had never learned anything worth knowing except from women.

The former graduate student was not the only woman with whom he had an affair during his first marriage. Shortly after renewing his acquaintance with her, he began seeing a Sarah Lawrence freshman who was a student of Anita's in 1930. She was "a lovely slender young woman, graceful, with boyish figure, dark-complexioned, with violet eyes and a soft seductive voice." Although only eighteen, she had already imbibed the changing sexual mores of the time. They would meet in Manhattan and make forays by subway or "el" into the countryside, carrying the picnic basket that has been a time-honored pretext for amorous adventures *en plein aire*. It was all in the "approved Edna Millay fashion": the picnic basket included a bottle of wine and a couple of anthologies of poetry. She taught him more than he already knew about the varieties of sexual play, and their outings continued when the Lerners moved to Bronxville. Anita seemed to suspect nothing, often inviting her to the evening suppers for students and relying on her to baby-sit.

Once, while eagerly setting out for one of his dates with Anita's student, Lerner's cockiness almost got him into trouble. He had bought a second-hand car but had not yet gotten a driver's license. He had picked up the student at her dormitory and was on the uphill street leading to his house when the car "somehow collided with a tree." Panic-stricken that he would be arrested for driving without a license, his first impulse was to extricate himself and the girl and flee the scene. Instead, he went home with her, left her with Anita, and returned to the site of the accident, fully expecting to find a policeman. He was relieved to see only a knot of curious onlookers. To his further relief, the car started up and he was able to drive it off, resolving to get his license without further delay.

He continued the affair for some years. The student dropped out of college to spend a year in Europe. When she returned to school, they resumed where they had left off. One summer, while teaching summer school at the University of Wyoming, he made a side trip to visit her at her home in the West. Years later, when both were living in Manhattan, they saw each other again. Finally, she married, and the affair came to an end. Lerner found himself wondering what a marriage between them might have been like: "If being forewarned about each other's strayings could make a marriage work this one might have. We would have richly deserved each other."

As his work on the *Encyclopaedia* was drawing to a close, Lerner too was offered a job teaching at Sarah Lawrence, at a starting salary of $4,000 a year. He accepted eagerly, anticipating he would find the opportunity attractive in more than one way. Mixing metaphors with heady abandon, he would explain candidly: "Where else could I have found a more complete Eden, with the dazzling Faustian mix of knowledge, hunger, power, and a whole bevy of Helens?" This first academic post did in fact prove to be a very satisfying introduction to teaching and at the same time an opportunity for extracurricular dalliance. At the time such affairs were not unknown at women's colleges like Sarah Lawrence and Bennington, where liberated sexual sentiments blended with liberal social attitudes.* For Lerner, Sarah Lawrence was a "budding grove" full of attractive young women about to flower. He was twenty-nine, unhappy in his marriage, with a wife and home he seemed to take every chance to get away from. And here was a garden of virgins ripe for the plucking:

> The young women were nubile as well as beautiful, the male faculty (including the married ones) lived in perpetual dazzlement with Springtime always in their hearts, their wives at home were worried and defensive (and rightly), and the students in turn were fiercely jealous of them for having snared the man who (had he had the sense to wait) would have preferred *them.* It may have looked like a campus but it was in essence a jungle, reeking with desire, generativity and enchantment—and not only with ideas.

Lerner's most ardent foray in this arcadian jungle of desire involved an intermittent campaign of stalking issuing in a long delayed conquest. Anita made what eventually turned out to be a fatal mistake for her marriage when she introduced him to an especially handsome and bright Sarah Lawrence freshman. He learned of her before he joined the faculty, when Anita came home one night and reported that one of her students was the most beautiful girl she had ever seen. A few weeks later, they went to a college concert and he saw the girl sitting on the floor facing them. He caught his breath as he saw for himself that Anita had not exaggerated. Some time later, when Anita asked him to take over her classes for a week, he saw the same girl again in one of them. She was Genevieve Edna Albers, then seventeen. He put a question to her in class (something like, "Miss Albers, what was your first encounter with the state?") but found her so captivating that he was utterly unable to pay attention to her answer.

In later years, he was to marvel that they might never have met except for a quirk of fate. Edna had applied to Vassar and was on her way to take the Scholastic Aptitude Test when the car she was driving ran out of gas. Because she was unable to take the test, she

---

*When reports of Lerner's extracurricular activities reached college administrators, they took no action to admonish him but ordered windows installed in the doors of instructors' offices.

was not admitted to Vassar, even though she had done well in school. A boyfriend, who was attending Princeton, mentioned that he had met some Sarah Lawrence girls who talked of the school with enthusiasm. She applied there and was admitted.

Lerner was immediately enthralled by Edna's appearance. She had an intense face encased in a bone structure embodying what he thought of as the essence of classic beauty, with a figure to match. He was also impressed by her intelligence. She was, he thought, the ablest of his Sarah Lawrence students. Her mind had been honed in a home library collected by her surgeon father, an avid bibliophile, and in the excellent Brooklyn Friends School where she had prepared for college. She took to Lerner's classes with delight, excited by the chance to explore the universe of ideas he was opening to her.

She soon realized that Lerner was smitten with her, but she had no thought of becoming romantically involved with him. She was put off by the double consideration that he was married and ten years older, a difference of age which, to a teenager, seemed impossible to bridge. She was not put off by his Jewishness but was simply unaware of it, never having encountered anyone who was Jewish. As much as she admired him, however, she sensed that he came from a very different social background. Although she shared his love of books and had come from a home in which education was highly valued, hers was also a world of country club dances, sailing, and college football weekends. She had many suitors, foremost among them Donald, the Princeton varsity football player who had told her about Sarah Lawrence. Lerner became Edna's "don," supervising her extracurricular learning and meeting with her now and then for "don conferences." She would see him in and out of class, often in a small group which clustered around him outside McCracken Hall to carry on discussions begun in class, sometimes alone for coffee in a Bronxville hotel. But they were never intimate at this time. Edna had been raised in a strict Episcopalian home and was not about to have a premarital affair with anyone, let alone a married man.

Anita could see that Lerner was attracted to Edna, but she could not imagine that he might one day leave her for a girl so young. Edna was regularly invited to the supper evenings at their home—which routinely ended, after the children had been tucked in, with the singing of labor union and radical songs. Anita had a foolhardy confidence, even suggesting that Lerner take Edna on "field trips" to Manhattan, as he sometimes did for students in his course on American Civilization. Even though Edna was at first put off by him as an "older man," he felt later that he had enjoyed an advantage over her other suitors just because he was shaping her way of thinking. She took all his courses, moving into a new intellectual orbit that revolved around him and his teaching. On one of the outings to Manhattan, they went to a public defense rally featuring Samuel Liebowitz, then the lawyer for the Scottsboro boys, a group of illiterate young black men condemned to death for an alleged gang rape in Alabama. On another he took her, alone, to a burlesque show on 42d Street, where the strippers and the audience of beady-eyed men frightened her out of her wits. One evening, along with several of her Sarah Lawrence friends and their dates, she accompanied him to the Savoy Dance Hall in Harlem, a showcase for the great entertainers of the Harlem Renaissance. While they were inside the theater, the trunk of Edna's big Stutz roadster was broken into and Lerner's ratty Yale raccoon coat was stolen—to Edna's secret relief, because she hated it.

Throughout her college years, Edna and Lerner drew closer and closer. He expressed an interest in meeting her parents, and she obliged by driving home with him to Kenilworth, in Long Island. He thought they suspected that there might be more to this friendship than an academic relationship and did not blame them in the least for being cordial but frosty. She thought he was imagining things and that her parents simply thought him an odd type for a college professor. The summer before her senior year, Edna and two classmates went off to the Soviet Union, and he wrote long letters to her.

In later years, their recollections of how their relationship at Sarah Lawrence ended differed considerably. When she was about to graduate, Lerner recalled, they had a serious talk at her prom, and he decided that their "strange and bootless courtship" should end. Donald, her Princeton suitor, was pressing her to say yes or no to his proposal of marriage. Lerner did not feel he could ask her to wait for him to gain a divorce from Anita, even though he was convinced the marriage, now stretching into a seventh unhappy year, could not last. He was unwilling to take the initiative and reluctant to abandon his daughters while they were still so young. He told Edna that although he had no claim on her, he would love her as long as he lived. But he added that he thought she loved Donald and owed it to him as well as to herself to give their love the test of marriage. He came to feel that although this was probably the best advice he could have given her, it was also in his own interest, because it would give him time to test his own marriage and overcome his guilt if he had to break it. If Edna would be free again and come to him, she would do so without ever wishing she had not foregone the other opportunity. Edna recalled no such discussion. She remembers only that while she admired Lerner, she did not think of him either as a beau or a possible husband, only as her teacher. Their acquaintanceship lapsed after she was graduated and went off to Muncie, Indiana, to work with the sociologists Helen and Robert Lynd as an interviewer for the second of their *Middletown* studies, and she married her Princeton beau.

Meanwhile, Lerner's marriage to Anita was deteriorating, and he sought solace in the company of other women. "The trouble with our marriage," Anita later recalled, was that "he was never content with our daisy field. He felt that bigger, more perfect flowers might bloom in the nearby cow pasture. So while I kept my eye on him, his neck was craned, watching the passing parade. That one had style, the other daring, the third an ankle or a muted, husky voice." It never occurred to Anita that any of Lerner's amours would stick:

> His affairs didn't please me, particularly when they involved a network of lies. But I didn't think they would break up a twelve-year marriage. We felt easy, companionable and warm together, sang riotously together and felt proud of each other when company came. He called me "Eve" and left books around with dedications that only we would understand. He used to say that we have more in our marriage than most people we knew.[6]

A Life on the Left

For a time, the marriage persisted mainly because Lerner was preoccupied by career changes and absorbed in a left-wing literary milieu. He took on the role of left-wing intellectual with ease, together with the Bohemian attitude toward life that went along with it. The common aim of those in his circle was to be liberated from the oppressions of capitalism and Puritanism—from robber barons like Carnegie and censorious Victorians like Anthony Comstock.

But if there were no bounds to Lerner's Bohemianism, there were limits to his political radicalism. In 1932, when a number of his colleagues on the *Encyclopaedia* staff came out for the Communist candidate, William Z. Foster, Lerner balked. Although they argued that Roosevelt was merely a potential Kerensky, a transitional figure who would have to be removed for the final overthrow of capitalism, Lerner was unwilling to risk a revolution in the hope that it would be followed by a socialist utopia. He supported Roosevelt, though his endorsement was lukewarm. Those were the days when Roosevelt's talents were commonly underestimated, even by experienced observers like Walter Lippmann, who dismissed FDR as "a kind of amiable Boy Scout" and, still more derisively, as "a pleasant man who, without any important qualifications for the office, would very much like to be President."[7]

In coming to terms with the New Deal, Lerner was working through the thinking of Veblen in order to develop a position of his own. Just as Veblen had all but endorsed communism, so Lerner concluded that collectivism was destined to replace individualism. American Progressivism, he thought, was too tame. Its social vision, rooted in Midwestern populism, suffered from an agrarian bias and a poor understanding of the problems and the potential of the heavily immigrant and urban working class. Marxian analysis, which posited the rigidity of the class structure and the inevitability of class conflict, fit Europe better than it did America, with its open and highly mobile class system. The task for American intellectuals was therefore to develop a more appropriate program for economic reorganization.

In this connection, Lerner thought that his fascination with the lives of business titans could be a springboard for the kind of analysis that was needed. In 1930 he submitted an article to H. L. Mencken, then the editor of *The American Mercury*. Entitled "Jupiter on Wall Street," the article concerned the financial tycoon J. Pierpont Morgan. To Lerner's delight, Mencken accepted the piece even though it had a Veblenian tone and Mencken, although he lampooned everyone, had great respect for businessmen and detested Veblen. Lerner's essay mixed admiration for Morgan as a kind of heroic buccaneer with antagonism to capitalism as an obsolete system. This success with Mencken led indirectly to a meeting with Lincoln Steffens, then the dean of American muckraking journalism. Steffens had asked his friend Alvin Johnson to help identify someone who might be able to do a biography of Louis Kirstein, a successful Boston businessman. Johnson recommended Lerner, saying the Morgan piece should interest Steffens. When Lerner presented himself at Steffens's Manhattan home in the East 50s and was introduced to Kirstein, he was perplexed to discover that Steffens wanted someone who would be critical of his friend. "Kirstein," he told Lerner, "wants someone to write his life as a success story. I tell him he's been a failure. That's the way the story should be written." Kirstein frowned. Steffens asked to see the Morgan article and went off to read it by himself. Left alone with Lerner, Kirstein protested Steffens's view: "My life has not been a failure, in spite of everything Steffens says. I've made money, sure, but I've shared it with my employees and I run model stores. Is that a failure?" When Steffens returned, he handed back the *Mercury* article to Lerner saying, "This won't do. You admire the man. In spite of everything you have written about him, you do admire him. It simply won't do. Kirstein has to be written about by someone who sees businessmen as failures."

Kirstein was downcast, and Lerner was devastated. He had been told by Johnson that the fee they had in mind was the then colossal sum of $10,000. Apart from the money, he wanted more than anything to work for Steffens, the most famous left-wing journalist of the day, who had discovered Reed and licked the cub reporter into shape. Lerner soon recovered and consoled himself with the thought that he was probably better off on his own. Besides, he thought, Steffens was suffering from a typically myopic Progressive moralism. He could not understand that it was possible to admire the achievements of an entrepreneur and at the same time show that the system requiring entrepreneurs had outlived its usefulness. He was too much of a sentimentalist, with too little a sense of history, to be able to make that kind of distinction. That was why Steffens could lurch from Progressive muckraking to a resigned acceptance of Soviet communism. He had begun by exposing the corruption of the municipal bosses and "rings" and ended with his fatuous whitewash of Bolshevik Russia: "I have been over into the future and it works." Lerner's more flexible thinking was his undoing with Steffens, but the encounter left him resolved to approach social realities with a more complex and more hard-boiled attitude.

After the disappointment with Steffens, Lerner had better though much less lucrative luck with Allen Johnson and Dumas Malone, the editors of the *Dictionary of American Biography*. They liked a sketch he did of John Warne ("Bet-a-Million") Gates and commissioned him to do seven more entries. Lerner consoled himself that his talent for biography was not going altogether unappreciated and honed his radical axe by recounting the often rapacious careers of the great entrepreneurs.

Teaching and Writing: Yaddo, Wellesley, and Harvard

The Great Depression and the election of Franklin Delano Roosevelt as president gave Lerner's thinking and writing a more immediate political focus. Early in 1933, Roosevelt electrified the country with his inaugural address and the legislative blizzard of the first hundred days. Lerner teetered on the brink of accepting the New Deal as the answer to America's problems or rejecting it as yet another spurious reform that did not address the systemic failings of capitalism. At times he feared that Roosevelt would end up sponsoring a corporatist fascism like Mussolini's and that populist demagogues like Huey Long and Father Coughlin would replace him by trumping his appeal to the disaffected and downtrodden. But as some of the New Deal's experiments took hold and roused the country from defeatist torpor, Lerner came to see its reforms as the best immediate alternative to fascism, one that reflected a level-headed American pragmatism that was the best antidote to populist panaceas. He saw Roosevelt as a shrewd democratic politician with the talents needed to achieve democratic legitimacy. He began to rethink the view of Veblen and Marx that "the state was the vessel and capitalism the content, the state the glove and the class struggle the mailed fist." The images, he came to think, should have been reversed: "Democracy was the substance Roosevelt would have to save and capitalism only the form."

During the summer of 1932, Lerner was given an opportunity to formulate a position of his own, but his first efforts were unsuccessful. He was invited to attend the retreat known as "Yaddo" in Saratoga, where creative writers and artists lived together in a secluded setting free of distractions. Those invited were all left-wing luminaries, and Lerner felt honored to be included. He found himself attracted to the beautiful Marion Greenwood, a painter with long red hair and striking features, who reminded him of a pre Raphaelite Madonna. She would later be drawn to the Mexican muralist José Orozco, but at the time she was attached to two other writers in residence, Philip Stevenson and Josephine Herbst,[8] so Lerner had to be content with sitting for a portrait by her. The composer Marc Blitzstein, then at work on an anticapitalist opera, *The Cradle Will Rock*, was the center of attention—dark-haired, intense, with

a gift for mixing satire with horror. Lerner was supposed to be working on his first book, to be called *The Modern State*. He made numerous starts but found that he was not ready to do a book and also
that the assumption behind the Spartan atmosphere of Yaddo did
not work for him. The "Yaddo scenario," he thought, was based on
the "false premise" that what creative people need most is leisure
and solitude:

> Not so. I have written my better books in the midst of life, with too
> many other things to do and with my small sons clustered around my
> typewriter or galloping through my study in wild Indian garb. . . .
> There were times, alone in that monastic room, where I would get an
> overpowering urge to play solitaire, or retrace some sexual encounter
> in memory, or sneakily lie down on the cot for a brief nap, and each
> time I would fight it off with combined virtue and guilt.

His thinking was better stimulated during the following summer at an Institute for Social Progress held at Wellesley College,
attended by hundreds of people of all ages. Lerner, by then a faculty member at Sarah Lawrence, was asked to serve as chairman of
the Institute's faculty. He not only contributed but gained from listening to both the students and civic leaders, including Roger Bab-
son, a keen student of business statistics who was to found the Bab-
son Institute, Benjamin Graham, who became an acute analyst of
the stock market, and Henry Dennison, a manufacturer who had
ideas about how to organize business that would make him a godlike
figure in postwar Japan. The foremost economist in attendance was
Gardiner Means, a New Englander who also had a small factory in
which he wove beautiful rugs. He was better known for having
written, in 1932, with Adolf Berle, the *wunderkind* of the Columbia Law School, *The Modern Corporation and Private Property*, a
highly influential study that became the bible of the New Deal and
vindicated Veblen's view that in mature capitalism ownership and
control would become separate and antagonistic. In these meetings, the faculty and students covered every phase of the economy,
the New Deal's alphabet agencies, the labor movement, the youth
corps, the price-fixing mechanisms, the planning agencies, and the
wheeling and dealing behind the scenes.

In 1934, he went to Washington briefly to become director of a
New Deal agency designed to encourage consumer activism, but
although he enjoyed the enthusiasm he found in the capital, he soon
realized that he was not cut out to be a government administrator

and returned to the more congenial academic environment of Sarah Lawrence. A year later he was elated to receive an offer of a one-year lectureship from the Government Department at Harvard. Laski had held a similar appointment fifteen years earlier when he caused a sensation (and scandalized President Lowell) by giving a speech on the Boston Common in support of a strike by the Boston Police. Lerner quickly accepted the offer, though he decided not to leave New York but to commute to Cambridge.

At Harvard Lerner taught one course on constitutional law, a subject on which he had already written major law review essays. Asked to teach another, for freshmen, on classics in political theory, he found himself reading for the first time the political writings of Plato, Aristotle, and Machiavelli. Mims, his *Encyclopaedia* colleague, who was also teaching at Harvard, suggested he read Machiavelli's *Discourses*. When he did, and realized that the *Prince* and *Discourses* had not been put out in a single edition, he decided to write an introduction to a translation to be published in the Modern Library series. For the same series he also did an introduction to a translation of Aristotle's *Politics* and an edition of Adam Smith's *Wealth of Nations*.

In Cambridge Lerner also began a long friendship with Felix Frankfurter, then a professor at the Law School, to whom he had been introduced by Laski. Frankfurter knew and liked Lerner's work and had already reprinted an essay of his on Brandeis in a book he had edited. They maintained a steady correspondence when Lerner left Harvard and before and after Frankfurter received an appointment to the Supreme Court. Whenever Lerner wrote about judicial decisions, he braced himself for reactions signed "FF," sometimes laudatory and sometimes hectoring. When Lerner published an article in the *Yale Law Journal* in 1937, Frankfurter wrote playfully to chide him for being overly pedantic in resting so much of his argument on authorities (especially Frankfurter) rather than relying on his own judgment:

> Do you know the Talmud's parable about drunkenness? "If one man tells you you're drunk, knock his teeth out. If two tell you you're drunk laugh at them. But if three tell you you're drunk, go to bed."
>
> Not less than three of your friends have commented on the fact, as phrased by one of them, that your [essay] was "too elaborately aware of the sources of some of your thinking." I concur.[9]

Frankfurter was especially anxious that Lerner gain a proper

understanding of the need for judicial restraint, his most passionately held belief. In April 1936 Lerner wrote an editorial for *The
Nation* criticizing an opinion written by the conservative Justice
George Sutherland, a Harding appointee who had spoken for the
Court in the Carter Coal case. The opinion invoked Brandeis's belief in judicial impartiality to strike down the Bituminous Coal Act,
a major piece of New Deal legislation allowing control of production, prices, and wages in that depressed industry. Lerner had described Sutherland's reference to Brandeis as a smokescreen designed to cover a conservative bias. Frankfurter, who knew from
Lerner's previous writings that he preferred to see the Court bow to
the will of the majority rather than behave impartially, objected
sharply to his reading of the opinion, accusing him of deliberately
trying to tar Brandeis by associating him with the Court's "inex-
cusable . . . defiance of the Brandeis technique":

> But you were trying to hit two birds with one stone. You saw a good
> chance to take a crack at the Brandeis technique by showing how the
> enemy can use it. And really, Max, you quite missed the point. The
> thing is very serious business and I wish you would realize a little
> more the kind of a fight we've got on our hands. You know radicals
> can also be doctrinaires. Sometimes I wish you'd spent a year with
> me instead of a year with Hammy. This is nothing against Hammy,
> and certainly nothing in my favor. I merely think you would under-
> stand the tools and techniques of the other side a little better and
> therefore would be more effective in the employment of your own
> great resources.[10]

Obviously feeling trapped, Lerner replied deferentially, assuring Frankfurter that what he had written was not meant "as a slam
at Brandeis" for whose work on the Court he had nothing but admiration. He tried to escape Frankfurter's wrath by explaining that
he had relied on Cardozo's dissenting opinion in the case, and ac-
knowledging that Frankfurter understood these matters better than
he did—in the process committing a revealing Freudian slip:

> What I meant to say was merely that Justice Sutherland is using—
> not genuinely but meretriciously—the idea that the Supreme
> Court should not pass upon the constitutionality of an act unless it
> has to, and that he is concealing behind that screen an outrageous
> partisanship. If I didn't convey that by the context of the two para-
> graphs, I am sorry for my clarity [sic]. . . .
> Do not misunderstand this letter. I know perfectly well that

you have an enormously greater understanding of what the actual struggle is like at the present time between the forces of the big interests and the liberal forces. If I had one-tenth of your knowledge, I should be one hundred times more confident than I am in tackling this job that I have. I am not trying to defend what I wrote. I am trying only to say that I did the best I could within my limitations, and you must not set it down to any malevolence toward Brandeis, or any irresponsible haste. I think we start our analyses of these cases from somewhat different intellectual premises. But I can assure you that my own anxiety about the struggle that is now being waged equals that of any other person in the country, and my own sense of responsibility for the small role I am playing is continually growing. I am learning what tools and techniques the other side has, although I am probably learning very slowly. Do forgive me if it is too slow for your own anxiety.[11]

After this exchange, when Frankfurter had not written for a while, Lerner wrote to ask whether he had "done something more than I ordinarily do to hurt you." Frankfurter's reply was typically sardonic but reassuring:

Dear dear dear—
Don't you record that I remained friends with Walter Lippmann more than ten years after he broke my heart—which is not to compare you with WL, but to give you an indication of my cardiac coefficient.[12]

He ended on a conciliatory note by claiming that what he had problems with was not Lerner but journalism. This was a continuing theme of their correspondence. "Maybe Herbert Croly was right," he wrote to Lerner in 1945 and several times afterward, "and the Lord intended me to be a journalist but perversity took me into the law."[13] In 1949, after a visit to Brandeis University, he wrote to say that he urged the university's president to make some arrangement for Lerner that would draw him out of journalism so as to free him from the habits of mind it begets in its practitioners. Lerner thanked him but defended his addiction to journalism: "The simple fact is that it pays rotten,* but I like it, and I have a pride of craftsmanship

---

*Just how "rotten" the pay was, and how eager Lerner was to keep his journalistic foothold, may be gleaned from an exchange he had in 1963, after he had been the leading political columnist of the *New York Post* for fourteen years. The publisher, Dorothy Schiff, wrote to turn down his request for a raise, insisting that she could afford to pay no more than a hundred dollars apiece for the three

in it not dissimilar to the pride you have in the judicial process . . . When you read again Holmes's speeches asserting that the study of the law need not narrow or truncate the minds of its students, provided it is carried on by 'seeing the relation between your fact and the framework of the universe,' you may get some notion of how my defense of journalism will run." * [14]

The Nation, the Purge Trials, and the Court-Packing Controversy

Lerner found his Harvard teaching assignments challenging and made friends with other faculty members as well, but he felt torn between two worlds—the academic world of Cambridge and the political-literary world of New York. At Christmas of 1935 a call came from Maurice Wertheim, publisher of The Nation, inviting him to become its political editor. Lerner informed Elliott of the offer and told him he was tempted by it but would consider turning it down if Harvard would convert the lectureship into a tenure-track assistant professorship. Elliott and Friedrich assured Lerner they could manage that, but when they took the proposal to Harvard's president, James Bryant Conant, he reacted coolly. A chemist, Conant thought that someone who would seriously consider leaving Harvard to become the editor of a weekly political magazine had better do so. Lerner knew that in accepting the position at The Nation and losing the prestige of a Harvard faculty appointment he was taking a risk, especially since he might not be able to keep the job at The Nation. He took the gamble because he thought he could achieve enough prestige on his own and that one day he would

---

columns he wrote each week. He replied, with as much firmness as he could muster, that he could settle for no less than $325 a week (n.d., YMA, I, 7, 358).

*Lerner's admiration for Frankfurter is evident in a description he later offered of Frankfurter as a Supreme Court justice: "His mind is a little like the structure of his sentences, generally a long sentence, at once serpentine and brittle, that winds and crackles its way into a subject by the help of many subordinate clauses and parentheses. It is involved, magisterial, and enormously alive . . . His diminutive size, round face, the dancing eyes behind his pince-nez, the unending stream of mocking wit which is punctuated by a radiant and explosive laugh: all these combine to form an unforgettable image. If it is totally unlike the reserve and repose one associates with the aristocratic figure of Oliver Wendell Holmes, who was his friend and is still his idol, it only serves to underline the fact that Frankfurter is like no one else" (Lerner, "The High Tribunal," ms., 1951).

return to academic life having benefited from his encounter with the world of political journalism. Lerner would not forget or forgive Conant's dismissive attitude. In May of 1943, Conant wrote an essay for *The Atlantic Monthly* entitled, "Wanted: American Radicals," evoking the memory of such figures as Thoreau and lamenting the absence of radicals from current American life. In response, Lerner wrote a column for *PM* called "Conant's American Radicals" in which he remarked tartly that evidently the only radicals Conant liked were dead ones.[15]

Wertheim had decided to offer *The Nation* position to Lerner after reading his review of Harold Laski's *The State in Theory and Practice* in the *Herald Tribune* book review section. The truth was, Lerner was later to observe, that "I knew less about the state than Laski, who knew little, and Wertheim knew even less than either of us." But there was an odd chemistry that brought together the British socialist intellectual, the American professor of radical leanings, and a shrewd Wall Street broker who was bored with money-making, admired Roosevelt, and wanted to influence public opinion to support the New Deal. Wertheim introduced Lerner to his talented young daughter Barbara, who had been to Spain and Japan, had done graduate work on the Far East, and had lived in London where she had been involved with the anti-Fascist Left. Wertheim suggested that she might be a helpful research assistant. Since she was not only the boss's daughter but well qualified, Lerner was happy to take her on. She was later to become a widely read historian known under her married name as Barbara Tuchman. Throughout her career, she valued Lerner's advice and remained his warm admirer, as he was of her.

Lerner moved his family to a fourth-floor walk-up on West 12th Street, in Greenwich Village where he haunted the neighborhood cafes that had become radical shrines. Here was where Reed had lived with Louise Bryant, where Max Eastman edited *The Masses*. Later, when Lerner saw the film "Reds," in which the actor Warren Beatty played Reed, he would observe that "in one way or another we were all Reds in those days." Not to be on the Left was to risk becoming a pariah among the circle of friends in which he and Anita moved. Connie was enrolled in the progressive City and Country School. With her younger, red-headed sister, Pamela, she would wait at the top of the stairs for him to return from the office and tell them bedtime stories about the supposed adventures of King Ludwig of Bavaria, the character he invented for all the children. On weekends the apartment was often the setting for large parties attended by Sarah Lawrence students and alumnae, fellow staffers on *The Nation* and *The New Republic*, faculty friends from Harvard and Columbia, visitors from Washington, and others involved with writing and publishing. The atmosphere was heavy with dogmatic Popular Front certitude, even in the face of the great unknowns that loomed domestically and internationally. At times, he would survey the scene and the bright, self-assured cocktail chatter and think of a glittering Belgian ballroom on the eve of Waterloo.

The Nation had been published for some seventy years when Lerner joined it in 1936. It had been founded by Edward L. Godkin in 1865 as the organ of liberal Republicanism. The magazine had passed to Henry Villard, newspaper publisher and political reformer as well as railway financier, and then to his son, Oswald Garrison Villard, named for his grandfather, the abolitionist William Lloyd Garrison. Villard *fils* became editor in 1898. He surrounded himself with an admiring court and held sway for thirty-five years. Under his editorship, *The Nation* remained a passionate advocate of Godkin-style laissez-faire liberalism and also of pacifism. Villard had opposed U.S. entry into the First World War and would later oppose Roosevelt's effort to get around the Neutrality Act in order to come to the aid of Britain.

When Wertheim acquired a controlling interest from Villard in 1935, he set up an editorial committee presided over by Villard as editor-in-chief. Lerner joined the committee as political editor, along with Freda Kirchwey, the managing editor, and Joseph Wood Krutch—not yet the celebrated naturalist he would become—as the literary editor. Lerner liked the arrangement at first because it enabled him to concentrate on editorial work and avoid the chores of running the magazine. Because of his coequal status, however, he had to battle for his editorial positions at the Thursday morning editorial conferences—frequently at the cost of bruised feelings. It did not take long for Lerner and Villard to rub each other the wrong way. Villard saw Lerner as a brash, abrasive, young New Deal radical—and a Russian-Jewish immigrant to boot—who would threaten his cherished classical liberal beliefs for the sake of untried, utopian social reforms. Lerner returned the compliment, describing Villard as "a symbol of the feckless paleo-liberalism that was stuck with free trade, anti-regulation of big business, and isolationism, and had left the field to the corporate barons and the dictators." [16] He saw pre–New Deal liberals like Villard as sleepwalkers, unaware that a new world was dawning. The other members of the editorial board also felt Villard was something of an old fogey but did not want to break with him sharply. Lerner was not part of their circle and was too impatient to be tactful. Kirchwey had welcomed his arrival at first, but she came to resent his brashness and the impact he was having through his writing, especially since she herself was not as polished a writer. He got along better with Krutch, who was less political than Kirchwey and less beholden than Villard to the prevailing liberal dogmas.

Despite personal frictions, the editors initially shared a strong common bond because of the Civil War in Spain. In 1936, embattled Republican Spain became the focus of the Left's hopes and anxieties. Here, it was hoped, the Popular Front would prove itself and defeat the Fascist coalition led by right-wing generals and reactionary clerics. This hope was the magnet that attracted idealists like André Malraux, George Orwell, and Arthur Koestler, and the young Americans who enlisted in the Abraham Lincoln Brigade. At the time, Malraux was a dashing figure who had raised a brigade of volunteer pilots to aid the Loyalists. His widely read novel, *Man's Fate*, loosely based on his experiences in China, combined Communist theory with revolutionary fervor. Malraux offered to come to America to raise funds for the Loyalist cause, and *The Nation* was chosen to sponsor the effort. As the magazine's political editor, Lerner was asked to chair a meeting at which Malraux spoke.

Lerner's rising status made him a target for cultivation by those farther to the Left. He agreed to speak at a celebration of the work of Maxim Gorky arranged by Joseph Freeman, editor of the Marxist journal *New Masses*. At the meeting Freeman set out to win Lerner over to the Communist camp, saying, "Our people like and admire you," and the flattery persuaded him to chair another meeting exploring the affinities between Marx and Freud. At Freeman's instigation, Lerner was invited to have dinner with Vito Marcantonio, the radical New York congressman elected on the American Labor Party line and tagged by the press as "Red Marc." Lerner noticed two dark-looking men hovering near the table. They were Marcantonio's bodyguards, Freeman whispered. "You can have that too if you join us," he added. Lerner was unmoved. "I enjoy working with you," he told Freeman, "but as for joining you, I have to tell you that I will never enroll as a soldier in any political army." Occasionally, during the turmoil caused by reports of the purge trials, little delegations of Communist Party functionaries would come to his office at *The Nation,* ostensibly to give him information but actually to try to give him "guidance." One night, when there must have been a serious crisis, V. J. Jerome, whom Lerner recalled as a "dour, prissy clerk of a man whom we used to call the 'Cultural Commissar,'" came with two other comrades to his apartment:

> They had heard that I had written an editorial on the trials. Could they see it? Reading it in galleys Jerome said it wouldn't do and showed where I had to change it. I laughed. "I don't think you understand" I said. "This is my editorial, not yours." I showed them to the door and never saw Jerome again.

The furthest Lerner went in associating himself with the Communists was in expressing intellectual admiration for Lenin's accomplishments. He admitted later that just as he had been drawn to the Horatio Alger "strive and succeed" myth in admiring the Robber Barons, so now he felt a hunger for militancy which expressed itself in admiration for mythic revolutionaries like Lenin and Reed—despite Lenin's dictatorial style and Reed's political innocence.

Reports from Spain about the political interference of Soviet agents and from the Soviet Union about internal repression caused Lerner discomfort, but did not lead him to join those denouncing the Soviet Union. To condemn the Soviet Union at a time when it was the only country supporting Republican Spain, he thought, risked weakening the unity of the Popular Front and endangering the Loyalist cause. News of the purge trials was brought back from Moscow by *The Nation*'s correspondent Louis Fischer, a close friend of Kirchwey's, who had gone to Russia sympathetic to the aims of the Revolution but had been shaken by the trials. Upon his return he had hinted at his disillusionment in talks with the editorial board, though he remained reluctant to give up on the Bolsheviks entirely, and ended by urging the editors to pay more attention to the need to support the Spanish Republic. Lerner agreed and found himself walking a tightrope, condemning Stalin and Stalinism but not the Revolution that had spawned his iron dictatorship:

> I expressed the ambivalence of our whole group in my editorials, condemning Stalin but not the Revolution itself—a dubious paradox since Stalin was the evil flowering of the totalitarian party and the GPU state. No longer wholly bemused by Russia itself I still clung to the democratic potentials of collectivism elsewhere, especially in Spain and America, and I was fearful that the focusing on Stalin would "play into the hands" of Russia's enemies in the fascist

regimes, who were also America's enemies. It was politically as well as morally blinkered thinking, but I shared my ambivalence not only with the *Nation* staff (except Joe Krutch) but with the liberal community we wrote for. It was a case of the blind leading the blind. It would be a decade before I could face the Gorgon's head that the Soviet Union presented to the Left.

For America, throughout the period from the New Deal to the end of World War II, Lerner championed a more thoroughgoing but democratic economic reorganization, presenting his ideas in his classes and in a cascade of writings, most of which appeared in *The Nation* and *The New Republic,* and supporting Roosevelt and the New Deal with growing if still qualified enthusiasm. In the 1936 campaign, Roosevelt was at his most militant, attacking the demagogues of the Right while also pouring scorn on the anti–New Deal Democrats, including Al Smith, whose "American Liberty League" he derided as a clutch of frightened corporate managers. When FDR trounced the Republican candidate, Governor Alf Landon, Lerner wrote a triumphant editorial for *The Nation* claiming that Roosevelt's reelection was a victory not only for a man but for a cause—a cause he identified as "progressivism" rather than liberalism. Later, when the alarming economic slump in 1937 seemed to show that the jerry-built programs of the New Deal were not working, Lerner called for a more militant program of government initiatives.

Economic theory was no more Lerner's strongest suit than it was FDR's. Like the president, he was committed to a few nostrums, but his were more Keynesian than FDR's: antitrust, higher consumer demand, especially through trade union bargaining, deficit financing, and planning. He was considerably more knowledgeable about the Supreme Court and in favor of reforming it via a constitutional amendment that would have ended the life terms of justices. From Cambridge, Frankfurter encouraged Lerner to attack the Court's activism:

> You will profoundly disappoint me if you do not write a rip-snorting piece on the deeper significance of the Supreme Court's discovery that, for a hundred years, it has been usurping power and itself violating the Constitution. Or maybe you don't know—for how should you, since not a single New York paper that I saw mentioned it—that the Supreme Court last Monday in *Erie Railroad Company* v. *Tompkins* did what I have just stated.[17]

Controversy over the Court's resistance to the New Deal had

mounted since May 1935, when a Court majority struck down the National Recovery Act, the linchpin of the New Deal's regulatory apparatus, in the critical Schechter case, popularly known as the "sick chicken case" because it involved the conviction of a small poultry firm for selling diseased chickens. This first blow was followed by others, notably the rejection in 1936 of the legislation establishing the Agricultural Adjustment Act. Roosevelt responded by making a campaign issue out of the Court's "horse and buggy" conservatism. Two weeks after taking the oath of office in 1937, he proposed to deal with the problem by asking Congress to reform the judiciary act. He wanted the act to provide that whenever any federal judge reached the age of seventy and failed to retire, another judge be appointed to the bench on which he served—the total number of such new judges not to exceed fifty. Six of the sitting justices on the Supreme Court had already reached that age, so the proposal would have permitted the president to increase the number of justices on the Court from nine to as many as fifteen. The anti-Roosevelt press promptly dubbed the proposal a plan to "pack the Court." The proposal triggered an avalanche of criticism from FDR's enemies, who were eager to paint him as an overreaching dictator. Lerner took the president's side, arguing that something had to be done to prevent the Court majority from reading its capitalist predilections into the Constitution. He saw the battle between FDR and the Court as a contest for the American future between democracy and reactionary conservatism—between the new course chosen by the people and the stubborn resistance of "nine old men." The Legal Realists with whom Lerner was in philosophical agreement maintained that neither the law nor legal institutions could be thought of as "above the battle." To him, however, this was not just an abstract question of judicial philosophy but a political question of whether unelected judges should be allowed to thwart the clear will of the majority.

But how to break the impasse? Even many New Deal sympathizers were put off by FDR's proposal. Lerner thought it a coy tactic which did not address the major issue, which was not the age of the justices but their arrogant presumption. In editorial meetings, Villard argued against Roosevelt's proposal, but a majority of the editors decided the magazine should support Roosevelt. Villard was outraged, and Kirchwey made sure his dissent appeared prominently in the magazine. Unfortunately for Lerner's tenure as political editor, Wertheim agreed with Villard. In an effort to resolve the dispute, Wertheim invited Lerner to his home in Greenwich for the weekend, then to his Manhattan penthouse. "I have plans and dreams of other publications," he told Lerner, "and you are part of my plans. But you have to understand how I feel. I can't face my friends downtown on this court-packing plan. They read your editorials and they think I'm either a fool or crazy." Lerner promised to reconsider his position, but when he went back to the office and reviewed an opinion piece he had written for the next issue on the subject, he decided he could not in conscience back down. Wertheim countered by writing a column for publication in the magazine disagreeing with Lerner's view. From that point on, their relationship never returned to what it had been.

Roosevelt was doing even worse than Lerner until his luck changed. The president was learning that many Americans opposed presidential tampering with the Court, and on this issue he lost the support of a number of his closest allies in the Senate. But then came several developments that enabled him to set aside the proposal. Justice Van Devanter retired, Justice Roberts switched positions on New Deal legislation—prompting a neat pun on an old adage about a "switch in time saving nine"—and a new Court majority now upheld two major pieces of the New Deal, the Social Security Act and the Wagner Labor Act. Lerner too was able to breathe easier. Roosevelt's next move was to nominate Van Devanter's replacement. The first justice he appointed was the most militant liberal in the Senate, Hugo Black of Alabama. FDR was confident that the Senators would have a hard time refusing to confirm one of their own, and in fact Black was quickly confirmed. In *The Nation* Lerner hailed the appointment as the harbinger of a judicial renaissance. Almost immediately, however, a cloud appeared on the horizon when the sensational news broke that Black had been, at an earlier time in his life, a member of the Ku Klux Klan.

The shock caused by this discovery threatened to force Roosevelt to cancel the appointment, and Lerner played a role in saving it. Black had been on a visit to England when the story hit the press. Laski, who was among Black's hosts, cabled from London asking Lerner to meet with the prospective justice aboard his ship when it docked at Hampton Roads, Virginia. Lerner hurried to the port of entry along with a horde of reporters. He managed to slip a note under Black's stateroom door, and Mrs. Black emerged to whisper that they would meet with him after a press conference. When the Blacks debarked, Black said little to the reporters, adding that he would say what he had to say directly to the public in a radio address. Black then asked Lerner if he would like to accompany them back to their home in Alexandria. Lerner agreed and later spent the evening with the couple, beginning a long friendship with an interview which was a political journalist's dream scoop. Lerner returned to his office and wrote a story recounting Black's conversion from Alabama redneck to New Deal liberal. Black admitted that he had been an opportunist when he accepted Klan support in running for the Senate, but contended that he could not have won election without it. Once in office, he said, he had been swept up in the New Deal fervor and had broken completely with the Klan. Although Lerner thought that Black remained an opportunist, he was convinced that his political views had indeed changed, and that he could be counted on to become a great progressive jurist. Lerner's sympathetic article in *The Nation* helped sway opinion leaders in the groups who would otherwise have been most strongly opposed to the nomination. When Black told the same story to a national radio audience, the *New York Times* reported incorrectly that Lerner had helped write the address. What Lerner had done was to serve Black as a kind of test audience for his account. For his support of Black, Lerner was bombarded with abuse from readers. He recalled a typical letter from Alfred A. Knopf, the publisher, who said that if Lerner could support such a Fascist as Black, it was the end of their friendship. The article had considerable impact, but it only reinforced his co-editors' doubts about Lerner's moral and political judgment. When Black joined the Court and turned out to be a champion of First Amendment rights and social reform, Lerner felt vindicated.

In defending Black's appointment and the New Deal, Lerner became convinced that what was happening under FDR's leadership was a pragmatic prelude to a fuller transformation to come. In 1942, he began but never finished a book he had planned to call *The New Federalist*. In a draft chapter he reflected on what had happened:

> It was less than a decade ago, yet it seems a whole generation removed. What stabbed at us in America was a combination of economic and constitutional crisis. In Europe the continent was being darkened by the Nazi racial madness and the Nazi imperialist dream. Few saw at the time that Hitler, just beginning to build his military machine, was counting on internal crises within the democracies before he struck. Roosevelt was then in his first term, having come into office just when the industrial crisis turned into a bank panic. The Lords of Creation came to him pleading for government inter-

vention as the faithful might plead for supreme unction. These men of action on the Right, always certain of themselves, had abdicated their rule; the men of thought on the Left were convinced that this was the end of capitalism, and that if Roosevelt acted it would be toward fascism. As for the President himself, he never lost his buoyancy and his unflagging will, even though he had little idea of what he would do.

Roosevelt had "neither plan or program," he went on, "only a list of things about which something had to be done," notably the security of the banks, the structure of debt, speculation in the security markets, the collapsing wage and price structure of overcompetitive industries, the relief of impoverished "independent farmers," increase of labor's purchasing power through collective bargaining and the setting of a minimum wage, the need for immediate relief, and, for the long run, a social security system. "Blind and blundering" as the first steps were, "they accomplished the purpose of giving the people an image of decisiveness as they gave the economy an emergency scaffolding of support." They did not reflect a philosophy so much as a mood—"the mood of an affirmative state." The mood came close to being shattered in 1935 and 1936 by the decisions of the Supreme Court. The business interests who stood to lose from economic reform fought back with every weapon they had but mainly through the Court, "which since Jefferson's day had been the final defense line of the owning groups against every drastic reform program."

Lerner heaped scorn on Roosevelt's enemies on the Court. "The greatness of the tradition of John Marshall and Roger B. Taney was gone," he wrote. "Lesser men had come, with narrower minds, and with economic doctrines that no longer bore any relation to the real world outside; but they spoke with a magisterial assurance that to them alone was the freedom of the country entrusted as a sacred charge." Of the four "die-hards," Willis Van Devanter was the leader, "even though there was some insurmountable barrier that kept him from putting pen on paper." The most articulate was George Sutherland, "a man who wore Constitutional blinkers with the same primness with which he wore his *pince-nez*" and who wielded a lethal axe against New Deal measures. The third was James McReynolds, "a man of consuming hatreds, a feudist rather than a jurist," who "did not trouble to adorn his economic primitivism even by a humanism of language." Finally, there was Pierce Butler, a railroad lawyer "to whom even elevation to the Court had not given either distinction of mind or tolerance of spirit." These four voted almost always as a monolithic bloc, leading Homer Cummings, the attorney general at the time, to remark from bitter experience that they would vote against a New Deal measure "even if the Angel Gabriel himself made the argument."

Having four votes, the die-hards needed only one more to make a majority. For that vote they looked to the "balance-of-power group," consisting of the chief justice, Charles Evans Hughes, and Owen Roberts. Hughes was the very model of a Supreme Court judge in bearing and demeanor, through his commanding presence, his piercing eyes, and whiskers—a "picture-book Jove," as someone remarked at the time, who might at any moment hurl his thunderbolt at some mere mortal. Hughes, Lerner thought, proved to be a master political strategist whose ruling passion was to keep the Court safe from attack. As long as he could carry Justice Roberts with him, during 1933 and 1934, he could join the three liberals to form a majority, but when Roberts swung to the side of the die-hards in the Railway Retirement cases, Hughes had to follow to keep every decision from being split five to four. Despite his lesser status, Justice Roberts "proved to be the tail that wagged the judicial dog":

> He was a Philadelphia lawyer who had been government prosecutor in the Teapot Dome frauds, and had thus rubbed shoulders with liberalism. The thing about Justice Roberts was that he was so true to type. There were thousands of lawyers like him all over the country—honest, able, alert, but without the capacity to look beyond the limited horizon of one whose life has been spent guarding the interests of corporate clients. The Pecora Senate investigation, early in 1933, had revealed his name on the now famous House of Morgan "preferred list" of "inside clients" who were "cut in" on securities below the market price. This was no fault of the Justice's, but it showed how the Lords of Creation thought of him. While still a lawyer he had adjured them, perhaps unnecessarily since it was in a speech before the American Bankers Association while Coolidge was president, not to let the government "go into a state of socialism," but to "get out, take off your coats, and root for good old-fashioned Anglo-Saxon individualism." Today he is the Forgotten Man on the Court, but from 1934 to 1937 history, by a cruel irony, cast him in the role of the Marginal Justice, on whom everything else turned.

If he was contemptuous of the die-hards, Lerner venerated the three liberals on the Court. Louis Brandeis, the friend and associate

of Holmes, was the enemy of the "curse of bigness," whether in government or business. Harlan Fisk Stone was "an amalgam of business experience and 'Puritan conscience.'" The youngest but most
highly regarded for his legal knowledge was Cardozo, "sensitive, a
recluse, a man who could write like an angel but who was no Poor
Paul about economics and administration." During the whole period of crisis, the liberals behaved well, Lerner thought, showing a
readiness to make every possible concession to the majority, even
leaning over backward to vote against the administration in doubt-
ful cases. At the time, their work seemed "heartbreakingly futile,"
but in retrospect it had been crucial:

> They carried on the liberal judicial tradition from the era of Justice
> Holmes into the era of the New Deal. Without their dissents and their
> cool but devastatingly reasoned opinions, the nation might have con-
> cluded that the New Deal was in reality unconstitutional, and the
> affirmative state might have died even before it was born. As it was,
> it became ever clearer that the Court majority was not writing into
> its decisions an inexorable Constitution but its own economic pref-
> erences; and President Roosevelt was able to appeal from the Court
> Hyde to the Court Jekyll. When finally in 1938 Justices Hughes and
> Roberts swung back to a liberal Constitutional view, the three dis
> senters reaped what they had kept alive in the dry season.[18]

As he looked back at the constitutional crisis, Lerner had mixed
feelings. Compared to what had happened in world affairs since, it
seemed like a tempest in a teapot, but at the time "no storm over a
matter of domestic policy had equaled it since the Civil War." For
a year beginning with "Black Monday," May 27, 1935, when the
Court had struck down a section of the National Recovery Act as an
improper delegation of power to the president, the conservative
majority had waged a war of annihilation against the New Deal,
and Roosevelt had picked up "the gage of battle." Lerner remembered how in his first year as an editorialist he and his colleagues
waited eagerly each week for each new turn in the fight. The Agricultural Adjustment Act was ruled unconstitutional because the
regulation of farming was not a national concern but had to be left
to the states. The Court majority surprised its critics by upholding
the act authorizing the Tennessee Valley Authority—but only because it was put forward for the purposes of national defense and
flood control. "It is interesting to speculate," Lerner mused, "what
might have happened had the Court majority insisted on holding

the dam unconstitutional." A *New Yorker* cartoon appearing while the decision was being considered showed two workmen on the construction site as a third came running toward them, saying, "My God, Henry, the whole damn thing's unconstitutional." One of the justices was reported to have said wistfully, "We couldn't very well ask the government to rip up the dam and plug up the hole." In the case of *Jones* v. *Securities and Exchange Commission,* Justice Sutherland accused the SEC of being "a star chamber." In the *Carter* v. *Carter Coal Co.,* the National Bituminous Coal Commission was destroyed even before it had much chance to function. In *Morehead* v. *Tipaldo,* a New York state minimum wage law was held invalid. "Since the Court had in 1923 held that the federal government did not have the power which was now denied to the state governments, the President had a heaven-sent chance to point out that the Court had created a 'No-Man's Land' in which the power to govern did not exist." [19]

By the logic of these early decisions, it was clear that the rest of the New Deal was doomed as well, including the Public Utility Holding Act, Social Security, and the National Labor Relations Act. But Roosevelt fought on undaunted and rallied the electorate behind him in the 1936 election. The Court had succeeded mainly in giving the president invaluable campaign material. In the wake of the election, the Court might have capitulated on its own, but FDR decided to force the issue in February 1937 by announcing his plan to enlarge the Court in order to break the impasse over New Deal legislation. Ironically, one of the incidental beneficiaries of the sharp dispute that followed was Frankfurter. Up to then, his name had been anathema to conservatives, but now the word went round, based largely on an earlier encyclopedia article he had written in disapproval of Court packing, that he was against the president's plan. It did not take long before the Bar Association took him to their heart in gratitude and passed a resolution recommending him for the next Court vacancy.

In retrospect, Lerner thought the president had been wrong to be so disingenuous as to claim that the Court calendar was too crowded and the justices afflicted by the ravages of old age. Had he said directly that the Court had played politics rather than respect the Constitution's broad grant of legislative authority to Congress, and therefore that it was necessary to put new blood into the judiciary, there was at least a slim chance the country might have followed him. But "to give his enemies the weapon of accusing him of lack of candor was to court open disaster. He tried to make up for it later by his admirably candid fireside talk to the nation, but it was too late." Finally, the Court executed its famous turnabout and the president gleefully declared victory and dropped his proposal. But he had aroused public opposition because he had not reckoned with the strength of the constitutional image in the minds of the people:

> To be sure, the people were wrong in their associations with the image: the Supreme Court is not the only guardian of the Constitution, and for a year the Court had been doing its best to destroy the effectiveness of a democracy in action without which the Constitutional image could not survive. Yet one does not argue with a symbol-structure. One reckons with it. And the President failed to reckon with it. He had paid a price, having been left open to continuing attacks claiming that he had "dictatorial" ambitions. Fear of fanning such accusations may well have inhibited him from lifting the embargo on goods to the Spanish Republic and made him think twice before tampering with the Neutrality Act to help Britain before America's entry into the war. The country also paid a price in the ruined lives the Court had callously prevented from being rescued, but the result was nothing short of a miracle in political economy— to have our cake and to eat it. Economic recovery was sustained and the Court retained its authoritative status as interpreter of the Constitution and arbiter of the federal system.[20]

The Court's resistance to the New Deal only confirmed Lerner's view, expressed in an often reprinted 1933 law review article, that the Constitution had been made into a weapon for the defense of economic inequality and used against all attempts to modify property rights for the sake of "economic democracy." "The impact of American capitalistic development on the Court," he wrote, "has been at once to pose the problems and condition the answers."[21] In other essays he drove home the same point. John Marshall's genius was not just to assert the national power but to do in the interest of property—he turned up "at just the point where a rising capitalism most needed him."[22] Justice Roger B. Taney too could not escape the belief in the supremacy of property rights over human rights, a belief that led him and the country into the turmoil of Dred Scott.[23] The judicial resistance to the New Deal, far from moving Lerner to the political center, at first only reinforced his radicalism and his reputation for advocating bold measures. Despite the precarious position he had put himself in with the publisher of *The Nation,* his incisive writings—both journalistic and academic— were making him a major figure on the democratic Left.

FOUR

Popular Front Progressive

By the late 1930s Lerner had be-
come a luminary among those on the American Left calling for a
"Popular Front" against fascism and a transition from the New Deal
into the era of what he described as "democratic collectivism." The
boldness and freshness of his thinking, coupled with his rhetorical
skills, won him loyal followers and all but compelled those who disagreed with him to take him seriously. As a rift developed on the
Left over whether to condemn the Bolshevik experiment as inher-
ently repressive or to see it more indulgently as a kind of latter-day
French Revolution that could still outgrow its reign of terror, Lerner sought to straddle the breach. Reluctant to weaken the unity
of the Popular Front—especially after the Soviet Union alone had
come to the aid of the Spanish Republic in its struggle against fascism—he criticized the lack of political democracy in the Soviet
Union but held out hope for eventual reform. As war clouds loomed,
he threw himself into the campaign to oppose isolationism and combat a new wave of anti-Semitism. It was as a spokesman for "Popular Front progressivism" that Lerner became best known in the
years just before America entered the war. After the attack on Pearl
Harbor, he plunged into the effort to mobilize public opinion in

support of the war effort. Meanwhile, the turmoil of his personal life was resolved by a painful divorce followed by a second, happier marriage.

The New Deal and Beyond

V. I. Lenin is supposed to have described George Bernard Shaw as "a good man fallen among the Fabians"—the society founded in the 1880s to promote democratic socialism in Britain. Had the Bolshevik leader survived into the 1930s, he might have made a similar assessment of Max Lerner in the America of the Great Depression. Prepared by Veblen's theory of business crises to expect the worst from the American economy, Lerner was among those who thought that the economic collapse proved that the "price system"—Veblen's term for capitalism—was incompatible with sustained economic growth and any semblance of social equity. Veblen died shortly before the stock market crashed in October 1929 after remarking to a friend: "Naturally there will be other developments right along, but just now Communism offers the best course that I can see." [1] As fascism—with its brazen appeal to the irrational sentiments of race, national chauvinism, and hero worship—emerged as one "other development," Lerner recognized that Veblen's detached, ironic analysis did not go far enough either in anticipating the threat from the Right or in mobilizing resistance on the Left. Along with other American radicals who had previously relied on domestic social critics, he now turned with greater interest to the theories of Marx and Lenin. He did not become a full-fledged Marxist, however, still less a Leninist. His closest affinity was to the Fabians, whose writings he had already come to appreciate.*

Like many on the Left, Lerner was convinced that the widespread appearance of Fascist movements and their rise to power in Italy, Spain, and Germany showed that the privileged classes would do whatever they could to block the transition to socialism, even to the extent of supporting fascism. Although mindful of the constitutional barriers to dictatorship in the United States, he saw fascism

---

*At Brookings, Walton Hamilton had assigned R. H. Tawney's *Religion and the Rise of Capitalism,* the classic study arguing that, contrary to Max Weber's thesis, the "Protestant ethic" did not inspire capitalism but served the bourgeoisie as a convenient rationale. Lerner was impressed by Tawney's thesis, as he was by his moral critique of "the acquisitive society."

as a domestic danger as well—unless the newly elected Franklin Roosevelt could point the way toward an effective alternative. While welcoming the New Deal as a needed palliative, Lerner saw it not as an end in itself but as a possible step toward a more fundamental transformation. If he could be described in these years as a socialist in economics, he was at the same time a democrat in politics and a gradualist, neither an apologist for a dictatorship of the proletariat nor an advocate of violent revolution. Like the Fabians, he was confident that the mass of the people, once fully enfranchised and educated in the values of trade unionism, would wrest control of the "commanding heights of industry" from the "economic royalists" and entrust it to accountable public servants committed to the common good. This was the radical vision that emerged in the 1930s to inspire those on the Left with hope and those on the Right, including skeptics like the economist Joseph Schumpeter, with foreboding.* It was not the Bolshevik example that fired Lerner's radical imagination in the 1930s, rather it was the seeming failure of American capitalism and the vision of a new democratic future the new Deal seemed to prefigure.

The special task for radical intellectuals, Lerner thought, was to think through the character of the transition and formulate the principles with which political leaders could mobilize a following. If working people were to become an effective force, unity would be essential. There could therefore be, as the saying went, "no enemies to the left." Although Lerner scoffed at the notion that the fractious and marginalized Communist Party of the United States could become "the vanguard of the proletariat," he was prepared to cooperate with Communists and opposed "red-baiting." He joined no conspiratorial cells, supported no party line, and took no orders as to what he should or should not write. He allowed his name to be used by causes and organizations he believed in (like the American Civil Liberties Union), but sought to stay independent of movements and political parties and aloof from the factional struggles that made the Left as fractious and sectarian as any religious movement. Struggling to find an Archimedean point from which to grasp

---

*Despite his certainty that the market economy would always outperform a state-managed economic system, Schumpeter concluded gloomily, in *Capitalism, Socialism, and Democracy* (New Haven: Yale University Press, 1942), that leftists were correct to expect that universal suffrage would lead to the adoption of socialism.

what seemed to be the great revolution of modern times, he plunged into the flow of events as a political journalist, while seeking to keep enough detachment to articulate a new political outlook.

While working on his *Encyclopaedia* assignments, which included writing numerous entries, Lerner broke into publishing elsewhere, first by book reviewing, then through magazine articles. He wrote a series of reviews for the American Federation of Labor trade-union newspaper and then for the *New York Post*. In the *Political Science Quarterly* he reviewed Harold Laski's study of communism—in which Laski virtually announced his conversion from pluralism to socialism. Finally he succeeded in gaining entree to the Sunday book review section of the *New York Herald Tribune,* then the premiere medium for reviews, as well as the *Yale Review* and *The New Republic*. In 1931 he published his first article, "Veblen and the Wasteland," in *The New Freeman,* a short-lived liberal weekly. Then came "What is Usable in Veblen?" for *The New Republic,* followed by a series of sharply written articles for the Ivy League law reviews.

Soon he was attracting attention and interest. He was thrilled one day in 1936 to receive a letter from Laski, a preeminent political theorist and socialist intellectual, who was planning to visit New York and wanted to meet him. When they met for tea at the Biltmore, Laski struck Lerner as a bird-like personality, dapper, dark-complexioned, with glossy combed-back hair, "his round glasses making his face even rounder, walking swiftly on ballet-dancer feet, yet with incredible self-possession and authority." Even before the tea came, Laski served up a pleasant surprise, telling Lerner that he was about to refer to him in an article in *The New Republic* as the most promising and important of the younger political theorists in America. Lerner was dumbfounded but elated, unprepared for such an act of generosity from someone he had known only from his writings. Laski's praise boosted Lerner's stock and made the editors more receptive to his contributions. He and Laski were to remain close friends and mutual admirers. In 1938 Laski dedicated his book *Parliamentary Government in England* to Lerner, and they kept up a warm correspondence. Laski made his affection especially clear in a letter in 1941: "There are not many days when you are out of my mind; and when I see something of yours in a journal I give a whoop of joy." [2] Until Laski's death in 1951, Lerner was to see himself, and be seen by others, as Laski's American counterpart.

A Machiavellian at Williams

Any credit Lerner may have earned by supporting Black was not enough to save his job at *The Nation*. Wertheim expected to control his own magazine, and Lerner's support of the Court-packing plan as well as of the Black nomination had caused the publisher embarrassment among his friends. In the spring of 1938 Kirchwey informed Lerner that Wertheim had turned the magazine over to her. Lerner learned from Barbara Wertheim that her father had sold it to Kirchwey for a nominal sum[3] on condition that Lerner would no longer remain political editor. Lerner did not resent Wertheim's behavior, because he saw it as in keeping with a businessman's view of the way of the world, but he did resent Kirchwey's complicity in the maneuver. She was an editor, not a financier, with whom he had made editorial compromises in a process that involved a sense of journalistic ethics. Now she had in effect colluded with Wertheim to fire him—something Wertheim was unwilling to do openly. Lerner felt betrayed by Kirchwey but tried not to show it. He finished the articles he was working on and left without making a scene, feeling good about his life and prospects despite the dismissal.

He would not be jobless for long. The academy beckoned again, this time at the initiative of James Phinney Baxter III, who had come to know Lerner at Harvard, where they were both attached to Adams House. Baxter had just become president of Williams College, nestled in the Berkshire hills of western Massachusetts, and he invited Lerner to join the Williams faculty. Lerner gladly agreed. When Frankfurter wrote to congratulate Baxter on his courage in making the appointment, Baxter replied graciously that it was due not to his courage but to "simply extraordinary good luck . . . Nothing has made me happier this year."[4]

At Williams Lerner found himself among a lively group of radicals, none more than ten years his senior. Two of his colleagues, Alan Sweezy and Frederick L. Schuman, had been appointed by Baxter's predecessor. Sweezy was a Keynesian "progressive" whose brother Paul, a leading Marxian economic theorist, Lerner had come to know at Harvard as one of a group of bright young intellectuals, including Frank E. Manuel and Norton Long, who would later be his colleagues at Brandeis. Schuman, a specialist on international relations and a popular lecturer, was given to flights of rhetoric and could be curt in dismissing views with which he disagreed. Lerner and Schuman got on while they were colleagues, though they had a kind of sparring-partner relationship, and later debated in public. Baxter, determined to make the faculty even more challenging to the students, proceeded to appoint Raymond Walsh, a specialist on trade unionism, Robert R. R. Brooks, a more moderate liberal than the others, and Robert Lamb, an economic historian. This unusual collection of critical intellectuals attracted attention. The literary historian Howard Mumford Jones wrote an admiring piece about the group in *The Atlantic Monthly*. The radicals were pleased to become celebrities, though the publicity probably left the college's trustees wondering how they had become host to such a den of vipers. Lerner became a particular *bête noir* to Williams's conservative alumni. Baxter once called him to his office and showed him a stack of letters from alumni threatening to cut off financial support for the college so long as he was retained, along with a "Dear Alumnus" form letter he had prepared in reply:

> Thank you for the strong interest you express in the college and its welfare, especially as it relates to the activities of Professor Max Lerner. I need scarcely remind you that my responsibilities as President are limited to the quality of his scholarship and teaching and do not extend to his activities outside the campus, which are in the sphere of his freedom as a citizen. However, if you know of anything in his writing and teaching which reflects on his scholarship or the exercise of his teaching duties, I shall be interested to have you write me again.[5]

But the atmosphere on campus was warm to Lerner. On one Alumni Weekend he taught a class with a number of parents in attendance. The class ended to thunderous applause. Baxter heard about it and was delighted.

In the stimulating environment of Williams, Lerner was exceptionally prolific. He continued to write for a variety of journals, mainly for *The New Republic*, of which he became a contributing editor. He drafted introductory essays to the Modern Library editions of Machiavelli and Aristotle and prepared two compilations of essays, *Ideas Are Weapons* (1939) and *Ideas for the Ice Age* (1941). The Machiavelli introduction was an especially vivid piece of writing. It has been assigned over many years to thousands of undergraduates, giving them a lively sense of the relevance of Machiavelli's thinking to modern events. Although Lerner was not a specialist in the history of Renaissance Italy, he had a keen sense of Machiavelli's importance in stripping the veil from the play of royal ambition and thereby prefiguring the "power politics" of the modern state system. "We live today in the shadow of a Florentine," he began memorably,

> the man who above all others taught the world to think in terms of cold political power. His name was Niccolò Machiavelli, and he was one of those rare intellectuals who write about politics because they have had a hand in politics and learned what it is about. His portraits show a thin-faced, pale little man, with a sharp nose, sunken cheeks, subtle lips, a discreet and enigmatic smile, and piercing black eyes that look as if they knew much more than they were willing to tell.

Machiavelli, he went on, was at once the first scientific observer of political mechanics and a kind of Renaissance artist painting the portrait of power:

> Where others looked at the figureheads, he kept his eyes glued behind the scenes. He sought the ultimate propulsion of events. He wanted to know what made things tick; he wanted to take the clock of the world to pieces to find out how it worked. He went on diplomatic missions, organized the armies of Florence, carried through successfully the long protracted siege of Pisa. Yet always he was concerned about the nature of power. In an age of portraiture it was natural that he too should be a painter, but his subjects never knew they were sitting for him. He studied Pope Julius II, the secular princes, the condottieri; above all he studied Cesare Borgia, the Duke Valentino, who came closer to embodying the naked ideal of power than any other person Machiavelli had met. There was in Machiavelli, as in Savonarola, an intense and searing flame, but it was a secular flame, and the things it fed on were not such things as religious dreams are made of.[6]

The theme of the essay, first presented at a public lecture at Williams, had a present purpose, which was, he later wrote, that

> Machiavelli had to be rescued from "Machiavellism," that he was in his own day a liberal New Dealer, but a hard-thinking, tough-minded one, that his dissection of power was like Harvey's study of the circulation of the blood and marked the transition from the normative thinking of Dante's *De Monarchia* to a detached and dense thinking of the unfooled and unclouded intelligence. And that between the realm of what must be and the realm of what is there is the third realm of what can be—that in speaking to the Prince and in writing about the lessons of Roman history Machiavelli was acting as a possibilist, which we must do in our own time as well.

Lerner attracted good students. One with whom he became especially close was James MacGregor Burns, later to become a brilliant political scientist and historian. Burns was in his junior year in the spring of 1938 when Baxter sent him to the train station at Albany to pick Lerner up and bring him to Williamstown. Lerner was so impressed by Burns that he later said that he decided to teach at Williams because he formed such a good impression of the student body upon meeting him. Burns was to form an equally warm admiration for his teacher:

> He was arresting in appearance to begin with—quite different from the generally WASP teachers we had—and he had that deep, resonant voice, which he employed quite effectively. I vividly remember him sitting in a small seminar and holding us spellbound with the way he spelled out ideas. He had a technique of putting a central question or idea on the blackboard and then working out from it in a series of spirals, until he covered the whole blackboard, rather than simply listing them vertically.[7]

Burns did not do his senior thesis under Lerner, but during his final year as an undergraduate he had the option of taking independent study and did so with Lerner. In 1940–1941, while pursuing graduate study at Harvard, Burns helped Lerner put together his edition of the writings of Justice Holmes. When Burns returned to Williams to teach, they continued to see a good deal of each other. On December 7, 1941, Burns and a fellow graduate student were visiting the Lerner home in Williamstown in the company of two Red Cross nurses they had invited for the weekend. The telephone rang, and Lerner returned from answering it with the news that Pearl Harbor had been bombed. Later on, when Lerner began to write for *PM*, he had to cut back on his teaching at Williams, and Burns sometimes substituted for him. Burns recalls that "having Max in class only half-time or two-thirds time was equivalent to any other teacher in terms of value received."[8] After Burns was drafted into the army in 1942 they maintained a warm and steady correspondence by "V-mail." Writing from Saipan, where he fought in one of the typically ferocious battles of the Pacific campaign, Burns noted: "I've had my share of bombing, shelling, and incessant sniping. Occasionally I've had to take quite literally your dictum that 'History is written by the survivors.' " Lerner was moved to learn that Burns had taken *The Mind and Faith of Justice Holmes*— for which he and a Harvard Law School student, Lawrence F. Ebb, had done research—along with him to read. Lerner wrote back: "I am touched . . . that you should have taken Holmes along with you. It would have moved the old man very much to know that he was being read amidst the Saipan battles." [9] When Burns returned home and went on to win the Pulitzer Prize for a biography of Franklin Roosevelt, Lerner felt a keen teacher's pride. Later, when Burns introduced him at a lecture in northern Berkshire County as the best teacher he had ever known, Lerner warmly returned the compliment by describing Burns as the best student he had ever had.

Had the times been less tumultuous, Lerner might have been tempted to settle down and rusticate at Williams, where he had come to be greatly admired; in 1941 the class yearbook was dedicated to him. But the times were very tumultuous, and he was torn between journalism and academia. In effect, Lerner strove to maintain two cultural homes, one in Williamstown, the other in New York, now mainly through *The New Republic,* then headquartered in Manhattan. His writings, as in the essay on Machiavelli, sought to bridge the academic and the political. Power had to be understood as the art of the possible, and great leaders with Machiavellian virtù were needed. Although his work was in the history of ideas, it was written with an eye on the present. It was no accident that he called one of the first compilations of his essays *Ideas Are Weapons.* He was criticized by the philosopher Sidney Hook for seeming to imply that political ideas were merely ideological instruments for manipulating opinion. [10] Although Hook properly identified ambiguities in Lerner's thesis, Lerner meant to suggest by the title that ideas mattered in history, and that in the struggle with fascism it was necessary to see clearly what the alternatives were.

Meanwhile, his marriage continued to founder. Anita, although shy and awkward with men, was driven to have an affair of her own with Louis Fischer, Lerner's colleague on *The Nation.* She confessed and asked Lerner whether he wanted a divorce. He was tempted to say that he did, but he could not bear the thought of leaving his children. They decided to make the first year at Williams a test of whether the marriage could be saved in this idyllic setting away from New York, far from the temptations it held for both of them. Anita had taken a leave from Sarah Lawrence and sublet their New York apartment. When she became pregnant with their third child, Joanna, and hinted she had allowed herself to become pregnant in the hope of holding the marriage together, he reached the limits of his patience. In the spring of 1939, they took a long walk around

Williamstown and decided to take steps toward a divorce. He was reminded of a stanza in George Meredith's sonnet sequence, *Modern Love:*

> We saw the swallows gathering in the sky
> And by the osier isles we heard their noise
> —as lovers asked what sword it was
> that had come between them on their nuptial bed.

A Manifesto for the Masses

While still at Williams, Lerner sharpened his analysis of the contemporary political condition. He continued to have ambivalent feelings about Roosevelt. He admired FDR's political skills, thinking of him as a Machiavellian who combined the boldness of a lion and the cunning of a fox, who recognized political problems and addressed them with patriotic virtù. But he had been disappointed that FDR gave only lip service to the Loyalist cause in Spain while allowing Secretary of State Cordell Hull to maintain the arms embargo. He found an odd ally on this issue in none other than Eleanor Roosevelt. Once when they shared the dais at a dinner meeting, she made a point of telling him not to let her presence inhibit him from calling for more support for the Loyalists. "We have to build a fire under Franklin," she said.

It was Hitler, however, who built the fire. As the German chancellor ordered troops into the Rhineland, concluded the Anschluss with Austria, and then persuaded Chamberlain and Daladier to allow him to occupy the Sudetenland, Roosevelt grew alarmed and began to prepare the nation for the possibility of war. In a speech in Chicago in 1937, he announced his intention of imposing a "cordon sanitaire" between the democracies and the Fascist powers, so as to "quarantine the aggressors," provoking an immediate isolationist backlash. Unintentionally, the president saved the New Deal by launching a major program of deficit spending in the name of preparedness. Until then, the president had resisted the advice of Keynesians by winding down the temporary relief spending he had ordered—with the result that millions of Americans were once again unemployed. Lerner sought to put these dramatic events into a framework for analysis and action.

Lerner's thinking resulted in his first book, to which he gave the provocative title, *It Is Later than You Think.* He took the title from

an inscription he noticed on a sundial, attributed to a Chinese saying he thought was indeed timely. The manuscript was begun in the
offices of *The Nation* and completed during the summer of 1938 on
Martha's Vineyard, in time for the Christmas book season. He presented his thesis at a faculty meeting at Williams, and in the fall of
1938 *The New Republic* ran three excerpts—"Wasteland," "Power
Is What You Make It," and "Six Errors of Marxism"—the last of
which predictably called down upon his head the editorial wrath
of *New Masses.*

In this manifesto, written with passion and a sense of crisis and
dedicated to his three young daughters, Lerner began by echoing
Laski's critique of classical liberalism as the threadbare intellectual
garment of capitalism. But his diagnosis differed significantly from
Laski's, in ways that had emerged in his review in 1936 of Laski's
The Rise of Liberalism. There he suggested that liberalism had split
into four tendencies: the atrophied classical liberalism espoused by
Landon in the 1936 election campaign; the Progressive liberalism
of Louis D. Brandeis that championed human rights but was leery of
big government; the New Deal liberalism that turns increasingly to
government and the social service state to protect basic rights; and,
finally, "the liberalism of the progressive labor movements" which
reaffirms the original aims of liberalism but extends them beyond
the protection of property rights to guarantee the rights of all. In
choosing to describe Laski as a liberal of the fourth type, Lerner was
actually making it easier for himself to agree with his views. He
knew perfectly well that Laski had rejected liberalism as nothing
more than the defense of private property, much as Engels had described Calvinism as the disguise of the bourgeoisie. The liberalism
Lerner fathered on Laski and accepted himself was one that retained
the principles of moral and political liberalism but rejected economic liberalism.[11]

Unlike Laski, Lerner found Marxian theory only partly persuasive. He agreed with Marx's explanation of the class basis of social
conflict, but thought his analysis of the prospects for change defi-
cient and his materialistic philosophy of life uninspiring. Rather
than reject liberalism in toto as the ideology of capitalism, Lerner
urged retention of its core moral belief in the liberty of the individual. The great problem for the future would be how to persuade
a majority of the people that old-style capitalism would have to be
replaced by a full-scale democracy—one that combined the popu-

lar sovereignty inspired by liberalism with "economic democracy," the planned economy that would rectify the mistakes of economic liberalism. Lenin had asked, "What is to be done?" and had proposed revolution. Lerner's answer was different in being resolutely democratic. He looked forward to the gradual replacement of old-style capitalism by a democratically adopted form of socialism in which the fruits of labor would be shared more equitably.

Marx, he thought, had been right in predicting that the high bourgeoisie would put up a strong fight before yielding control, but overconfident of the revolutionary potential of the proletariat. Experience had shown that workers goaded into general strikes and "direct action" could as easily be misguided by nihilistic demagogues as mobilized to become "class-conscious" trade unionists. Marx had too little appreciation for the power of nationalism and of lingering barbaric tendencies in human nature, evident in fascism. Fixated as Marx was upon abstract social forces and historical determinism, he allowed no role for "great men," thinking of individuals as mere instruments of historical forces. The reality was that revolutionaries like Lenin and Hitler or charismatic politicians like Roosevelt and Churchill affected the way these forces took shape. Marx had the moral passion of a biblical prophet, Lerner thought, but too many of his followers had a spiritless, mechanistic view of life which had no room for humanism—for liberty and love, for creativity and personal warmth. Lerner also rejected Leninism, arguing that the Bolshevik leader had been far too casual in supposing that a dictatorship of the proletariat would be less malevolent and easier to get rid of than other forms of dictatorship. Similarly, he rejected Lenin's belief that a conspiratorial "iron core" party could act as a midwife to help the forces of history give birth to a new society. With the Nazi rise to power in Germany obviously very much in mind, however, he called for unity on the left:

> The basic soundness of a Popular Front as the radical tactic in the present dilemma rests on the immediate need for democratic survival. We are in a period when the collapse of a capitalist democracy is bound to lead not to a proletarian democracy but to the certainty of a capitalist dictatorship. A revolutionary attempt from the left, under such conditions, would be adventurist; and even its small chance of success would depend on a ruthless use of violence, which would array the marginal middle-class elements with the Right. Under

such conditions the policy of a Popular Front is not a choice. It is a necessity.[12]

The Popular Front was the tactic; the goal was "democratic collectivism." Lerner was reluctant to spell out the character of the end he had in view in too much detail, suggesting that it would have to be the work of many minds and the project of an American labor party. But he did offer an "agenda" of what should be avoided and what should be the aim. It would not require rationing, or the abolition of private property and profit making, or the leveling of income and the standardization of consumption. It would leave consumers free to make choices among a range of products. Planning would not be directed at the entire economy but only at the basic industries. In more positive terms, the first aim would be to expand national income by improving productivity. The objective would be to expand income for all, and to distribute it more equitably, not to redistribute a dwindling economic pie. An expansion of at least a third in the first five years, as much as a doubling in ten, could be accomplished by estimating consumption schedules for major products and stepping up production accordingly in the twenty or thirty basic industries. A government fund would guarantee the success of the program to the owners of industry by providing that any unsold production would be bought by the government. Relying on increased productivity, government could simultaneously guarantee rising real incomes to workers. The banks would have to be nationalized and credit controlled in order to regulate the money supply and keep inflation in check. The government would also supervise foreign trade and seek to regulate investment, "determining the total national product and the allocation of that product among industries." A planned economy would only be the first step in a fuller transition to socialism: "Our hope is to make that transition gradual enough to prevent violence, yet effective enough to prevent breakdown. Eventually private ownership, with the economic and cultural power that it carries along with it, must be the exception rather than the rule." [13]

In later years, Lerner reflected on what his basic aim had been in these years:

I believed in the creativeness of the city masses at the base of the income pyramid, and especially of the immigrant influx of which I was a part. I was certain that the access to social mobility was still open and the American promise not yet foreclosed. I wanted better ways of organizing the economy that would put more stress on high technology and less on the price and profit system.

I. F. Stone, another budding political writer of similar views, wrote a long review of the book mixing praise and criticism. "No other writer," he observed, "has been so successful in articulating the feelings, doubts, dilemmas, hesitations, beliefs and gropings of the contemporary middle-class Leftist intellectual." But Lerner was not fully successful, according to Stone, because he typified those in a revolutionary age "whose understanding of history and social change has been enriched by Marxism but who cannot shake loose from the liberalism whence he sprang and to which he constantly looks back with mingled contempt and longing." [14] Lerner frets that democratic governments have been unable to manage their economies and that those that do manage them are autocratic. He would like to have the planning but not the autocracy: "Mr. Lerner would like to take capitalism from the capitalists—but peacefully." [15] History, Stone argued, simply does not allow such luxuries.

Sidney Hook, who then also thought of himself as a socialist but was intensely anti-Stalinist, criticized Lerner for supposing that the tactic of forming a Popular Front with Communists, which had failed elsewhere, could succeed in America, and for downplaying the similarities between Stalin's regime and the domestic terror of Hitler. In particular, he criticized Lerner for completely ignoring the findings of the 1938 commission headed by the philosopher John Dewey which had investigated the Moscow purge trials and found them to be a scandalous miscarriage of justice. Hook saw acutely that in order to make a case for the tactic of the Popular Front, Lerner was tempering his criticism of Soviet-style communism and its adherents: "He wishes to distinguish himself from Stalinists and yet to escape their slanderous vituperation." [16]

Stone was right to suspect that Lerner was unorthodox in his adherence to socialist principles and unwilling to endorse any form of reform or revolution that entailed autocracy. Hook was also right in recognizing that Lerner had not denounced the Soviet Union and its supporters as strongly as he should have, given his commitment to political liberalism and democracy. Lerner's aim, however, was to promote unity on the Left in order to avoid the factionalism that seemed to him to have gravely weakened the European Left in confronting fascism. In this radical phase, he wanted to go beyond the

Marxist canon, which he found provincial and reductionist. His work on the *Encyclopaedia* had taught him respect for cross-disciplinary thinking and for the views of other radicals. His aim was to help create an American Left that would move beyond the New Deal but would not imitate the Soviet example, as he made clear in an exchange with an American Communist in *New Masses* in 1943:

> Ultimately only a democratic socialism can fulfill the promise of American life. Communism is not that. I do not ask the Communists to dissolve their party. No one has the moral right to ask that. And I shall fight every attempt to ban it—not because I care for the Communists, but because I care for American liberties and do not want totalitarian methods to crush them. But in the long run I regard American communism as rootless and feckless. All our energies must be channeled toward fulfilling American democracy—that is our dream of home and our hope of Heaven.[17]

A Bitter Harvest on the Vineyard

While Lerner was prescribing a new future for American society, he found himself increasingly unable to manage his own personal life without another sort of radical transition. In 1938, he and Anita agreed to try a trial year of separation. Anita and the girls moved back to New York, and she resumed her teaching at Sarah Lawrence. They spent another, final summer together at Martha's Vineyard in 1939. The scenery was different but the people much the same as in New York, except for the presence of liberal lawyers like Morris Ernst and Arthur Garfield Hays along with the coterie of liberal and radical writers. The psychoanalyst Lawrence Kubie, who also summered at the Vineyard, became a lifelong friend and counselor. At midnight, there would be swimming in the nude at the beach home of Roger Baldwin, director of the American Civil Liberties Union, and his wife Evie. Baldwin, though he was the "purest distillation of the New England Yankee," was no Puritan. Freudianism was in the air and in the writings of Eugene O'Neill, F. Scott Fitzgerald, and Edmund Wilson which set the tone for the avant garde. The atmosphere was libertine. The feeling among them all seemed to be that even if they could not restructure their society as the Soviets were doing in Russia, at least they could restructure their own lives and find the love they had lost or not yet known.

It was on the Vineyard that summer where the marriage finally disintegrated. Edna had reentered the picture earlier while Lerner was still teaching at Harvard, having found her marriage unsatisfying. Although Donald was a loving husband and had everything Lerner lacked—good looks, an athlete's physique, and social position—she wanted even more what Lerner had to offer, which he was to describe as "the appeal of the foreign, strange, intellectual, radical, risky, forbidden, in short the *Other.*" Torn between the two men, Edna arranged for them both to visit her psychiatrist separately. The psychiatrist, a woman, reported that of the three of them, Donald was the only one who knew clearly what he wanted in life. Of Lerner, she said only, "*ach*—he is not a man to marry, he is a man to have an affair with."

For Lerner, Edna's appeal lay in her beauty, youth, intellectual depth, and brilliance as well as in her emotional fire and integrity. With her he experienced the full passion of love—intellectual, emotional, and sexual—he had not found with Anita. He pursued her ardently. When she was doing research for the Progressive Education Association at the New York Public Library, he would manage to come from Cambridge and show up at her desk. She gradually succumbed to his attentions, though she felt terrible over leaving Donald for him. They met whenever they could manage it, in Cambridge and Connecticut, and in New York for long lunches at Village restaurants, for cocktails at the Ritz bar, and blissful afternoons at a furnished hideaway walk-up rented by the month. With Lerner separated from Anita, she visited Williams several times and stayed discreetly at the Williamstown Inn. Anita refused to recognize that Lerner himself was becoming increasingly unhappy in their marriage and was pursuing Edna. She preferred to think of Edna as a siren who was luring him away from her:

> It didn't happen overnight but over a period of time like a great snowball, far, far away winding its way relentlessly toward you instead of the neighboring tree. I didn't try to compete with her. I was furiously involved with my own life and saw nothing to be gained by imitation. She was my junior by ten years, a passionate, unpredictable person more aggressive than I, putting everything she had into her wardrobe . . . He flourished with his two women. With me he felt at home, with her footloose and rebellious. He would have liked things that way indefinitely. For while he held out marriage to her, he told me not to worry, that she was essentially ordinary and I the real thing. This went on for five years. I wrote to her: "Take him if

you wish, he is free, only make up your mind quickly . . . " When we were together, her telephone calls bombarded us. Her suicide gesture did the trick; it captured his imagination, and in the end she determined the issue.[18]

According to Edna, however, Anita was simply fantasizing. It was Lerner who pursued her, not the other way around. She never telephoned him, dressed simply in the style of the time, and never contemplated suicide. Clearly, Lerner had come to feel that his marriage to Anita was a loveless trap, and he was intensely drawn to Edna. For her part, although she felt guilty about leaving Donald, who had been kind and loving and offered the stability of a life in the suburbs, complete with golf at the country club, she found Lerner "fascinating, so alive, so connected with the world" that she could not resist him.

Crises—Personal and Global

In the summer of 1939 matters came to a head. Lerner's personal crisis coincided with the international crisis that came to its fateful climax during the same summer, with the Hitler-Stalin pact and soon afterward with the German invasion of Poland and the start of the Second World War in Europe. Lerner's diary for the year (in which Edna is sometimes still referred to not very cryptically as "ea") records the intersection:

Thursday, AUGUST 24
Chilmark
Up a little before 9 after a night of dreams. Take the children to the riding field. They are beautiful. Home, + unsuccessful attempt to call ea at Hewitt Lake. Call for children again. Then to work on my "Hitler as Thinker" essay; ironic, since the news is all about Hitler as doer. Today's papers announce Soviet-German non-aggression pact. Great excitement among everyone. Swim and lunch at Larry and Ellen Rees, with Helen Marot and Caroline Pratt. Learn how to ride the breakers in, like an arrow. Anita high on a drink, and brilliant. Conversation on Russia, of course. On way back, meet Margaret Lamont, who says Corliss is heartbroken (his new book [19] is now ironic—), + that everyone is deserting SU like rats and he is wavering. Study papers in afternoon. I feel by no means *distrait* over it. It spurs me to plan out my little essay, "Ideas Are Weapons." Wire from Viking. Remaining ms. due today. Plan to stay up all night to

From the 1923 Yale Yearbook. Manuscripts and Archives, Sterling Library, Yale University.

With parents, Bessie and Benjamin Lerner, New Haven (c. 1930s). Courtesy of
Joanna L. Townsend.

Thorstein Veblen (date unknown). Courtesy of Carleton College Archives.

Walton Hamilton. Courtesy of the Brookings Institution Archives.

Max Lerner, with first wife Anita Marburg Lerner, and daughters Connie
(left), Joanna (center), and Pamela (1939). Courtesy of Joanna L. Townsend.

As war correspondent for *PM* (1944–45). *PM* photo. Courtesy of Edna
Albers Lerner.

Edna Albers Lerner, Lerner's second wife, mother of his three sons (1955).
Photograph by Mary Morris Lawrence.

With youngest son Adam Lerner at Southampton, New York (early 1950s).
Photograph by Mary Morris Lawrence.

Teaching at Brandeis University in the 1950s. Courtesy Brandeis University Library.

Max Lerner, at Yaddo (1932). From a color painting by Marion Greenwood.
Photograph by Beth E. Warach. Courtesy of Adam Lerner.

At Brandeis University, with Professor Frank E. Manuel (c. 1960s). Courtesy of Edna
Albers Lerner.

At Southampton, New York, with sons Michael (left), Adam (center), and Steve, and the two Bouviers, Shadow and Aquarius. Photograph by Hans Namuth. Courtesy of Hans Namuth Ltd.

With two of his protégés, Martin Peretz, editor-in-chief of *The New Republic* (left), and Congressman Stephen Solarz of New York (c. 1970s). Courtesy of Edna Albers Lerner.

Teaching Hugh Hefner how to flip potato pancakes *(latkes)*, Playboy Mansion West
(February 23, 1986). Photograph by Tom Cummins. Courtesy of Hugh M. Hefner.

At the Playboy Mansion West (May 31, 1982). Photograph by Larry Logan.
Courtesy of Hugh M. Hefner.

Max Lerner (1972). Courtesy of Edna Albers Lerner.

finish. Somewhat sad, and sick with desire for ea, torn by beauty of children.

Friday, AUGUST 25
But I didn't stay up all night—only part of it. Stormy talk with Anita all morning. Then came wire from Edna to meet her in NY tonight. I break the news to Anita. Tempestuous day—weeping and recrimination. Call Edna + tell her I shall be in NY tomorrow. The news in the papers about the Soviet-German pact is bad. Even in the midst of our personal grief, we scan it with anxiety. We drive into town in afternoon to get Margaret [Collins, chauffeur and stenographer], Anita a bit calmer. We walk through the streets of Oak Bluffs together. We go to The Barn for dinner, as guests of Mildred Adams, and I feel very tenderly toward Anita. Most of the night in talk and affection, with not much more on my book. Before bed, I dictated a bunch of letters to Margaret to send out after my departure.

Saturday, AUGUST 26
Up very early, to make morning boat for New York. Anita practically disintegrated and very bitter. I try to joke with children at breakfast, and take my leave from all three with a frightened sense. It's a drizzly drive to town, and Anita to my surprise comes to the dock and stands there as tragic a figure as I have ever seen her . . . Taxi to Holter's + the quick sick feeling in stomach as it approached house. Edna was in the hallway to meet me. Everything went blind. We made love feverishly. Then a late dinner, then a 14th St movie, then back to sleep and love.

Sunday, AUGUST 27
9th St NY
Up late, and Sunday breakfast with Edna at Alice McCollister's. Talk and work most of the day, trying to finish my "Ideas Are Weapons." Worked feverishly and against time. Trying to write a title essay almost overnight is no hilarity for me. But happy. Edna and I have never loved each other so much or known that loving could scale such heights and still find heights to scale.

Monday, AUGUST 28
Again working on "Ideas Are Weapons." Have been up a good part of the night with it, and I finish it this morning . . . War tensions increasing. My prediction is that Hitler will somehow get what he wants without a general European war—that Chamberlain will

find a face-saving formula. Have good chat with Freda [Kirchwey], Bob [Bendiner], Jimmy [Wechsler] at *Nation.* There seems to be a *rapprochement* between us again. We disagree on many things but agree that the Hitler-Stalin pact has dealt a death blow to the Comintern . . .

Tuesday, AUGUST 29
Great tension in Europe. Notes are being exchanged, but Hitler's troop movements look ominous. I work on my Hitler essay all day. I am very happy here with Edna, but there is a sense of impending reckoning for both of us.

Wednesday, AUGUST 30
I spend the morning on Hitler, and also on proofs of my new book. Work all afternoon . . . Maggie arrives for dinner. Anita calls me up and asks to have dinner with me. I am surprised at her cheerfulness and strength. She has been to see F[elix] F[rankfurter] and has a plan: a year's separation, with no one saying anything about it. I accept it. We have a friendly dinner + then see a movie, and I leave her at Anne Harvey's. I come back to 9th St to find Edna, Holter, Maggy + Stefan. We all go for a drink, but it is a cheerless party. Edna very distressed. We spend night at Albert.

Thursday, AUGUST 31
Up late, and read the papers in bath at hotel. War close. My calculations seem to have been wrong. Edna calls Don and arranges to see him. She plans to come back for the night, but I have a hunch she won't—and she doesn't. I feel pretty miserable, and fall asleep in my clothes . . .

Friday, SEPTEMBER 1
Edna comes back in the morning, while I am out to breakfast with [I.F.] Iz Stone. He tells me he is sorry about his article on me.[20] We go up to *Nation* office after breakfast, + find them all listening to radio. Germany has invaded Poland and is bombarding her cities from the air. I go back to find Edna. Don has agreed to a Winter's separation. But Edna is sick . . . She arranges to go to Dr. Stone's office . . . Chamberlain is still writing notes—obviously Hitler is seeking to get a headstart in his attack on Poland. I come back to find that Anita has called—auto accident—car smashed but no one hurt. I called her and found her completely unnerved . . . Maggie and Eddie and I go to dinner at Gene's and have a hilarious time. Then Eddie + I go to see "In Name Only" with Carole Lombard. Then home.

Saturday, SEPTEMBER 2

A very troubled day. Real tension between Edna + me. Finally after lunch she goes off to her mother to break the news to her. I spend the afternoon reading Margery Allingham's *Flowers for the Judge*—reading an imaginary murder while mass murder is going on in Europe + an imaginary love affair while my own real one is careening like a wounded ship. Then a quick dinner at a lunch wagon, and "The Adventures of Sherlock Holmes" at the movies at Roxie's. War still undeclared, but France and Eng have issued ultimatum. Home to listen to the radio + write this diary. Fall asleep in my clothes.

Edna and Anita both got their divorces at about the same time in 1940. Before that, Lerner became a father for the third time, with the birth of Joanna. Guilt over the abandonment of the children wracked him and kept him from marrying Edna immediately:

> The overmastering sadness of the whole story for me was less the breaking of a marriage bond that had never been strong or true than the grievous fracturing of my ties to my children and of the home setting which had held us together. There are many marriages that look outwardly satisfactory but carry no real home with them, and others—like ours—that retain the aura of a home even when the fire of the marriage itself has died or was never there.

In utter despair, he blurted out, in a conversation with a friend and physician, that he was thinking seriously of freeing himself from the guilt he felt by committing suicide. He was dissuaded and in time recovered his equanimity, though Edna and he had to endure the skepticism of their friends and the intense social disapproval that still attached to divorce. Her friends thought she was a fool to throw over the comfortable life she was assured with Donald for the grab-bag existence she would have with Lerner. His friends—and Anita's—thought it monstrous of him to abandon his daughters and break up the marriage, however imperfect. But Lerner and Edna would not be dissuaded, feeling that they were destined for each other. Lerner and Anita separated. She would move first to Boulder and then settle in Baltimore, continuing to teach Russian literature but never remarrying.

Rumors of the impending divorce swept through Williamstown like a brushfire. James Phinney Baxter III, the president of the college, was having enough trouble as it was fending off complaints from wealthy alumni that their offspring were being indoctrinated by a left-wing Svengali. He warned Lerner that if he were to divorce and marry this younger woman, there would be such a scandal that he might be asked to resign his faculty post. Lerner had been the first Jew to be appointed to the Williams faculty; a radical to boot, and now he would be divorced at a time when that too was socially disreputable. Lerner nevertheless went ahead with the divorce. Baxter asked him not to bring Edna to Williamstown so soon after the divorce, and he reluctantly complied, waiting until the spring of 1940 to marry her. Finally, they went off to be wed, he at thirty-eight, she at twenty-seven, by a clerk of the court in Concord, Massachusetts—hoping the name of the town would prove symbolic. When informed of Lerner's divorce and remarriage, Baxter appointed a committee headed by the Williams historian Richard Newhall to assess the impact of this behavior upon the Puritan sensibilities of the community. Lerner, who had met Baxter at Harvard and remembered watching him recreate the Civil War gunboat battle between the Monitor and the Merrimack atop a lunch table at Adams House, saw the choice of Newhall as a shrewd tactical maneuver. Among the members of the faculty Newhall was a conciliatory John Winthrop, not a censorious Cotton Mather. Baxter must have anticipated that Newhall would issue a reluctant exoneration, which the president could rely on as a shield against criticism. This was in fact the outcome, and the controversy subsided.

Although the couple settled in an idyllic little house near a pond, the marriage got off to an inauspicious financial start, in the first place because Lerner signed over $4,200 of his $6,000 Williams salary to Anita. He had to scramble for writing and lecturing opportunities to find means of support. They would never amass wealth but would live comfortably, eventually acquiring a townhouse in Manhattan and a summer home on Long Island—on their combined earnings, almost all of which came from his multifaceted career as a teacher, writer, and lecturer. They very much wanted children and were delighted when the marriage produced three sons.

The relationship between Max and Edna—"Jenny" * as he called her privately, from her first given name—remained passionate, and their relationship was deepened over the years by a sustained intellectual partnership. He encouraged her to develop a career of her own as a clinical psychologist, shared his thoughts with her, relied on her to criticize his work, and took her suggestions and ideas

---

*He said jokingly that when he loved her he would call her "Jenny," and when he got angry with her he would call her "Edna."

very seriously. She wished he would not try to do as much as he did and travel as much. She recognized, however, that he was restless by nature and a man of extraordinary energy who would not be satisfied if he could not do more than anyone else and go practically to the ends of the earth to enthrall yet another audience. In their constant concern for each other and their delight in each other's company, they were a loving couple with a warm family life for the nearly fifty years of their marriage.

That he loved her dearly and appreciated both the warmth and vitality of their relationship and the joys of family life is apparent in many ways. He expressed his affection to her directly and in countless diary entries and letters written when he was away from her. During his first prolonged absence from her, in 1944–45, when he went to Europe to cover the last stages of the war, he recalled writing letters to her that were "sulphurous with sexuality and generally ended with fantasizing which must have scorched the envelopes and convinced some poor Army censor that he was dealing with a sex maniac . . . I was very much in love with her and my absence from her made me more so." His later diary entries vividly record how much he missed being with her. The letters he wrote to her shared his experiences and reflections and expressed his physical yearning for her. The terms of endearment in the private letters that survive (most were destroyed by Edna because she felt they were too personal) show beyond any doubt that his feelings for her were intense and passionate. Especially in the late years, Lerner's life came increasingly to center on his family, as illness made him less mobile and more dependent on Edna's care and supervision. Although he was as restless and as adventurous as ever—as if determined to maintain his independence and to deny that he was growing old—his relationship to Edna was a continuing engagement of mind and heart. However much they might differ and even quarrel from time to time, they were devoted to each other and constantly in each other's thoughts, bonded above all by their delight in language and literature.

But Lerner remained all his life, as he had been at boyhood, determined to demonstrate his virility and enjoy the pleasures of the senses, sometimes heedless of the emotional pain he was inflicting upon his wife and children. Neither the rupture of his first marriage nor the bliss of the second dampened his enthusiasm for the chase. The marital turmoil he went through in the 1930s had not interfered with his efforts to establish a reputation as a writer. In fact, he came to feel that his erotic adventures and his efforts to gain literary celebrity were mutually reinforcing, as if the desire to court women and the desire to court readers arose from the same erotic impulse. In later years he would sense in himself the same motivation Dreiser had ascribed to the hero of his novel, *The Titan:*

> Was Dreiser's hero, Frank Cowperwood, moved to nail down fame and money because it could make his erotic satisfactions easier, or was he moved by his sexual hungers to become a conqueror in the world of men? . . . In my own case there was the hunger for erotic acceptance, still unsated, and the impulse to storm the city and conquer the domain of ideas and letters, and again—as in Cowperwood—they were connected in a circuit. I was moved by each to attain the other.

Lerner relished the company of attractive and intelligent women. He was by no means insensitive to the feelings of the women he courted; on the contrary, he showed great solicitude and friendship toward them and encouraged their intellectual pursuits. But monogamy was simply not enough to satisfy him, even though he continued to love and appreciate his wife, who raised the children, managed the family finances, took care of his needs, and suffered his infidelities. In a column on the ideal marriage, he hinted at a rationale for his own behavior:

> The key to a true man-woman relationship lies, I suspect, in having searched for—and perhaps found—a life-style and therefore a set of values on which both can tolerably agree, in terms of inclusions and exclusions. If they succeed, it will come close to satisfying the needs of both.[21]

Edna never agreed to his request that she consider theirs an "open marriage," and although he entered into other liaisons, he remained devoted to her for the rest of his life. From the moment he first caught sight of her, in 1932, he was to write fifty years later, "she has been—through years of turbulence and delight—the life center to whom I have kept returning, and to whom I have been faithful—in my fashion."

Pearl Harbor: A Prophet Vindicated

The turmoil Lerner experienced in his marital life did not keep him from playing an active role as a public intellectual. As the largely domestic concerns of *It Is Later than You Think* were overshadowed by the looming clouds of war, Lerner turned his attention to building American support for the struggle against fascism in Europe. With Lewis Mumford *(Men Must Act),* Waldo Frank *(Chart for Rough Waters),* Archibald MacLeish *(The Irresponsibles),* the literary critic Malcolm Cowley, and the theologian Reinhold Niebuhr, he sought to promote awareness of the need for "collective security"—a term he helped popularize—and to allay fears that the country would become a "garrison state" by girding for war. When the Hitler-Stalin pact in 1940 made a mockery of the Popular Front and American Communists duly called for the United States to stay out of Europe's "imperialist war," Lerner criticized liberal isolationists and joined with the writer and ex-Communist Granville Hicks to urge formation of an "independent left" that would campaign to awaken Americans to the need to help Britain and France. Ruth McKenney, later to be known for her popular novel *My Sister Eileen,* but then an editor of the slavishly party-line *New Masses,* denounced him for advocating intervention, warning that "the blood of the workers will be on Max Lerner's hands." Disagreeing publicly with his Williams colleague, Frederick L. Schuman, who at first praised Stalin's cleverness in staying out of the war and then recanted when the Soviet Union invaded Finland, Lerner argued that Nazi Germany was a menace to democracy everywhere and should be resisted. In the neutralist *New Masses* he was denounced as a warmonger who was betraying the socialist cause: "Mr. Lerner started out to organize an 'independent left'—he winds up furnishing pseudorevolutionary apologies for a war administration." [22] Once Germany invaded Russia, the American Communists changed their tune and Lerner renewed his support for a Popular Front, again in the hope that once Nazism was defeated, democratic reform would take hold in Russia.

Meanwhile, from the anti-Communist Left he was criticized for clinging to the belief in the Popular Front. On August 10, 1939, only a few weeks before the stunning news of the Hitler-Stalin pact, a letter had been issued by a "Committee of 400" critical of an anti-Stalinist statement issued by the Committee for Cultural Freedom, the forerunner of the Congress for Cultural Freedom. The statement, of which Lerner was a signatory, criticized those who were equating the Soviet Union with Nazi Germany for sowing division among anti-Fascists. For this he was taken to task by Sidney Hook. [23]

If Lerner's endorsement of Roosevelt's campaign to win support for helping Britain without directly entering the war offended American Communists, it raised his standing with liberals and won him an audience with the president. Sometime before Japan's attack on Pearl Harbor, Roosevelt's brain truster, Tom Corcoran, in cooperation with Mrs. Roosevelt, arranged for Lerner to go to Hyde Park to visit FDR. The president and the professor had a wideranging conversation about political ideas as well as immediate issues. Lerner left deeply impressed:

> I marveled at how this man, not an intellectual, displayed a sense of perfect ease with ideas and concepts rather than confining himself to issues and tactics. He was troubled by the problem of how to make American power effective without committing American troops. When we got into the question of managing public opinion he became engrossed. "They use the propaganda of the word against me," he said, "but I answer with the propaganda of the deed." We canvassed every theme. Then came the inevitable secretary to say his next appointment was waiting. "Not yet, not yet," he said, "we're having a good time talking philosophy. I'll call you when we're through." I came away feeling that I had talked with my Prince and that he didn't need any Machiavellian instruction from me.

The bombing of Pearl Harbor had the initial effect of vindicating interventionists like Lerner, even though few of them imagined that the country would be drawn into the war by the outbreak of hostilities in the Pacific. At Williams, Lerner felt a sudden change in the attitude of his faculty colleagues. He was no longer looked upon as the stormiest petrel in a small outlying flock. Invited by the college chaplain to lead a chapel service, he gladly agreed, choosing a scriptural passage for the lesson. A few months later, on Memorial Day 1942, he was invited to speak at a ceremony in a little graveyard where the dead of previous wars lay buried, remarking in retrospect that "it was a new experience for me to feel close bonds not only with the faculty but with the tradesmen, farmers, villagers, who gathered on that Memorial Day when none of us knew what lay ahead."

The declaration of war also had the effect of dampening, at least initially, hostility toward Jews and the corresponding anxieties they felt because of it. Another wave of anti-Semitism had arisen in the mid-1930s, stimulated both by the association of Jews with domestic radicalism and by Nazi propaganda. Within months of Roosevelt's taking office in March 1933 rumors spread that Jews were "running the government." In some quarters the New Deal was referred to as the "Jew Deal." Tales circulated that Roosevelt himself, referred to by anti-Semites as "Joosevelt," was of Jewish ancestry, having descended from "Rosenbergs, Rosenbaums, Roosenvelts, Rosenblums, and Rosenthals." [24] In Europe as well, the Nazi venom was taking effect beyond the borders of Germany. In 1936, Laski wrote to Lerner to express his dismay over the rise of anti-Semitism in Britain. It "gives one the horrors—not least because of its power over the Jews themselves." [25] In the years leading up to Pearl Harbor, the German Foreign Ministry encouraged the formation of anti-Semitic groups in America. From 1933 through 1941, over a hundred anti-Semitic organizations were created, compared to five in all previous American history.[26] In addition to the usual charges, Jews were being accused, notably by the members of the newly formed German-American Bund, of promoting American involvement in Europe only out of concern for their coreligionists.

The rising tide of hatred alarmed leading American Jews. In 1939 Lerner was one of five men invited to meet with Justice Frankfurter in Washington, under the auspices of the American Jewish Committee, to consider what could be done about it. The conferees agreed that Jews should proceed openly in whatever actions they took, so as not to give any semblance of credibility to the notion that Jewish leaders operated as a secret cabal. They decided to concentrate on promoting democratic ideals as the single best way to combat anti-Semitic prejudice. Frankfurter stressed that the "innate decencies of the American people" could be counted on in the long run to resist intolerance against any minority group. But the conferees were worried enough to consider mounting a special effort to promote toleration. Lerner was assigned the task of examining ways to "reach the American public," and Frankfurter was to prepare a statement on the meaning of democracy in relation to anti-Semitism.[27] America's entry into the war made the project seem less urgent.

Frankfurter himself had become the target of vicious defamation upon his nomination to the Supreme Court earlier the same year—so much so that other leading American Jews, specifically Secretary of the Treasury Henry Morgenthau and Arthur Hays Sulzberger, publisher of the *New York Times,* were reported to be urging President Roosevelt not to appoint Frankfurter to replace the deceased Justice Cardozo because he had "come to symbolize

Jewish radicalism in the New Deal." To put a second Jew on the
Court, while Brandeis was still serving, would, they warned, "play
into the hands of anti-Semites at home and abroad." But Frankfurter
had been a valued adviser to Roosevelt, and the president thought
that, just because persecution and discrimination were rising around
the world, it was all the more important "that we in this country
make it clear that citizens of the United States are elected or selected
for positions of responsibility solely because of their qualifications,
experience, and character, and without regard to their religious
faith." [28]

Like Frankfurter, Lerner aroused concern among Jews fearful
that his radical reputation would rub off on them. Some wrote to ask
him to take a lower profile, because his radicalism, coupled with his
divorce, made him an attractive target for anti-Semites. Lerner's response was that silence had not helped the German Jews and that one
had to be the person one was. He did not see himself as a Jewish
spokesman, but he worried that anti-Semitism was helping fuel
home-grown fascism. Only weeks before Pearl Harbor, on September 20, 1941, he expressed serious alarm in a letter to Laski* over the
coalescence of an extreme American right wing with a distinctly
anti-Semitic undertone:

> The America First group has become the center of a genuine honest-
> to-goodness Fascist alignment. Lindbergh has become a real Fascist
> symbol. There is talk of the formation of an American peace treaty,
> to be made up of an alliance of Americans, the Coughlinites, the
> Christian Front, the Western Populist senators, the John L. Lewis
> group and the CIO, the reactionary Republicans[,] the worst ele-
> ments of the Irish Democrats, the Townsendites, the Ku Klux Klan,
> the Pacifist[s] and the anti-war Socialist[s]. This unholy alliance
> aims to contest the 1942 congressional election and hope to win
> about 50 seats, which will give them the balance of power. As you
> know, anti-Semitism has now come out in the open, with statements
> by Lindbergh and Nye. It has grown a great deal also in the labor
> movement—within the AF of L, largely because of the Irish feeling,
> and within the CIO largely because of Lewis' hostility to Sidney
> Hillman.[29]

*Laski replied a month later mentioning a "grim adventure" when a hotel
in which he was staying in the north of England was bombed "and I found myself
precipitated through three floors—on to a bed; physically untouched, if somewhat shaken; but fiercely anti-Nazi when I had put myself together again" (Letter, October 29, 1941, YMA, I, 5, 392).

The outbreak of the war left the isolationists in disarray and at least temporarily silenced organized anti-Semitic propaganda. The German-American Bund disintegrated. Father Charles E. Coughlin's *Social Justice* was banned from the mails under the provisions of 1917 Sedition Act that prohibited speech aiding an enemy. William Dudley Pelley, head of the pro-Fascist Silver Shirts, was tried and found guilty under the same act and sentenced to fifteen years in prison. For Lerner, the change in the political climate meant that for the time being he did not have to fend off isolationists and anti-Semites and could instead concentrate his energies on the common cause. The respite, however, proved temporary. In 1942 Gerald L. K. Smith, a one-time associate of Huey Long, began distributing *The Cross and the Flag*, an anti-Semitic sheet, and a year later he founded the America First Party. Coughlinite agitation instigated a plague of anti-Semitic incidents in the Northeast. On Capitol Hill, Senator Theodore Bilbo and Congressman John Rankin, both of Mississippi, were the most notorious but hardly the only members of Congress who commonly used anti-Semitic epithets in public remarks. Popular anti-Semitic sentiment grew so strong that government officials, from the president down, became hesitant to express sympathy for European Jews or take any steps to ease entry for Jewish refugees.[30]

Lerner could not altogether ignore the recrudescence of anti-Semitism, especially since some of it was directed at him, as an increasingly visible commentator who could now be attacked not only as a domestic radical but as an internationalist. Now, however, he could and did appeal for American unity in the face of the dire threat to national survival, and he was free to devote his energies to the common cause without having to defend his right to do so.

FIVE

PM and the "People's War"

America's entry into World War II did not engage Lerner directly, but it did draw him into full-time editorial journalism and make him a commentator on world affairs—a Walter Lippmann of the democratic Left. By coincidence, a New York daily named *PM* had been launched in 1940, and it was as its chief editorial writer that Lerner became an especially prominent public figure, even though in these years his newspaper work was not yet syndicated. His previous work for *The Nation* and *The New Republic*, grounded on his studies of economic history and constitutional law, had prepared him to deal with domestic issues, but he was not as well versed in international affairs. He had made no previous study of diplomacy or warfare and did not so much as visit a foreign country until he went to Europe as a war correspondent in December 1944. Like many other Americans, he was suddenly forced to contend with a new set of conditions in which it was hopeless to imagine that the country could remain unaffected by turmoil elsewhere. The sheer force of events, coupled with a passionate conviction that democracy was facing a life-and-death struggle with fascism, greatly enlarged the focus of Lerner's thinking. With the outbreak of war in the Pacific, the fate of the world hung in the balance. The question, as he saw it, was whether humanity would descend into a new barbarism—a man-made ice age—or whether a "people's war" would usher in a "people's century"—in which the Western countries and the Soviet Union would cooperate in building a new peaceful community of nations.

It was as a spokesman for this hoped-for future that Lerner made his mark in the war years. By the time Henry Wallace staked his political career on this vision by running for president as the candidate of the new Progressive Party in 1948, however, Lerner felt such misgivings about Soviet expansionism and about Wallace's willingness to accept the support of Communists that he disappointed his more radical followers by refusing to endorse him. While he continued to argue for superpower cooperation, he was losing confidence in Popular Front pieties. Before long, he accepted the view that the Cold War was largely the fault of the Russians and that America had no choice but to resist the spread of communism, adopting a stance unreconstructed leftists derided as "Cold War liberalism."

PM: A Noble Experiment in Journalism

Exempted from the draft because of age and family status, Lerner wanted to be of use in the war effort. He took leave from Williams in 1942 to accept a minor post in Washington helping Archibald MacLeish in the new "Office of Facts and Figures" but did not find the work satisfying or important enough. Just as a decade earlier he had felt uncomfortable and out of place in the New Deal bureaucracy, so again he felt that his talents for expression were not being well enough used in the back room anonymity of a government agency. He returned to Williams but parted amicably from the college in 1943 to write regularly for *PM,* for which he had previously been only a book reviewer. As the newspaper's leading commentator, he became a powerful voice at the liberal-to-Left band of the national political spectrum. Although *PM*'s readership was small and concentrated in metropolitan New York—circulation never exceeded 150,000 and sometimes fell well below that peak—its influence exceeded its circulation because it took a more radical stand than any other major national newspaper and because it numbered among its readers some who were prominent in government and the media.

If prohibition was a noble experiment in reforming social behavior that failed, *PM* was a noble experiment in reforming journalism that also failed but was exciting while it lasted and had an exhilarating influence upon the profession. When it first appeared, in June 1940, it became the first daily to enter the New York market since 1924, when two tabloids, the *Mirror* and *Evening Graphic*, revolutionized the newspaper world. In the interim, four papers had folded: the *World* and the *Evening World* (in 1931), the *Graphic* (in 1932) and Hearst's *American* (in 1937).[1] Before *PM* itself succumbed in 1948, it made a valiant effort to recreate the American newspaper in a more serious but lively form. The paper was the brainchild of Ralph McAllister Ingersoll, an inventive maverick whose forebears included Robert Ingersoll, the controversial nineteenth century freethinker. Like Lerner, Ingersoll had lived in New Haven as a boy and attended Yale, but there the similarity ended. Ingersoll had been born in New Haven, with the right pedigree, stood six feet two inches tall, and fit in perfectly among his classmates. After college, he had worked in Luce's shadow to develop *Time, Life,* and *Fortune* but left of his own will determined to do something for which he would get full credit.

Ingersoll envisioned a paper that would be run by its editors and writers solely for the enlightenment of its readers. It would cover labor affairs but run no stock market tables or "society" news. It would be innovative in everything from the superior quality of its newsprint to a policy of not "jumping" stories from the front pages to the back but letting them run, column after column, until the entire tale was told. Reporters would be free from restrictions, such as the convention that everything of importance in a news story must be encapsulated in a "tell-all lead" after which the remaining facts "dribble away." In politics, the paper would be "scrupulously non-partisan." Its writers and editors would not be completely unbiased, but their bias would be in the public interest. To protect editorial independence, the paper would rely for support mainly on circulation, not advertising. It would accept only those display ads that met strict standards of truthfulness and served the reader's interest; and it would apologize whenever it published an ad that turned out to be misleading. By selling for five cents at a time when competitors cost two or three cents, it would gain more revenue than they—for a paper smaller in size and therefore less costly to produce. Ingersoll thought it could break even with a circulation of 200,000, a goal that seemed within reach, given the size of the market. In 1939 the *Daily News* sold 1,800,000 copies, the *Times* 500,000, and the *Evening Post*—the weakest of the remaining six—250,000.[2] To avoid having to compete in the overcrowded morning field, *PM* would appear in the afternoon (hence the name). It would look and feel like it was worth five cents by comparison with the competition, and readers would find it worth ten times the price. Although he admitted that the analogy was imperfect, he pointed out that *The Saturday Evening Post* was having trouble getting five cents a copy, whereas *Life* sold well at ten cents.

Ingersoll expected readers to flock to *PM* both because it would be committed to "the service of the truth" and because it would use the latest techniques for making a newspaper attractive. Like *Life*, it would recognize the importance of pictures—not just photographs but paintings, sketches, diagrams, and isometric maps—to tell stories. It would use the newest printing methods, so that it would look like the magazine section of the *New York Times*, but it would be in four colors (a goal never reached).* Above all, it would be a crusading paper, fighting for the "little guy." In the words of its prospectus, often reprinted in the paper:

> We are against people who push other people around, just for the fun of pushing, whether they flourish in this country or abroad. We are against fraud and deceit and greed and cruelty and we will seek to expose their practitioners. We are for people who are kindly and courageous and honest. We respect intelligence, sound accomplishment, open-mindedness, religious tolerance. We do not think all mankind's problems are soluble in any existing social order, certainly not our own, and we propose to applaud those who seek constructively to improve the way men live together. We are American and we prefer democracy to any other form of government.[5]

To attract backers, Ingersoll put together a dummy issue, edited by the detective story writer Dashiell Hammett and his consort, the novelist and playwright Lillian Hellman—fueling rumors that *PM* would be the mouthpiece of the Left because both were known for their radical sympathies. Ingersoll's psychiatrist, Gregory Zilboorg, put him in touch with the prominent lawyer Louis Weiss, who became the newspaper's guardian angel. With the attractive dummy

---

*Not all the proposed ideas worked out. The designer Norman Bel Geddes came up with a new format: a newspaper designed like an accordion printed on thirty-two feet of uncut newsprint. When he appeared with a specimen, the staff was intrigued until Ingersoll asked to hold it, opened it as if it were a book by holding the first and last pages, and all thirty-two feet sprawled out on the floor. Everyone in the room imagined what would happen if it were opened on a subway train (Roy Hoopes, *Ralph Ingersoll: A Biography* [New York: Atheneum, 1985], p. 216).

as bait, Ingersoll managed to sign up a number of wealthy backers with liberal sympathies, including Marshall Field III, the son of the wealthy owner of the famous Chicago department store of the same name and also one of Zilboorg's patients.[4] The paper was launched, and William Benton, the advertising prodigy, orchestrated the fanfare, building great excitement. When the first issue went on sale, in June 1940, the delivery trucks were mobbed by eager buyers. In the cutthroat world of New York newspaper publishing, however, the ballyhoo only frightened one of its competitors into sabotaging its prospects. Joseph Medill Patterson, publisher of the *Daily News*, had his circulation manager, Ivan Annenberg, warn the city's 4,200 city and suburban newsdealers that any of them who sold *PM* would lose their allotments of the *Daily News*. Ingersoll protested to Mayor Fiorello La Guardia that the city, which licensed the newsdealers, could foil that tactic, but La Guardia was unwilling to tangle with Patterson. Instead he suggested that Ingersoll sell *PM* from coin-operated racks. The result was that throughout the city the paper could be bought only from its own racks attached to newsstands. In the suburbs, it was available mainly by home delivery.[5] To make matters worse, in an excess of idealism, the newspaper refused to accept any advertising at all.

But the product itself had an original flavor and character, thanks to an extraordinarily talented if motley crew. Elizabeth Hawes, a dressmaker for "arty" New Yorkers and an iconoclast known for a popular book entitled *Fashion Is Spinach*, was put in charge of a "News for Living" section which reported sales and singled out stores offering good values. The film reviewers listed all movies being shown in the metropolitan area, along with check-mark ratings. The feature staff included the critics Louis Kronenberger and John T. McNulty, who had previously been reviewers for *Time*, and Dalton Trumbo, who in the 1950s would become a screenwriter blacklisted as one of the "Hollywood Ten." Among the professional journalists were George Lyon, a Scripps-Howard executive who was made managing editor; Penn Kimball, who came from the magazine *U.S. News;* Kenneth Stewart and his wife Evelyn Seeley, both experienced and idealistic journalists; James A. Wechsler, who had edited the Columbia College *Spectator* and worked with Lerner at *The Nation;* copy editor Rae Weimer; the sports writers Joe Cummiskey and Tom Meany; and, briefly, Hodding Carter, who later made his reputation editing *The Delta Democrat-Times* in Greenville, Mississippi. Albert Deutsch pioneered a column on physical and mental health (and did a ground-breaking expose on the appalling conditions at the city's mental hospitals).[6] Sidney Margolius opened a consumer column. Arnold Beichman reported on outbreaks of religious and racial bias and served as city editor. Leon Edel, who would go on to write a classic biography of Henry James, served as night editor. I. F. Stone, who had previously written editorials for the *Post*, served as Washington correspondent.

Other staff members were George Reedy, who was to become press spokesman for President Lyndon Johnson, the photographers Margaret Bourke-White and Mary Morris, and the novelists Erskine Caldwell, Ben Hecht, Ernest Hemingway (who reported on the war in the Far East), and Jerome Weidman. Frank Sullivan, who would later write a famous Christmas greeting poem for *The New Yorker*, wrote a regular humorous column. Jimmy Cannon, who became popular for his Hemingwayesque sports prose, started on *PM*. Theodore Geisel, the future "Dr. Seuss," did three cartoons a week before he was drafted. James Thurber wrote for *PM* until he joined *The New Yorker*. Dr. Benjamin Spock did a series on baby and child care. The artists Ad Reinhardt and Joseph Szyk contributed cartoons.

Although even this galaxy of star staff members and contributors failed to boost circulation to a figure close enough to Ingersoll's projections, it did win the paper many fans. On *PM*'s anniversary in June 1941, hundreds of congratulatory letters and telegrams poured in, including tributes from political leaders and a host of celebrities, ranging from Jack Benny and Eddie Cantor to Albert Einstein and even, most remarkably, FBI Director J. Edgar Hoover—a sign that the newspaper's support of Roosevelt and the New Deal had made it politically respectable, at least until then. The humorist Dorothy Parker raved about "Barnaby," one of the paper's several original comic strips (featuring Mr. O'Malley, Barnaby's blundering but lovable ghostly godfather, whose favorite imprecation was "Cushlamochree!"). The strip, Parker wrote with pardonable hyperbole, was "the most important addition to American arts and letters in Lord knows how many years."[7]

From the beginning, however, *PM* was dogged by a "Communist problem." Ingersoll tried to head it off as early as December 1940 by announcing his intention of battling with the Communists on at least one key issue:

> I do not agree with the Communists in their foreign policy. I propose to fight them . . . We're going to ignore the pressure groups

and special pleaders, to get out a paper so square and straight and able and intelligent and interesting and dramatic and generally satisfying that we will have earned the faith of the common people of New York, who alone can make our reputation or break it.[8]

Before taking this tough line, however, Ingersoll had sent word that he wanted to meet privately with Earl Browder, the head of the CPUSA, reportedly to put him on notice that he intended to publish a completely independent newspaper but also to assure him that the paper would be open to the Communist point of view, which he considered "an important factor in contemporary politics." He even offered to appoint a Communist reporter of Browder's choice with the understanding that the reporter's influence would be restricted to the presentation of the party's point of view "in council." Such a reporter was appointed but quit after a few weeks, saying he could not go along with the paper's professed objectivity. After publication began, however, articles appeared in *The American Mercury* and *The Saturday Evening Post* citing the number of known Communists or fellow travelers on the staff—as many as sixteen by one count. Intense ideological battles broke out in the newspaper's offices between a pro-Communist and anti-Communist faction. The Communist-dominated Newspaper Guild was intent on promoting the party line and getting as many party members and fellow travelers hired as possible.[9] Leo Huberman, a mediocre journalist of pronounced Communist sympathies, became a cause célèbre. Ingersoll thought Huberman's "emotional involvement with a single faction of the labor movement so intense that he could not write or edit objectively." The Newspaper Guild protested, and the dispute went on for months until Huberman was finally fired.[10]

Ingersoll later thought that this internal warfare had ruined *PM*'s prospects, but there were other serious problems as well. The newspaper was attacked for being pro-Communist by *The Saturday Evening Post* and for "red-baiting" by the *Daily Worker* and *New Masses*. The pro-Fascist "Christian Front" protested its editorials as well as its penchant for running photographs of bathing beauties, ostensibly for the benefit of subscribers in the armed forces. Before Pearl Harbor, the pro Nazi German-American Bund denounced it for "war-mongering." Militant anti-Communists circulated a handbill in newspaper offices listing allegedly Communist staffers and contending that they were controlling its copy. *The New Leader* ran an article by labor writer Victor Riesel titled "Million Dollar

Daily Follows CP Line." Even the U.S. army listed it as a "dangerous publication." [11] Ingersoll fired back at the newspaper's enemies, labeling them either Fascists or Fascist sympathizers, but the charge hung around the newspaper's neck like an albatross. The paper suffered from Ingersoll's readiness to hire too many staffers who had no experience running a newspaper and from the failure of the paper—in part due to the hiring policy—to meet the extravagant expectations aroused by the advance publicity. Although some of its readers remained intensely loyal, circulation dropped steadily, falling well below the 200,000 break-even point. Ingersoll tried to stem the decline by firing staff, hiring replacements, and changing assignments, hoping to find the right combination. The main result was a prolonged war with the Newspaper Guild. By August, 1941, circulation had plummeted to a mere 31,000, and the paper was on the verge of bankruptcy.

Suddenly, its fortunes revived. Field bought out the other stockholders at twenty cents on the dollar, and the paper was saved for the time being. Advertising, having at first been disdained, was now solicited. Ingersoll's personal coverage of the war in Europe helped boost readership. His dispatches from London and Moscow sent daily circulation soaring by 50,000. By the end of the year it had reached over 90,000—still well short of what it would need to survive—but when the United States entered the war, circulation spiked up again, jumping another 77,000 by the end of March 1942.[12] Finally, *PM* seemed to have turned the corner. At that point, however, events beyond Ingersoll's control removed him from his role as editor and left the paper to find its way without him. Classified 1-A, he received a draft notice in 1942. He appealed the classification, and some readers wrote to the newspaper agreeing with his contention that he was worth a division editing *PM*.[13] Ingersoll took the unusual step of airing his case in the pages of the newspaper, to no avail. When his appeal was rejected, he decided to volunteer and received a commission. He was inducted and did not return to *PM* until the end of the war.

"The Professor Will Do an Edit"

Lerner was among those who read *PM* with admiration from its debut. As he grew increasingly impatient with the detachment of academic life in wartime, he tried to get a job on the newspaper. His first effort proved to be a disheartening failure. By prearrangement,

Front page of the newspsper *PM* (May 23, 1947).

he met Ingersoll in the lobby of the Waldorf Hotel, bringing with him two trial editorials. Ingersoll was a big, hulking figure whose very size made the diminutive Lerner feel insecure. Ingersoll glanced hurriedly over Lerner's trial editorials and said, "These won't do. Not enough punch," adding, to rub salt in the wound, "You'll never be a journalist," and stalked off. Lerner was keenly disappointed, but by year's end Ingersoll had enlisted in the army, and Lerner was encouraged to try again. Fortunately for him,

Ingersoll had been replaced by John P. Lewis, who had previously become managing editor and was interested in having Lerner write for the paper regularly. Mary Morris, a friend of Edna's from Sarah Lawrence days, served as go-between. Again Lerner brought a trial piece, and this time it met with approval. "Will do," Lewis said, and offered Lerner a job on the spot on a week-to-week basis at $7,500 a year. To circumvent guild restrictions, he was given the title of "Assistant to the Publisher," an odd and patently contrived designation inasmuch as the newspaper had no formal publisher.

There was no written contract, only a handshake, and Lerner knew that he could expect no job security. Nevertheless, after getting a leave of absence from Williams, he accepted eagerly. He arrived at the paper's offices late in January 1943 just in time to be asked to write a commentary on a breaking story: the summit meeting between Roosevelt and Churchill at Casablanca. At an editorial meeting, Lewis nodded toward Lerner and announced, "The Professor will do an edit on the Summit; either it will run, or not." Lerner had done similar editorials for *The Nation* and *The New Republic* but rarely under this sort of time constraint: it was noon and the editorial was to appear the next day. He sat down at an unfamiliar typewriter, banged away, and at 3:30 handed an editorial over to Lewis. "Will do," said Lewis, "get yourself settled. See you tomorrow."

For Lerner, this was the start of what was to prove to be a long career as a newspaper columnist and a shorter role as the leading journalistic voice of the non-Communist Left. Unlike *The Nation* a decade earlier, whose subscribers consisted of a motley national collection of progressives, pacifists, and believers in free trade, *PM*'s readers were mainly from the greater New York area and were either liberals (the term increasingly used to denote those who strongly supported the New Deal, civil liberties, and civil rights) or democratic socialists. They were education oriented if not college educated, reform minded, with a keen sense of justice and idealism. Some of the male readers were in business or government; many were professionals with an intense political consciousness, and some were affiliated with trade unions, either as organizers or rank-and-file members. Lerner felt from the start that the readers wanted to be represented by an articulate spokesman and that he was better suited for the role than Ingersoll had been—more intellectual, Jewish like many of its readers, more committed to a Left-liberal point of view, and more at home with ideas and literary culture.

But he saw then, and even more clearly later, that the newspaper had serious problems. He thought the idea of an adless newspaper "idiotic," having never cared for this sort of misplaced idealism. He had learned from his *Nation* experience that the real need in journalism is for financial independence. The function of advertising, he thought, was to provide that independence. At the time, he did not fully appreciate the editorial paradox that also afflicted *PM*. In retrospect he realized that *PM*'s politics and the initial total ban on advertising prevented it from becoming as widely read as its prospectus had envisioned: "*PM* had two strikes on it: it was too left to get enough readers, and it had no advertisers. Either one was wounding, the two together were to prove fatal after eight years."

Other critics thought that the newspaper's main shortcoming was its fixation with the plight of the politically oppressed and socially downtrodden. One said that its idea of a good story was "man bites underdog." [14] Another, A. J. Liebling, in his *New Yorker* column, "The Wayward Press," observed of *PM* that "it was pure in heart" but not as broadly public-spirited or enough in tune with a wide spectrum of readers to win the loyalty of a larger audience:

> The injustices it whacked away at were genuine enough, but an awful lot of whacks seem to fall on the same injustices. A girl to whom I made a present of a subscription to *PM* in 1946 called to ask me after a time, "Doesn't *anybody* have any trouble except the Jews and the colored people?" *PM* couldn't get the second hundred thousand unless it changed, and it couldn't change without losing a substantial number of the first hundred thousand. Once, in a bid for popular appeal, the sports department picked an all-scholastic Greater New York football team. The paper received a flock of letters from its readers reproaching it for exalting brutality and asking why it didn't pick an all-scholastic *scholastic* team. [15]

While it appeared, however, *PM* was an exhilarating experience for Lerner and the others on the staff and for many readers who became avid admirers. Lerner's "think pieces" appeared at first on page 2 under the boxed title, "Opinion." In *PM* these were always signed, in pointed contrast to the standard practice of using the "editorial we" to make a newspaper's opinions seem those of the editors rather than of the publisher to whom they were beholden. Those opinion pieces meant to convey the views of the entire editorial staff carried a special designation, often "Max Lerner for the editors of *PM*." The opinion pieces became particularly important as *PM* came to be thought of as a "newspaper of opinion"—giving rise to the joke that *PM* was really an eight-cent newspaper, because it cost five cents to buy *PM* and three cents for the *Times* to find out what was happening.

Some of Lerner's essays were random observations of wartime America, knit together by a fascination with the country, especially its popular culture, and embroidered with literary references. When he put together selections from them in the books *Public Journal* and *Actions and Passions*, he included some of his forays into what he described as "cultural anthropology." In one lyrical piece, written in 1943, when the wartime ban on lighting was lifted for New York, he celebrated his love of the city's distinctive neighborhoods as "a mosaic of memories and images" but noted that something was missing:

> I think it is a heart, and I mean this in a literal and not a sentimental sense. In almost every culture the town or city is built around some center to and through which the blood of the community flows. It may be the *agora*, the commons, the pub, the crossroads store, the market square, the "green" or the church. But in each case it is the pole between which and his home a man can move. It is a place of quiet talk, of bantering association. There is no such place in New York. Broadway and the movie houses and the bars and night clubs are what New Yorkers turn to, but they are places of movement and amusement and unquiet, not the secure core of a community. New York, which is the center of our national culture, has in itself no center.[16]

In the New York of that time, however, the newspapers served as a marketplace of ideas that made them a modern equivalent of the ancient Greek *agora*. The 1930s and 1940s were the Golden Age of New York newspaper journalism before television networks and local stations began to eclipse the print media as the primary purveyors of news reports, opinion, pictures, and advertising—adding insult to injury by substituting animated cartoons for the unique American institution of the newspaper comic strip. Before the primacy of print journalism went down the tube, so to speak, there was a New York newspaper to suit every taste and every political nuance. *PM* appealed to its readers mainly because they identified with its Left-liberal point of view.

Democracy against Fascism

PM was an idealistic newspaper that sought to expose corruption, fight racial and religious prejudice, and champion the rights of labor and the policies of the New Deal.[17] It defined the central issue facing the country and the world as the struggle for democracy and against fascism. Lerner used his editorial podium to rail against Fascists and against those he considered their unwitting allies because they were trying to undermine the alliance with the USSR. His favorite targets were the "lunatic fascist press" and the "Hearst-McCormick-Patterson axis," a reference to Randolph Hearst, publisher of the *Daily Mirror* and *Journal-American;* Col. Robert R. McCormick, publisher of the *Chicago Tribune;* and Joseph Patterson, McCormick's cousin and the publisher of the *Daily News.*[18] Drawing on such studies as Robert Brady's *Business as a Structure of Power* (1943), Lerner articulated an explanation of fascism that was then a widely held view on the Left and was prefigured in Marx's analysis of the coup d'état of 1851 in *The Eighteenth Brumaire of Louis Bonaparte.*

As Robert C. Tucker has noted,[19] this analysis became "a sort of prologue to later Marxist thought on the nature and meaning of fascism." Marx explained Louis Napoleon's coup as a result of the upper bourgeoisie's effort to crush its erstwhile allies, the petty bourgeoisie and the proletariat. As the bourgeois dictatorship of Thermidor had paved the way for the rise of Napoleon, now the same class enthroned his nephew, a mere *remplaçant* without the strategic gifts of his uncle or his army. Lerner offered essentially the same interpretation in updated form. Fascism, he contended, was the product of the failure of governments to impose enough economic planning. When the "anarchy of capitalism" led to economic collapse, the working people turned to the labor movement and the Socialist parties. To forestall the inevitable adoption of socialism by electoral means, industrialists courted right-wing paramilitary groups like the Black Shirts of Italy and the Brown Shirts of Germany, hoping to use them to stage preemptive coups d'etat. The fact that during his rise to power Hitler had gone to Dusseldorf and convinced German business leaders to support him was cited as clinching evidence that fascism was an instrument of last resort used by the bourgeoisie to stave off socialism. To gain popular support, the right-wing cynically appealed to the racist and nationalist sentiments of the German middle class, as well as to its hostility to the trade unions. By assuming a populist mantle, they attracted the *lumpenproletariat*, damaging the domestic and international solidarity of the working class. Fragile democratic governments led by weak leaders with little help from the press readily succumbed, and the Fascists, once in power, worked hand-in-glove with the upper bourgeoisie.

This general formula did not seem to need much modification to take account of Japan, which was assimilated, however roughly, to the Western model: the *zaibatsu* industrialists were taken to be the counterpart of the German and Italian cartels which had given Mussolini and Hitler the money they needed to finance their takeovers; nationalism and Japanese ethnic chauvinism were seen as the equivalent of the Nazis' racism and Mussolini's imperialism. Noting that Veblen, in *Imperial Germany and the Industrial Revolution,* had predicted that both Germany and Japan, because they had industrialized late, would become autocratic, Lerner saw little difference between what was happening in Europe and what was happening in Asia:

> The case of Japan is the case of the most perfect setup for a fascist military ruling clique that history has ever invented. Their purpose and need are the same as the purpose and need of the gang around Hitler; to entrench and expand their power, and to stifle any stirrings among workers or any ideas among students and writers. But whereas Hitler had to strive to make himself God, the Japanese Hitlers have a homegrown and ready made God on hand. Behind him as a screen, they build their armies, exploit their people, stifle all "dangerous thoughts" and lay their plans for world domination.[20]

Could fascism come to America, as its leading American intellectual advocate, Lawrence Dennis,[21] expected it would? In view of experience throughout Europe and in Asia, Lerner thought that this was not an altogether far-fetched prophecy. What if "right-wing reactionaries," supported by the giant corporations and their allies and spokesmen in the press, should succeed in preventing the New Deal from regulating capitalism? Another even worse economic collapse could trigger a resort to Fascist repression, instigated by the National Association of Manufacturers—an organization with a political influence he thought fully comparable to that of the European and Japanese cartels. Press barons like Roy Howard struck him as little different from German industrialists like Fritz Thyssen.[22] The reactionaries would be able to exploit American nativism, a powerful force since its emergence in the 1850s, which remained virulent in the form of anti-Semitism and dovetailed with a long-standing hostility to blacks. Lerner saw evidence of nativism in the relocation of Japanese-Americans at the outset of the war, which he denounced as "a lethal attack on the Bill of Rights." [23] His hope was that the record of fascism in Europe and Japan, and the aggressive threat it had come to pose, would bring enough Americans to their senses in time to prevent a repetition of what had happened in Europe.

The international and domestic threat could be met, he thought, only by a combination of political leadership, militant trade unionism, and a press that would champion the ideals of democracy. FDR was providing the leadership, with the help of the trade unions, though Lerner agreed with Laski that only a labor party could guarantee that New Deal reforms would be carried forward. The American Labor Party of New York might have become the basis of such a national party, but the internal squabbling between its Communist and non-Communist factions had damaged it irreparably. For the press, *PM* would set the example of a socially responsible, progressive approach to reporting and editorializing.

Motivated by this conception of the great struggle between fascism and democracy, Lerner and *PM* became strong supporters of the New Deal and of Roosevelt as its leader—all the more so as Roosevelt rallied the country in the struggle against the Axis powers. Lerner praised FDR for making a success of the New Deal by institutionalizing government regulation of industry and protecting collective bargaining. He also credited him with adopting a foreign policy more progressive than that of any president since Wilson. "His great shaping ideas in this field have made history: the Good Neighbor idea in Latin-American affairs; the idea of 'quarantining' Nazi aggression; the idea of America as the arsenal of the democracies; the idea of Lend-Lease; the idea of the Four Freedoms; the idea of the United Nations." [24]

Defending Roosevelt's concessions to big business, Lerner explained that the president had no real alternative as long as the war lasted. Given the prevailing system of economic power, the captains of industry could either sabotage the war effort or enable it to succeed, and Roosevelt was simply recognizing their indispensability. But Lerner urged him to bear in mind that this was a war to end exploitation, and to be prepared, once the emergency was past, to restore the principles of the New Deal—already, he noted, under attack. The Dies Committee, named for its chairman, Congressman Martin Dies of Texas, was denouncing New Dealers as subversives. The "radio monopolies" were trying to weaken the regulatory power of the Federal Communications Commission. An "Unholy Alliance" in Congress between the Republicans and the "Tory Democrats" was finding support in the press, the advertising agencies, and the business lobbies. "The object is to smash FDR and the New Deal. The strategy is to cripple one after another the important administrative agencies and then accuse them of doing a bad job." Lerner urged the bureaucrats to resist, by doing such a good job that the enemies of positive government would have nothing to criticize. The reactionaries, he charged, had kept soldiers from voting and protected the poll tax to keep Southern blacks from exercising their right to vote. By supporting Sewell Avery of Montgomery Ward in his refusal to pay taxes, they had put the right to private property above the national welfare in time of war.[25] They were trying to hamstring the Office of Price Administration by forcing it to appoint as administrators only people sympathetic to big business.[26] This was not just a "technical fight" but a moral fight, he wrote, "and the one that has the greatest moral stamina is the side that will win."[27]

In foreign policy, Lerner feared that the United States, under the aegis of the State Department but with FDR's approval, was pursuing a policy that in effect repeated the folly of appeasement, by siding with reactionary forces in North Africa, France, and Spain. FDR was too preoccupied with the military needs of the moment, Lerner argued, and too heavily dependent on certain advisers, notably Admiral William Leahy and Adolf Berle, who were advocating a "realistic" policy of supporting the status quo, fearing that to encourage "economic democracy" abroad would stir sleeping dogs on the Right at home. The great looming struggle seemed to be the effort to shape the postwar world, which Lerner and *PM* hoped would finally be free of the imperialism they held responsible for aggressiveness and division.

In a preface to a reissue of *It Is Later than You Think*, in 1943, Lerner looked forward to a great postwar reconstruction. Hitler did not reckon with the "potential strength of the democratic idea, and with the new vitality it could take on once it had been shaken loose from the fetters of minority complacency by the impact of the war itself."[28] The nations in which capitalism and democracy moved in an uneasy partnership—chiefly Britain and the United States—had enough attachment to democracy, and enough sheer strength, to join the Soviet Union in turning the tide against the Fascist aggression. Looking to the postwar world, he sided with those who hoped that the United Nations could become the basis of a peaceful world, while recognizing that the ardor for nationhood would survive. Respect for national autonomy would require the abolition of imperialism, the creation of regional federations, and help for the newly emerging countries. In the United States, what would be needed most would be social harmony, an end to racism and economic privilege, and a recognition by the people that only the democratic principle "can open the career to their talents and give them that stake in the future upon which the release of their energies depends."[29]

Lerner's passionate exposition of these views, especially in *PM*, won him many liberal admirers, even among those who found his earlier writings too radical. Thurman Arnold, the author of one of the most original books of the decade, *The Folklore of Capitalism*, and by then a federal judge, wrote to congratulate him even as he repeated his disagreement with *It Is Later than You Think*, which he thought the best expression of a wrongheaded socialist diagnosis. "Now you are attacking specific instances of special privilege—things on which you can't go wrong—and you are doing it better than any one writing today."[30] The philosophic historian Hannah Arendt congratulated him on a "wonderful" column criticizing the expanding powers of the FBI.[31] Justice Black wrote to praise an article by Lerner in *The Antioch Review*, adding only that he wished it were presented in terms more accessible to ordinary readers: "It is because I like what you say that I want your messages to have a far greater audience. The people need them."[32] (Lerner reciprocated, assuring him that his friendship had been very encouraging, frequently referring to Black as "the gentle giant from Alabama," and writing to him: "Your friendship has been most encouraging to me.")[33] When the military services banned Catherine Drinker Bowen's study of Justice Holmes from service libraries, Lerner wrote to defend the book, even though he did not care for it. She wrote to thank him: "It is good to know that we have people like you to fight for things here at home that need support—more than support, a kind of cold and logical fury you know how to impart in print."[34]

Laski responded with delight to Lerner's writings, and encouraged him to cooperate in developing a revolutionary vision for the postwar world. He found Lerner's essays "a joy" and encouraged him to see the American role as a catalyst in a worldwide revolutionary movement. In April 1942, Laski wrote to say that he was confident of allied victory but disagreed with Frankfurter (and Churchill) that all efforts should be concentrated on winning the war, leaving the principles that would regulate the postwar world to be determined later:

> It is no longer enough, pace Felix, to fight with courage for victory; we have got to make it quite sure what the victory is to be for, and to do that while we are fighting. Otherwise I am quite certain that there will be a drift to complete dissolution of the European system with no prospects of any enduring social peace. Benes sees this quite clearly; and to some extent [U.S. ambassador to Britain] John Winant. But most of our people are the victims of Felix's tragic obsession that you can separate victory from postwar reconstruction. That, of course, is Winston's view, and I think it may well lead to changes grimmer than any we have so far encountered. For the more you see into the mind of at any rate our people the more you can see that a revolution is already psychologically complete and that it will seek expression at the first moment when danger is past. It is so clear to anyone who meets the men in the forces and the factories that though they will fight the Nazis till they are broken, they are not fighting to restore the old order, and that the traditional society does not interest them. We have got to find new categories of political thought, new institutions, a new social contract. The Russian Revolution was merely a stage in a process which is world-wide . . . the democratic phase of bourgeois civilization is over . . . The basis of society must be seen and felt to be in transformation or we shall move straight into an era in which Terror will be king.
>
> This is where I think American influence is fundamental. For you are vital, experimental, still capable of deliberate revolutionary adjustment. Privilege hasn't with you the prescriptive graces of four hundred years. Your culture is democratic. Your political differentiations are democratic. Your social heritage is democratic. If you can make it understood that all your influence as a great power will be thrown on the side of fundamental change the impact on Europe will be immense. In power the next century belongs to America and Russia, as the one after belongs to China and India. The question is what canon will you establish for it. Can F.D.R. restate the Jeffersonian ideal in 20th century terms? Can he give all America could give to the re-establishment of faith in reason? It means a new content for freedom and for justice, and it means a change in the basis of American life even more profound than in the Civil War.[35]

Lerner agreed with Laski that the future of America was tied to the future of democratic socialism in Europe. Whether America would repudiate the New Deal and thereby invite a return of economic chaos and with it the danger of an American version of fascism, he thought, hinged on its policy toward the Soviet Union. He was convinced that by "demonizing" Soviet communism, the reactionaries wanted to frighten Americans into resisting further experiments with collectivism at home. To help thwart them he joined the National Citizens Political Action Committee, formed in 1944 by the CIO leader Sidney Hillman. Its aim was to unite "independent progressives" behind a program aiming to "crown a people's war with a people's peace"—words Lerner himself had been using. The sponsors included liberals like Bruce Bliven, the editor of *The New Republic;* Reinhold Niebuhr; and the labor leader Philip Murray; as well as pro-Soviet figures like the great baritone Paul Robeson and the Marxist economist Paul Sweezy. Lerner expressed their commonly held view when he wrote in *PM* in 1945: "Do not reject an imperfect ally when you are working for a common aim." [36]

In December 1944, Lerner traveled to Britain aboard the Queen Elizabeth, then a troop carrier, to report on the climax of the war and assess the prospects for postwar reconstruction. The puckish anarchist Dwight Macdonald reprinted in his magazine *Politics* a *PM* photo of Lerner in the military uniform worn by war correspondents, to poke fun at some middle-class intellectual leftists only too ready to do the bidding of their capitalist warlords. In London, Lerner got to know Aneurin Bevan and other Labor Party leaders. He went next to Paris, where, while waiting to be allowed to go to the war front, he took in the sights and got to know the foreign correspondents, playing poker with them until the wee hours of the night. He also had a long talk one evening with the Existentialist writer Albert Camus and was gratified when the next day a package of Camus's writings was delivered to his hotel. Lerner wrote to Edna to record his excitement at listening to Camus explain why he had taken part in the Resistance even though he despaired for the future of humanity:

> It was one of the most moving experiences I have had. And the most moving thing about it was finding a man who didn't fool himself, who fought for the material things that can make his people great within a framework of moral values, and didn't let the darkness of life strip him of either dignity or effectiveness. I have met no one since Malraux who impressed me as much, and this man is more ordered and disciplined than Malraux.

Given permission finally to move to the front, Lerner set foot on newly captured German soil in February 1945. He sent a dispatch back to *PM* describing his thoughts upon seeing dead German soldiers and wretched civilians as he reflected on the "whole terrible train of events since the Nazis first laid their withering hand on Germany":

> I have seen in my mind Walter Rathenau lying in the back seat of his car riddled with the bullets of the Vehme gang. And Karl Liebknecht and Rosa Luxembourg, with their skulls bashed in by fascist hoodlums in the prison yard. And the underground fighters on whom the Gestapo refined its torture methods, to refine them still further on the resistance movements in the occupied territories. And the concentration camps of Germany which were a prelude to the charnel houses and human furnaces in Poland. I saw in my mind a Europe in which the human spirit had been all but crushed from Spain to the Ukraine. I saw the burned books, and the writers who had escaped, but had been stripped of hope on which a writer lives, as surely as a musician is stripped of it when his hands are broken, and who—like Ernst Toller and Stefan Zweig—had ended by hanging themselves. I saw a whole blasted generation.

It was wrong, he cautioned his readers, to rejoice over the enemy dead or seek revenge against the living, "who were human even if they were German." The tragedy, after all, was that "the Nazism of the Germans was allowed to befoul our world."[37] The scenes of devastation and the stories he heard from survivors of the concentration camps were to remain with him the rest of his life; he would sometimes awake in the middle of the night screaming from nightmares recalling his experience of the war.

The Soviet Question

Once the outcome of the war in Europe became clear, Lerner turned his attention to the prospects for a "people's peace." For many European leftists like Laski, there could be no question of the need to maintain the Soviet-American alliance; for American liberals this was a more troubling and divisive issue. In 1942, while still at Williams, Lerner addressed it in a lengthy article for *The Atlantic Monthly*. At the time, the Russian forces were being pressed back steadily, but he was confident that eventually they would prevail. Why were the Russian people putting up such a determined fight?

Partly out of patriotism and fear of the consequences of defeat, Lerner conceded, but also, he insisted, because they had what Veblen had called an "industrial" rather than a merely pecuniary economy, with a serious level of military technology and administrative skills based on the principle of "the career open to talent." Did Stalin's earlier willingness to sign a pact with Hitler make him likely to be an untrustworthy postwar partner? Echoing Schuman, Lerner argued that the pact with Hitler was a Machiavellian response by Stalin to "the treachery of the British and French ruling groups"—one "likely in the end . . . to be more devastating to antifascist opinion and more costly to Russia than it was worth as a maneuver in gaining time." The record did not justify fears for the future, he thought. Stalin, whether or not he betrayed the revolution, "is no revolutionary adventurer, but one of the men who come after a revolution to consolidate it. His natural conservatism will be fortified by the need Russia will have of getting back on its feet." Even if democracy and the Soviet system were polar opposites, "nations with divergent ideologies can remain at peace." It is only when a governing group (as with the Nazis) holds an ideology which by its very nature pushes toward an imperium over other peoples that an ideological war becomes inevitable. The question was whether the world would move forward to a "people's century" mediated by the United Nations or leave power vacuums in which new forms of fascism would arise or in which either America or Russia would behave imperialistically. Reaffirming his belief in democratic socialism, he concluded by sweeping the Soviet experiment under the democratic tent:

> There is something dying in our world. It is the idea of state irresponsibility for the welfare of the people, and the correlative idea of an unplanned and chaotic system of power politics. There is something being born in our world. It is the idea that men are brothers more than they are enemies—the idea of a framework of united peoples determined to organize a people's century. Nor is the framework one that needs to be spun out of our innards. The habits of common action that are now being forged on the battlegrounds, in the factories and schools, even in the concentration camps all over the world in the struggle against a common enemy, must not be broken. If we extend them into the future we can win that future.[38]

In editorials for *PM*, Lerner continued to defend the Soviet system. As the tide of war in Europe turned against Hitler Germany, and the people of the Soviet Union, through terrible sacrifices, were defeating the seemingly invincible *Wehrmacht,* he expressed the gratitude shared by many in the West. He did not stop at expressing gratitude, but went on to praise the Red Army as the product of the leadership of Lenin and Trotsky and the "moral strength" imparted by the Communist system. Ignoring the devastating effect of Stalin's purges on the officer corps and the willingness of many non-Russians and anti-Communist Russians to join the German invaders, he cited the spirit of the Red Army as an example of the collective spirit Americans needed to emulate.[39]

As the war in Europe was ending, anti-Communists renewed their attack on the Soviet Union and called for the forging of a new alliance against it. Lerner devoted much of his work to denying that the wartime alliance must necessarily fall apart. He locked horns first with the ex-Communist Max Eastman and then with the diplomat William C. Bullitt and the writer James Burnham. Eastman, in the *Reader's Digest,* had urged that Americans "face the facts about Russia." Claiming that Vice President Wallace, Wendell Willkie, and Ambassador Joseph E. Davies had all disguised the truth about Stalin's repressiveness, Eastman urged Americans to recognize that however important it was to keep Russia as a wartime ally, there must be no delusion about the difference and animosity between the Soviet system and Western-style democracy. The stubborn resistance of the Russians to Hitler, he contended, no more justified communism than the stupendous assault of the Germans justified Nazism. Eastman argued bluntly that Russia was a vast concentration camp, with 10 million political prisoners, that it was impoverished and relied on slave labor, and that the Russian leaders hated and despised democracy and were plotting to overthrow democratic governments wherever they could.

Lerner pounced on this article first of all to defend Wallace, Willkie, and Davies. They were, he argued, far more realistic than Eastman because they saw that the war could not be won unless Americans and Russians won it together. Nor could the peace be made secure, he added, unless America and Russia organized it together. Against the notion that there is a moral equivalence between German fascism and Russian communism, Lerner argued first that the heroism of the Soviet people belied the claim that their social system was so terrible. "As I read Eastman," he wrote, "I kept thinking: if these people are slaves, why do slaves fight so well? Why do starving people form themselves not just into a nation with an army, but a nation in arms?" Why do Russian children "die for their country with a deep joy that would do honor to grown and mature men? Why do Russians have the sense that they are fashioning a New World, with new meanings—a sense that we in America seem sadly to have lost?" Besides, he argued, was there no moral difference between a nation that makes an assault upon another, and one that resists it stubbornly? And "is there no political difference between a nation whose life and aim are war and a nation that wants to build its own social system and, to do so, requires to live at peace with the world?"

As to Eastman's prescriptions for American policy, Lerner was equally dismissive. Eastman did not say that America should demand that Russia change its social system as a price for collaboration. If he did, "imagine what the Russians could say about our distribution of income, our treatment of Negroes, our class system of education." Eastman's only specific suggestion was that the Communist Party be banned in the United States and that the schools and media be kept safe from the agents and apologists of communism. Lerner replied that Eastman would have America fight communism by adopting the repressiveness of free thought for which he properly blamed Soviet communism. Lerner himself had more faith in America's democratic institutions, so much faith that "I believe they can compete in the world with those of a totalitarian socialism—and without our having to resort to suppression." [40]

In retrospect, both Eastman and Lerner may be said to have scored points in this debate, though Eastman came out ahead. He was right to emphasize the totalitarian character of the Soviet Union under Stalin and to charge that liberals were ignoring realities for the sake of maintaining the wartime alliance. Lerner was disingenuous in denying what was known by then not only about the denial of political freedom in the Soviet Union but about Stalin's show-trial purges and the persecution of enemies of the state and the party. The willingness of the Russians (and non-Russians) to fight in what they called "the great patriotic war" was due to a desire to repel a brutal invasion and defend "mother Russia" rather than communism. The ferocity of their struggle was also a response to the savagery shown by the invaders—a self-defeating policy that kept the Nazis from attracting even more of those chafing under Soviet rule than the considerable number they did attract to their side.

Lerner was on better ground, however, in arguing that anti-Communists like Eastman were too ready to ape Soviet totalitarianism in order to deal with dissent at home and even to smear the New Deal as "creeping socialism." He was on defensible pragmatic ground in urging that if the forces of fascism were to be defeated, "we must put Russia's strength and its qualities as a going concern in the foreground, and communism's sins in the background."[41] He was also right to warn that if the alliance broke down in the postwar period, a third and even more devastating world war would become a serious threat.

Bullitt, in a lengthy article in *Life,* had for the first time in the mainstream media put forward an argument Lerner described as "the slimy whispered agitation for a split between America and its Russian partner in the war . . ." all but issuing a direct call for a war between England and America on one side and Russia on the other. Lerner answered that there was an "imperative need" to maintain the wartime coalition "all the way to a complete victory" and an equally great need to maintain it "as the base of a new peace structure for the world." He attacked Bullitt for repeating "the old slanders" about millions of Poles having been deported to Siberia by the Russians, and for inciting the Finns and Rumanians not to break with their German partners, and Yugoslavs to struggle against each other rather than unite under Tito. Lerner admitted that the biggest problem of the peace was what to do with Germany, but he argued that the allies must stand together on that question or fall out about all the others. Bullitt was arguing for the creation of a new *cordon sanitaire* under British leadership, a coalition of Western European states that would resist the spread of communism.[42] To Lerner this was calculated to wreck the wartime alliance and destroy all hope of peace afterward.

In 1947 Lerner took on Burnham, a philosopher and ex-Communist, who was also given an audience by *Life* to summarize his book *The Struggle for the World,* in which he claimed that the Russians were intent on world conquest. Lerner answered that if this were true, perhaps the only sensible defense policy would be a preemptive atomic war. Fortunately, it was not true. Since the showdown over Iran, Lerner argued, the Soviet leaders seemed to have become willing to compromise, and in any case they had a doctrinal hatred of militarism and a stable economic system which "makes it unnecessary for them to expand in order to create jobs." The rulers would be "insane" to want to risk the survival of their system on a drive for world conquest and would be content to "share a partnership of a world power inside a UN organization."[43]

These debates over Western policy toward the Soviet Union marked the resumption of the ideological battle between Left and Right that had been muted by the war. As the wartime alliance broke apart, and anti-Communist zealots again sought to expose both Communist Party members and "fellow travelers," liberals and radicals were thrown on the defensive. The House Un-American Activities Committee gave this crusade official blessing, and the Truman administration adopted new "loyalty and security" regulations that made left-wing associations suspect. In 1946 Laski suffered the profound embarrassment of losing a libel suit against a writer he claimed had misrepresented his views on revolution. In June 1945, he had spoken at a political rally during the General Election campaign in Britain. A heckler, quoting from a Conservative Party speakers manual, had challenged him to explain why he had advocated revolution during the war. Laski replied that the accusation was false and that what he actually said was that unless serious popular grievances were addressed, the events of 1789 and 1917 had shown there was a real danger that people might take matters in their own hands and resort to violence and revolution. Several newspapers, including Lord Max Beaverbrook's *Daily Express,* reported that in the speech in question Laski had said that if the Labor Party could not achieve its ends by fair means it would resort to foul. Laski immediately sued the paper and several others as well as the writer who had reported the claim. At the trial he was cross-examined for two hours, and his counsel argued that the accusation was a fabrication, resulting from taking words out of context. In his instructions to the jury, however, the presiding judge noted only that Laski had in fact mentioned violence and revolution. The jury found for the defendant with costs, and Laski had to raise the substantial sum of 20,000 pounds. Lerner solicited contributions from Americans to help Laski pay the fine and succeeded in raising $6,500 from a long list of prominent writers and political figures. Laski was deeply grateful, writing to say that Lerner's gesture of friendship "has moved me more than I can say."[44]

The political climate grew threatening for Lerner as well. He became a target of right-wingers who saw no great difference among liberals, "creeping socialists," and Communists. Walter Winchell, with whom he had previously had cordial relations, took to referring to him as "Marx Lerner." The atmosphere even invaded Lerner's correspondence with Frankfurter. In 1948, when Lerner wrote in unusually courtly style ("May I presume on our friendship . . . ")

to pass on Laski's concern that he had not heard from Frankfurter about his book on American democracy, Frankfurter chided Lerner for being so formal: "How Victorian, Max! Or is the state of the country so panicky that you resort to Victorian formalism to cover up your 'red' past!" At the bottom of the letter he made sure to add a postscript:

> Dear Mr. Hoover:
> If by some chance the above should fall under the eye of one of your F.B.I. agents, you of course will be able to tell that I'm kidding in my "red" reference to Lerner's past.[45]

With the intensification of the Cold War, the debate over American foreign policy became polarized between those like Lerner who clung to the hope that the wartime alliance could be saved and those convinced that the West must gird for a showdown with international communism. For the Left, a critical turning point came when Roosevelt dropped Wallace as his vice-presidential running mate when he decided to run for a fourth term in 1944. The decision was made not because FDR was unhappy with Wallace's views on foreign policy but for domestic political reasons. The president had been warned by Democratic Party leaders that Wallace's image as a fuzzy-minded idealist (and his involvement with a "guru") made him a campaign liability. FDR vacillated, but in the end, fearing a fight over the nomination at the party convention, agreed to replace Wallace with Truman and tried to mollify Wallace by offering him the cabinet post of his choice, secretary of commerce.

Ingersoll had by then returned to the editorship of *PM.* Convinced that Wallace represented the hope of the future, "the age of the Common Man," Ingersoll used *PM* to help popularize Wallace's ideas, printing the texts of his speeches and making him the newspaper's political poster boy. Lerner was at first caught up in the general euphoria and reluctant to challenge Ingersoll on an issue so critical to him, but the more he saw of Wallace's naiveté in allowing the Communists to play leading roles in his Progressive Party, and the more convinced he became that Stalin's aggressive behavior had to be confronted, not appeased, the more he became disenchanted with Wallace.

By February 1948, when Wallace decided to run as a Third Party candidate, Lerner moved away from him, gradually and reluctantly. Schlesinger, whose views he took very seriously but who was often ahead of his own thinking, had expressed misgivings about Wallace in a letter from Harvard in 1947, contending that Wallace could not have subscribed honestly to the consensus on foreign policy among members of the newly formed Americans for Democratic Action. At the time, Lerner demurred:

> You say that Wallace believes in the possibility of working with Communists. Does this mean that liberals are to organize a secondary boycott and exclude from their organization not only the Communists but also the genuine liberals who (however mistaken) may hold differing views of working with Communists? I say this . . . because I think the great danger that any liberal organization runs these days is that of Communist control on the one hand and that of sterile parochialism on the other.[46]

In *PM*, Lerner tried to defend Wallace, portraying him as neither the demagogue his enemies claimed nor a visionary "dreamer"; he was rather an insurgent in the Midwest Populist tradition of Bryan and LaFollette. A stubborn sense of conscience kept Wallace from repudiating Communist support, Lerner argued, but he was far from being a Communist himself. Wallace's thinking was Populist—" 'agin' the trusts, 'agin' imperialism, 'agin' Wall Street." He was, however, also a believer in capitalism as the engine of economic progress, and his Christian ethics gave him a strong sense of justice. As an insurgent Republican who joined the New Deal to help improve farmers' incomes, he had broadened the base of his popular support to include workers, intellectuals, and minority groups. "As an agronomist," Lerner wrote, explaining Wallace's sympathies for the Russians, "he approaches politics experimentally, with the practical purpose of improving the breed of political man and social institutions. Such a man could not be caught up in a holy war against Russia, for the simple reason that he sees the Russians as a scientist might—sees them as adapting their political forms to their historical needs." His vision was of a world in which an amalgam will emerge of "the economic planning of the Russians added to the political freedom of the Americans." Lerner even agreed with Wallace's supporters that both capitalism and socialism were guilty of imperialism. Wallace was "somewhat naive about the Russians and the nature of their foreign policy; he does not recognize the extent to which the ruthlessness of the police-state has led to a Communist imperialism, just as with us the power of the monopolies has led to a capitalist imperialism."

But Lerner thought Wallace "a wretched tactician." His decision to run as a Third Party candidate, Lerner contended, would divide liberal voters and result in the election of a reactionary Republican president and Congress. His campaign, Lerner predicted correctly in February 1948, "will be a futile insurgent gesture, with the main organizational strength provided by the Communists, whose prize victim and trophy Wallace has become. And the movement he leads will go down in history as a valiant but mistaken fringe-movement, instead of part of the central current of American liberalism." [47]

As the 1948 election approached, Lerner was frustrated with the available choices. He again identified himself with "what seems to me the last best hope of America—the group that I call the critical and independent left," but he felt that this group had no sure home in any of the existing political parties. It included, he thought, a considerable number of liberal Republicans of the Willkie variety, Democrats who preferred Justice William O. Douglas to Truman, and those in both the Progressive and Socialist Parties who wanted reform and internationalism but were not naive about communism and the Soviet Union. This group had no candidate of its own. At first, Lerner announced, he would keep an open mind among Wallace, the Socialist candidate Norman Thomas, and Truman. [48] If Lerner could not bring himself to endorse Wallace, neither could he summon enough enthusiasm to back Truman, though he supported Truman's tough line against the Soviets. Shocked by Lerner's approval of Truman's support of efforts to block Communist takeovers in Greece and Turkey, the apoplectic Frederick Schuman, Lerner's old Williams colleague, had already canceled his subscription to *PM* in protest, though he managed somehow to see enough of Lerner's editorials to accuse him of the foulest treason to the Left and to demand that he recant:

> Never, since the Social Democrats in the Reichstag unanimously voted confidence in Hitler (May 17, 1933) and Blum betrayed the Spanish Republic in 1937, have I seen such a performance of base treachery to all that Progressivism stands for. I am inexpressibly shocked by your editorials. Never have you been so wrong, Max. You will of course come to your senses before November. Let me know when you do.
>
> With profound disgust and regret,
>
> Fred

Schuman, no doubt like other *PM* readers, expected Lerner to come around to endorsing Truman eventually: "You will, I suppose, continue to support that filthy, nauseating, putrid little prototype of the coming American Fascism who wants to build a balcony on the White House. I will support Wallace. We will both meet in the same concentration camp. I promise not to gloat." [49] But Lerner surprised Schuman, if not his more faithful followers. Convinced that Truman could not win, Lerner announced, in his column in the *New York Star*, the brief successor to *PM*, that he would waste his vote on Norman Thomas.

Lerner's reluctance to endorse Truman was not just a result of a faulty calculation that Truman would be defeated. It was more an indication of the crisis for liberals caused by the outbreak of the Cold War. Truman was responsible not just for the Marshall Plan but for the Truman Doctrine, which laid down limits beyond which Soviet expansionism would be resisted. He had tightened loyalty and security rules to respond to claims that Communists were being allowed to infiltrate the federal government, dismaying civil libertarians. At first Lerner tried to resist the pressure to join in denouncing the Soviet Union, for fear that this would play into the hands of the enemies of domestic reform. An exchange of correspondence with Joseph Alsop captured the dilemma tellingly. Responding to a column by Lerner critical of Alsop and his brother Stewart for their views on domestic politics, Alsop explained that they remained in favor of New Deal objectives but could not agree with the conventional liberal view on foreign policy. They did not believe that the CPUSA should be suppressed, because that would represent a denial of free speech, but, he added significantly,

> it is time for the Liberals to get the Communists out of their hair. There was a period—a very long period—when the Communists were valuable as a sort of ginger group. That period, I am sure, has definitely passed. They do harm, now, both to American Liberalism, and to the American Labor movement, because they are animated by entirely different motives than the Liberals and Laborites who work with them, and thus tend to distort situations and arouse otherwise avoidable opposition to what Liberals and Labor want.

The basic problem, Alsop continued, was not posed by Communists in America but by the Soviet Union. A great contest was underway, he thought, not between those who believe in economic planning and those who do not, but between two political systems, in one of which the idea of freedom was paramount, whereas in the other "the individual occupies the same relation to the state as the ant to an ant-hill—to borrow a comparison from Mr. Churchill." The Soviet rulers, he warned, had embarked on a program of expansion which, if not halted, would ultimately engulf most of Europe and Asia. The threat, Alsop warned, would inevitably generate fear in the United States. This fear might promote a political movement toward the Left but was far more likely to result in "a native brand of Fascism." He therefore thought that political steps must be taken to halt Soviet expansionism and remove the conditions which lend themselves to it. Eventually, the Soviet leaders would conclude that they cannot compete and "then sincerely seek our cooperation." Then the United States would move in the direction of economic planning and social welfare, while the USSR would relax its control over the individual and abandon its more ruthless methods, under the influence of prosperity. Otherwise, there was a serious danger that appeasement of the Soviet Union by American liberals would taint the cause of liberalism at home, just as Chamberlain's appeasement of Germany had harmed the Conservative cause in England.[50]

The analysis was to prove both cogent and prescient, but at first it did not sway Lerner. He replied that he disagreed with the underlying premise of the Alsops' position, which seemed to put "the stigma of unpatriotism on liberal ideas which the popular mind has been conditioned to associate with Russia." Lerner was arguing, in effect, if not explicitly, that in order for the domestic agenda of the New Deal to be sustained, it was important that Russia continue to be portrayed in a favorable light. Besides, what exactly did it mean to compete with the Soviets in moving into the "soft spots of the world?" Should it not be done by showing that "on crucial issues— such as Franco Spain—that we are against feudalism and poverty and reaction?" Was it not essential to build democracy at home rather than practice an American form of imperialism? And what about atomic weapons? Lerner argued for international control, as would soon be envisioned in the Acheson-Lilienthal report to the State Department and proposed to the UN by Bernard Baruch on behalf of the United States. Besides, Lerner argued, the analogy with the Fascist threat was grossly overdrawn:

> Surely I am not in any way under the spell of the Russians when
> I say that the Russian idea system, their attitude toward war and
> militarism, their attitude toward racism and the stability of their

economic system, are in no way comparable to the Nazi situation before the war. There is one point of similarity—that of expansionism.
But that makes the comparison a metaphor rather than a simile . . .
Do you really believe that our national survival is endangered today
by the Russians as British or American survival was endangered in
1938 by the Germans? I don't believe it. If it were true, then the only
logical policy would be to use the atom bomb on Russia immediately
and wipe out the threat at any cost. Neither you nor I would dream
of going that far, and the reason is because the comparison doesn't
hold. Let's both be honest enough to say so.

. . . My program is a simple one: deal realistically with the Russians on every issue across the diplomatic table. Use the United Nations machinery to settle problems and not to embitter them. Stick
as far as possible to the Roosevelt policy of Big-Three common action, where it can be used without sacrifice to our own interests.
Make it clear to the Russians that we will not tolerate their further
expansion, but make it equally clear that we are ready to join in
common action to give them access to natural resources, harbors, and
economic aid. Back up the democratic cause as against the fascist
cause in questions like the Spanish question. Make it clear to the
people of the world that we are ready to help them fight poverty
and reaction, famine and feudalism, through democratic means." [51]

As the Cold War intensified, Lerner clung to his hope that the
wartime alliance could somehow be maintained, or at the least that
America and Russia would compete peacefully for the affections of
the rest of the world. Schlesinger complained privately that Lerner
seemed not to appreciate the futility of such hopes:

It would seem to me that if the experience of the years since the war
suggests anything it suggests that agreements with the USSR are futile in advance of the underlying political and economic conditions
which alone can guarantee the agreements. Do you seriously believe that any conceivable paper agreements with the USSR would
deter it from pressing its disruptive activities in Western Europe so
long as conditions in Western Europe give Communist disruption
the slightest hope of success? My own belief is that the time for use-
ful direct negotiations with the Russians will come only after solid
foundations for such negotiations exist in the economic recovery,
political independence, and military strength of Western Europe.

When the Marshall Plan will have brought about a strengthen-
ing of Europe politically, economically and militarily to the point
where it becomes relatively immune to Communist activity, then we

can perhaps hope for a stable agreement with the USSR. But to argue that we can get such an agreement now, that somehow an international miracle can be achieved by two men sitting around a table which would relieve America of the grim task of working for peace the hard way, is to play into the hands of both the isolationists and the Communists. [52]

In a matter of months, Lerner was to come to agree with the Alsops' and Schlesinger's views.

Apart from the problems created for him by the onset of the Cold War, Lerner had no doubt where he stood on another issue. In 1947, when the British mandate over Palestine was terminated and the United Nations adopted a partition plan that the Arabs rejected, *PM* became sharply critical of the British position and warmly supportive of the effort by the Jewish settlers to establish a Jewish state. Lerner became a major editorial spokesman on the issue. Again, Joseph Alsop wrote privately to express disagreement, and to warn Lerner of what he saw as the danger that domestic anti-Semitism might develop if American troops had to be sent in to help the Jews. "I am absolutely convinced that enforcing the Palestine decision of the UN, if it is in fact enforced, will involve the sending of American troops . . . as the major component of a UN force," he wrote. Congress, however, would refuse to authorize this, he was sure, and even the proposal would "cause the strong, unspoken, anti-Semitism of many of the more extreme isolationists to burst out in a manner that would not be slick, but would certainly be very poisonous." To invite this outcome, he thought, was irresponsible and dangerous: "I say to you solemnly, that this is the risk that you are running." [53] Lerner and *PM* persisted in opposing British policy and welcoming the establishment of the Jewish state. Laski too found himself an embattled supporter of the Jewish settlers against leaders of his own Labor Party. Of Ernest Bevin, then British Foreign Secretary, he wrote to Lerner, "I am not sure E. B. hates Jews more than Communists; it must be a near thing—you can imagine what I feel after giving half my life to this party and still feeling that its rank and file are the salt of the earth." [54]

Looking Backward

In hindsight, Lerner was to be harshly self-critical of his first opinion piece on the Casablanca conference and of the rest of his work as a *PM* editorial writer. On domestic affairs he was often on unassail-

able ground. When Lerner denounced the notorious lynching of
Leo Frank in Atlanta, for example, the often caustic Frankfurter
did not stint in his praise: "Nothing, I venture to believe, that today appears in print is as relevant to the eternal issues regarding
the nature of man—and therefore of civilization—as your piece
on the Leo Frank case. And so I say this word of gratitude to you
for writing it." [55] But on foreign policy, Lerner recognized that he
had been in the grip of delusions:

> Rereading that first column I am struck by its amalgam of confid-
> ence and ignorance. I laid down the law brashly with the theorems
> of the liberal Left—what F.D.R. had done wrong, what he had to
> do, what dire things would follow if he didn't, what post-war har-
> monies would ensure if he did. I fear I was to set the pattern and
> style for much of the *PM* liberalism that dominated the 40s.

There is some truth in this self-indictment, though a similar judgment can just as fairly be addressed to any of the other editorial
pundits who must try to make sense of the day's news under immi-
nent pressure of deadlines. Lippmann, who earned an almost godlike aura as a "realist" for his analysis of world affairs, thought, before Pearl Harbor, that the armed forces of the United States could
respond to an attack from Japan by using naval and air power alone.
He also praised the Yalta accords, before they became a subject of
East-West acrimony, as a "triumph of diplomacy." [56] The Alsops
proved wrong in supposing that if an independent Jewish state were
proclaimed in Palestine, it could not be defended against Arab attack except by American troops. Although the Alsops were right to
be concerned about Soviet expansionism, they grossly exaggerated
its dangers. "Like many others of their generation," a sympathetic
biographer has noted, "they initially supposed—incorrectly, as we
may say now with perfect hindsight—that world communism was
a menacing monolith, reflecting and manipulated by a conspiratorial Kremlin." [57] Lerner and those for whom he spoke were struggling to come to grips with great historical forces that were often unfamiliar to Americans and baffling in their complexity. From the
perspective of the time, it was hardly clear whether the wartime alliance among the Big Three would survive and on what terms;
whether the postwar world would return to the old patterns of power
politics and business cartels, or move toward a new era of cooperation
and democratic socialism. On these distant affairs, Lerner articulated the views shared by many of *PM*'s readers. Neither he nor they

were willing to admit that a Cold War loomed on the horizon. "I wish I could say, thinking back to the mid-30s," he would later write, "that I was clear in my thinking about Russia and Communism. I wasn't. Marxism as a historical system drew me powerfully. The Soviet Union as an adventure in collectivism, for all its shabbiness as a system of power and a way of life, wouldn't let go of my imagination."

Nevertheless, the harsh judgment of William L. O'Neill that Lerner had "rationalized the crimes of Stalin" [58] is too strong, because it ignores the criticisms he did make of Stalinism in the 1930s and tears his view of the Soviet Union out of context. Lerner was certainly carried away by a wartime wish, naive at best, to interpret the heroic resistance of the Soviet peoples as evidence of a commitment to socialism. In a special issue of *The New Republic* on "Russia Today" he suggested that the strength of Russian resistance was proof that socialism worked as an organizational system and that it gave ordinary people a stake in their society which they would fight to defend. The Russian people, he claimed, "have been given a sense of participation in a process of social and economic reconstruction. The great reason why the Russian people are fighting as they are is that they are fighting in defense of something they believe they themselves had a hand in building, and something that they believe belongs to them." [59] Praising their heroism, he depicted them as fighting a "people's war" on behalf of democratic ideals. He was even guilty of presenting a ridiculously rosy picture of Stalin, as when he remarked in a passage quoted by O'Neill with understandable relish: "The men around Stalin have learned his sense of power, but they have little of his saving humor and flexibility," thus "showing," O'Neill could not resist adding, "an intimate knowledge of Stalin's jolly ways." [60]

In those dark days, however, Lerner was hardly alone in allowing the critical importance of the wartime alliance against the Fascist threat to cloud his judgment. Harry Truman referred to Stalin as genial "Uncle Joe." The American mass media, including Luce's *Life* magazine, carried glowing accounts not just of the heroism of the Red Army but of the strength of the Soviet social system that supposedly shored up the fighting forces. The Hollywood film "Mission to Moscow" also bathed the Soviet system in a warm glow of wartime sympathy.

But Lerner did not cover up Stalin's crimes or altogether ignore the failings of the Soviet system. In *It Is Later than You Think*, in 1938, he noted that the purge trials "completed the process of disillusionment with the views of those on the extreme left," and sharply criticized the monolithic party structure of the Soviet Union. He also criticized as naive the supposition that a dictatorship of the proletariat would necessarily be temporary:

> [T]he question arises, how long this dictatorship will last, and what form it will take. From the past decade of Soviet history we have begun to understand that political power may have its inner structure and its life history fully as much as economic power; that the problems of group conflict and tyranny are not automatically solved when the means of production are socialized; and that the need for a proletarian dictatorship must be minimized, its time-span shortened, and channels found for the expression of political opposition in the socialist states of the future.[61]

In the same work he warned with keen insight that a totalitarian socialism was not only morally wrong but a recipe for stagnation:

> Socialism cannot remain totalitarian and still achieve a socialism of the spirit. When it becomes totalitarian, it lets itself in for the instability of the praetorian state, with its succession of military garrisons and adventurist leaders . . . The real indictment of a totalitarian socialist regime is not that it may become corrupt, but it may become sterile—as sterile as the fascist regimes have already proved themselves. Even on the streets of socialism, there is the danger of blind alleys.[62]

A *New Masses* reviewer was under no illusions about Lerner's attitude toward Stalinism, complaining that the book was "studded with unfavorable references to the Soviet Union" and that "the author too often tends to lump socialist USSR with fascist Germany." Lerner, he regretted, had "succumbed to the inverted type of Red-baiting that afflicts other liberals as well."[63]

As victory in the "good war" was succeeded by the Cold War, Lerner's consistent attachment to political liberalism, coupled with a growing attachment to America, led him to lose all sympathy with the Soviet Union and all patience for the prospect that it would be reformed. From a Popular Front progressive, he became a "Cold War liberal," as radicals would derisively characterize those who still thought of themselves as progressive on domestic issues but endorsed "containment" in foreign policy. Increasingly his views on the events of the day were framed by an ambitious effort to understand the character of American civilization, as the leading carrier of the liberal democratic tradition of the West.

Discovering America
Brandeis Years

In the fall of 1949, a year after Lerner became a columnist for the *New York Post*, he was appointed to the faculty of the new Brandeis University, which had admitted its first freshman class a year earlier. The campus, acquired from the defunct Middlesex Medical School, occupied a sylvan hundred-acre hilltop in the quiet suburban Boston community of Waltham, best known until then for a once thriving watch factory. Lerner was named to the Max Richter Chair of American Studies, the first chair donated to the university. Brandeis was to be Lerner's academic pied-à-terre, if not a home in the fullest sense, for twenty-five years. From an apartment on East 92d Street and then a brownstone on East 84th Street in Manhattan, he commuted by air to Boston throughout the academic year. Although he normally spent only two days a week on campus, arriving early one morning and returning home the next evening, he was an active presence at the university, as a teacher, program builder, faculty recruiter, and speaker at fundraisers. Some of the university's recruitment efforts took place in the Lerner apartment in Manhattan, where he and Frank Manuel, the historian of ideas, both suitably fortified with alcoholic spirits, interviewed candidates. Lerner offered several different courses for politics majors and introduced a required undergraduate course, and afterward a field of study, on "American civilization," the subject he had first taught at Sarah Lawrence. The crowning scholarly achievement of this period and of his career was the publication in 1957 of *America as a Civilization*, a work in which he shed much of his radical past and celebrated mid-century America as the archetypal modern society.

Liberal Arts and Liberal Politics

The founding of Brandeis and Lerner's absorption with American civilization were both symbolic of the rapid assimilation of Jews in a country to which most of them or their forebears had emigrated only within the previous half-century. The proposal of a Jewish-sponsored university had arisen earlier in the century but kept being deferred so as not to detract from more pressing needs. When, just after World War II, studies showed that barriers to Jewish enrollment, especially in medical schools, were still in place, the project acquired fresh impetus. Ironically, however, by the time the university opened its doors, quotas against Jews in admissions to private colleges and graduate schools were being eliminated, except for the indirect effects on admissions of alumni preferences and geographical distribution policies. So dramatic was the change in medical education that the founders' intention of establishing a new medical school under the university's auspices was quietly forgotten. The trustees and fund-raisers now downplayed the original impetus and instead stressed the university's positive mission. As a "Jewish-sponsored, non-sectarian" institution of higher learning, it would join the impressive ranks of privately endowed schools founded by other religious groups as "a corporate contribution to American higher education."

Brandeis admitted its first undergraduate class of ninety-one students in the fall of 1948. By coincidence, it was in the same year that the modern state of Israel came into being. But whereas Israel was the fulfillment of the Zionist dream of "the ingathering of the exiles," Brandeis was a token of the realization of the "American dream" of assimilation and prosperity. The great majority of American Jews had left Eastern Europe to come to "a new world," as Irving Howe has remarked, "perceived as radically different from the one in which they lived." [1] While they welcomed the restoration of

Jewish statehood in Palestine with pride and enthusiasm, few, even among those who thought of themselves as Zionists, wanted to uproot themselves and settle there. They had come to think of America as something much more than another temporary and precarious way station in the diaspora. Extended families had begun to take root and prosper, not only in the original areas of settlement but almost everywhere in the country. It was fitting that the university should have been named for Justice Brandeis. He was not only the first Jew to achieve so high a public office in the United States, but he was also a Progressive, a pluralist, and a supporter of Zionism.

The university's founders were especially anxious that it be regarded as a secular institution, unlike Yeshiva University, which inculcates orthodox Judaism along with instruction in secular subjects. They decided that Brandeis should be modeled after other American universities and colleges which had been founded by religious denominations but offered a mainly secular education and were open to all. Rather than only being "guests" at universities sponsored by other religious groups, Jews would now also be "hosts." (Hence the title of the book by the university's founding president, Abram L. Sachar, *A Host at Last.*)[2] To emphasize its nonsectarian character and remove any confusion between its Jewish sponsorship and the "Yeshiva image," the founders were reportedly advised by a public relations consultant to field a football team which, like other college teams, would play its games on the Jewish Sabbath. To coach the team, a former Michigan All-American quarterback, Benny Friedman, was recruited. He scoured the East for high school football players who might reasonably be accommodated by the admissions requirements* and did manage to put together a team

---

*The university's short-lived effort to maintain a football team had its comic aspects. *Newsweek* reported that, when Coach Friedman first arrived on campus, he was dismayed to notice no students who looked as though they might be varsity material, until he spotted one wearing a sweater with a high school athletic letter—only to be informed that the student had been awarded the letter for managing the tennis team. In these early years Brandeis had so many foreign-born faculty speaking thickly accented English that some of the students thought it only appropriate to introduce a somewhat unusual cheer at football games: "Ve vant a touchdown. Vere? Vere? Over zere!" The football squad, recruited with the help of athletic scholarships, was known to some equally irreverent faculty members as the "ECMs" ("Early Christian Martyrs").

for a few seasons until football was replaced by basketball, which, under the capable direction of a former Boston Celtics star, K. C. Jones, proved a more practical undertaking.

The same concern to promote a double image of a university that would be Jewish-sponsored and in the mainstream of American higher education, influenced the choice of the founding president. When Albert Einstein, the first to be approached by the trustees, declined, he wrote to Laski to offer him the post, claiming (to the surprise of the trustees) that he had been authorized to do so. The trustees were relieved when Laski indicated he did not want to leave England. He was thought unsuitable because his appointment would give the university an undesirable political tinge, especially in Boston, where he was still remembered for encouraging a police strike during the time he was a lecturer at Harvard. Instead they recruited Sachar, the recently retired director of the national Hillel foundation which sponsored Jewish programs at universities and colleges.

Sachar was a nonpolitical choice who turned out to have a Midas touch with donors, but the school nevertheless acquired a political coloration reflecting the generally liberal leaning of the Jewish community from which it drew most of its students and all its support. Few faculty members were especially active or outspoken in politics, and some who were refugees from Hitlerism had been cowed by their experience into political quiescence. In its first two decades, however, Brandeis attracted to its faculty and student body many who were either liberals or radicals. Philip Rahv, who joined the English Department, had been an editor of the Trotskyist *Partisan Review.* Two eminent faculty members, the sociologist Lewis Coser and the literary critic Irving Howe, founded *Dissent* magazine, the democratic socialist quarterly. Herbert Marcuse, who was to become one of the most prominent radical gurus of the 1960s, first came to public attention while teaching at Brandeis.

The trustees and Sachar were concerned that campus radicals, especially those who might have had ties to the Communist Party or Communist Front organizations, might give the university a bad name. "We live in a goldfish bowl," Sachar liked to admonish students anxious to advertise their political views. In the early 1950s, he had a well-publicized row with one faculty member in the Art Department who refused to cooperate with the House Un-American Activities Committee. Later, at the time of the Cuban missile crisis in 1962, David Aberle and Kathleen Gough, a married couple with appointments in the Department of Anthropology, denounced the Kennedy administration's demand that offensive missiles be removed from Cuba as an impudent instance of American imperialism. Gough, a British subject, said that if she were still in London she would join the protesters at the American embassy shouting, "Viva Fidel, Kennedy go to hell." Sachar claimed afterward that he made it clear to Gough that, despite community protests, he would defend her right to express her views, though he added that freedom of speech gave her no right to make a "wild attack." In the following year's budget, however, he denied a merit increase to her on the ground that there was no reason to "reward her conduct."[3] Aberle and Gough decided to accept appointments elsewhere, and Sachar was reprimanded by the American Civil Liberties Union, though not by the Brandeis faculty, which in those years could be counted on to support him almost without question. When Marcuse turned sixty-eight, Sachar refused to guarantee him more than a two-year extension of his appointment, effectively encouraging him to pursue other prospects. Marcuse's Brandeis student, Angela Davis, followed him to the University of California, San Diego, where she embarked on a career as an avowed Communist and a sympathizer with "armed resistance" by black power militants.

A few other notorious examples of political radicalism had links to Brandeis. Abbie Hoffman, who gained notoriety when he was one of the "Chicago Seven" arrested during the melee outside the Democratic convention in 1968, had been a Brandeis undergraduate, though he dropped out before graduating. Two women undergraduates, intent on raising money for a radical faction, took part in a bank robbery in which a Boston policeman was killed. One was captured and sentenced to a jail term, the other managed to elude capture for many years before turning herself in and being sentenced to prison for her role in the robbery. The crime caused so much distress and chagrin in the university community that a scholarship fund was established for the children of the slain police officer.

These instances of political extremism were in no way typical. The great majority of the faculty and staff, and the thousands of students who were graduated from the university in the early years resembled those at comparable liberal arts campuses. In the 1950s and 1960s, the university associated itself with liberal and moderate politicians like Adlai Stevenson, Hubert Humphrey, and John F.

Kennedy. Eleanor Roosevelt served as a trustee. In later years, the
campus would be preoccupied with the civil rights movement, the
Vietnam protest, and apartheid in South Africa, and, in keeping
with the image of its namesake, would honor liberals like Supreme
Court Justices William O. Douglas, Thurgood Marshall, William
Brennan, and Ruth Bader Ginsberg. In effect, the university took
on the liberal political coloration of the American Jewish community from which it sprang.[4] American Jews tended to be liberal because of two background factors well identified by Irving Howe.
One was the fading but still remembered tradition of Jewish socialism, the other the premise that Jewish interests and survival
were best served by "an open, secular society promoting liberal
values and tolerating a diversity of religious groups."[5]

Lerner fit the mold well. He was liberal enough to satisfy those
on the campus and in its supporting community who wanted the
university to be identified with the left-of-center of the American
social and political spectrum, but not so radical as to be an embarrassment. He was well-known enough to be very much in demand
as a lecturer for groups affiliated with Brandeis, and the university's reputation profited from the talks he gave under other auspices throughout the country.

The quality of the faculty also benefited from his diligent efforts
of recruitment. Although he himself suffered from the opprobrium
that some academics attached to "mere" journalists, he respected
those who were "pure" scholars and worked with colleagues, at first
especially with Manuel, to identify and recruit promising faculty
to the social science and history programs, such as the sociologists
Coser and Philip Rieff, the psychologist Abraham Maslow, the historians Leonard Levy and Merrill Peterson, and the political scientist
John P. Roche. Since the faculty was still too small to offer enough
course coverage, Lerner and his colleagues made sure that students
benefited from a steady stream of outstanding visitors, notably the
historian Henry Steele Commager and the sociologist C. Wright
Mills, both of whom flew up from Columbia to moonlight at Brandeis. And Lerner was himself an exceptionally lively and stimulating teacher, who taught both a required lecture course and smaller
advanced courses, and moderated the weekly course in which distinguished visitors—including Alfred Kinsey, Leo Szilard, Agnes de
Mille, Thurgood Marshall, and Margaret Mead—discussed their
career choices and beliefs.

At Home in America:
The Reconciliation of the Intellectuals

Lerner's teaching at Brandeis carried forward the interest in American studies he had developed at Sarah Lawrence and Williams, but he took a decidedly more favorable view of the country and its role in the world than he had in earlier years. This change of attitude reflected not just the growing assimilation of American Jews but also a change of heart among many intellectuals and writers of his generation, who came to feel more at home in their own country than they or their predecessors had felt in the 1920s and 1930s. The domestic reforms wrought by the New Deal helped promote this change of attitude. The smug confidence of Wall Street and Main Street alike in the "gospel of wealth" seemed to have been replaced by a new consensus recognizing the need for government to regulate swings of the business cycle, promote full employment, and provide "safety nets" for the needy. The Social Darwinist creed of "rugged individualism" seemed to have been overcome in favor of a more balanced individualism in which self-reliance was joined to a sense of social responsibility. Notwithstanding the threat to civil liberties posed by the postwar fixation on "loyalty and security," the reelection of Truman confirmed the strength of the country's latent democratic character that Lerner had stressed in his earlier writings. There was still much to be done, especially to end racial segregation—the country's major unfinished business, to Lerner and those who shared his values—but the persistence of the New Deal reforms showed that the country was deeply committed to the Jeffersonian ideals of liberty and equality. Lerner's growing admiration for the country was, he thought, not so much an indication that he had changed as that the country had changed, and very much for the better.

World events, especially World War II and the subsequent outbreak of the Cold War, also had something to do with this change of perspective among left-wing intellectuals. The war cast the United States in the role of savior not only of democracy but of civilization itself, and the subsequent disheartening collapse of the wartime alliance was attributed to Stalin's appetite for expansion rather than to anything for which America could fairly be held responsible. Lerner and others nurtured in the Wilsonian dreams of their youth had hoped for a "people's peace" in which the United Nations would guarantee collective security and foster a world order blending liberal democracy and democratic socialism. The outbreak of the Cold War frustrated this hope and divided the left-wing intellectuals into essentially two camps. In one were radical die-hards who blamed the Cold War on the West at least as much as on Stalin and Mao and who saw American resistance to the spread of communism as a futile last-ditch effort by the forces of capitalism to prevent the inevitable triumph of the proletariat. As targets of the Truman administration's loyalty-security program and the circuslike hearings of congressional investigations into "un-American activities," they saw the United States as a repressive, even fascistic nation in league with dictatorships in the developing countries. In the other camp were some disillusioned worshippers of "the god that failed" who were now militant anti-Communists. Many more in this camp, including Lerner, had previously suppressed misgivings about the Soviet Union but now favored a policy of containing the Soviet threat, coupled with efforts to prevent nuclear war by a combination of military deterrence and arms control. They saw the United States as the great champion of liberty and democracy, though they too were apt to be critical of alliances with unsavory dictators made in the name of stopping communism.

Lerner's change of heart was first revealed in an invited symposium in a 1952 issue of *Partisan Review.* He was not a part of the journal's inner circle or a regular contributor, but he enjoyed a certain peripheral status among its editors as "a public intellectual." The issue was devoted to a symposium on the theme of "America and the Intellectuals" and was later published separately. In the preface, the editors remarked that the purpose of the symposium was "to examine the apparent fact that American intellectuals now regard America and its institutions in a new way." While expressing serious reservations about the country's economic and political institutions, and even more about the dangers posed by its burgeoning popular culture, the editors noted the most important reason for this new attitude: "Politically, there is a recognition that the kind of democracy which exists in America has an intrinsic and positive value: it is not merely a capitalist myth but a reality which must be defended against Russian totalitarianism."[6]

In his contribution, Lerner admitted that he would have been embarrassed to praise America in earlier years. But in 1945, after a trip to Europe, he had begun to compose a "longish impressionistic essay" about the country—one that very likely would have reflected the fascination with the varieties of everyday life that had begun to make him a general columnist rather than exclusively a political writer. This "anthropological" eclecticism was already evident in the two collections of newspaper columns he already published, but he found himself unable to keep his thoughts within these limits and therefore decided to take on a far more ambitious task. So much was changing in American life "in the minds of most of us, including mine," that it was now necessary to "argue out on paper the issues and values of almost every major phase of American experience." This reconsideration, he reflected, was something neither he nor any of his contemporaries would have dared to try a decade earlier. "It would have seemed to us sentimental, conformist, even chauvinist." In the process, his "love for the subject[,] . . . long repressed," was finding release. At the core of this newfound emotional acceptance was the claim that America had been changed fundamentally and that despite its shortcomings it had become an example to the world of what democracy can accomplish:

> Consider, as an instance, the problem of American poverty. We cannot blink it as a fact, nor the spread between that poverty and the Babylonian living at the other extreme of the scale. It is the darker side of our moon. Yet it is also a fact that we are farther on the road toward reducing poverty to a very marginal phase of our life than any other social system in our history. Or consider the classic question of monopoly capitalism. The monopolies have grown in scope and power, and have crowded out many small concerns. Yet they have not been able to crush the unions nor overshadow the government: the unions are thriving, the government has shaped a welfare state, and those who own the country are not running it.[7]

This early declaration was a reflection of the thinking that went into *America as a Civilization* during the decade of its composition. It was to be a labor of love that would pull together what was known about the country's history and its social and economic structure in the hope of discovering its innermost character as it was being expressed at mid-century. In an afterword to the 1987 reissue of *America as a Civilization*, he explained how he had first conceived it:

> When I originally set out the structure of the book, I did it in part from the perspective of the cultural anthropologists and their emphasis on material reality—from the bottom up, so to speak. I laid a base in the land, stock, and human needs; then built on them the layers of technology, economy, polity, and class. On these in turn, with

help from the perspectives of psychology and the philosophy of history, I structured the life cycle, the high culture and popular culture, the value system and religious beliefs, with some closing reflections on America's world position and destiny.[8]

In his undergraduate lecture course at Brandeis, Lerner laid out his findings. Students were required to take two introductory social science courses as part of the general education curriculum. One was given by Manuel and dealt with European history. The second was Lerner's course on America. Manuel, his mind and work steeped in the intellectual history of Europe, his manner formal and traditional, though by no means humorless, looked upon his colleague's enterprise doubtfully. Convinced that Europe was the heartland of Western civilization and America only its offshoot, Manuel nevertheless admired the audacity and conviction with which Lerner boldly staked out his claim and the easy-going, "democratic" style in which he offered his ideas to the judgment of the immature. Manuel expressed this ambivalence in a description of Lerner:

> While many of us clung to the professoriate as a secular priesthood, and pontificated from a formal elevated rostrum, suddenly in sauntered a breezy man who laughed easily and made others laugh, and sat on the edge of the platform—not up at the rostrum—dangling his feet, and conversed with an astonished body of students, as if he were in a market place—Socrates at play. His vision was brilliantly clear at that time. He was evoking before the eyes of this fresh student body an American civilization of their day . . . Those of us who had thought of the institutions of our country as from across the Atlantic, an offshoot that could sustain itself only on European culture, were confronted by a bold, straightforward affirmation that America has brought forth on this earth a new civilization. And Max loved it with a passion I have recognized in no other man. He reveled in its variety of peoples and styles and thoughts; no perceptions were alien to him. In a brazen act of democratization, he offered his class for criticism chapter after chapter of the manuscript of his great work on America as a civilization, instructing, debating, challenging the young men and women who were the most recent embodiment of this civilization. Before us pompous professors who were committed to education as a rehearsal of the past, [Lerner] flaunted the primacy of present things and the presence of future things. At faculty meetings we balked, we kicked, we cried "sacrilege," but his human warmth won out.[9]

When *America as a Civilization* finally appeared in print, weighing in at over 1,000 pages, it represented a prodigious and extremely ambitious effort of synthesis, ranging over the country's social history, natural setting, literary and popular culture, economics, and politics, as well as its national character and style—all in an effort to define what was unique about the country and to analyze the factors that accounted for its development. It was meant to sum up everything he and others had come to understand about the country and its place in history. Until then, all the other books he had published were compilations of his essays and columns, anthologies, edited volumes, or tracts for the times. In order to grasp the character of the society, Lerner thought it was necessary to bring together the insights that could be gleaned from historical studies and the modern social sciences. Only in this way would it be possible to see the society whole and in its various dimensions: family and class; religious, ethnic, and regional diversity; and values and ways of life. The book was designed not to be narrowly political, or a history, but to be eclectic and wide-ranging, perhaps reflecting the belief (advanced by the German sociologist Karl Mannheim in *Ideology and Utopia*) that the time was ripe for a "synthesis of perspectives."

The Frame of "Civilization"

With Tocqueville's classic study in mind, Lerner sought a framework for his approach that would fit the country's experience into some larger analytical matrix. Whereas Tocqueville had singled out the American adventure as a laboratory experiment in democracy, for which the whole of Western history had been a preparation, Lerner chose to conceive of the country—even more audaciously, as Manuel recognized—as one of the world's great civilizations. As Lerner defined the term, it incorporated the concepts of society and culture but added the criteria of complexity and impact. He had come to think of the United States as more than just an appendage or projection of Europe. It was best understood, he thought, as a new civilization in its own right, not least because it was uniquely influential upon Europe itself and the rest of the world. At the outset, he readily admitted, it had been very much a colonial offshoot of Europe, especially of Britain, but it had acquired a separate and different character and was imprinting this character upon the world. The young people of the world were listening to American popular music, watching American films, wearing American jeans, and yearning for the same autonomy Americans enjoyed. Lerner contended that the test of whether a society deserves to be considered a civilization is whether or not it has this sort of extraordinary impact. Greek or Hellenic civilization, Roman civilization, and the civilization of modern Western Europe have been distinct not only in culture but in impact—on the peoples with whom they came in contact and on future generations. The same was now true, he thought, for the United States.

Lerner was aware that this scheme of classification was more arbitrary than that used by Arnold Toynbee, who had recently popularized the idea that civilizations are the most important units of historical analysis. Lerner was bold enough to suggest that his was a better usage because it took into account not just differences of time, geography, and continuity, but what Hegel had called the "world-historical character" of a society. Toynbee, he argued, had been idiosyncratic and overly dogmatic in supposing that religious belief was the predominant motif defining the character of a civilization. The idea that Europe and America were both expressions of Christian civilization, and well enough understood under that rubric, struck Lerner as too simple and even cramped, and not because it ignored the distinctiveness of Judaism and its contribution. Lerner did not quarrel with Toynbee's view that Christianity was the outgrowth and successor of Judaism. The problem was rather Toynbee's double failure to appreciate that a civilization acquires its character from the whole pattern of its beliefs and activities—to which religion alone is not a sufficient index—and that the most compelling test of whether a society deserves to be considered a civilization is its impact on world history. On the first score, America was evidence that modern religiosity is more secular than supernatural. "It might be truer to say . . . that instead of finding their democratic faith in supernatural religion, Americans have tended to find their religious faith in various forms of belief about their own existence as a people." [10] On the second score especially, Lerner thought, America had to be recognized as on a par with any of the great civilizations.

Earlier analysts, he thought, had been unable to recognize the importance of America as a civilization because they had seen it while it was still in its relative infancy and because the social sciences were not yet mature enough to provide the materials needed to prove the point. Now, just as one can conceive of the "whole man," not just of political or economic man, thanks to psychology, philosophy, and anthropology, it had become possible to conceive of a whole society, of a pattern of civilization. Thanks to the work of the cultural anthropologists, there was now general agreement that every distinct people, whether a tribe or a nation, had its own unique culture—an organic pattern of life that could be understood as a living whole. From the study of primitive peoples, anthropologists had extended the concept of culture to include all peoples. The "anthropology of everyday life" had begun to emerge as the study of contemporary society and culture, and efforts had been made to develop cross-cultural studies.

While he did not disparage the comparative approach, Lerner became convinced that the deeper truth lay in recognizing the wholeness of each particular culture. America deserved to be thought of as a civilization in this anthropological sense of the term, Lerner thought, even though the more dismissive of the European theorists still thought of America as a derivative of Europe, a pale copy without Europe's capacity for rebirth and renewal. To them America was an amalgam of Europe's flotsam and jetsam, diluted further with the overflow populations of Asia and Latin America. For Spengler America was an offshoot, possibly an excrescence of Europe. For Toynbee only five of the nineteen or twenty-one historic civilizations were still active— the Western, Orthodox Christian, Islamic, Hindu, and Far Eastern. He saw the United States as a nation-state on the margin of Western civilization, a latecomer affected with the latter-day scars but lacking in offsetting graces.[11]

Against those who assimilated the New World to the Old, Lerner insisted that America was not just a marginal fragment. "For good or ill," Lerner argued, "America is what it is—a culture in its own right, with many characteristics of power and meaning of its own, ranking with Greece and Rome as one of the great distinctive civilizations of history." What makes one culture or one society a civilization is that it reaches a degree of complexity and "cuts a swathe in history"—so much so that another term is needed to describe it—one that has the necessary overtones. Such societies—those of Greece and Rome, China and Britain, the Aztecs-Mayans and India, Renaissance Italy, Spain, and France, or Russia and America—are different. They are great "going concerns . . . leaving a deep imprint on the human consciousness, a scar on men's minds." They make an impression that becomes very much a part of human experience.[12]

In arguing for his frame of analysis, Lerner was not contending that America was completely distinct from the other nations of the West but rather that it was the fulfillment of tendencies developed in Europe and brought to completion in the New World. He was well aware that he was trying to unravel a riddle: America had developed out of the Old World and yet had become something new and different. He dramatized the riddle by describing it—in terms of the myth of origin reported by the anthropologist Frazer in *The Golden Bough* and used by Freud in *Totem and Taboo*—as the "slaying of the European father." Like a child in some primitive tribe, the American nation had been raised with a strong paternal influence, but its character had been formed in a rebellion against that influence. The rebellion could not fully succeed, as Freud had remarked. But Lerner introduced a new wrinkle on the Freudian version. Americans had reenacted the primal crime, the slaying of the father, by seeing themselves as constantly engaged in the slaying of authoritarian regimes. Thus the justification for the entry into World Wars I and II and the fight against Stalinism in the Cold War.

The European paternity, Lerner recognized, still exerted a powerful influence, but the "American imago" was one of a pastoral plenty Europe could not afford. America was more than just a mythic land of promise. It was the product of four great forces in European history that shaped the modern era: the rise of the new science, the commercial revolution that paved the way for industrialization, the secular humanism of the Renaissance, and the Protestant individualism. All these forces combined, paradoxically, to make it possible for Americans to reject the Old World. "Without taking over the European heritage the Americans could not have revolted against Europe . . . In America the vigorous European elements were brought into play as against the exhausted ones." The settlement of America helped drain off Europe's revolutionary energies and at the same time gave expression to those energies.[13]

The contrast between Europe and America was therefore as striking as the commonalities. The political sociologist Roberto Michels, Lerner remarked, had said that every nation has two myths—the myth of origin and the myth of mission. In the case of America, Lerner suggested, one myth points toward a European past, the other toward a uniquely American future. The founders were all steeped in European thinking, but the amalgams they made acquired new meaning in the New World. The waves of immigrants gave the country a continuing sense both of its rise from the Old World and its relentless effort to create a new society—a novus ordo seclorum, a new order of the ages. Partly because they were so determined to remain independent, Lerner contended, modern Americans reject political ideas thought to be European or Marxist and blame their influence for all the country's difficulties. To be sure, the best American intellectuals have recognized that they were missing something because of the separation from Europe: "From Henry James in the old London houses that drew him so, to the literary proconsuls of the 1940s and 1950s in Paris and Rome, American writers went to Europe seeking some quality—aesthetic sensitivity, a freer expressiveness in living, old traditions, a sense of community, dedication to artistic discipline—which the cruder energies of the American civilization had not provided." But from Emerson onward Americans have understood that self-reliance was necessary and that it should not mean fear of Europe or self-abasement before the Old World.[14]

It was with the two world wars, Lerner suggested, that the American attitude toward Europe changed from one of ambiguous regard and even subservience mixed with the desire for isolation. Europe was now revealed not as "a father demanding obedience and exerting his authority but an endangered civilization needing help." But Americans rationalized their coming to Europe's aid as a rebellion against authoritarianism. In this curious way, they could compensate for the sacrificial slaying of the father and yet continue to see themselves as rebellious sons. Although the act of rebellion was inspired by European thinking, it led to something new and different. "Without taking over the European heritage the Americans could not have revolted against Europe. The ships that crossed the Atlantic to America carried with them not only the European economy but also European aspirations and the European system of thought . . . In fact, the rise of American civilization was the product both of the revolution and dissolution in Europe." But in the New World "the vigorous European elements were brought into play against the exhausted ones. It was free enterprise arrayed against mercantilism, laissez-faire against cameralism, individualism against hierarchy, natural rights against monarchy, popular nationalism against the dynastic regimes, social mobility against caste, the pioneering spirit against the status quo." [15]

Dynamism and "Extended Genesis"

Like Tocqueville, who saw the New World as "the empty cradle of a great nation," Lerner was awed by the majesty of the American landscape. Perhaps the most beautifully written passage in the book, reminiscent of Tocqueville's depiction of the pristine setting, is the sketch of the American physical prospect as it must have appeared to the Europeans who first encountered it: "strange, untidy, uncompassable," a wild continent of grand proportions with a luxuriance of plant and animal life:

> There was the stretch of the Great Forest sweeping from the Atlantic dunes with a few breaks to the deep interior, and then the stretch of the Great Plains and the long-grass prairie lands across the Ohio and Mississippi and Missouri to the foothills of the Rockies, and then the short-grass grazing lands and the mountains and deserts to the fertile valleys of the Pacific Coast, with another expanse of Great Forest northward along the coast. It was a land riven by mountain chains, from the Appalachian range in the East to the Sierra in the West, scarred by canyons, watered by broad and tumultuous rivers, with a climate that spanned all the intervals, from the frost of the North Country in the Great Lakes region and the Far Northwest of the fur trappers to the mesas and tablelands of the swamps of Florida. It was filled, when the settlers first found it, with a fecund vegetation and wildlife: buffalo herds, deer, elk and bears, wild pigeons and geese, alligators and catfish, cod, sturgeon and salmon; with dense canebrake and coarse slough grass and needle grass and bluegrass and stands of prairie dropseed and tall-growing saw-tooth sunflower. And there were the trees: fir and spruce, maple and birch and elm, chestnut, hickory, and the always incredible sequoias, and that aristocrat of all American trees—the great white pine.[16]

What impressed Lerner most about what had happened within this setting over the two centuries of settlement was that America had become a leading force in world history because it represented so many of the great forces in modern history. These forces included capitalism and democracy, science and industrial technology, and mass culture. America was also different from other countries in that it absorbed a mixture of ethnic stocks that was unique in world history; that it was given to attitudes of experimentalism, not just in technique but in ways of life, from mass production and consumption to the sexual revolution. America had shown a flexibility and an adaptability—Lerner called them "dynamism"—that would keep it from declining as other great civilizations had in the past. He was convinced that this dynamism would ultimately enable the United States to prevail over the Soviet Union (which suffered from all the rigidities of a closed society). Although he did not anticipate the collapse of the Soviet Union, he thought the Cold War would end with a kind of truce, mediated by a secular arbiter like the UN—whose capacities he exaggerated, as he had a decade earlier.

America would triumph, he thought, because it was not backward looking but forward looking, not mired in the past but eager to embrace the new and uncertain. The secret to the success the country had already achieved and the reason it would exert continuing influence was that it had become the social equivalent of the natural process by which biological evolution assures the survival of the species. For Lerner, America was an example not of natural selection but of continuing adaptation, or what he called "extended genesis." It could not be imprisoned in tradition, because its tradition was one of constant innovation. It was not rigidly governed from the center but was in effect a network of forces, including those of business and technical elites and those exerted by the tastes and choices of ordinary people. Whereas the individuals in it would inevitably pass through the "life cycle" from birth to senescence and death, the society itself would constantly be reborn.

Why had America been so much more successful than other civilizations in assuring its own survival, Lerner wondered. Perhaps, he thought, because the nation benefited not only from sheer geography—the expanse of the continent, the protective expanse of oceans; and the richness of its resources—but from social factors as well, including its pluralism—its blending of different religious, ethnic, and linguistic strains. America had become a laboratory of biological and psychological integration. The country also drew great strength from the Constitution its founders had written, and from the interpretation given to the Constitution by successive generations imbued with faith in progress and a pragmatic readiness to adapt to new circumstances. The initial capitalist ethos produced great wealth and an emphasis on the limited state and a contempt for bureaucrats, but there had always been a countervailing anticapitalist strain in American history, beginning with Jeffersonian agrarians, emphasizing the wastefulness of capitalism and its unhealthy tendency toward concentration of ownership.[17] The frontier, as the historian Frederick Jackson Turner had first suggested, gave Americans a combination of individualism and democracy. As a result of immigration and expansion, the society has constantly been renewed and restarted, both vertically and horizontally. America became an especially "dynamic" civilization—animated by its founding principles but not handicapped by them from growing in complexity and accepting constant modernization.

The American as Archetype

Lerner thought that this continual growth and churning had produced an American character with two principal facets: self-reliance, coupled with endurance, friendliness, a democratic informality; and a sharp aggressiveness, coupled with an organizing capacity, a genius for technology, a sense of bigness and power. The two sets of traits were fused in the national character, he argued, because they were interwoven in the crucial phases of American history. As a result, American civilization had produced the "archetypical man of the West." Foreigners might still indulge a patronizing contempt for Americans, sometimes taking form in anti-Americanism, sometimes in the radical view of America as the centerpiece of a world order of hegemonic capitalism, imposing economic dependency and using naked military intervention where necessary to protect its interests. Yet the truth was, Lerner noted, that the imperialism America practiced most is "the imperialism of attraction." America is universally emulated because it is perceived as the most advanced of the Western countries in those respects most valued by ordinary people everywhere. The American may not be admired but he is envied.[18]

This influence suggested to Lerner an inner harmony between the American spirit and the spirit of modernity. That harmony explained why America had drawn to itself so much of what is new in the world—in the "brain drain" of scientists and engineers, the migration of ambitious and hardworking people seeking a better life, in newly acquired capital and new ideas for products and services. By "fusing its strength with the world's," the country produced a new cultural specimen, "the concentrated embodiment of Western man, more sharply delineated, developed under more urgent conditions, but with most of the essential traits present."[19]

To illustrate the traits embodied in Western man, Lerner drew on the work of Toynbee, Mumford, and Johann Huizinga, and he suggested that the modern man incarnate in the American is mobile, restless, no longer fixed in status hierarchies, thirsting for experience, and transnational—in the sense that America was becoming the epitome of all the world's societies. The modern American man is this-worldly, optimistic, drawn to material consumption and to innovations, and pragmatically indifferent to ideological nostrums. In his sex life, he is apt to be active, not too finicky about rigid standards of virtue but hungering for a sense of personal worth. Unlike those of previous ages, he is not drawn to salvation or virtue or saintliness or beauty or status but is "an amoral man of energy, mastery, and power—the double figure in Marlowe of Tamerlane and Dr. Faustus." [20]

In offering this imaginative portrait of the American character in its masculine form, Lerner made clear he was not endorsing nativism or chauvinism, but trying to identify a national style that had to be appreciated if the American experience were to be understood:

> While it is risky to attribute a national character to any people, as if its qualities and destiny could be ripped out of the living body of history, it is also true that nations are realities, that their cultures develop along different paths, and that the world inside the heads of their people is a characteristic world. Much of the chauvinist and racist treachery of the term can be avoided if it is remembered that national character is a doctrine not of blood but of culture. It consists of a body of values, social habits, attitudes, traits held in common by most members of the culture. Thus the psychological field of action, thought, and emotion into which an American is born differs not only from the Russian or Chinese but even from that of an Englishman. [21]

To find the sources of this national character, Lerner wrestled with various approaches but found no one "talisman." Laski, Lerner now recognized, had written a morality play depicting a bitter feud between democracy and capitalism in which democracy loses—a play like Clifford Odets's *Waiting for Lefty*, in which the stage is set for the hero, but he never appears. In Laski's drama democracy never appears because it is the victim of the forces of greed and reaction. Contrary to Laski, Lerner thought, there is no single cause to be discerned, only an interplay, a pattern. "The study of American civilization becomes the study of the polar pattern itself, not a search for some single key that will unlock causation." American character exists in the relations between opposites, "between power and ideas, science and conscience, the revolutionary machine and the crust of tradition, mass production and social creativeness, individualist values and collective action, capitalist economics and democratic freedom, class structure and the image of prestige and success in the American mind, elite power and the popular arts, the growth of military power and the persistence of civilian control, the fact of an American imperium and the image of an open constitutional world." [22] The country had a class system, but it was an "open class system." The society was stratified into ruling groups of the wealthy and powerful, a growing middle class "with a sense of well-being that defies all predicted dooms," a working class tenacious of its gains but "with none of the marks of a permanent proletariat," and minority ethnic groups whose peculiar status cuts across the class strata. Because of the openness of the system and the fluidity of movement among the classes, the class consciousness Marxian theory postulates "is almost absent from the American scene." Thus American studies of class tend to be examinations of relative status as determined by community evaluations rather than of objective class interest. Wealth and income are important determinants of class standing, but the image people have of themselves and of each other is no less important in placing them in the social hierarchy. The American "religion of equality" had created a kind of "democratic class struggle in America." Its purpose was "never . . . the extermination of the other classes, nor even class domination, but the effort of the majority to achieve access to the means of a good life . . ." [23]

Although on the whole the portrait Lerner painted of America was buoyantly optimistic, he expressed reservations on a number of scores. Well before the environmental revolution of the 1970s, he warned about the society's failure to protect its habitat. The country was in danger of forgetting, he feared that "the web between man and his environment is broken only at his peril." More was at stake, he thought, than material resources alone. If Americans were to lose their reverence for the very land to which they were bound, they would risk losing their capacity to sustain a great civilization, with all its complexity and interdependence of the human and the natural. [24] He wrote presciently of the "ordeal of the American woman," noting that although the country had done more than any other society to realize the vision of Mary Wollstonecraft's *Vindication of the Rights of Women*, it had left the American woman in a quandary, "groping for a synthesis of her functions in her home, her community, and her job." The American woman, he thought, would somehow have to learn how to lead a diversified life while retaining her sense of herself as a "life creator and life sustainer." [25] Above all other concerns, he set the condition of blacks in America, portraying it as a fundamental challenge to the country's professions of toleration and community but one he was confident would be met:

> It has been the context of American society and the American creed that has reduced the walls of the caste system. The American economy, with its impersonal relations in the market of buying and selling, gave the Negroes a new bargaining power. So also has the American political system, with its formal principle of counting each head once no matter what the pigment of the face, and its reliance on an equilibrium of pressure groups. The American legal system, with a tradition of growth to meet the changing demands of a changing society, gave the Negro a slow and belated but irresistible measure of justice . . . It is true that the progress in civil rights for Negroes came partly through their own bargaining strength and partly through the self-interest of the whites, but that progress could never have been achieved except through the operation of law and public opinion and the impulsion of the idea of equality. Without these even the needs of war and cold war would have been powerless to achieve the same ends.[26]

He continued to think that the individualism which had given such strength to the American character also had its pathological side. In a market society, "the great crime is to be 'taken in,' and the great virtue is to be tough and illusionless." As a result, there is a tendency to see fellow-feeling as a weakness. "The nightmare of American life is to be left dependent and helpless—a greater nightmare than failing to help others when they need help. The result is a desensitized man whose language is the wisecrack and whose armor is cynicism.[27] He worried about the rootlessness caused by the restless mobility so characteristic of American life in the mid-twentieth century:

> When two Americans discover that they come from the same place, a spark is lit between them. And when an American finds that you have not heard of the place his family came from there is a sense of loss and almost of shock. It is not only that Plainville is therefore denied as if it had never existed but that the whole rich experience that clusters about it is also denied. The dangers of a dynamic society are that they lead to a whittling down of those accretions which the sense of place gives to the personality. When you move from the place where you were known to one where you must make your way, you cling all the more to memories of place . . . That is why Thomas Wolfe, moving from Asheville to New York, wove a sense of place into the web of time and memory with his haunting evocation

in *Look Homeward, Angel*—"a stone, a leaf, an unfound door"—
to express his longing and his feeling of being lost.[28]

He was also sensitive to the cultural link critics of American life
have sometimes noted between sex and violence, which he saw
reflected even in the country's literature:

> In Dos Passos's . . . *USA*, the characters (mainly on the make) use love
> as a commodity of exchange, and are incapable of anything but its
> hollowest forms. Ring Lardner's short stories (as in "The Love
> Nest") lay bare the heartlessness behind the show of heart. In Faulk-
> ner the symbols of love are often associated with the violence of in-
> cest and rape. In Farrell the Studs Lonigan worthies gang up on a
> girl in a drunken brawl and use her in succession. O'Hara portrays
> with compassion, in *Appointment in Samarra* and *10 North Freder-
> ick*, and with more violence and disillusionment in *Butterfield 8* and
> *A Rage to Live*, the defeat and dissipation of the generous impulses
> of love. Even in Hemingway, whom two generations have found
> deeply moving, the symbol in *The Sun Also Rises* is that of the mu-
> tilated incapacity for love, in *A Farewell to Arms* it is the cup dashed
> from thirsty lips, in *Across the River and into the Trees* it is that of
> a mingled ritual of war and eroticism. I cite these almost at random,
> not as an accurate transcription of the operative force of love in Amer-
> ican society but because the reflections of American attitudes in the
> minds of sensitive and creative writers, however transmuted, are an
> index of what people believe about themselves.[29]

A Farewell to Arms: The End of Radicalism

In its examination of political economy, *America as a Civilization*
marked Lerner's farewell to the radicalism of his earlier years. In
discussing the country's radical tradition, he pointed out that it has
always had a hard time, thanks originally to the fact that the American Revolution was more of a colonial than a social revolution. Since
then, it "remained a series of sporadic and sometimes eccentric flare-
ups which kept alive the equalitarian dream but had no sustained
program, no continuing party, nor even a body of common doctrine."[30] The final failure of American radicalism reflects the pace
of social change and the constant sense of dynamism, the moving
frontier, and the persistence of an open-class system. Radicals could
not compete with liberal reformers in concrete programs and had
no effective long-term programs, because real revolution, measured
by technical and social change, was taking place all around them.

What the radicals have achieved is to reaffirm the egalitarian impulse and to keep both conservatives and liberals alert to the need to keep the system of production raising living standards for all.

Overall, Lerner was convinced that the America that had emerged from the Great Depression and World War II was a society in which the latent democratic tendencies of its founding mandate were finding expression in a new relationship between government and industry. The Marxist analysis of the contradictions of capitalism had been made obsolete by the changes that had taken place in the American economy. "The more strictly technical problems of production and scarcity, of income distribution, of bigness in the sense distinct from monopoly, even of the business cycle, are fairly on the way to being resolved." The trade unions had become a powerful network countervailing the power of the corporations. "While the two systems are often locked in struggle, they are part of the same firmament in the same universe." If Carnegie and Ford defined the course of American big business, Samuel Gompers understood best how the American labor movement could succeed in the American setting. He saw that the trade unions in America had to be an integral part both of the capitalist psychology and the democratic process. "The break with the European tradition of feudal rank kept the American worker from accepting the paternalism either of a tyrannical employer or a tyrannical government. Since he saw himself as the " 'masterless man' he did not feel the resentments of the class struggle at whose root is a master ridden proletariat trying to unseat its masters." Thanks to the success of Gompers-style trade unionism, the American economy had been constitutionalized.[31]

As a result, a kind of "democratic collectivism" had been achieved, but it was a collectivism in which two "collectives," business and trade union, balanced each other's power. The creation of the CIO in 1938 answered the need for a stronger labor movement to restore balance and promote purchasing power in the economy. The National Labor Relations Act served as the New Deal's charter of growth, and minimum-wage and social-security laws filled out the charter. The result was a "working partnership between the American labor movement and the principle of welfare democracy which was to affect the history of more than one American generation." The end product was a revolution—a conservative revolution "making possible a constitutional government of industry and trying to recapture for the worker his dignity as a human being." [32]

Because the trade union movement lacked a revolutionary

dynamic, it did not use its power to strike to paralyze the economy as it might have or to shape a labor culture for its members or to form the most powerful political labor party in the democratic world. This would have been incompatible with the national character.

> The reason is that Americans do not think of themselves as being exclusively members of any single group. A steel or automobile worker, a clerical worker, or a carpenter is not only a trade-unionist. He is also a homeowner, a stock investor, a Democrat or Republican, a Mason or Elk, a Presbyterian or Methodist or Baptist, a resident of Cleveland, Detroit, or Glendale. He may come from a farm family, and his children may be moving into the corporate managerial group or into one of the professions. He does not inherit from his father or transmit to his children a "working class psychology." Nor is he likely to be content as a member of a political party which seems to take him out of the mainstream of American political life.[33]

Lerner acknowledged that despite the efforts of the trade unions "there is still an inequality pyramid in America which the recent years of income expansion have not substantially leveled out." Compared with corresponding groups elsewhere, however, the American poor are better off; yet the society as a whole could be even more prosperous than it was: "America is the first civilization in history that has at its command the means for the total abolition of poverty." The result of the struggle between capital and labor in America had been the emergence of a new amalgam scarcely recognizable from their original form, one in which "the private sector is a form of business collectivism and the public sector is a form of state capitalism." The main remaining conflict was over techniques for assuring economic stability—such as taxation, encouragement of investment, and regulation. As a result the American economy was neither an example of pure capitalism nor of creeping socialism but a mixed economy—one which has achieved sustained economic growth without succumbing either to chaos or to "serfdom." In the aftermath of the New Deal, corporations became dependent on government contracts; a new managerial form of direction replaced the old economic individualism; government planning operated indirectly, by winks and nudges. The resulting freedom of movement was "the principal element in American dynamism."[34]

The reorganization of the economy had been accompanied by a changing attitude toward the functions of government. Americans have from the beginning of the country believed with Emerson that "all states are corrupt." But from the days of Jackson onward they have also approved effective government and strong presidents. In his approach to the Supreme Court and judicial review, Lerner took a very different approach than he had taken earlier. The Constitution had first been interpreted as a compact, whether among the states or individuals. Then, after the Civil War, it had come to be understood as the guarantee of Union. From the Civil War onward, it was seen as an instrument for restraining government actions aimed at interfering with the economy. With the Court's shift during the New Deal, it came to be seen as an instrument of government. Once it had accepted the New Deal, the Court could become an agency of social change. "The game of adapting constitutional doctrines could be played by a Miller, a Brandeis, a Black, and a Douglas, as well as by a Field and a Sutherland." Those who complain that the Court is not a democratic institution are right insofar as that means that it does not respond mechanically to changes in public opinion. The Court has split between believers in judicial self-restraint and in judicial activism. The trouble with self-restraint is that it leads to abdication; the trouble with activism is that it leads to judicial tyranny. One of the best instances of how the Court has acted with a sense of greatness, Lerner thought, was the landmark decision in *Brown* v. *Board of Education* outlawing segregation in schooling. In this decision, in which he later learned Justice Frankfurter had played an important catalytic role, the Court did not mince words or claim to be distinguishing school desegregation from other forms of segregation. It met a social problem boldly, summing up a series of decisions that had been moving in this direction, allowing itself to go outside customary legal categories to take sociological studies into account, and summed up the conscience and progress of the nation in civil rights.[35]

Underlying American politics, he thought, was a commitment to democracy, but democracy contains two sometimes contradictory polar ideals: liberty and equality. Liberty expresses the belief in natural rights beyond the reach of governments. Equality excited Lerner's passionate concern for democracy:

> It presents the spectacle of a demos unbound, a whole people striving however imperfectly to make social equality a premise of government. It shifts the emphasis from the narrowly political—from the ballot and the constitutional guarantees—to the economy and

  the class system. It stresses the conditions for putting within the reach of the ordinary man the opportunities of education and the making of a living, regardless of his confessional faith, his ethnic group, and his social level.[36]

Equality did not mean the complete absence of economic disparities. Income remained "malapportioned" in America, but it would be "less true to say that Americans would no longer tolerate great disparities in income than to say that no society would ever again tolerate the large-scale damming of aspirations and hope on the part of the plain people." [37]

  If he had been a Veblenian more than a Laskian in the 1930s, the Max Lerner of *America as a Civilization* might best be described as a Galbraithian, who embraced the new Keynesian consensus as popularly expounded by John Kenneth Galbraith. The word "collectivism" was not dropped from his vocabulary, but it took on new meaning. He now saw the managed economy of the affluent society as a reasonable approximation of the democratic collectivism he had earlier advocated. In the chapter devoted to the economy, he no longer indicts capitalism or assigns it to oblivion but seeks to balance its benefits and costs. The arguments in defense of its efficiency, he now admits, are "basically valid." On the critical test of productivity, he finds its performance is especially impressive. But this was a new capitalism, not the old Social Darwinist free-for-all it once was. "For all its individualistic slogans," he wrote, "the business class in America has effectively substituted its own form of collectivism for the old individualism." Dreiser's titans and Matthew Josephson's robber barons had been replaced by organization men in gray flannel suits, managers rather than buccaneers, people "likely to have a broader vision of the economy as a whole than the individual small businessmen . . . " Contrary to the logic of Marxism, American capitalism had not altogether captured the political system; its power is checked by countervailing forces. Thanks especially to the trade unions, America had achieved "the government of industry by constitutional means." Although inequality and poverty persist, and the dependence of the economy on military contracts is worrisome, the economy is productive and the welfare state accepted. All that is needed to preserve prosperity and extend its benefits is for the government to maintain "the New Deal amalgam of state capitalism and business collectivism." As to the need for planning, in this country planning occurs in a roundabout way: "That is to say, instead of nationalization or codes of regulation and control by government administrators, the planning is mainly by pressures, nudges, and prods. The Keynesian revolution in economic theory has largely taken over American economic policy." Ours is therefore "a loosely planned and indirectly controlled progressive capitalism" giving the biggest prizes to the rich but also generating prosperity for the nation as a whole.

To say that in accepting a progressive or Keynesian capitalism Lerner became more conservative in this period of his life would be inexact, if that were to mean that he was now reconciled to a status quo he had previously rejected. From his point of view, the New Deal and the aftermath of the war against fascism had profoundly altered the economy and the country, and mostly for the better. The America he had taken to task for the failings of capitalism had begun to direct the economy so that it would serve democratic ends. Continuing failings, including assaults on civil liberties and the denial of civil rights to black Americans, were the unfinished business of an "unfinished country."

With the new assessment went the less critical, more evenhanded tone characteristic of *America as a Civilization*. Judicial activism is needed to protect civil liberties, he contended, but there is a danger that by abandoning self-restraint courts will intervene arbitrarily in areas in which other branches have constitutional authority. Americans have been expansion-minded, even ready to practice interventionism, he conceded, but they have not been motivated by imperial ambitions. The Cold War, while costly and dangerous, was forced upon Americans by an expansionist Russia and a turbulent Third World. The people of the United States had no real choice but to defend themselves and freedom around the world.

In embracing the America of the New Deal, the Fair Deal, and of containment as well, Lerner was not seeking to ingratiate himself with the "establishment" so as to earn praise and emoluments or escape McCarthyite harassment. It was rather that whatever establishment the country had was changing enough to make room for him and others like him. He had shown himself tough enough to take all of the abuse thrown at him by right-wing journals like *The Saturday Evening Post,* whose editors once observed that they would not get down in the gutter to debate with the likes of Max Lerner. He must have known that defending liberal America would cost him the polemical niche he had carved out for himself, because many who had followed him earlier when he was more critical would now accuse him of having sold out.

No one in fact could have been more acutely aware than he of the intellectual advantages of being an outsider and of the corresponding costs to a social commentator of becoming too much of an insider. He had called attention to Veblen's essay explaining the intellectual preeminence of the Jews in Europe as a function of their marginality, noting that as the child of Norwegian immigrants, Veblen appreciated the advantage for the social critic of being an outsider. Lerner must have understood that in giving up his marginality, he would sacrifice stylistic boldness for the less appealing manner of the synthesizer and balancer. It is revealing of the change that came over him that when he cites Veblen, it is almost always in order to disagree with him.

Because it is a work of acceptance rather than of criticism, *America as a Civilization* rarely has the same literary appeal as many of the shorter, earlier pieces. The prose lacks the critical bite of the early work and with it the stylistic punch. But it was not intended to entertain or mobilize as much as to educate; it was written less for contemporaries than for the next generation, that of his eldest son to whom the book is dedicated. He wanted above all to help this generation appreciate that America was not just an offshoot of Europe but one of the great distinctive civilizations of history in its own right, on a par with ancient Greece and Rome; that this country's Revolution was more authentic than that of the Soviet Union; and that the success of its Revolution, with all its failings and unresolved problems, proves that the ideal of the open society is workable, indeed, that America's pluralistic and liberal democracy is a model the rest of the world could profit by emulating.

The Reception

The book was designed to be read by a wide audience and to pass muster with specialists. Drafts of the chapters had been vetted by a host of eminent scholars, some of whom had made suggestions that helped reshape various sections and bring out the overarching theme. C. Vann Woodward wrote to commend the section on "extended genesis" and to express skepticism about the claim that America was a distinct civilization:

> If, as you say, "the American is the concentrated embodiment of Western man as a whole," how can you insist upon an American as distinct from a Western Civilization? Granted that Toynbee and the

rest show inadequate appreciation for the American contribution, does that justify secession? . . . Granted we are a frontier civilization, were we not the frontier of Europe? But as I say we could pound the table endlessly on this point.[38]

The sociologist William H. Whyte thought the chapter on suburbia "excellent." [39] Lerner's young Brandeis associate, the historian Leonard W. Levy, was the most assiduous and the most helpful with historical details. Daniel Bell made penetrating suggestions for improvements on the chapters dealing with labor and business. Clinton Rossiter, who reported that he was "truly excited by it," made helpful suggestions on the section dealing with early history. George F. Kennan commented helpfully on the discussion of American foreign policy.[40]

Publication was greeted with many favorable and prominent reviews. Eminent historians and commentators hailed it as a book that could take its place along previous classic studies of America. The two reigning deans of American historiography, Samuel Eliot Morison and Henry Steele Commager, were unstinting in their praise. Morison called it "at once informing, stimulating and provocative . . . a great book." Commager, known to be an exacting scholar, wrote a very laudatory review and sent a warm personal note of congratulations:

> I want to tell you that I think with this book you take your place alongside Tocqueville and Bryce; it is the best book on American civilization written in my generation. What a massive achievement it is. How, o How do you do it . . . What with the Post and Brandeis, and all the rest. You are the first to incorporate the findings of the behavioral sciences into the findings of history, and that is a great pioneer task. I cannot congratulate you too warmly on this achievement . . . . Are you so exhausted that you will never write another line? . . . And have you really six children! What a man.[41]

Helped by such strong endorsements, the book sold well, was translated into several foreign languages, and was later reissued, in 1987, in a thirtieth-anniversary edition. It did not evoke universal admiration. Some reviewers complained that Lerner had tried to be so balanced that he ended up having no point of view at all. Others saw the work as too descriptive and insufficiently analytical. One of the more unusual critiques came to the publisher from the idiosyncratic Oxford historian A. J. P. Taylor:

I am most grateful for the copy of Max Lerner's America as a Civil-
isation. I have read large parts thereof, though not all. The industry,
grasp and range of the author stagger me. The mere physical effort is
more than I could undertake in a lifetime. But all the same: the book
is too long and too large at any rate for feeble readers of an old continent. I cannot even hold it with comfort. How then can I read it?

With great respect, American writers and publishers who produce books of this size earn from me condemnation, not praise. You
are killing literature. But of course you are an outsize nation; and
maybe it is all right for you. We have abandoned projects of this size.
We jog along from day to day, enjoying what comes—including
books of reasonable compass—until you or the Russians press the
button.[42]

Taylor might also have complained, as even sympathetic pre-
reviewers did, that the book was so comprehensive that it had more
the character of a dictionary or an encyclopedia than of a book with
a recognizable and sustained thesis. This was the initial reaction of
the insightful Louis Hartz, professor of political theory at Harvard,
when he saw the first three draft chapters. Although he politely
praised the "staggering dimensions" of Lerner's ambition, Hartz
raised the objection "that the work seems for all its panoramic brilliance too eclectic." In claiming that the work was "intended to have
no strategic relation" to issues current at the time, Lerner had made
"a surrender to the bad kind of detachment which you yourself have
assailed in many of your articles and books." He urged Lerner to take
a position so that there would be a "cutting edge" to the analysis.
Hartz went on to offer constructive help in this direction by pointing
out that the second chapter, in which Lerner discussed the cultural
continuities and differences between Europe and America, held the
key to a powerful overarching theme. Modestly noting that he "did
not want to ride a hobby horse of my own too hard"—a reference to
the fact that he only recently published a major study, *The Liberal
Tradition in America*, which took the contrast between America and
Western Europe as its framework—Hartz urged Lerner to make
more explicit his understanding of the distinctions between America and Europe. With his uniquely uncanny insight, Hartz put his
finger on exactly the point that Lerner himself was groping toward:

I was much taken . . . with the concept of the American as the "archetypal" figure of the West. I believe this is in some sense profoundly
true, but it does occur to me that in order to demonstrate this you

would have to make certain more explicit affirmations in connection with it. The American is the archetype, in my judgment, because he is a pure embodiment of the most dynamic elements of modern Western history. These elements are surrounded in Europe by hangovers and antagonisms, which have meant they have really never gotten beyond the incipient stage there. Here they have been permitted by history to reach fruition.[43]

Hartz went on to hint at his own analysis by pointing out that the notion of American exceptionalism, which he noted was an old preoccupation of Lerner's, is best understood as the obverse of the integration of America into the pattern of Western civilization. The real need was to explain the pattern of variation. This was just what Hartz set out to do in his *Liberal Tradition.* Beginning from Tocqueville's insight that the Americans were fortunate in being "born equal," in the sense that there was only a marginal feudal impact here, he went on to suggest that in contrast to Western Europe (especially England and France) Americans were preoccupied by the ideology of liberalism. Because of the weakness of feudalism and the presence of Lockian liberalism at the time of the Revolution, liberalism had become the national ideology, transformed into an unselfconscious, indeed mythic or "irrational" Americanism. For just this reason, and not because of "objective" or material consider ations, American political thinking had occupied a narrower spectrum than the European, effectively cutting off the extremes of reactionary neofeudalism and monarchism on the right and socialism and anarchism on the left. Hartz therefore put forward a thesis often identified by historians with the "liberal consensus" approach which, in part due to his efforts, became popular in the 1950s. Among other evidence Hartz cited was Lerner's earlier effort to deny American exceptionalism in order to sustain a Marxian analysis; Hartz criticized this effort as myopic.

Hartz did not intend his analysis in his *Liberal Tradition* as a Panglossian assurance that the country would always pursue enlightened policies. On the contrary, he intended to send the ironic and critical message that because liberalism (in the nineteenth-century sense of the term) had had the field all to itself, and as a result had become a mythic shibboleth, Americans had been blinded to the need for realistic reform to suit changing circumstances. Prisoners of their own "irrational Lockianism," they would strike out at "unAmerican" (i.e., un-Lockian) ideas, condemn dissent, and, perhaps worst of all, try vainly to impose their own ideology on the rest of the world, even though it might be altogether inappropriate for conditions elsewhere.

Lerner did not fully appreciate the novelty or brilliance of Hartz's analysis, perhaps because Hartz was too modest in his letter and merely hinted at the thesis he presented in his book, or because the book appeared too late for Lerner to assimilate it into his own thinking, which was already well advanced. Arthur Schlesinger, Jr., wrote to urge him to pay attention to Hartz's thesis, but he emphasized only Hartz's reprise and elaboration of Tocqueville's emphasis on the importance of the absence of feudalism as the key to distinguishing American from European experience.[44] Lerner recognized this point and made use of it, but failed to appreciate the difference between Tocqueville's thesis and Hartz's reworking of it. For Tocqueville, the absence of feudalism meant that American society had begun with an "equality of conditions." He feared that eventually the envy lurking in demands for equality might produce a servile form of socialism just as it would in Europe. Hartz saw the same experience as the matrix not of an open-ended egalitarianism but of a liberal unanimity—so unrecognized as to be called "Americanism"—that would not tolerate a socialist ideology. Because of the profoundly informing and inhibiting effects of its founding ideology, he argued, America had not taken the same political path as Western Europe. For Hartz, the very fact that liberalism had been so exclusively influential in the founding experience meant that the American mind was inoculated against the fevered dialectic of reaction and revolution that convulsed Europe in the nineteenth and twentieth centuries. Because of the hold of this Lockian consensus, Hartz explained, both right-wing and left-wing movements had been marginalized in America. On the right, only the South, with its antebellum "reactionary enlightenment," challenged the consensus, but its defeat in the Civil War rendered that effort, schizophrenic from the start, altogether vain. Socialist and anarchosyndicalist movements rose with immigration and subsided with assimilation. Lerner would have been right to object that Hartz's analysis minimized the significance of the division within the American consensus between the right and left wings of traditional liberalism, producing the twentieth-century split between liberals and conservatives, but he simply did not recognize what Hartz was driving at. Instead he argued that analyses like Hartz's pointing to American exceptionalism were correct but overdrawn.

Hartz really argued not for exceptionalism (or American "unique-ness") but rather for a recognition of the differences between Amer-ican and European ideologies based on comparative analysis, em-phasizing the importance of the founding conditions.

The shift of Lerner's thinking reflected in *America as a Civiliza-tion* is in fact a prime vindication of Hartz's thesis. What it showed most of all is that the effort to arouse class consciousness among Americans is doomed to failure. Here Lerner expressed a view of the country considerably different from the one he had adopted in his Veblenian years. His thinking had moved away from an earlier fixa-tion with the critique of capitalism toward an appreciation of Amer-ican society as something much more complex than it seemed ei-ther to Veblen or to Laski. Veblen saw it as the ultimate expression of the pecuniary culture; Laski fastened on the question of whether democracy or capitalism would predominate in shaping America's future. Although Lerner remained concerned about the inequities of distribution resulting from the American system of political economy, he now saw it as essentially successful in promoting both economic efficiency and widespread opportunity for a decent and rising standard of living. But he also recognized that political econ-omy was only one dimension of the American experience.

Lerner thought, mistakenly as it turned out, that the "new con-servatism" which had appeared in the mid-'50s was "likely to have a difficult time finding a stable intellectual base amidst the tensions of the years ahead." He was right, however, in recognizing that the characteristic American ideological impulse—even the one that animates conservatives—is that of liberalism, in the original sense of the term. The weaknesses of the liberal tradition, he thought, were clear enough: the atomism of the early liberals made it hard for them to conceive of social linkage. Its association with pragma-tism sometimes robbed it of a sense of vision. Its emphasis on reason ignored the force of the irrational. For all its weaknesses, however, it is "the central expression of the American democratic faith." [45] Its "basic premise has been in a majority will capable of organiz-ing itself effectively when the obstructions are blasted away by the dynamite of facts and ideas." And it was the strength of this un-derlying liberal tradition, with its encouragement of change and adaptation, that inspired the confident note on which he ended:

> There are many who feel . . . that, whether through conformism,
> fanaticism or rigidity, American society will succumb to the final

impersonality of the Age of the Insects. The long journey we have made through these pages should lead to a different conclusion. There is still in the American potential the plastic strength that has shaped a great civilization, and it shows itself in unexpected ways, at unpredictable moments, and in disguises that require some imaginative understanding to unveil. What Emerson said a century ago I would still hold to: "We think our civilization is near its meridian, but we are yet only at the cockcrowing and the morning star." [46]

As this confident encomium suggests, Lerner had reached a critical turning point in his understanding of the country and his attitude toward it. In earlier years he had been a sharp critic of the American social and economic system. Now he became an unabashed admirer of its achievements, its future promise, and its example to the world. He had achieved an understanding of the country that would inform all his future work, including the newspaper commentaries that became his most widely read writings.

SEVEN

Liberal Pundit of the *New York Post*

Well before he became a news-
paper columnist himself, Lerner was inspired by the work of three
predecessors—Heywood Broun, William Bolitho, and Walter Lippmann—all of whom began their journalistic careers on the *New
York World*, founded by Joseph Pulitzer. When the *World* was sold
to the Scripps-Howard chain and merged with the *Telegram* in
1931, Broun, who had courageously criticized the tactics used in
prosecuting the anarchists Sacco and Vanzetti, joined first *The Nation* and then *PM*, where Lerner became his colleague. Bolitho,
who had an eye for the passing parade and an ear for the vernacu-
lar of the jazz age, flashed across the journalistic sky like a comet,
dying at the age of thirty. He left an impression on other writers,
including the playwright Noel Coward, who considered Lerner a
worthy successor. "I mean it as the greatest compliment," Coward
wrote to Lerner, "when I say that your use of suddenly unexpected
words and similes reminded me of him frequently." [1] Lippmann
moved to the *New York Herald Tribune* and began writing the column he called "Today and Tomorrow," for many years the country's most widely read commentary on foreign affairs. Lerner had
criticized Lippmann in the 1930s as a "reactionary" [2] and later

187

regarded him as a rival, but in 1973, at Lippmann's death, Lerner saluted him for having given all political columnists "a sense of our intellectual role in a profession which would otherwise be halfway between the newsroom and the cracker-barrel . . ."[3]

At *PM*, Lerner began as a Broun-like contributor to its "Opinion" section, gradually added Bolitho-style short essays as he gained a following, and often emulated Lippmann in pronouncing on world events. The Hindu word "pundit," meaning a teacher and critic, came into popular use in this period and fit Lerner well, especially when he became a columnist for the *Post*. For over four decades, beginning in the spring of 1949, he was New York's leading liberal pundit, writing some 6,000 columns for the *Post* and eventually for a larger syndicated audience.

Newspaper columns attracted a considerable following in these years, thanks in part to the special place print journalism occupied among mass media. Until television became the prime disseminator of news and magazine-style "documentaries," newspapers were the main conduits for news reporting and analysis. Editorial writers, including the leading political columnists, had a role in shaping public opinion second only to that of the most prominent political leaders. Radio was mainly an adjunct to the press, relied on for news bulletins, commentaries by journalists, and FDR's innovative but unique "fireside chats." Although the radio networks reached national audiences, they offered relatively skimpy news coverage and only a modicum of commentary. Even their public affairs programs, such as "Meet the Press," underscored their auxiliary role. For a time Lerner did a Sunday broadcast commentary, but it was not as successful as his column.

In the densely populated New York metropolitan area, the competition among newspapers was the keenest in the country. There were enough readers to support an extensive mainstream press as well as a remarkable array of ethnic and foreign-language papers. In the morning market, the *Times* was the most prestigious of the general circulation dailies, followed closely by the livelier *Herald Tribune*. Two racy pictorial tabloids, Joseph Medill Patterson's *Daily News* and Hearst's *Daily Mirror* (both modeled after the defunct pioneer, the *New York Graphic*), competed for the mass-circulation audience. The *News* boasted the most popular comic strips, including the craggy-faced detective Dick Tracy and the adventurous waif, Orphan Annie. The *Mirror* relied heavily on the popularity of

Walter Winchell's staccato-style chronicle of celebrity gossip and "insider" scoops. In the afternoon market, Scripps-Howard's *World Telegram & Sun*, Hearst's *Journal-American*, and the *Post* all courted the general reader. The *Daily Compass* and the Communist *Daily Worker* competed for a dwindling audience of radicals. The *Wall Street Journal* was read mainly by financiers and business executives. Brooklyn still had its own *Daily News* and the *Eagle*—for which Walt Whitman had written—and Long Island, the *Star-Journal* and *Press*. There were also Italian-, Polish-, Spanish-, and Yiddish-language dailies and a variety of local, ethnic, and religious weeklies. Suburban Yonkers boasted three dailies; and northern New Jersey seven more. S. I. Newhouse had traded an interest in the *Bayonne Times* to acquire the *Staten Island Advance*, with which he was beginning to build a media empire to rival those of Hearst and Scripps-Howard.

This bright burst of activity would prove to be the twilight of a Golden Age of competitive newspaper journalism. By 1967, the ten general-readership New York dailies that flourished in 1949 had dwindled to three: the *Times*, the *Daily News*, and the *Post*. In a column marking the passage of the *Post*'s last afternoon competitor, the merged *World-Journal-Tribune*, Lerner attributed the decline to several factors, among them the loss of "personality" due to the mergers. The three survivors, he pointed out, all had a distinctive character attractive to a segment of the public. The *Post*'s identity was mainly "the continuity of a liberal stance since the days of the New Deal." [4] Over the next several decades, the *Post* too shed its identity and emerged as an imitator of the *Daily News*.

When Lerner began to write for it, the *Post* was the nation's oldest continuously published newspaper. Founded by Alexander Hamilton, it had been owned by liberal publishers for some time, since it was acquired, before the turn of the century, along with *The Nation*, by Henry Villard. He passed it on to his son Oswald Garrison Villard who sold it in the 1930s to J. David Stern, under whose ownership it became the only New York newspaper consistently to support the New Deal and Franklin Roosevelt. By the end of the decade it was in serious financial difficulty until, in 1942, Stern managed to persuade a politician and writer, George Backer, to take it over. Backer was able to buy the paper because he had recently become the second husband of Dorothy ("Dolly") Schiff, the wealthy granddaughter of the financier Jacob H. Schiff and a friend and admirer (and rumored one-time lover)* of FDR. Backer became president of the paper, but Schiff soon tired of him and took the advice of a staffer, Ted O. Thackrey, to turn the *Post* into a tabloid and merge it, in 1946, with the *Bronx Home News* in what proved to be a successful effort to raise circulation. In succession, Thackrey became editor, Schiff's third husband, and co-publisher. In 1948, however, he came out editorially for Wallace while she wrote editorials against Wallace and eventually endorsed the Republican candidate, Governor Thomas E. Dewey of New York. The couple broke up in 1949. He opened a new paper, the left-wing *Daily Compass*, to fill the gap left by the demise of *PM* and the *Star.* Schiff became sole publisher of the *Post* and appointed James A. Wechsler, Lerner's former *PM* colleague, as editor.

In 1949, the *Post* appeared in two editions, late morning and afternoon, and sold 366,000 copies six days a week—more than the *Sun*, about the same as the *Herald Tribune* and *World-Telegram*, but less than the 707,000 of the *Journal-American*, and far less than the combined 3 million copies (even more on Sunday) sold by the *News* and *Mirror.* Lerner now had a larger readership than he had enjoyed on *PM* though it was still only one segment of the New York newspaper audience. That changed, but only temporarily, in 1963 when one of a series of devastating strikes stopped the presses of all the New York dailies except the *Post.* Schiff broke ranks with the other publishers and agreed to a costly deal with the typographical unions. As a result, Lerner suddenly acquired readers normally drawn to more conservative pundits. A *New Yorker* cartoon captured their frustration, depicting a railroad commuter car full of suburban businessmen grimly reading the *Post*, as one of them scowls and asks, "Who *is* this Max Lerner?"

In the mid-'60s, the paper managed to stay afloat in the face of escalating costs and shrinking advertising revenues until it enjoyed a temporary reprieve thanks to the collapse of all its afternoon rivals. The *Post*'s circulation rose to a peak of 700,000 but soon fell back to 500,000, as all the newspapers except the *Times*, which had acquired a growing national readership, and the *News*, which still sold 2 million copies a day, fell victim to a variety of pressures. These

---

*Lerner told Schiff's biographer that "Dolly knew Roosevelt intimately. I imagine he saw her for his political self-interest, as well as for his sexual interest" (Jeffrey Potter, *Men, Money & Magic: The Story of Dorothy Schiff* [New York, 1976], p. 184).

included rising labor costs, stiffer competition from television, and a changing demographic profile. Middle-class families moved to the suburbs, taking department stores to malls and their advertising with them, to be replaced by an influx of poorer and non-English-speaking immigrants. Buffeted by these winds of change, the *Post* almost went out of business until it was taken over in 1977 by the Australian media entrepreneur Rupert Murdoch, who remade it, with the help of experienced tabloid staffers from London's Fleet Street, into an even racier version of the *News*. It now became notorious for purveying celebrity gossip and digging up the details of the goriest murders. Its editors were proud of using headlines such as HEADLESS BODY IN TOPLESS BAR.* Circulation jumped and Lerner's column was featured in a less prominent and less regular format.

But it was not just the change in the newspaper's form and target audience that knocked Lerner's column off its old pedestal. A conservative mood was rising in the suburbs where population and newspaper readership were increasing. Otherwise, the New Left's disdain for liberals and its admonition never to trust anyone over thirty may have deterred some younger readers who might otherwise have taken to him. Others were growing skeptical about relying on established authorities in general. In 1964, another *New Yorker* cartoon hinted at the changing attitude, depicting a wife asking her anguished young husband, "Now that you've read James Reston,

---

*This initial degradation was not enough to assure its survival. In 1993, when Murdoch sought to acquire other, more lucrative media properties, he was required by the Federal Communications Commission to give up his ownership of the *Post*. The paper spun out of control, lost circulation, and was on the verge of final collapse when it was rescued again and eventually restored to Murdoch. In defense of the paper's preoccupation with scandal, its 1990s editor, Steven Cuozzo, noted that, whatever "establishmentarians" and "elitists" might say in criticism, it was simply catering to the popular taste for stories that "illuminated the gaudy spectacle of American life—the interface of sex, crime and celebrity that defines the national mysterioso." Hamilton, he claimed, would not have been surprised, having unwittingly prophesied the rise of tabloid journalism, when he noted that "men are ambitious, vindictive, and rapacious"—"an observation," Cuozzo remarks, "that might serve as a tabloid manifesto" (Steven Cuozzo, *It's Alive! How America's Oldest Newspaper Cheated Death and Why It Matters* [New York, 1996], pp. 6–8). Hamilton also remarked, in *Federalist* 9: "It is impossible to read the histories of the petty republics of Greece and Italy without feeling sensations of horror and disgust at the distractions with which they were continually agitated."

William F. Buckley, and Max Lerner, what's your opinion?" In 1959 and 1960 Lerner dispatched his former Brandeis student Martin Peretz to visit newspapers around the country in the hope of drumming up business, but Peretz could report only sporadic interest. When the column was picked up by the Los Angeles Times Syndicate some years later, it did only marginally better. Lerner could count on the column being picked up fairly regularly by papers in most of the major cities, but it never achieved blanket coverage of the nation as a whole.

In his heyday, however, Lerner was a major columnist at a time when newspaper columnists had a major influence over public opinion. Until newspapers began to lose their separate followings, they were often fiercely competitive. Their leading political columnists were apt to be revered as tribunes of the people by their loyal readers and reviled as demagogues by those angered by their viewpoints. In cities where there were too few newspapers to assure a full spectrum of opinion, the newspapers usually offered at least token representation to points of view other than the publisher's. Densely populated New York offered a more luxuriant variety until the late 1960s, as each newspaper catered to a different segment of the political spectrum. The *News* and the *Mirror* were outspokenly on the right editorially, but apart from the *News'* once isolationist Washington editor, John O'Donnell, and "insider" reporters like Drew Pearson and Robert S. Allen, their columnists (including Ed Sullivan, Hedda Hopper, Dorothy Kilgallen, and Winchell) traded only in celebrity gossip or entertainment news. Otherwise the newspapers ran the political gamut, from the right-wing *Journal-American* to the middle of the road *World Telegram & Sun* to the moderate Republican *Herald Tribune*, the independent but increasingly pro-Democratic *Times*, the liberal *Post*, the radical *Compass*, and at the extreme left the *Worker*—in its prime an attractively laid out and professionally edited organ of the party line. In two particular cases, ethnicity also played an influential role in determining newspaper loyalty: the *Journal-American* had a large following among Irish Catholics, and Jews made up the largest segment of the *Post*'s readership.

Apart from the morning tabloids, each of the papers had a stable of columnists reflecting a particular point of view, except for the *World Telegram & Sun*, which specialized in offering features to cater to all interests and downplayed partisan politics. The *Herald Tribune* featured Lippmann, nationally syndicated by Scripps-

Howard, along with the domestically liberal but stridently anti-Communist Joseph and Stewart Alsop, the independent-minded Dorothy Thompson, and the conservative George Sokolsky, who later moved to the *Journal-American*. The *Times* offered readers a choice between the conservative Arthur Krock and the moderately liberal James Reston, both of whom enjoyed privileged access to the politically powerful in Washington. The *Journal-American* boasted the right-wing fulminations of Westbrook Pegler, who was syndicated by Scripps-Howard, and the acerbic Fulton Lewis, Jr. The *Compass* had I. F. Stone, who had become a Washington columnist, and who wrote to Lerner in 1950 expressing his amusement that some readers were accusing him of "Lerneritis": "That means I don't follow the party line." [5]

Under Wechsler's editorship, and afterward, under that of his successor, Paul Sann, the *Post* had an extensive stable composed almost exclusively of liberal columnists, all highly regarded both by readers and by their journalistic peers. From the 1950s through the mid-1970s, they included, along with Lerner and Murray Kempton (a favorite of fellow journalists), Clayton Fritchey, Samuel Grafton, Frank Kingdon, Oliver Pilat, three African-Americans (a novelty at the time)—the poet Langston Hughes; the civil rights leader Roy Wilkins, and the soon to become legendary ex-baseball player Jackie Robinson. The *Post* also ran the syndicated columns of Marquis Childs, Doris Fleeson, Mary McGrory, Joseph Kraft, Drew Pearson, Eleanor Roosevelt, and Eric Sevareid. The editorial cartoons were by the *Washington Post*'s Herblock. The paper also carried Walt Kelly's acclaimed "Pogo" comic strip and, for a time, a column by Harry Golden, famous for his book (and phrase) *Only in America*. When the merged *Herald Tribune*'s presses fell permanently silent in 1966 (after which its logo survived only in an international edition published in Paris), the *Post* picked up Lippmann, along with William F. Buckley, Jr.—something that would have been inconceivable earlier. (More important for circulation, the *Post* also acquired the extremely popular comic strip "Peanuts.")

Pride of place among the columnists, until the change wrought by Murdoch, went to Lerner, who carved out a special niche for himself as a commentator on both foreign policy and domestic politics. He became in effect the spokesman for liberal New York opinion, and developed a broader following once the column was syndicated. The 900-word column appeared three times a week, except when he was on vacation or traveling, until 1970 in a classic double-column format headed by a box with his photo and a brief title. For several years its location was opposite the editorial page, flanked at first by Leonard Lyons's column of celebrity anecdotes, "The Lyons Den," then by one written by Kempton or by another of the *Post*'s premiere columnists. From 1970 to 1978, the column appeared in a three-column layout in a separate magazine section, still featured prominently. Thereafter its format often reflected the racier, less formal style the newspaper assumed, sometimes carrying a headline and photograph relevant to the subject, and in the later years it appeared twice weekly.

Many of the columns carried foreign datelines and were written on makeshift desks in exotic locales, including

> a long table at our house in Sundar Nagar in Delhi; on a hotel veranda overlooking the marketplace in Pnom Penh; on a houseboat in Kashmir; in the dappled sunlight of an enchanted garden in New Orleans; in a heatless room of a Roman winter; in the Trastevere; on a sundeck in Malibu and another in Topanga Canyon in California; on a Venice balcony opposite the Church of Santa Maria; in a tiny room at the King David in Jerusalem; on the small boat wharf at Santa Barbara; in a pygmy forest in Zaire; in a little grove at a sunny *finca* in Ibiza.[6]

Although most of the columns were devoted to public affairs, Lerner sometimes wrote about whatever else struck his fancy. "In American journalism," he noted, "there are exclusively political commentators and general ones. I fall in the latter category." He liked to think that through his columns and his academic books he was addressing Virginia Woolf's "common reader," not separate audiences, though his was mainly the liberal fragment of the larger national audience. Sensitive to the disdain among American academics for "mere journalism," he pointed out that European intellectuals did not share this prejudice, citing writers from Defoe and Swift to Sartre and Orwell. Like them, he wanted to be a social historian, social theorist, and man of letters, but one who would be engaged with the "actions and passions" of the time. "I have been a man of my time," he wrote, "responding to its felt needs, mirroring its hopes and fears, caught in its intellectual battles, breaking lances again and again in its political struggles."[7] He enjoyed the polemics column-writing invites:

> [M]y own best medium seems to be the polemical. I don't know whether it is glandular or a matter of biographical accident. But once

I get sore at a man or an idea, it is hard for me to pull back and say,
"This bastard is only 75% wrong." I generally push on until I reach
the limits of the 100%.[8]

With coarse rivals like Westbrook Pegler he had no civil relations,
but with literate, intelligent conservatives like Krock and Buckley
he was on good terms. In 1968, Buckley sent a note saying, "Sorry I
missed you. Don't say anything subversive. You've been reasonably
well-behaved lately."[9] When Lerner publicly scolded Buckley for
making misleading allegations concerning Vice President Humphrey's campaign for the presidency, Buckley replied indignantly,
but added praise for Lerner's criticism of the radical student uprising at Columbia University:

Sapientissimus Max:
When you scold me for inaccuracy, *mon vieux*, get straight what I
said. What I said was that Humphrey let go the filing date for California because he did not have the financial assurances he needed.
That is true, everything else I said was in the conditional mood, If
not A, then not B, etc. . . . Your thing on Columbia was not bad, not
bad at all. Another fifty years or so and you will make up in wisdom
what I lack in factual knowledge.
Affectionately,
Bill[10]

Lerner replied in the same spirit:

Dear Bill,
Even with your explanations of it, I fear I must still count your analysis of Humphrey's financial plight something less than your finest
hour. I must add, however, that a few of your columns recently have
been disturbing because they tremble on the brink of making sense.
At this rate you and I may find ourselves, somewhere in the calculable future, with too little to quarrel about to give that fine edge
to our friendship.
As ever,
Max*[11]

*Lerner also had an amusing exchange with the lyricist Alan Jay Lerner, who
forwarded a letter from France addressed to "Max Lerner." He attached this note:

I am enclosing a letter from one of your French fans which came to me
by mistake. It is, however, a mistake that has cleared up a great mystery
for me.

If Lerner's point of view became fairly predictable, he sometimes surprised his readers, and his way of putting things could be striking. Writing from India he questioned the common view about India's spiritualism: "Despite everything I have read and heard about how the Asian religions despise life on earth, Bombay is clamorous with people who seem to be holding on to life like men slipping off a mountain and digging their fingernails into the rock." [12] Contrary to the image of ethereal Eastern serenity, he observed that "the formlessness of the East is alien to serenity and can in fact drive you batty." To live in urban India was hardly a serene experience, but rather one "I can only describe as a machine civilization in which the machines don't work." [13] But he was inspired to rapture by a visit to Jaipur, one place that did live up to its Eastern mystique:

> Your first impression of Jaipur is of complete unreality. You look at it, drive and walk through it, see its housefronts and shops and stalls, its hundreds of temples everywhere, including the small ones plumped right in the middle of the street, its balconies and minarets, latticework everywhere, its rows of tiny windows, and you feel it to be a city that never was on land or sea. It is a filigree city, spun out of nothingness. [14]

In most of the political columns, the prose was more workaday, but moving moments sometimes evoked moving prose. On the first anniversary of the assassination of President Kennedy he spoke for many when he remarked that "the memories still carry pain, like an unhealed wound." A column on the Watts riots of 1965 began:

I have not received any royalties from France in years and I assumed it was due to the fundamental French belief that one only takes money from Americans but never gives them any. Now I understand thoroughly what has happened. Obviously your books are being published under my name, and my songs and plays under yours. So would you please be a good fellow and send me all those royalties you have been pocketing for all these years?

If you're a little short I will be happy to wait until the newspaper strike is over.

Good try, old man.

Lerner replied that he found this theory of "the transposition of our identities . . . not wholly persuasive." He preferred to think that "you and I form a composite person, who all along and all alone has been writing weighty works of political theory along with delightful social comedy, both the *Age of Overkill* and *My Fair Lady*. The purpose of this human monstrosity is to make the world weep and laugh at the same time, thus driving it into a schizophrenic frenzy (Letters, n.d., YMA, I, 5, 231).

"Writing about Joyce, Rebecca West said that he was a man who in order to breathe felt he had to break all the windows." [15] After interviewing Lyndon Johnson in 1968, when the war in Vietnam was going badly and protests were mounting against him at home, Lerner wrote of the beleaguered president:

> The impression that comes through to visitors is that of a terribly stubborn man and a terribly lonely one, whose massive power only emphasizes his isolation, turning increasingly inward for support, showing few signs of how shaken he was by events, blistered by his own past decisions and miscalculations, confident of vindication by history if not by the people. Above all, one must be impressed by the naked will power of the man, as if he were exerting sheer will to hold everything together at once—the war, the nation, and his own inner universe. [16]

Lerner was as mesmerized as most Americans by the unfolding scandal of Watergate. At first he thought President Nixon would escape unscathed. Then, as the evidence of the president's complicity in the cover-up mounted, he supported the effort to compel the White House to release all the relevant evidence in its possession, including the now famous oval office tapes. But he tried to keep the affair in perspective, as when he took issue with the hyperbolic reaction of Senator Sam Ervin, chairman of the Senate committee investigating the scandal:

> It will be a long time before we have fully assessed the dimensions of the Watergate tragedy. Carried away by emotion, as he sometimes is when wrestling with the perversities of witnesses and of President Nixon, Sen. Ervin called it the greatest tragedy in American history, greater even than the Civil War. The two are not really comparable . . . It is hard to think of anything more tragic than brother killing brother, for over four years. It has left an ugly scar across American history which has still not wholly healed.
>
> The ugliness of Watergate is of a different order. It was a betrayal of law and of moral values, a power drunkenness which used national security to cloak the excesses of arbitrary power. It was pretty bad, but civil war is far worse. In fact, one of the impressive things about the mood of Congress and the country thus far has been the hesitation to push an impeachment movement which might indeed polarize emotions, bring social divisions, and split the society. [17]

A year later, when Richard Nixon was finally forced to resign the presidency in disgrace, Lerner called attention to the paradox at the heart of his makeup and behavior:

> Although one of his purposes was to contain the turbulent rebellions of the '60s, he was himself a kind of anti-establishment rebel. He fought the Eastern Republican establishment, loathed the liberal intellectual establishment, despised the traditional leadership of Congress, the press, and the courts except where he could use it to his purpose. He saw himself as a maverick, at home only with the close circle around him who shared his contempts and his tough-guy talk.
>
> The one thing that touched him deeply was his place in history, and his hope of being remembered as the peace-bringer who had eased the tensions and threats to a new equilibrium of the Great Powers. The irony—as the historians are bound to see it—is that he tried to achieve this by methods of inner manipulation and fire-storming which broke the Constitutional safeguards.[18]

The death of prominent people inspired some of Lerner's most telling writing. "One felt the wit in him," he wrote of Bertrand Russell, "and the bubbling irreverence, and the iconoclasm: everything but depth." [19] Of Dwight Eisenhower, whose election he had twice opposed, as a loyal supporter of Adlai Stevenson, and whose administration he had often criticized as lackluster, he offered this final assessment:

> Eisenhower had no corrosive or original mind, but the mind of a unifier who reached for what people had in common, whether in a football squad, an Army, or a nation. If some heads of state govern by fear and others by love, Eisenhower governed by good will and heart—which is why he was so widely loved.
>
> He lived and governed just before the cracking of the social covenant in America. His deepest intuition was to try to keep it from cracking. If he failed it was not from lack of goodwill but from relying too heavily on it alone. But those who followed him also failed, with their innocent faith that the sheer dynamism of "getting things done" would somehow provide cement for the splits that a mindless dynamism inevitably brings with it."[20]

Lerner had come to know and admire the poet Robert Frost. At Frost's death in 1963, he recalled their friendship, savoring the lines and images from Frost that gave him pleasure:

> When he reflected whether the world would end in fire or ice, when he swung birches or mended fences or tried to clap his hand at a

minor bird, when he stopped by the woods on a snowy evening and remembered that he had promises to keep, when he placed his two-pointed ladder against an apple tree, when he mused on the hill wife or the death of the hired man or the witches of Coos and Grafton or the two tramps who came out of the mud into the farmyard, when he looked up at the constellations or remembered the road he had not taken or confessed himself acquainted with the night, Frost's themes and symbols broke through the particular and the now into the universal and the forever. That was why we read him and—wonder of wonders in our hurried time—why we took the trouble to memorize him.[21]

Of Henry Wallace, to whom he had been drawn but could not support for the presidency in 1948, Lerner still had mixed opinions. Wallace, Lerner observed in 1965, had been "a shy, awkward man, in rumpled clothes, with gentle gray eyes that were usually averted from you, with the suspicion of corn silk still in his hair—a strange mixture of hard-hearted plant geneticist and gullible mystic both in religion and politics." In retrospect, Lerner admitted, Wallace "would have made a disastrous President."[22]

He had greater admiration for Hubert Humphrey, though he thought that Humphrey had had a weakness that handicapped him in politics. Humphrey, Lerner wrote in 1978, had been a courageous and devoted man of reason—"in a world of brutal power he defended the life of the mind"—and a champion of the downtrodden, but he lacked the toughness needed to succeed in the rough and tumble of electoral politics:

> Humphrey lacked the iron of ruthlessness in his makeup. He had ample courage himself, as his last months of facing intolerable pain and the certainty of death showed, and he had endless gallantry. Yet he didn't have the savagery for the great power struggles—a savagery a man must have to get to the White House and stay there.[23]

Lerner also admired Nelson Rockefeller, politician and patron of the arts, whom he saw as an odd mixture of American and European influences:

> I think of him as some figure out of the Renaissance—merchant prince, art patron, adventurer, wielder of power, active in friendship and love and every web that life weaves, the last Venetian doge we are likely to harbor on these American shores. It is curious that such a figure should come out of his Puritan heritage, but the pride

of vocation and the hunger for public evidence of personal effectiveness were part of the Puritan mind.[24]

Sometimes Lerner tried to winkle cosmic significance out of a trivial event. Noting the crowds rushing to see the film *Cleopatra*, for example, he wondered whether the interest in the film was due not just to the appeal of its stars, Elizabeth Taylor and Richard Burton, and their off-screen love affair, but to a morbid association moviegoers were making, somewhere deep in the recesses of the mind, between the pomp and decadence of ancient Rome and Egypt and that of modern America.[25] Similarly, in explaining his attendance at a boxing match in Miami, he claimed that "aside from the excitement of our modern form of the Greek *agon* . . . anyone who wants to study mythmaking in America cannot neglect the Listons and Clays of our time . . . We live in concentric circles of violence, as Dante's people lived in circles of Hell . . . One way to express undestructively some of the sense of pervasive violence is to identify with the flailing fists of Sonny Liston and Cassius Clay."[26]

A parody of the *Post* that appeared during the newspaper strike of 1962 (under the logo *The New York Pest*) skewered Lerner for such overwrought interpretations. In a column supposedly reflecting on the significance of the death of a dog named "Wags," "the spotted and lovable pet of little Jane Schwartz of the Bronx," the parodist has Lerner observe that "the lessons in this microcosmic human drama" call to mind "the current East-West struggle and of course the fate of America as a civilization," not to mention "the even darker, deeper-flowing stream of Freudian motivation infusing, if not pervading, the entire sordid—and yet, in a curious way, heartening—little tale." And it goes on—and on:

> . . . The fact that little Wags happened to be a mongrel does not in any sense lessen our grief at his passing; we mourn him with all the feeling we would mourn a poodle of the finest pedigree. Our Judaeo-Christian tradition, leavened with the wisdom of Freud, Schweitzer, John Dewey, Justice Holmes, Jefferson, Thoreau, Vance Packard, Jane Addams, Liz Taylor, David Riesman, Shoeless Joe Jackson, Arthur M. Schlesinger, Jr. and Charles "The Bird" Parker has created a kind of socio-cultural zeitgeist culminating in a sense of fair play . . . These are only a few of the implications of the drama upon which I will have more reflections tomorrow, and tomorrow, and tomorrow . . . I shall no doubt find more lessons . . . to be drawn from this story of love and death, hope and heartbreak, passion and pity, for this, indeed, like life itself, is an Unfinished Column.[27]

Others were more appreciative of his forays into popular culture, especially the writers, playwrights, and filmmakers whose work he discussed. The playwright Edward Albee, who was to become a close friend of the Lerners, and who would dedicate a play to them, wrote to thank him for his comments on an early work, saying he only wished Lerner would become a theater critic.[28] Lerner's discussion of Tennessee Williams's *Sweet Bird of Youth* evoked a similar response from its author: "You are very perceptive, you bring keen sensitivities with you when you walk in a theatre, sharp ears and a responding heart. I wish I could be sure that I was always working with audiences like you: I mean all of them, always."[29] The film director Louis Malle also became a friend and correspondent. He enlisted Lerner's help in organizing a conference in Europe to help him think about a projected film on a utopian society. A column in 1950 discussing Charlie Chaplin's just-released film, *Limelight*, evoked a warm response from Chaplin:

> What you write in one paragraph would take me six months of polishing, then I doubt if I could say it as well as you do. However, I'm a better pantomimist.
>
> But joking aside, the last paragraph in which you describe the blind girl seeing the tramp for the first time and which you end by saying, "But it is Charlie's triumph that he keeps joy, shame, and apprehension in a balanced tension, and makes it a triumph," is, I might say, damn good writing.[30]

Norman Cousins, the editor of *The Saturday Review of Literature*, reviewing a collection of Lerner's earlier editorials, praised his writing:

> He is first of all a writer, and one of the best in the business. He has a respect for the word. He doesn't fondle words or flaunt them. There is a discipline here, an ability to turn words properly, with a sense of rhythm in the sound and in the phrasing. Improvisation, glibness, incompleteness—the three principal weaknesses of "spot" writing are nowhere in evidence in Lerner's editorials. Instead, we find a superb literary fabric, its material strong and evenly knit.[31]

Not everyone shared this enthusiasm for Lerner's writing style. In 1960, Sydney J. Harris, a syndicated columnist for the *Chicago Daily News* and a writer with fastidious standards, wrote a scathing review of *The Unfinished Country*, a selection of the first decade of Lerner's *Post* columns, for *The Saturday Review of Literature*. While praising Lerner's political commentaries and his columns on education, he was sharply critical of his excursions into literature and philosophy, accusing him of misquoting "from Shakespeare to Thoreau to Gershwin" and using "Great Thoughts" to make his platitudes more plausible. Harris was even more unsparing of Lerner's use of language, which he thought showed "an appalling triteness of expression":

> In his prose, people "skate on the edge of disaster," they weep "rivers of tears," they make "May-and-December marriages," they "break lances," they undergo "grueling experiences." His corpses are "pronounced dead," his tourists come "in droves," his silences fall in "mantles," his law is "stern-eyed," his midnight is "the witching hour," his civilization is a "veneer," his objects are in "sad repair," his promised gifts "turn to ashes," his widows are "grief-stricken."
>
> He mistakes "anxious" for "eager," confuses "masterly" and "masterful," uses "fulsome" incorrectly, confounds "healthy" with "wholesome," and calls for a "small legion" of men, which is rather like asking for a "poor millionaire." [32]

Elizabeth Taylor and "My Little Professor"

Some of his *Post* readers who took Lerner's work rather more seriously were troubled by his seeming obsession with the doings of Hollywood stars, especially Elizabeth Taylor. One reader (who would have been even more troubled had he known what was to become of the entire paper) wrote to express the distress he and his wife felt, after having read Lerner faithfully for many years:

> In recent years we have been disenchanted with your writings because they've lost their previous incisiveness + cogency. They are written by a man who has mellowed + and is therefore ill-equipped to really deal with liberal-oriented problems of today's world. In addition, we are sorely disturbed by your Elizabeth Taylor syndrome. For the life of us we can't understand why you concern yourself so drearily with a subject + personality handled so much "better" elsewhere in the Post. You sound, whenever you write about her, like an upper case press agent trying to convince your readership that that product of Hollywood in its vilest form is some profound manifestation of our culture to be raised up + examined minutely so that very nuance can be savoured. [33]

There was in fact more than just a cultural concern in Lerner's "Elizabeth Taylor syndrome." Lerner first met the actress in London in 1959, where he had gone to cover a summit meeting between Eisenhower and the British prime minister, Harold Macmillan. Lerner was then fifty-eight, she twenty-seven. In a *Post* column, he had written sympathetically about her anguish at the accidental death of her previous husband, Mike Todd, and defended her remarriage to Todd's protégé, the popular singer Eddie Fisher. They met in her suite at the Dorchester, where she and Fisher told him they had appreciated the column, and then all three went off together on a pub crawl. As Lerner and Taylor became friends, she admitted to him that her new marriage was not what she had hoped because Fisher was no Todd. "I thought I could keep Mike's memory alive that way," she said, "but I have only his ghost." Lerner took the admission as a hint that she might prefer someone more mature like himself. He chaperoned her in London, and they spent a weekend together in Paris. As if to underscore the intellectual character of the affair, somewhat in imitation of the courtship of Marilyn Monroe by Arthur Miller, he took her to the café *Aux Deux Magots*, made famous by Jean-Paul Sartre's patronage. She referred to him as "my little professor" and compared their liaison to that of Sophia Loren and Carlo Ponti—"the perfect complement of brain and beauty."[34]

He found her dazzling, an "extraordinary, enchanting, passionate, exasperating, impossible woman," and at least considered asking her to marry him. When the gossip columns reported the affair, Edna challenged him to make up his mind and offered a divorce. While he dithered, apparently unperturbed by the publicity, Taylor went off to Rome to film *Cleopatra* where she and Richard Burton became romantic co-stars on and off the set. Lerner later told Kitty Kelley, who reported the conversation in an unauthorized biography of Taylor, that he had decided not to propose marriage because he was well aware she "would use me the way a beautiful woman uses an older man"—as a front while she would go on having relations with other men.[35] He told others that he had been passionately attracted to Taylor and would have asked her to marry him had she not succumbed to Burton. He continued to see her from time to time in 1960 and 1961. When they met in California in 1961, they agreed to collaborate on a book about her physical and psychological problems (she had been accidentprone since childhood and had survived serious illnesses), to be called *Elizabeth Taylor: Between Life and Death*. "I'll do the recalling, you can do the heavy thinking," she said. They drew up a contract for the book and began work on it using a tape recorder, but they later tore up the contract when both became preoccupied with other commitments.[36] He thought of writing an article about her to be called "Elizabeth Taylor, Survivor." He outlined a story, perhaps a play, to be called "Cliffhanger Love," that would fictionalize the breakup of her marriage with Fisher, her stormy romance with Burton, and include a composite character of an older intellectual challenger, compounded, improbably, of Norman Mailer, Arthur Schlesinger, Jr., and himself. Later, he thought of writing a play about her on the theme of the femme fatale and did actually write several pieces about her for women's magazines, in which he discussed her appeal as someone who had "played the marriage game" in "a kind of non-stop sequential polygamy." One article, written for the *Ladies' Home Journal*, pursued the theme of the femme fatale. Duly identified as the author of *America as a Civilization*, Lerner offered the readers of the *Journal* a potted history of the romantic ideal, tracing the lineage of the heroine in love from the legends of Eleanor of Acquitaine, Tristan's Iseult, and Abelard's Heloise, to the cult of beauty in aristocratic Europe, until it reached a climax in modern America and Hollywood:

> Nowhere in the world and at no time in history has the idea of romantic love held as much sway over the mind—especially the minds of women—as in contemporary America. It was almost inevitable that the two most bruited romantic episodes of our time should be connected with the American movie industry—the case of Ingrid Bergman in the 1950s and of Elizabeth Taylor in the 1960s. It is worth noting that in both cases the dramatic enactment took place against the backdrop of Italy, with all the romantic memories associated with its historic cities. Miss Taylor's took place in the queen of cities, Rome. Miss Bergman's was linked with Stromboli and its volcanic lava flow.

Lest any readers miss the significance of the metaphor, he went on to add that "this eruptive turbulence is inseparable from the whole notion of romantic love."[37]

Lerner never publicly avowed his own passing part in Taylor's "eruptive turbulence." When Kelley's account of their affair appeared in 1981, he tactfully denied its report of their sexual intimacy.

Kelley stood by her account, insisting that she had quoted him accurately and that he had been very explicit, even boastful, in relating the details she provided. Whether the details were true or invented, he told the same tales to friends. In his *Post* column, he was careful to stress that his meetings with her had all been in the line of journalistic duty. In 1960 he told his readers of going to a boxing match with Taylor and Fisher, explaining that he had spent some time with both of them in London the year before, where he had met the heavyweight contender, Ingemar Johannsen, and his wife. In 1961, he wrote of attending another boxing match, this time in Miami, in Taylor's company. When she came through a life-threatening illness, he visited her and devoted another column to her, describing her as "ravishingly beautiful" and recounting that he had spent several days talking to her during her recovery. "She is deeper, gentler, a bit muted," he rhapsodized. "The fire that has always burned in her is still there, but it is as if it were a more secret fire, drawing its flame from a source on the boundary between life and death, where most of the rest of us have not been." [38]

Liberal Spokesman

Regular readers of Lerner's column turned to him not for culture criticism or because of his rumored romantic forays but for his political commentaries. These were written from the point of view of an American liberal, as the term came to be used from the late 1940s, to denote a strong belief in freedom of thought, equal opportunity, and government regulation of the economy. Although he liked to think of himself as independent-minded and nonpartisan in his affiliations, he was, like most of his readers, strongly committed to certain core policy positions: the post–New Deal politics of an expanding welfare state and the struggle for civil rights and civil liberties, and in foreign policy, containment of communism coupled with the quest for arms control agreements to reduce the dangers of nuclear war. Like many liberals, he began by supporting American intervention in Vietnam and then turned sharply against it. As protests against the war mounted and became entangled with a new youth-oriented counterculture, he found himself increasingly out of touch with a younger generation rebelling against the war and against liberal values. Although he tried to be tolerant of the cultural experimentation of the young, he became a sharp critic of the politics of the New Left of the 1960s, especially its most militant forms.

In the early 1950s, to be a liberal in America was a fairly straight-forward matter on domestic issues, though not necessarily on foreign policy. President Truman's Fair Deal was seen as a postwar contin-uation of FDR's New Deal. Liberal Democrats like Eleanor Roose-velt, Hubert Humphrey, Estes Kefauver, Justice William O. Doug-las, and Adlai Stevenson were the political bellwethers on domestic issues, championing such goals as full employment, steadily in-creasing income for working people, a progressive income tax to narrow the gap between rich and poor, and both civil rights and civil liberties. Under the intellectual guidance of Arthur Schlesinger, Jr., and John Kenneth Galbraith, the newly founded Americans for Democratic Action became an organizational rallying point. In 1948 Lerner did not support Truman's bid for the presidency only be-cause he did not think Truman could win. He also judged him a me-diocre machine politician who was unlikely to carry on the liberal agenda. But when Truman showed so much grit and popular appeal as to win an upset victory, and when he then earned the enmity of forces on the Right that Lerner had always opposed, by interven-ing on the side of labor in the steel industry dispute and promoting his social legislation, Lerner rallied to his side. The fact that the right-wing press spewed out the same hatred for Truman as it had for FDR made Truman seem an especially worthy successor. Later, although he was at first cool to John F. Kennedy, he became a strong supporter of both Kennedy and Lyndon Johnson.

Lerner's views on the Supreme Court were also typically liberal for most of this period. He supported the Court when it defended civil liberties and civil rights, especially when the Warren Court is-sued its landmark school desegregation decision. But he tried to be consistent with his earlier position in criticizing the Court when it went too far in imposing its own political and economic views. In 1952 he irritated Frankfurter by criticizing his conservative col-league, Burton, as "a gentle, insignificant Republican" who "likes to avoid deciding broad Constitutional issues." Frankfurter wrote to rebuke Lerner, saying that this description of Burton "shows how [little] even so informed and discerning a fellow as you knows or can know about the work of the Court." There is not one justice, he went on, "whom I hold in higher esteem." Burton's reluctance to decide Constitutional issues reflected a conscious, not merely personal, choice: "It is an alert effort to obey the rules of adjudica-tion which we all profess, but which too often in the Court's history has, on disastrous assumptions of what the public good requires, been disregarded." [39]

Foreign policy proved far more divisive for liberals, and Lerner was among those who shifted ground. The outbreak of the Cold War caused a rift in their ranks and forced many, including Lerner, onto the defensive against right-wing attacks. Some New Deal stalwarts followed former Vice President Wallace in contending that it was a tragic error to "demonize" the Soviet Union and risk the hard-won peace. They resisted the advice of statesman like Winston Churchill and diplomats like George F. Kennan that it was essential to thwart Stalin's expansionist ambitions by adopting a policy of containment and military deterrence. At first, Lerner straddled both sides of the debate. He agreed with the critics of the Soviet Union that its ideology and form of government were deplorable, but he clung to the hope that the wartime alliance might be preserved through the United Nations and saw the anti-Communist crusade as a mischievous effort intended to energize reaction at home. He sought to distinguish between what was good in the Soviet system—its socialism—and what was bad—its denial of liberty. He was therefore reluctant to make common cause with the anti-Communists even as he refused to align himself with the Wallacites. The best way to deal with the dangers of the Cold War, he thought, was to defuse tensions by diplomacy rather than trigger a nuclear arms race. He agreed with Secretary of State Dean Acheson and Atomic Energy Commission Chairman David Lilienthal that the best way to deal with atomic weapons was to achieve international control in accordance with the proposals advanced at the UN by Ambassador Bernard Baruch. Otherwise, he argued that stress should be put on the Marshall Plan and "Point Four" aid to developing countries, so as to undercut the appeal of undemocratic ideologies, both of the Left and the Right.

In the 1950s, Lerner's attitude changed sharply as he came to recognize that the Soviet Union's expansionist ambitions, coupled with the postwar weakness of Western Europe and the opportunity presented by decolonization posed a real danger to the United States and its allies. Like other liberals, he had been trapped in the middle of the debate over foreign policy, siding fully with neither side, until a series of events—beginning with the conflicts in Iran, Greece, and Turkey, and finally in Korea—forced him to get off the fence. He then became a centrist liberal—of the sort derided by those to the Left as a "Cold War liberal." He supported containment, opposed preventive or preemptive war, and endorsed American participation in limited peripheral wars, as in Korea and Vietnam, to prevent Communist expansion into the Third World. He opposed Secretary of State John Foster Dulles's "brinkmanship" as a reckless threat to peace. He did not agree with those who favored "limited nuclear war" using tactical nuclear weapons in the event deterrence failed. He feared that any war in which nuclear weapons would be used against a nuclear-armed adversary was likely to escalate into an all-out nuclear exchange. As it became clear that nuclear disarmament would remain only a long-term goal, he endorsed reliance on nuclear deterrence and NATO to check Soviet ambitions in Europe, but opposed intervention in Eastern Europe lest it entail nuclear war. How to defend Berlin was a difficult issue for him, but he generally agreed with President Kennedy that an attack on Berlin must be treated as an attack on the entire alliance. "There can be no freedom for the free world," Lerner wrote in 1961, "unless its people learn how to stand together, even for a symbol as unpopular as Berlin." [40]

All liberals, Lerner included, had misgivings about how intensively the Cold War should be fought, especially about the growth of nuclear stockpiles and the danger of nuclear proliferation. Lerner tried to look beyond the arms race and the immediate threat to discern a larger pattern. In 1962, in *The Age of Overkill,* he identified a movement beyond "the power principle" and state sovereignty toward a recognition of the need for collective security based on international law. The struggles over communism and the fate of the developing countries would continue unresolved for at least another generation, he thought, but eventually the political and arms-control dialogue would "transform the containment principle of a mutually poised murderousness into a principle of world collective security." [41]

In developing these views, liberals like Lerner found themselves edging toward the center of the political spectrum, though they remained at odds with conservatives, for whom foreign and domestic policy were two sides of the same coin. To the conservatives, the Cold War was a battle between freedom and state control, and the game was zero-sum: any encroachment of government power diminished the sphere of freedom and vice versa. In their eyes the United States was in grave danger of "creeping socialism" because of the impact of the New Deal. Denouncing liberals as "big spenders" and big taxers, the conservatives launched a counterattack against one after another of the major reforms. The sensational charges of treason against Alger Hiss by Whittaker Chambers threatened to taint the liberal cause, because they seemed to show that the New Deal had been a Trojan Horse for communism— "twenty years of treason," as McCarthy charged. Alistair Cooke aptly noted that the charge put a "generation on trial." Chambers's dramatic production of the "pumpkin papers" made it clear that Hiss had lied under oath and put liberals like Lerner on the defensive. Chambers's *Witness* convinced him that the case against Hiss was "very strong . . . not wholly airtight, but damning enough to make the burden of breaking it a terribly hard one." Although he thought Chambers himself unsavory, Lerner thought the book one of the most important documents of the time.

The espionage trial of Julius and Ethel Rosenberg was a different matter, and in no way an indictment of the New Deal, but it caused tensions of a different sort for Jewish liberals like Lerner. Although he knew that the mostly Jewish readers of the *Post* were upset about the imposition of the death penalty on the Rosenbergs, he initially agreed with the punishment, even though he thought it would make them martyrs for the Communist movement around the world. But when experts testified that the espionage committed by the Rosenbergs had not done as much harm as the government claimed, and as protests mounted against the impending execution, he joined those who vainly urged President Eisenhower to commute the sentence to life imprisonment.

Predictably, Lerner also became a champion of Israel in its struggle to maintain its precarious independence. Some liberals, like George Ball, were inclined to think that both American interests and concern for peoples in the developing countries (in particular in the Middle East) required a "more even-handed" policy. The columnist Dorothy Thompson, who had been outspoken during the war in denouncing the Nazi crimes against the Jews of Europe, angered American Jews by criticizing American support for Israel. She wrote to Lerner to complain that for expressing this view she was unjustly being accused of being anti-Jewish (and even of being an Arab secret agent) and threatened with an economic boycott by Zionists. Warning that the methods being used by Zionists against her "will ultimately redound against all Jews," she raised the issue of dual loyalty, arguing that Israel could not "go on claiming that all Jews, throughout the world, owe a special loyalty under all circumstances, and one that takes precedence over other loyalties, to a foreign state, without getting repercussions." [42]

In reply Lerner assured Thompson that he abhorred boycotts against individuals "without reservation." He had spoken out in defense of her right to express her views and would continue to do so, but he took exception to her characterization of Jewish support for Israel as "Zionist fanaticism":

> My own experience of working with a number of Jewish organizations that you would describe as Zionist is that they are fighting hard for the survival of several million people who are themselves the residue of millions of others who were butchered. When this kind of genocide is attempted against a people, and almost succeeds, it is hard to expect their survivors to keep quiet or always to be moderate on issues of life and death. Surely you know this, yet I miss the recognition of it in your letter. I have the same response when Southerners—either racist or moderates—complain to me about the activities of the NAACP.

Her claim that Zionists oppose America's friendship with other Middle Eastern countries, he added, did not describe his own view or that of the overwhelming majority of those considering themselves Zionists. He rejected her charge of dual loyalty as well:

> [T]he implication of what you write is that American Jews will feel very sorry for their behavior because of their opposing the power politics of oil and air bases and advocating what seems to them the only way to prevent a Middle East war. I have in my time taken many positions on American foreign policy, and some were right and some were proved wrong, but always I have done so out of a deep belief in the rightness of what I advocated. The position I take on the Middle East I should take equally in the case of Burma—a country and people that I love dearly, but with which I have no ties of kinship or religion. I should consider myself a poor American and a very poor human being if I did not speak out as I do, and if I did not exhort others to do so. Surely what applies to me applies to other American Jews as well, even if they happen to be—as I am not—members and officials of Zionist organizations.
>
> You say that you never have discriminated against Jews and do not hate them. I accept your word for it. But that is not the only question. There is also the question of what are the consequences for the whole of the Israeli community and for Jewish communities elsewhere—as indeed for the peace of the world—of the position you

are taking. It is here that I ask you to examine your conscience, as all of us who write for audiences must continually examine our consciences.[43]

The End of Ideology

In the 1950s, Lerner was among those who became convinced that a new consensus had developed with respect to American economic policy. In effect he agreed with the sociologist Daniel Bell that an "end of ideology" had been reached in which there was widespread agreement on principles, even if there was still disagreement over the means of achieving them. Echoes of the old controversies remained but only because of a lag in social recognition:

> Something interesting has happened in the controversies over our American democracy: The area of controversy has moved steadily away from economic issues to those of ethnic equality (civil rights), foreign policy, national survival and the presumed threats to it (hence the controversy about treason and traitors, and the problems of judicial safeguards they raise). The days of bitter dispute over free silver, collective bargaining, the farm problem, social legislation, deficit spending and the New Deal are largely over. This does not mean that commentators have stopped writing about them, but that (as [John Kenneth] Galbraith shrewdly suggests in his *Economics and the Art of Controversy*) the sounds of battle continue even after both sides have largely agreed on the stakes of conflict.[44]

He saw the Eisenhower years as years of vacuum—a return to the Coolidge-Harding-Hoover philosophy of letting nature take its course: "The harsh fact for a harsh age is that our fate is being ground out in these years of the vacuum. In the three great areas of policy—domestic economics, foreign relations and nuclear weapons—the watchword is to stay as we were and react (always too late) to events not willed by our decision makers. In dealing with recession, they do nothing at all. In foreign policy, John Foster Dulles merely trusts to holding firm. In nuclear policy, Lewis Strauss and Edward Teller act to frustrate disarmament." [45] The 1950s "will be remembered as the decade in which humanity caught a glimpse of its own possible brutish ending and shrank back from what it saw in the mirror of the future." Nevertheless he predicted, wrongly as it turned out, that the 1960s would see the spread of the bomb among the dozen or more countries on the verge of being able to produce it.[46]

In the 1960s, Lerner became an outspoken supporter of the containment policy, and of the use of military force in peripheral conflicts where it was necessary and likely to be successful. Convinced that the Soviet Union was indeed an aggressive totalitarian state whose aim was to undermine freedom wherever it could, he thought that the United States had to take the lead in opposing its expansionism. Unlike some conservatives, who wanted to see communism "rolled back" regardless of the risk, if necessary by a preemptive nuclear war, most liberals believed it was possible to contain the Soviet Union without risking nuclear war. Lerner sought to stake out this middle ground. Despite the embarrassment caused by the U-2 incident and the resulting cancellation of a major summit between Eisenhower and Khruschev, he defended the American policy of gaining military intelligence in order to maintain vigilance. There is no use denying, he observed, that "the democratic imperium and the Communist imperium are locked in a struggle." [47] Outside Europe, he thought the struggle allowed for a more militant form of interventionism, on the model of the Korean War, where it might be needed to rescue friendly states determined to maintain their independence or to take the side of domestic forces resisting injustice: "Whatever affects basic human rights everywhere in the world cannot be a purely internal affair." [48] But he was leery of military adventurism that might backfire. In January 1961—several months before the attempted invasion of Cuba at the Bay of Pigs—he warned that an American-sponsored invasion would be a fiasco. *The Nation* had printed reports that anti-Castro guerrillas were being trained for an American-led invasion of the island, and a *New York Times* reporter, Paul Kennedy, thought that preparations were under way for hostilities between Guatemala and Cuba. Lerner read between the lines and realized that anti-Castro guerrillas were being trained under American auspices for an invasion of Cuba. He foresaw that such an invasion would fail and warned against it:

> To overthrow a regime like Castro's, its enemies must agree on leaders—which they have not done. They must also combine internal revolt with invasion. It is too early for the first and too late for the second. An invasion now would be bloodily repulsed, with a howling triumph for Fidelism and a disaster for American influence, whether or not the U.S. kept clear of it.

Although a revolution was bound to come, he added, a premature uprising would hurt rather than help. It would "feed the fires of Fidelism in the grand arc of Latin-American discontent, justifying . . . Castro's indictment of the U.S. as a bully-boy imperialist." Instead he counseled patience and a shift of attention to the rest of the hemisphere that would confound Castro's intentions.[49]

When the disastrous invasion did come to pass, rather than crow about his prescience he defended the young and inexperienced president and his liberal civilian advisers. Praising the gallantry of the Cubans who died in the invasion, he lauded Kennedy for manfully accepting responsibility, and refrained from condemning what had been done. "What is worth doing," he wrote, "is worth doing even badly."[50] He disagreed with Lippmann that the "new men" around Kennedy should resign for showing such poor judgment. The democracies, he argued, must not limit themselves to passive containment of aggression; "everything was wrong about the Bay of Pigs but the intention."[51]

Vietnam—the Quagmire of the Liberals

If the Vietnam conflict was, as the reporter David Halberstam suggested, a "quagmire" for the country, it was especially so for centrist liberals like Lerner, who initially defended the American role in Vietnam. Having endorsed intervention in Korea, liberals like Lerner reluctantly followed Kennedy and Johnson into intervention in Vietnam. When President Kennedy first sent Secretary McNamara to Vietnam in 1961 to assess what sort of American aid was needed, Lerner did not mince words in endorsing American involvement. He agreed with the view that the Communists were pursuing a global strategy using "anticolonial wars of liberation" to whittle down the bulwarks of free world power. The West had "no choice but to answer these wars in kind." War was an evil, but this sort of war was a lesser evil.[52] When President Ngo Dhin Diem was overthrown in a CIA-sponsored coup, Lerner did not flinch. The ruling clique, he wrote, by waging war against the Buddhists, risked losing popular support. Kennedy, having failed to bring Castro down, could not afford to let another dictatorship mock U.S. power. "Let's face it," he wrote, "this has become, whether we like it or not, an American war."[53] As the American involvement intensified under Johnson, he became even more resolute. It was wrong to abandon Vietnam "to the mercies of the Vietcong." It would also be wrong, he thought, to extend the fighting to North Vietnam, because that would make the war a massive conventional war and risk Chinese involvement. Neutralization of North and South Vietnam might be an option, though it was "hopeless to conceive of them being united in our lifetime." The United States had no choice but to help Vietnam defend itself with whatever means were necessary. Conceding that it was a "nasty" war, he argued that "it would be a perfectly feasible (and completely 'nasty') limited war."[54] If the United States were to withdraw from South Vietnam and the country were to come under control of the Viet Minh, the consequences would be disastrous in southeast Asia and elsewhere in the world.[55]

Lerner was scarcely the only liberal commentator to support the government's policy in Vietnam into 1964. The editorial writers of the *New York Times* took the same view. As Harrison Salisbury has remarked, "There was no American antiwar movement at this time. No bands in the streets. No sit-ins. No colleges ablaze with indignation . . . There was no major editorial opinion against the war."[56]

Lerner often reiterated his support of the Johnson administration's war policy, attacking both the argument for all-out war advanced by the Alsops and the antiwar views of Lippmann, Hans Morgenthau, Senators Wayne Morse, Ernest Gruening, and Frank Church. The stakes in Vietnam, he thought, were very high, and the Communists were counting on a failure of American will. Although it would be no easy matter to sustain a willingness to fight in Vietnam, since no war is easy for Americans, especially in times of prosperity, he thought that American leadership in the world would be gravely weakened by a pullout. He realized that the cost would be high; domestic support could waver and decline because the war might take another three or four years; and the continuation of casualties, the draft, and the drain on the budget would strain public willingness to maintain the fight. It was a false argument, he thought, to say that America could not contain communism everywhere in the world; the country was managing to do so successfully wherever the challenge had arisen. Besides, the war would not be ended by an American withdrawal. The United States would only have to return later and fight a more difficult and dangerous war. Despite ridicule of the domino theory by critics of American policy, "an American withdrawal from Vietnam would have waves of confusion far beyond Vietnam. It would throw Laos and Cambodia wildly to Peking, make Sukarno's residual resistance to communism in Indonesia impossible, doom Malaysia. It would make the position of Thailand and the Philippines difficult." It would also "cast a dark shadow over India and Burma," and Vietnam itself would not be able to resist Chinese control. Although he initially opposed bombing North Vietnam, lest it trigger the entry of Chinese "volunteers" and enlarge the scope of the war, when the Johnson administration did bomb North Vietnam, he defended the policy as one of "limited airstrikes" and expressed confidence it would not provoke Chinese entry and would bring the enemy to the peace table. The Johnson policy, he thought, was exactly right—tough-minded, not tender-minded, one that "refuses to cut and run and faces the challenge of Communist expansion in Southeast Asia." [57]

To the student protesters he pointed out that China, not America, was the imperialist power in Asia. An American withdrawal, he argued, would vindicate Mao's view that the United States was a paper tiger. To suppose that China would not be able to digest Vietnam was to take a bad gamble. Why did the protesters demand only that United States unilaterally cease its bombing; why did they not demand reciprocity from the Viet Cong? To the complaint that in Vietnam the United States was hardly coming to the rescue of democracy, Lerner answered that this was a fight to preserve national independence, which alone could lead to democracy. "Communism is a one-way street," he argued, "with no return allowed. Non-Communist regimes can be changed and improved, as the examples of Brazil, Peru, and Chile showed." The United States was not fighting, as the students charged, to prevent land reform in Vietnam or to maintain economic hegemony over it. Besides, it was the other side, not ours, that was refusing to negotiate. Did the integrity of American democracy at home depend on getting out of Vietnam? "No, it depends on not flinching from the reality principle, in showing that democracy has what it takes for survival against ruthless forces both at home and abroad." [58]

Lerner's support of the Johnson policy embroiled him with his eldest son, Michael, then an undergraduate at Harvard. In an article in the *Harvard Crimson*, and in a private letter, Michael took issue with his father's views. Pointedly invoking William James's distinction between the tough-minded and the tender-minded, frequently cited by his father, Michael contended that "the liberal establishment" was deluding itself in supposing that it was tough-minded to imagine that the United States could impose its system and its control over every country in the world. Michael denied that the war continued only because Vietnam received aid from China and the Soviet Union and contended that the United States was taking the

side there of the landlords, not social reform. He rebuked liberals
who were applying outworn lessons from containment in Europe:

> It is hard for those old-line liberals who watched what the Russians
> did in East Europe to alter their conception of how Communism op-
> erates, or to learn to distinguish between Communisms and make
> decisions based on those distinctions. Yet the time has come when
> the learning process must take place.[59]

In a private letter, Michael disputed his father's view that the
Vietcong was not acting independently or under the control of Hanoi but out of supranational Communist discipline, arguing that the
evidence suggested strongly that if the Vietcong was controlled
by anyone, it was by the North Vietnamese. The evidence also suggested, he added, that the Vietcong was an indigenous force. He
strongly doubted that the Vietnamese would allow the Chinese to
take control of their country. If the United States struck an agreement with Hanoi and pulled out, the North would very likely unify
the country without allowing Chinese control.[60]

Lerner acknowledged the *Crimson* piece and the letter and answered both at length, noting that he was proud of his son's "reason-
ableness and maturity." He objected first to the equation of American and Soviet imperialism—perhaps forgetting that he himself
had made the same equation two decades earlier. "To define imperialism merely as " 'ideological and economic hegemony' simply
won't do: America stands in no way to profit from it." Nor had the
United States attempted to extend its hegemony everywhere out of
some Communist-style grand design. Michael had cited I. F. Stone's
figures to show that the Vietnamese were receiving little help from
China and Russia. Lerner doubted the evidence: "I know too much
about Stone's statistical methods from *PM* days to place much reliance on his figures now." Besides, that "does not go to the heart of
the matter. The movement has a double origin: in real social protest
(to be found in very social system, including the Communist if it
were tolerated), and in Communist launching and oversight; it has
since taken on an autonomous energy, but its roots and fruits belong substantially with Communist power." The United States had
not fought reforms, he contended; it had been pursuing a land reform program since 1955. It was proper to distinguish between the
varieties of communism, but that did not help in Vietnam, "unless
you assume that an 'independent Communism' is likely to emerge
in Southeast Asia as a result of American withdrawal—which is a

big assumption." To suppose that the United States is involved in Vietnam to protect investments is "tender-minded archaic mechanical Marxism that has no relation to present fact." [61]

A year later, as the war dragged on and the hold of the South Vietnamese government became more and more tenuous, and as Arthur Schlesinger, Jr., whose views he respected very much, publicly urged, in a *Look* magazine symposium, that the war be ended somehow, Lerner began to have second thoughts. "Looking back at the whole tortured history of the war," he wrote, "it now seems clear that we need not have gone in as deeply as we did." He no longer thought of the war, as he had previously, as a moral crusade on behalf of freedom and as one that the United States could afford to carry on. The war was no more immoral than other wars, he observed, "but in terms of political prudence it would have been better to stop at some point, before the war becomes overwhelmingly American." He no longer thought the war would have a domino effect, the non-Communist states of the region having proved stronger than had been earlier envisaged. He knew that he was backtracking from his earlier stand, and he did not deny that he was doing so: "This is hindsight, but it is worth saying, even if it means eating some of my own earlier words." But he also noted that none of those taking part in the *Look* symposium endorsed a unilateral American withdrawal, and he did not do so either. He continued to think that Johnson and the American people would have enough tenacity to continue the war until the Communists would finally realize that they could not win and would have to agree to a negotiated settlement.[62] In July of 1967 he finally expressed deep misgivings about the war:

> We are all caught in an endless, impossible war which strips us of some of the best energies of our youth, drains us of our manpower, our economic power, our scientific talent, our executive talent. Although the battlefield is small, the war is like a big maw swallowing up everything. It dampens what would otherwise be the ebullient energies of a society in a process of great revolutionary changes. It involves us in bitter internal strife. It erodes the belief of students and teachers, writers and artists, in their society. It confuses the moral sense of the nation as a whole.

And he added: "What makes it all worse is that there is no tolerably clear way out." It was obvious that Johnson would not be willing to preside over a unilateral withdrawal. Neither would any likely Republican replacement. The prospect was therefore bleak: "What this amounts to is that America is caught in an endless, fruitless war, with no exit." [63]

By August 1967 he came close to agreeing with those in favor of a pullout. He could not bring himself to criticize the architects of American war policy, whom he praised as fellow "humanists," but he could not restrain his misgivings. "I fear they have gotten stuck in the war's mire more and have allowed their options to become unduly narrowed." Perhaps, he wondered, they should blockade Hanoi harbor, even at the risk of angering the Russians, so as to see whether it would bring the North Vietnamese to the negotiating table. If it did not, "then America should use its other option, and write the war off as a massive blunder." [64] In October he grew so uneasy as to observe that Secretary of State Dean Rusk's claim that the issue was containment of China "seems pretty tinny to me." In November, while praising Johnson's advisers as "humanist" in intention, and insisting still that American leaders had the tenacity to stay the course, he pointed out that the worst cost of a "war of attrition" was "the anguished splitting of the nation." [65] When Vietnam became no longer Lyndon Johnson's war but Richard Nixon's, he became if anything still more critical. After the My Lai massacre, he urged that the nation "get out of the war—systematically, unequivocally, with every possible dispatch" [66] though he still expected the pullout to come through a negotiated phased settlement.

Coming to Grips with the '60s

As Lerner's change of mind indicated, supporting the Vietnam war was hardly a comfortable position for liberals to take, and in increasing numbers they broke ranks on the issue, as the war dragged on and brought sharp polarization and conflict. The tension was brought home to him in Chicago at the time of the 1968 Democratic convention, when he found himself caught up in the melee that erupted outside the convention hall. The polarization had the effect of driving a wedge between liberals and radicals. The liberals found themselves rejected by the New Left because they were presumably just as much a part of "the establishment" as conservatives. For their part, liberals like Lerner were angered by the tactics of the radicals, who deliberately chose "direct action" and confrontation over electoral politics and civil debate. It was a replay of the tensions of the Popular Front in the 1930s except that this time none of the liberals had any patience with the antics of the radicals. Lerner found himself trapped between the attacks of the New Left and the conservatives, a 1950s centrist unwilling to move in either direction. He was especially appalled by the outcome of the New Politics conference in September 1967, which had been taken over by black power militants who had proceeded to adopt an anti-American and anti-Semitic platform. The whole affair struck him "as the end of the radical left in any meaningful sense in America, at least in this decade." [67] It was really more the end of his tolerance for the radical Left than the end of the Left. He denounced the Left's attack on Governor Pat Brown in California for helping elect Ronald Reagan, comparing it with the behavior of the German Communists whose assaults on the Weimar Republic helped bring Hitler to power.[68] He had no sympathy with the philosophers of the counterculture. In 1968, he devoted one of his columns to criticism of the "moralizing gurus" such as Paul Goodman, whose teachings, he complained, only got young people into trouble.

Goodman wrote to object:

> I assure you we are equally sensitive to the right of the young to risk heavy penalties only on their own initiative. But you do not understand the realistic situation. The young come to us—it is not the other way; they have made up their minds but are solely in need of support.

It was essential, Goodman added, to say frankly what the political facts were about the war and the draft. At an earlier time, Lerner might well have been on the other side of the barricades. "Frankly," he concluded, "your own avowed policy of the gran rifiuto is contemptible."

By the end of the decade, Lerner had become unqualifiedly critical of the New Left, though he recognized that the turmoil of the decade could not be laid entirely at its door. The '60's, he wrote, had been a "crazy, contradictory, confused, mixed-up, too-much decade . . . a decade of wildly implausible tragedies . . . a decade of assassinations, riots and confrontations and of internal violence—a monstrous chamber of horrors, a wax museum of outrages, among which the Biafran starvings, the killings at Hue and My Lai, and the cruelties of the 'cultural revolution' in China represented heights (or depths) of the desensitized or impassioned." [69] But none of this turmoil either explained or justified the "generational revolt" reflected in the New Left. He rejected the "stock liberal" notion that the

times were out of joint and the young were showing how to set
things right. "The truth is," he wrote, "that some families are far
too permissive, mainly among the upper middle and professional
classes, while others—mainly the blue collar and some of the white
collar families—are too constrictive."[70] Those who succumbed to
"infantile leftism" were grossly misguided in supposing that a militant student movement could revolutionize American workers or
that the university could become the base for a seizure of social
power.[71]

Increasingly, and in almost every respect, he found himself re-
pelled by the new radicals and their "counter-culture." As to the
"hippies," "their language bothers me in its impoverished repeti-
tiveness of phrase." The drugs they suppose will expand consciousness "may become crutches to hobble the free vigor of mind and
imagination." Most of all, he was "dismayed by the failure to develop a sense of limits, with an 'anything goes' result in word and
deed and code, as much in the disruptions of the campus as in the
exploration of drugs." Students who disrupted campus activities for
political purposes should be reasoned with, but if reason failed to
dissuade them, they should not be allowed to prevent the campus
from functioning. If the terrorist Weathermen should be considered "radicals," "give me the humanist liberal, with no apologies
and no defensiveness about his humanism or his frame of limits."
Street demonstrations may be permissible, so long as they are non-
violent, but when mass marches are designed to provoke confrontations, they usher in the sort of anarchy that invites autocracy and
repression:

> There are ghosts from history that stalk through our minds: Na-
> poleon's "whiff of grapeshot" that dispersed an assembled crowd;
> the Left-Wingers and the Brown Shirts in brawling confrontations
> during the Weimar Republic in the 1920's; the crowds on the streets
> in the Arab capitals, pressing their governments to a harsher fight
> against Israel; the millions of teen-agers marshaled on the streets
> as "shock troops" in China's recent "cultural revolution." . . . It is
> because of these memories that I have some anxieties about seeing
> policy—even peace policy—made in the streets.[72]

In the polarization that resulted from the confrontational tactics
of the New Left, Lerner, once characterized as a dangerous radical,
found himself lampooned in *Ramparts,* the radical monthly. In one
installment of a regular feature, entitled "Sorel's Bestiary," the

artist Edward Sorel drew a caricature of Lerner's face on a "Common Boar (pontificus maximus)" and underneath offered a snide satiric caption:

> The Common Boar (or Slow Lerner as he is sometimes called) can be recognized by his short stature, unkempt appearance, and his small but sensitive snout, which enables him to tell exactly which way the wind is blowing. He is also known for swimming along with the tide, which may account for the fact that he once jumped head-long into the Bay of Pigs. Psychoanalytic naturalists attribute this behavior to intense Castro-ation anxiety. Although not a hunter by disposition, this pig once joined with the lower species to prey upon the Horn-Rimmed Rosenberg (vita extincta).
>
> Pontificus is in great demand for cocktail parties, television panels, and Hadassah gatherings due to his ability to deal with the insignificant in a profound and condescending manner. While boars are quite common in the academic community, this one must feed alone at the academic trough due to his malodorous position on Vietnam. The young boar is covered with distinctive Marx, but the mature animal would rather be fed than red.[73]

From Harvard, Martin Peretz, then identified with the New Left, wrote loyally to complain that the lampoon was "malicious and in bad taste" and the innuendoes false. (Indeed, the claim that Lerner supported the Bay of Pigs invasion fails to note that he warned against it.) He wrote, Peretz said, not just out of filial duty but with respect for the honesty with which Lerner came to his points of view.[74] Lerner himself later dismissed the attack as coming from a "shrill bizarre sheet." [75] Later in the decade, he would find it "incredible that this form of infantile oppositionism should ever have taken hold on the American mind." [76]

In the mid-'70s, Lerner outlined a book that would examine the decade tentatively entitled *Latter-Day America: Death Drives and Life Force.* In it he intended to extend his analysis of American civilization to take account of what was happening in this tumultuous decade. Although he never completed the book, he drafted an opening chapter that may well represent the most perceptive understanding he had of the decade. "The American air," it began, "is full of constant talk of crises—war crisis, campus crisis, race crisis, constitutional crisis, energy crisis—and their whole spawn." Crises are testings, he went on, whether of a person or of a civilization. But it seemed to him that American civilization had entered a phase of chronic crisis and continuous testing. The crux of the reason was that "a society committed to the fulfillment of the democratic dream should be committed also to the dynamics of constant and continuing change." This was of course the underlying if not fully developed theme of *America as a Civilization,* and it is therefore not surprising that it should have emerged again under the stress of the obvious challenges of the '60s. There had been earlier periods of crisis—in the runaway pace of the 1830s and early 1840s, the guilt felt over an imperialist war in the 1850s, constitutional crisis during the run-up to the Civil War and in the impeachment struggle of the late 1860s, and of course during the New Deal. But he was convinced that "no one period in American history combined so many forms of tension and testing as the fifteen years from John Kennedy's election in 1960 to the closing pages of the Watergate agony in 1975."

These crises faced by Americans had a world-historical significance, Lerner thought, because "the American" was still the archetypal man of the modern world, "summing up its best and worst energies, serving as test and model even for his detractors." The test of this or any other society would be how it rides out the crisis period. The fact that the country had survived and even profited from a host of setbacks augured well for the future, though the modern crises were more divisive than most past crises. They were "polarization crises" which threatened to divide the society and undermine its basic beliefs and institutions. On most issues, he thought, democracies do not have to achieve consensus in order to function, because most people do not care about most issues. In America, moreover, social memory is blessedly short and has a generally benign function:

> Even the interesting issues around which passions have swirled—abortion, busing, gun-control, marijuana, monochrome public housing, quotas—lose their fire after a time and are replaced by others. They may even serve a useful purpose by giving their partisans, on the one side or the other, something to care deeply enough about so that life doesn't lose its savor for them. The remarkable thing about the free-wheeling, change-ridden, pluralist American society is not that it generates such divisive issues but that it moves on from one to another with a minimum of residual scars. Or at least, the "issue" scars die with the people who carry them. They are not passed on, generation to generation, as religious hatreds are, or sectional grievances, or racial resentments, or class differences, or the heavy oppressive burden of poverty.

But the modern issue debates seemed more worrisome because they revealed a deeper sense of social division—a division over basic values and life purpose:

There can be little doubt that there is a more pervasive and continuing sense of strain and discontent in latter-day America than there ever was in earlier America, whatever crises it successfully survived. The tensions arising from disillusionment, anxiety, guilt, and pessimism can be more corrosive than those arising from hardship, hard ground, and class and sectional conflict. Hence the fact that Americans managed to resolve their earlier crises, and were even strengthened by them, is no assurance that they will be equally capable of resolving the crises of a very different character that may lie ahead. In that sense the American future is problematic.

Lerner tried, however, to discern a potentially positive outcome. Perhaps the turmoil had a revolutionary potential, sprawling, diffuse, and nondirected as it seemed. A case could be made, he thought, for the notion that the "new consciousness" Charles Reich described, in *The Greening of America*, was a kind of renaissance, and that the moral elements in the movement constituted a kind of reformation. In the '50s and '60s Lerner had begun to explore the new frontier of sexual candor, beginning with the research of Kinsey and such cultural phenomena as Genet's play about sexual perversity, *The Balcony*, and Federico Fellini's film, *La Dolce Vita*. As yet, however, he would praise them only for presenting sexuality in realistic terms. Fellini, he wrote, had produced "an inspired documentary of the diverse and distorted ways in which *Eros* expresses itself in a society which seeks to imprison it but secretly worships what it imprisons." [77] But he expressed concern at the lack of a moral framework in the film. He had no respect for Harold Robbins's steamy best-seller about Hollywood, *The Carpetbaggers*, which he saw as a mechanical description of sexual escapades and violence wholly lacking in a vision of life. There was a hint of a more complex view of the subject in his initial encounter with the neo-Freudian thinking of Norman O. Brown's *Life against Death*, in which "the plea is for breaking through the crust of restraint—not just for individual life expressiveness, but out of the conviction that it is the only way to cure a sick society and world." There was much in this message, he thought, with important bearing on the lives of most Americans:

I think the lives of most Americans, in their secret hearts, are dominated by love and the lack of it, by sex and the anxieties and repressions linked with it, and by the loneliness of people who will settle for something less than love and sex—simply for companionship and a bit of warmth.[78]

In 1970, he was still leery of endorsing the "sexual revolution" though not necessarily its ultimate objectives: "I should prefer to move slowly toward the total abolition of sexual restraints, as one might feel one's way, by degrees, into icy or scalding water." The pace of change was too fast, too much of a shock to the social system.[79] It was this fascination with *Eros* in all its dimensions, sexual and social, and with its expression in American mores, that was to preoccupy the next stage of his life.

EIGHT

Eros in California

In 1974, as he began his seventh decade, Lerner entered a new phase of his teaching career and of his intellectual and personal life. He kept up his interest in politics, the primary focus of his newspaper column. Increasingly, however, he was drawn into the vortex of ideas and experimentation spun off by the "sexual revolution" and the increasing popularity of new forms of psychotherapy. He had already begun to experience some of the novelties of life in California. Now he spent more time there, teaching graduate courses, becoming a frequent guest and resident sage at Hugh Hefner's "Playboy Mansion West" in Los Angeles, and pondering the meaning of the changes in values and behavior both he and the country were experiencing.

But Lerner did more than just ponder. In California he adopted a much more adventurous life-style than he was prepared to endorse in his New York newspaper column. There he remained an advocate of what he characterized as humanistic family values, defending the open discussion of sexuality but not sexual license, erotic literature but not pornography, and strongly favoring family ties over evanescent "relationships" and sexual promiscuity. Meanwhile, his own bi-coastal way of life came to resemble the plot of the film comedy, *Captain's Paradise,* in which Alec Guinness plays a sea captain with

a properly English homemaker wife in one port and a passionate
Mediterranean lover in another—except that Lerner did not confine himself to one paramour.

In deliberate defiance of the aging process, he set out to prove that
he was as vigorous as ever. He kept up the same busy pace as before,
wrote his column regularly, from wherever he happened to be,
taught and lectured widely, read voraciously, embarked on new writing projects, kept close touch with his children, maintained his
home and friendships in New York, and entered into new relationships with women on the West Coast. He often bragged about the rejuvenating effect of all these activities. "I mean to die young as late
as possible," he wrote determinedly in a journal, "hopefully in my
90s, conceivably after 100." Serious illnesses frustrated this ambition and ultimately denied him more extended longevity, but almost until the end he pursued both work and women despite all
obstacles. "I was in the midst of an autumnal period of sexual and
intellectual flowering," he would say in 1988, "and I loved the sense
of openness and infinite possibilities I found in California. It was a
tumultuous and exciting time, and I was living a very Faustian life,
reaching out in every direction, living hard in every way. But with
great zest and exultation." [1]

California became for Lerner, as it did for many others in these
years, a metaphor for novelty, renewal, and uninhibited behavior—
the national El Dorado in which guilt-free happiness was available
to everyone willing to shed eastern inhibitions. "New York," he
wrote in a column datelined La Jolla, "stands as a symbol of economic power, the intellectual elite and the communications empire.
Washington stands for political power and the political elite. California is the end of the road where extremes meet, illusions fuse and
anything is possible." Intrigued by Norman O. Brown's inquiry into
the clash between the two Freudian metaforces, *Eros* and *Thanatos*,
love and death, he saw each of the three places as "a source of decay
and the death drive" and at the same time as "an envelope through
which the life force bursts, streaming across the nation. The point
about America, which both its haters and lovers miss, is that the
death drive and the life force operate in it together, interlocked in a
mortal embrace." Although he could never give up New York, where
his roots went deepest, he looked forward to finding renewed vigor
in California, "the Newfound-land of Americans, whose dreams
start and end with it, whose violence and creativeness seem part of

its backdrop, and who feel less absurd about acting out their fantasy life here than wherever they come from." [2]

California seemed to be the symbol of a profound change in the American way of life, and Lerner wanted to understand what was happening and be a part of it. The sociologist Daniel Bell had pointed out that America was moving into the postindustrial stage of history, leaving behind the struggles of the industrial era between capital and labor. The new knowledge-based economy would conquer scarcity, greatly enlarge the middle class, and provide an unprecedented degree of leisure. Herbert Marcuse foresaw that the liberation from scarcity would lead to a new liberation in which Freud's pleasure principle would replace the "reality principle" of the work ethic and "surplus repression." With Marcuse and Brown, Lerner thought of *Eros* as the life-force behind not only the sex drive but all creativity and all striving for unity. "I think Freud was right in seeing the double heritage in which man has been endowed—the life-affirming and the life-denying," he wrote in a column.[3] "We have to work with the endowment we have but shift it toward *Eros* rather than *Thanatos*" by building "connections of trust and empathy." Lerner sought to make himself a popular exponent of this utopian vision and a participant observer in the movement to realize it. By experiencing it firsthand, he hoped to explain it in social scientific terms that would complement the philosophical analyses. In 1981, he described this intention in a magazine article:

> The California sector of my life, and my long and strong friendship there with Hugh Hefner, at whose mansion I often stay, have occasioned some surprised comment in the press and raised eyebrows in the academies. In a recent piece on me, *People* magazine seemed understandably absorbed with photos of the young beauties at the mansion who humor an aging man, remarking that I had become a "sex symbol in my 70's." Even Bill Moyers, in several hours during which we talked about Presidents, civilizations and Eros, kept coming back to how I manage my bicoastal life.
>
> My answer is—with delight. They are counterpoint to each other. I couldn't live without either. Bicoastal living, or even bipolar living in space and on the hard, good Earth, may well be the wave of the future—if flying costs permit. I love the excitement of New York intellectual life and cultural life, its stirrings and strivings, which I shall never give up, and the rooted and secure bonding with my wife and our children. I love also the warmth and freedom of

my newfoundland—that curious, exhilarating subculture of California, which no one has yet grasped in its full meaning.[4]

This was a version intended for popular consumption which only hinted at what he understood as the "full meaning" of this "newfoundland." The deeper significance of the remark was that the Max Lerner who had once been a political radical was now intent on remaking himself, in this late stage of life, into a cultural radical. He wanted to be in the vanguard of a great cultural transformation, just as he had earlier wanted to be in the vanguard of political change. Whereas Veblen, and later Marx, had given focus to his first radicalism, now he turned for guidance to Freud. Already in 1962, toward the end of *The Age of Overkill*, he had discussed Freud's speculation that existence was somehow pervaded by a never-ending struggle between the instincts of life and death. Lerner plainly felt a kinship with the Freud of the later years. As others turned to religion late in life, both these emancipated Jewish humanists turned to what the Germans speak of as *Lebensphilosophie* and *Weltanschauung*. After expounding Freud's views, he added that he had done so because no one had raised a better case against the easy optimism of those who suppose that human nature is pacific and that civilization represents a gradual triumph of reason and compassion over instinct and aggressiveness. Lerner's friend Robert Ardrey, in *African Genesis*, had reinforced Freud's arguments about a primitive death instinct by showing that the basic drives of animals in their natural habitat are those of hunger, territoriality, sexual possessiveness, the need for enemies as well as friends, and the drive to fight both for territory and for status. Man, Ardrey contended, is in his origins the most sophisticated predator the world has ever known. Lerner agreed with Ardrey and thought that modern humanity's persistent war-like behavior made Freud's pessimism especially compelling. But Lerner also believed that because of the plasticity of human nature and the countervailing power of the life-force, social institutions could be created that would use the means of violence human beings had developed to police behavior in order to preserve civilization. In this way the aggressive impulse might be sublimated into institutional mechanisms of collective security, turning the death instinct into a force for preserving life.

Having urged this dialectical notion as a basis for controlling international conflict, Lerner now set out to make it the basis of a philosophy of life in which *Eros* would be understood as a vital force which, if properly nurtured and expressed, could create a healthier and happier way of life free of irrational fears, neuroses, and possessiveness. It was this erotic impulse, he maintained, that continued to drive him and would keep him youthful and productive until the end. "Socrates said that the unexamined life is not worth living," he quipped to Hefner, "I would add that the unlived life is not worth examining," a witticism he had once heard from a college student. The "lived life" he had in mind included writing and teaching along with "play," including sexual expression and experimentation. This synthesis of work and play, he speculated, would also characterize American society, as it moved from the industrial to the postindustrial age. Although he recognized that the Cold War continued to pose a grave menace to civilization, he had dealt with this question as well as he could in his previous writings; now he wanted to address the working out of the "pleasure principle" in the American society of the 1970s and beyond.

Going Native, California Style

Lerner's decision to commute to California was to some extent forced upon him. He was determined to keep up his teaching career and needed to make up for lost income when he was compelled to retire from Brandeis at the age of seventy, a decision for which he never forgave President Sachar. At first he took temporary teaching jobs at the University of Florida in Gainesville and Pomona College in Claremont, California. Then, in 1974, he accepted an open-ended appointment as Distinguished Professor of Human Sciences at the United States International University in southern California. Though not then itself an especially distinguished university, USIU bolstered its faculty by appointing superannuated academic stars like Lerner and the psychologists Rollo May and Carl Rogers. The school offered both undergraduate and graduate programs at three domestic campuses—one located in the outskirts of San Diego, another in Los Angeles, a third at Irvine in Orange County—and another overseas outside London. Although accredited, the university was in such precarious financial condition that it was sometimes referred to locally as "USIOU" and eventually came near to bankruptcy until it was rescued and soundly restructured early in the 1990s. Lerner taught his courses in a program grandly styled "the Graduate School of Human Behavior," where students prepared for careers in such fields as psychological counseling and business management. He threw himself into his teaching with the same zeal he had always shown and the same knack for making students feel that he was opening the world to them, dazzling them with his ability to synthesize the elements of knowledge and draw them into his own patterns of thinking. He was especially pleased to be offering seminars, because they were more lively and interactive than lecture courses, and to be teaching older, career-minded graduate students after a quarter-century of teaching callow undergraduates with little experience of the relationships of love and marriage he now wished to explore.

The USIU appointment seemed to offer a new lease on life in an exhilarating and exotic venue. It gave him the excuse and wherewithal to spend winters in California, where his eldest son, Michael, and eldest daughter, Connie, were settled. For several months each year, he taught at all three of the southern California campuses, cultivating friendships, gaining new disciples, and investigating experiments in alternative forms of living that had blossomed there in the '60s. He had already taken part in encounter groups in northern California and reported that they "seemed to take the shape of an emerging America far better than the old exclusive therapy does."[5] He gave seminars at the Esalen encampment on Big Sur, where he experienced sulfur baths and the sensual style of "human potential" therapy: "With all its faults—and they are many—the movement still offers much to the human spirit in search of fulfillment."[6] Since his wife Edna was a clinical psychologist, he knew that she would be interested in the new forms of therapy, so he described them in detail in a letter to her:

> Esalen was quite sweet and almost homey, not at all the kind of place it is represented as. A more monogamous place I have not seen except, of course, that the couples are not married. But it certainly is a couple place. Bill Schutz turned out to be a genial host and so did his girl friend Christine. They have a perfectly beautiful home on a cliff overlooking the ocean, and I went to the hot baths with them and sat around nude in the sun (and got a sunburn) and watched an encounter session and a Tai Chi class (Chinese body rhythms) and met everyone there. They are a fascinating group including a man who is an Alexander Lang figure and goes off on psychic trips and bio-pharmacological psychoses who is carrying on experiments with schizophrenia along Lang's lines. Finally, I got Rolfed. You probably know Ida Rolf's "structural re-integration" which is a way of rediscovering muscles and tissue in the body that you long ago

lost sight of. She is one of the new gurus at Esalen now, having replaced Fritz Perls in stature and the current thing is "rolfing" and
"being rolfed." Schutz is one of her best technicians and he gave me
the first hour of the course of 10 hours. It was the most painful experience I have had in my life. Every thrust of his powerful hands
evoking incredible pain and I still carry the bruises on my chest and
under my arms. At one point I felt like giving up and calling a halt
because the pain was so intolerable but I didn't want to chicken out
and besides I really trusted his knowledge and skill even though I
wondered if I would ever be alive again. But it was an exhilarating
experience. I guess I not only discovered unused muscle and fiber
but also an unsuspected streak of gung ho masochism in myself.[7]

In the mid '70s, he also lectured at and took part in the activities
of the Sandstone Retreat, an experimental community which became notorious for open, communal sexuality, but which he saw as
a quest for meaning through sensuality. Looking back on this
phase of his life, he wrote that the years of his seventh decade were
"still full of travel, classes, lecturing, writing." In terms of activity
and work, "it was as if nothing had changed: I acted as if there
were to be an endless succession of such days. I saw my world and
its life force as an inexhaustible treasure trove, and almost fancied
myself immortal. The ground I walked on was the familiar ground
of my life—firm, tangible. The solid earth held, or seemed to."[8]
The ground he particularly liked was that of Hefner's comfortable
mansion in Los Angeles, where he spent much of his time and
where he sought to gain a better understanding of the erotic revolution of which Hefner had been a symbol and a moving force.

Max and "Hef": Playboys of the Western World

Lerner and Hefner ("Hef" to his friends) first encountered each
other in New York in the early 1960s on the set of a television talk
show hosted by the producer David Susskind. Thereafter, from time
to time, they were invited to appear on similar programs. Hefner
was under attack for challenging conventional standards of decency
in *Playboy*, and Lerner came to his defense on the television pan-
els, though as yet not in his newspaper column. Lerner rarely looked
at the magazine, but he thought its success symbolic of a social revolution in which old Puritan inhibitions were being shed in favor of
sexual liberation, first on the part of men and then also of women.
The movement had been catalyzed by the findings of Alfred Kinsey,

and *Playboy* had become its guiding star. "Kinsey gave Americans permission to reject the destructive mind-body separation. Hefner showed them how it could be done—how the legislating of sexuality could be fought, how the absurd antiplay and antipleasure ethic could be turned into a stylish hedonism and a lifeway which includes play and playfulness along with work."[9] This liberation, he added, was not just for men. Rather than being appalled at what *Playboy* and its bunnies represented, Lerner thought, feminists should have recognized that they were indebted to *Playboy* for breaking old stereotypes and leading women to reexamine their social roles and sexuality. "The women's movement wouldn't have been possible," he claimed, "without the revolt of the males."[10] The controversy aroused by Hefner's way of life and by his magazine was the best evidence of their social importance: "Americans carry out their revolutions by taking an idea, personalizing it, wrapping it in a flaring, vendable package, and then shredding it half to death in a firestorm of controversy."[11]

Hefner was pleased to have so erudite and articulate a defender and invited Lerner to write an article for the magazine presenting his views on the sexual revolution. Hefner had already established a precedent of including serious writing in the magazine—something he had learned to do working earlier at *Playboy*'s tamer predecessor, *Esquire*—so Lerner knew he would be in respectable company. Besides, the magazine's rates for contributors were quite high, and Lerner was hard pressed for income. He was offered $2,000 for an acceptable article and gladly accepted. Hefner invited Lerner to stay at his mansion in Chicago whenever he visited that city. Lerner took up the invitation and pointed out that he was not the only culturally prominent person who did so. Hefner liked to tell the story of what happened when Lerner came home from visiting the mansion in Chicago for the first time and told his wife he had stayed there: "She was outraged. 'How dare you! How can you stay at *that* place?' 'It's not the way you think,' he replied. 'My roommate was Bishop Pike.'" When Hefner hosted an anniversary celebration for the magazine to which he invited contributors, Lerner was among the guests, along with the humorist Art Buchwald, prompting one of the better-known episodes in the history of the Chicago mansion, which Lerner later recalled:

> [Buchwald] told his wife that he was going to the Playboy Mansion, and she got worried. What Helens of Troy would he see there? And

in what state of nakedness? And what would happen to him? Which, I must say, is quite understandable for a wife ... My wife, every now and then, has something of that feeling about my visits to that Mansion and this Mansion. But Art said he'd go, anyway, and he, too, had visions in his mind dancing around, of what this was going to be. And he got there ... and he came into the Mansion and into the large living room, and he was shown into his bedroom, and he thought there'd be things there, but nothing was happening. And after a while he thought he'd go down to the baths and the pool. And then he could really see it. And he went down there, and then there was this cloud of steam enveloping the whole place so that he couldn't really see very much. And he hoped that when it would dissipate he would see this raving beauty coming toward him. And as the steam dissipated, whom did he see but Max Lerner.[12]

The friendship between Lerner and Hefner took a political turn in 1968, during the tumult surrounding the Democratic convention of that year in Chicago. Lerner had joined Hefner's entourage, along with the cartoonist Jules Feiffer, on one of Hefner's rare expeditions to the outside world, to observe the demonstrations. Alarmed when they saw fires being set in metal trash receptacles, they hastened to get back to the mansion. Before they could retreat from the scene of the disturbances, they were mistaken for demonstrators and set upon by the police. Hefner tried to explain that they were not part of the protest. He identified himself to a policeman who replied that he did not care who he was and hit him with a nightstick. Afterward, Hefner called a press conference to denounce the police. From then on he became a particularly determined enemy of all forms of repression, political as well as sexual, establishing the Playboy Foundation to reward efforts to protect the First Amendment, and becoming a supporter of liberal causes and politicians. Lerner encouraged his political commitment, though that was not the main focus of their association. As they became closer friends in California, Hefner and Lerner became one of the odder couples of the period, something they themselves found amusing. "I teach him sex," Lerner joked, "and he teaches me politics."

Lerner's relationship with Hefner was not only one of convenience, though it certainly provided a variety of creature comforts. For Lerner the Playboy Mansion was both a symbol of the rejuvenating life-style he wanted to cultivate and a hospice that enabled him at first to deny his own aging and then, when serious illness struck, to convalesce. Hefner himself was at once the prophet and chief protagonist of the new, more erotically open American culture that Lerner found fascinating. In earlier years he had been drawn to the lives of the "titans" of industry who had been the social heroes of nineteenth-century America. In his middle years, he was fascinated by the great men with political power, presidents and prime ministers and the intellectual power broker, Henry Kissinger. In his late years he admired those like Hefner who were breaking the taboos of sexual convention. And he liked to be waited on. The staff of the mansion, with its kitchen open round the clock, specialized in catering to the whims of Hefner and his guests. Lerner basked in the luxurious ease of the Tudor-Gothic estate, originally built by an expatriate English millionaire to resemble the stately country homes he had admired in his youth, and situated on five-and-a-half acres of prime real estate near Sunset Boulevard in Los Angeles, in a wooded area adjacent to other large and expensive properties. The mansion brought to Lerner's mind the fabled pleasure dome in Xanadu of Coleridge's Kubla Khan.[13] Except for days when there were buffets or dinner with his host, his meals were brought to his room, to allow him to write without interruption. On festive occasions he would be invited into the kitchen to teach Hefner and the staff how to make Jewish-style potato pancakes *(latkes)* which he had enjoyed since boyhood. Following Hefner's lead, the staff treated Lerner as an honored guest, in respect both of his age and of his status as a resident sage. He enjoyed swimming in the Jacuzzis of the grotto, often pictured in popular magazines, walking the well-kept grounds, observing the strutting of the peacocks and the play of the monkeys—oddly mimicked by the goings-on inside the mansion among Hefner and his entourage of *Playboy* staffers, Hollywood personalities, and an ever-changing parade of "Playmates of the Month." In a journal entry for January 4, 1976, he wrote:

> Sitting on a window seat, in Room 4, on a Sunday morning with the sun shining on me and the waterfall below me and the long-legged exotic birds stalking the lawn. The sense of well-being. My sadness about time passing is less due to my fighting off death than to the enjoyment of every moment while I am alive, and the wish for it to linger.

He knew that he could never run fast enough to outpace the Angel of Death, but he added a lighthearted hope that his energetic efforts might win him reprieves: "I sometimes dream that if he pays me an inspection visit and he sees this aging hulk immersed up to the hips, shoulders, eyebrows in work and love, he may reflect, 'This fellow has started so many things—I want to see how they come out' and as in the 'Thousand and One Nights,' postpone the ending of my story."

He spent a good deal of the time in his room, reading and writing. When not working, he took delight in mixing with the attractive and glamorous models, and whether or not some may have found his invitations and attentions less than fully welcome, they generally played along, helping him maintain the illusion of being forever young.

For his part, Hefner liked the idea that the mansion could boast an intellectual-in-residence, just as he had made sure that *Playboy* magazine would be distinguished from other "girlie" magazines because it would include articles by serious writers and interviews with prominent people. But there was also a bond of affection, which grew in intensity over the quarter-century in which they knew each other, despite and in some ways because of the gap of twenty-three years in their ages and the differences in their backgrounds and intellectual interests. Hefner credited Lerner with making him more openly affectionate: Lerner would embrace people he liked when he met them, and Hefner found himself doing so as well. They found they had some things in common. One was that they were both unblushing narcissists: "We do not suffer from a lack of self-esteem," as Lerner put it. They were also both "unreconstructed romantics," he added.[14] In a recorded dialogue with Lerner, designed to help Hefner compose his autobiography, Hefner remarked: "What I have always searched for is a kind of quest for a romantic-dream relationship." Lerner replied: "That has been true of me . . . you and I share that very much." They neglected to mention that for both of them romantic dreaming had an ill-defined relationship to unabashed hedonism and womanizing, though Lerner came close to admitting this when he said that what he enjoyed most in the Mansion was "Hef himself, with his infectious lust for life" and the overtone of sexuality that surrounded the place, "because it imbued me with an enhanced sense of my own sexuality." When he first heard about Hefner and then encountered him on talk shows, Lerner said, he was drawn to him on the most elementary level:

> There was this nimbus around him of a man who not only talked about fucking, but did the fucking. The thing itself. It's like the wonderful *King Lear* passage, Lear looking to Gloucester on the heath,

> Gloucester coming around, saying, "Thou art the thing itself." Well,
> here was the thing itself. And I loved it.[15]

Their differences were also important to the chemistry of their friendship. Hefner admired Lerner's "wealth of knowledge, the quickness and depth of his mind, his curiosity and openness to new ideas." In their informal discussions and more formal dialogues, Lerner would often quote poetry and literature and explain such novelties as Gregory Bateson's theory of the double bind—a "Catch-22" hypothesis, introduced in a study of schizophrenia, that when someone in an intense relationship receives contradictory signals from the other party, any response he makes will necessarily be wrong.[16] Hefner found himself stimulated and intrigued by Lerner's erudition. And always there was the overriding theme of *Eros.* Hefner and Lerner both liked to say that Lerner's continuing interest in women even into his eighties gave Hefner reason to hope that his own sexual prowess would not disappear with age. At a roast to celebrate Hefner's fiftieth birthday, Lerner hinted broadly at this aspect of their relationship. He realized, he said, why he had been invited to the roast: "I'm old and you're scared," he said to a burst of appreciative laughter. That comment, he remarked only half in jest, had summed up their "inter-generational dialogue." If Hefner worried about impending impotence, presumably Lerner's display of continued virility was reassuring.

There were other bonds as well. When Lerner survived his first bout with cancer, Hefner invited him to recuperate at the Mansion. Lerner was touched when in 1980 he returned to lecture at USIU, still shaky from the illness, and Hefner insisted on sending a limousine to San Diego to bring him to the Mansion. A few years later, when Hefner suffered a stroke, Lerner immediately called Hefner's doctor and spoke regularly with Hefner to cheer him up during his recovery. Lerner was intrigued by Hefner's love of games, including backgammon, at which he was very good. Lerner thought it showed a typically American competitive impulse, but he was moved by a hint of vulnerability when Hefner said his interest in games was really another instance of a desire for "connectedness." Lerner was interested too in Hefner's attachment to the popular music and films of his youth in the '40s. They agreed that this background was one source of Hefner's sentimental romanticism. Hefner's daughter, who was to take over the magazine, had attended Brandeis as an undergraduate, though she had gone there too late to study with Lerner. Lerner had always admired great entrepreneurs, and Hefner had created a graphically innovative and very successful magazine, and then an international business empire—all out of nothing but the immaterial stuff of sexual fantasy. Hefner had succeeded, Lerner thought, not just because the time was right but also because he was literate and articulate and even more "a listener and a viewer." He heard the overtones in American consciousness and, more important, had "an eye for the effective image that counts in that consciousness . . . an unblinded Cyclopean eye, with every energy focused on the single revealing camera view." [17]

Even apart from Lerner's words of praise in print, what must have made him an especially welcome guest was that, in encouraging Hefner's efforts of introspection, he always reinforced his friend's sense of accomplishment and self-worth without challenging his beliefs or behavior. On the contrary, he made it clear to Hefner and to those who interviewed him about Hefner that he regarded him not only as a pioneer sexual liberator and thoughtful commentator, but also as a warm and caring person whose relationships with women were not sexually exploitative but romantic in the fullest sense. The closest he came to a critical appraisal was in pointing out an ambivalence in Hefner's attitude, involving both a rebellion against his Methodist upbringing and a feeling that down deep he remained the boy he had been brought up to be, thinking that what he was doing was wrong. Because Hefner recognized the same ambivalence in himself, he did not resent being told about it. They worked together on the scripts of programs and on other materials explaining Hefner's "Playboy Philosophy," and in preparing material for the autobiography Hefner intended to write. In an interview, when Hefner explained that he had grown up in romanticized but repressive circumstances, Lerner said he felt the same way about his own upbringing. Hefner's complaints about "the establishment" reminded him of William Blake's complaint against all those figures of power who sought to close the gates to the "garden of love":

> And I saw it was filled with black graves,
> And tombstones where the flowers should be;
> And Priests in black gowns were making their rounds,
> And binding with briars my joys & desires.

Lerner saw Hefner as a latter-day Blake—a rebel against his own personal upbringing and, at the same time, a symbolic figure in a more general American revolt against society's Puritan moorings:

Hef has a sense of his childhood as being sort of typically Puritan. More than anything else what he recalls are the repressions which both his family and the community—and the whole period— forced upon him. And his whole life has been in a sense a revolt against those repressions. And what he did, of course, that makes him an enduring figure in the history of American popular culture . . . was to project his personal rebellion until it became a rebellion of the whole period, of a whole era.[18]

Pressed by Lerner to explain his view of life, Hefner said he saw it as a "miraculous adventure" in which there should be no guilt over enjoying sexuality. Lerner explained to Hefner that in the evolution of American culture he and Kinsey would go down as "the guilt killers." But he wanted Hefner to understand that what was at stake in all this went well beyond him and even beyond social mores. In one of the more delicious moments of American cultural history, he introduced this prodigal son of Middle West Methodism to the *angst*-ridden outlook of fin de siècle Vienna, patiently explaining the Freudian theory of the slaying of the primal father that Lerner had invoked in *America as a Civilization*. Hefner was puzzled because he had never before heard of the theory, but he was a dutiful pupil: by the end of the Socratic exchange he professed he had come to understand himself better:

ML: [T]he reason I ask about the guilt thing—I think that guilt is very deeply part of all of life, all of our lives. I don't think it's just culture and society myself, although a particular society and culture can intensify—

HH: I don't quite understand what you mean by that. What else could it be? It ain't in the genes, and that's all that's left.

ML: In the history of the human race, we once killed our fathers very early, and this is how the human race developed.

HH: How do you mean?

ML: In the beginning of society, at some point, the sons killed the father.

HH: That's part of the tradition of Homo Sapiens? I don't know about that.

ML: In the beginnings of human society, the original society was the horde, with the father as master [of] the sons and the women.

HH: Oh, you mean when the sons grew to manhood, they killed their elders. Or they took their women away from—

ML: Killed the father in order to pluck the women.

HH: You keep saying the father. I mean was that a tradition in some area that I don't know about?

ML: In every tribe, the father—well, this is even pre-tribal. I mean this is all conjectural, obviously, but it is very much part—

HH: You mean the young males took what they wanted away from the older males.

ML: This was the original parricide, which Dostoevsky recreated [in *The Brothers Karamazov*].

HH: Does it happen in the lower animals?

ML: So far as we know, it happens in primates where the leader is killed or rejected and the younger ones come in; it happens with the apes; it happens with lions, and so on. I am not enough of an ethologist to know which particularly ... It comes out of Freudianism, but it's pretty much today an accepted [idea] about the origins of society ... There had to be at some point ... a leader of the pack who had the women ... [T]here's a remarkable book, called *Love's Body*, which readdresses this whole thing ... But I take it as accepted, as I see parricide as very, very deeply within us, although it takes many forms. But what I'm saying is that guilt is not just Western [or] American ...

HH: Without some repression and some guilt, you don't have what we call civilization ... These are controls. They're controls over the individual.

ML: I start with that by saying that guilt is part of us, and we are steeped in guilt, and ... every one of us has to, in some way, manage the guilt in ourselves. We do it for better or for worse. But there are a number of individuals in our history who, by grappling with the guilt in themselves in order to free themselves of that guilt, have managed also to free others.

HH: That is precisely what my life is all about.[19]

Indeed, Lerner added, Hefner had been living out his fantasies for himself and for others, in effect exorcising their guilt. Hefner's "Playboy Philosophy," he told an interviewer, was "a crystallization of Kinsey, applied through the lens of Hef's life," and one that he

felt very much in tune with, which is why he felt that he fit in at
the Mansion, despite his age. He enjoyed being there, he said, because it was a kind of extended family of creative people sharing each
other's joys and sorrows. During his own illness, Lerner was touched
by the care and sympathy he received from this circle of friends.
And he went so far as to tell the interviewer that Hefner had created not only a new American life-style and a new image of sexual
freedom but a new community as well:

> I often told him . . . he was not only great because he publishes an
> important magazine, but, in some ways, even more because of his
> art of being able to create a community and keep it going. One of the
> things we used to discuss was community creation. And I was at that
> point . . . writing the book I haven't yet finished, *Eros in America.*
> And one of the chapters was on the history of the . . . erotic revolu-
> tions in America. And a very important episode there was the united
> community . . . And I said, "Hef, you've got one here. This is a com-
> munity. May not be the united community but in many ways it is
> better.[20]

Lerner stopped short of comparing the Mansion with the Fourier-
ist communes of New Lanark and New Harmony or with the East
European *shtetl* of his forebears or an Israeli *kibbutz*, but he was
nevertheless sure it was somehow a model community for the
emerging America.

Lerner repaid Hefner's friendship and hospitality by defending
him and *Playboy* in two especially trying episodes. One concerned
Hefner's long-time associate and private secretary, Bobbie Arn-
stein, who in 1975, through her boyfriend, had become entangled
with narcotics. Arrested for possessing a small amount of cocaine
and for allegedly being aware of the boyfriend's trafficking, she was
given a harsh but "conditional" fifteen-year sentence—the condition being that she cooperate with the police in their further investigations. Hefner suspected that the police were really after him
and aiming to bring down the Playboy empire. Offered leniency if
she would implicate Hefner in drug activities, she refused. An assistant prosecutor called her and warned her that there was a "contract" out on her, implying that some powerful "friend"—presumably Hefner—was anxious to get her out of the way by having her
killed. Despondent, she went to a hotel room and committed suicide,
leaving a note blaming only herself, praising Hefner for his generosity toward her, and completely exonerating him of any involve-

ment with her drug activities. Hefner was extremely distraught and unable to forget the affair. Lerner wrote a column expressing his sympathies and concern over the alleged police misconduct.[21]

Later, when Hefner was under assault from feminists critical both of pornography and of what many considered the sexual exploitation of women in magazines like *Playboy,* Lerner again came to Hefner's defense. Peter Bogdanovich, the Hollywood director, had been on Hefner's authorized guest list at the Los Angeles Mansion, where he had met and fallen in love with Dorothy Stratten, the exquisitely beautiful twenty-year-old "playmate of the year." She starred in movies he directed and returned his affection, but she had earlier married a disreputable hustler who had coaxed her into posing nude for a *Playboy* competition. When she told her husband she intended to leave him, he brutally raped and murdered her and then committed suicide. Bogdanovich turned against Hefner and wrote a book bitterly denouncing all that he represented, endorsing the critique of *Playboy* advanced by feminists. Bogdanovich's version of the Stratten story and of Hefner's role as a "guilt killer"[22] painted a picture of Hefner and the life at the Mansion rather different from Lerner's. He thought of Hefner's way of life as a web he had spun out of a desire to gain revenge for his humiliation by his first wife. Stratten's tragedy seemed to Bogdanovich a symptom of a larger erosion of social values.

Shortly after Stratten's death, Hefner had a stroke, from which he recovered gradually, with a lingering speech impairment, and some of his entourage felt that the Stratten affair had precipitated it. Lerner defended Hefner and contended that Bogdanovich had misinterpreted his relationship with Stratten:

> So far as I know, the relationship between the two of them was not the kind of thing that Peter described in the book. I think this was a case where Hef really idealized this young woman. There were relatively few people in his life that he had this sense of an ideal—his notion of what a young woman should be like. And that does not mean, as Peter suggested, that he exploited her. I have no sense of his having exploited her in any way. But when this happened to her, then what happened to him [because of Bogdanovich's charges], this ideal of his had been somewhat soiled. And it was the soiling of it that gave him his sense of anger and injustice.[23]

When Hefner married Kimberly Conrad, the 1989 Playmate of the Year, Lerner saw his transition from bachelorhood to marriage as symbolic of a social transition. He reiterated his view that Hefner and Kinsey would be seen in American history as "guilt killers" but sought to distinguish what they represented from the nihilism of the counterculture. There was a difference, he contended, between a liberation that results in a "values relativism . . . that becomes personally and socially damaging" and an attitude that stresses freedom from guilt—with which "you may still find your sense of limits in strongly held personal values." Noting that Hefner's working title for his autobiography was *Hefner: Puritan Playboy*, he saw him as "the last Puritan of the modern American sexual consciousness and the first playboy of a hedonic life that had shed its guilt." Hefner symbolized, Lerner thought, a revolt against the hypocrisy of a moral code that condemned the vices of sex, drink, and gambling, but tolerated breaches of the code by those who could get away with them. Noting the accession to the helm of *Playboy* of Hefner's daughter Christie, with her feminist and humanist concerns, which "made the attacks of the feminist Left sound silly," he saw Hefner's marriage as in the vanguard of a social return to the ideal of romantic love: "The tumultuous young warrior is now back as the older and more serene warrior but he is still in the romantic vanguard." [24] Hefner, he thought, had always been a romantic, especially since adolescence, and marriage was merely a logical step in the evolution of that romanticism:

> He holds on to the romanticism. He will not let go. For him—how shall I put it—his feelings about beauty, particularly as embodied in young women—he sees life as a kind of Garden of Eden, filled with luscious Eves, and with himself as the only Adam around. For him it is a wonderful scenario, and he wants to hold on to this for as long as he possibly can. So he went through a succession of these Garden of Eden scenes until finally—by the way, each time there was a fall into vulnerability, guilt and so on—but finally he found the Eve and the Garden of Eden in which there was no fall. That was marriage with Kimberly. [25]

Like Bogdanovich, Gay Talese told a very different story. In 1980 Talese published an account of the sexual revolution, in some respects a *vade mecum*, such as Lerner wanted to write, but which offered a far less flattering portrait of Hefner and all he represented. Hefner himself, Talese wrote, "wanted not only to have the nude pictures but also to possess the women who had posed for them." In his early disillusionment with marriage, he noted, Hefner had not been unique. The divorce rate was beginning to rise as men home from the war were discontented with humdrum suburban lives, and as women, induced to enter the work force in World War II, began to shed their homemaker role and achieve an independence which made them willing to break out of unhappy marriages. Hefner dreamed of a better life for himself, Talese suggested, especially one that would be sexually satisfying, but when he launched *Playboy* he had no expectation that so many other men would share his dreams. In *Playboy*, he suggested, Hefner had created a magazine that for the first time presented young American males with the embodiment of their sexual fantasies: "a nude woman who appeared to be sexually approachable" to "a vast audience of suitors, each privately claiming her as his own." [26]

Eros in America

Had Lerner been younger, and not so beholden to Hefner, he might have been as critical of Hefner and his way of life as Bogdanovich and Talese, or at least have recognized the merit of their strictures. Already in *America as a Civilization,* he had expressed a cautionary view toward the sexual revolution. Although he saw it as a "revolt for a healthy expressive life" which "emphasizes the sustained relationship as necessary to a healthy sexual life," he was not sure where the revolt would lead:

> This may, of course, be wishful thinking on my part, discerning a stream of tendency where there is only a whirlpool of crosscurrents. Americans are probably engaged in a complicated struggle in the building up of definitions as to what is permissible and truly expressive in the area of sexual behavior. There has been nothing approaching an accurate account of this struggle, with its agonies and blindnesses and earnestness, taking place on the darkling plain of the American psyche. One possible outcome may be a reversion to a new form of the Puritan codes, with new and more indirect repressions. But the more likely outcome is the newer expressiveness which I have outlined here.[27]

In the 1970s Lerner decided he would write a book on "*Eros* in America" to come to grips with the changes taking place. In an early formulation, he set out his theses. The thrust of the changes in sexual attitudes, he thought, had been "largely life-affirming," but there could come a countervailing reaction. In a society where the belief in individual liberty is so ingrained, "there are few inherent limits to the expansion of sexual freedom. *Anything Goes* becomes King. The limits, if any, must be sought in a social backlash." They would come, he thought, from the class character of American society. In Rome decadence was spawned by a standard-setting aristocracy. In America, the lower-middle and middle-middle classes, "which serve as the inner limits of resistance to runaway changes," were apt to check the spread of libertinism. A dialectic of Puritanism and pleasure seemed to hold sway. Just as the country has been pluralistic in other respects, now it was tolerating and practicing a sexual pluralism influenced by the decline of religious taboos, the moral relativism introduced by anthropological studies, and the drive for self-expression and self-help common to many American movements. As a result, America had become a "pleasure society," much as Babylon was, or the French aristocracy of the Sun King, Edwardian England, or Weimar Germany. The American version was even more intense because it was driven by the same "metaphysical passion" as was behind immigration and the expansion of the frontier. Americans were not becoming obsessed with sex to the exclusion of love but were seeking a continuum of both: "[W]e are now focusing on sex and hope that love will come with it." The new openness about the sexual lives of American presidents was an indication of an "eroticizing of the political." Whereas sexuality and power were previously incarnated in the economic titans, now increasingly political figures are the social models, testifying to the growing importance of the political. But there were signs that erotic revolution might be checked:

> I raise the question, however, whether there can be a meaningful sexuality in a society which is not given both meaning and limits by some kind of religious framework. The current turning of the young to religions, West and East, seems to coincide with a slowing down of the movements for sexual change and a return to forms of self-restraint.[28]

In an essay of reminiscence, focusing on the link between *Eros* and power, Lerner reflected on the examples of Franklin Roosevelt, John Kennedy, and Lyndon Johnson. "In recent years," he wrote, "I have been absorbed, as a president watcher, to note how *Eros* has combined with the power drive in the forming of Presidential character." Perhaps Roosevelt was such a forceful leader, he speculated, because he was so passionately attracted to Lucy Mercer. "We pay little heed," he noted, "to the impact of the emotional content of a leader's private life on his public acts. I like to think now that this was not an emotionally starved man, channeling his unexercised erotic energies into public service, but a man at the height of his power of feeling and will and action, expressing again the sense of triumph which his renewed meetings with Lucy must have nourished." Lerner saw nothing surprising in the fusion of *Eros* and power in Kennedy, whom he admired for his tough-mindedness in office. "We must take Kennedy as a total man," he argued, "which means taking the sexual drive in him along with the power drive, the imagination, and the judgment." What was especially striking about Kennedy, Lerner thought, was the persistence with which he linked his sexual conquests with danger and mystery. "There were not two Kennedys but one, and . . . they were held together by *eros* not only as sexuality but as a life-force . . . To overcome a woman's resistance was like winning a campaign; to triumph in bed was like triumphing over Castro." In Johnson's case, Lerner was fascinated by his affair as a young congressman with a woman in Virginia, the mistress of a Texas tycoon whose newspapers were critical to Johnson's campaigns for office. He took an enormous risk in courting her, Lerner remarked, and although Johnson's biographer, Robert Caro, saw this as an anomaly in a career devoted to power and money and devoid of values, Lerner preferred to think of it as evidence of Johnson's complexity, including his capacity for romance.[29]

This analysis of the erotic life of men of power helps explain Lerner's own conduct in these years. He was determined to show that his own erotic self remained strong because that would show that he too was a "conqueror"—a cultural conqueror rather than a political leader or a financial titan. Hefner noted that Lerner took particular pride in boasting about his virility:

> His bedroom shared a bath with the bedroom that Harry Reems [a pornographic film star] occupied, and he would quip: "He is the sex symbol of the '70s and I'm a sex symbol in my seventies." While at the Mansion, Max enjoyed interludes with young women, and an ongoing relationship with a woman in her forties. The rest of the year he would return to the Manhattan apartment he shared with Edna . . . As Max told *People* in 1979, he and his wife held opposite opinions on the subject of sexual freedom, but their union survived. Edna deadpanned to *People,* "I've never been to the Playboy Mansion, but Max seems to enjoy it."[30]

Lerner also enjoyed the Sandstone Retreat. Sandstone was an experiment in communal sexual exchange founded on the belief that possessiveness was ruinous to human social relationships and that recreational and "varietal sex" between men and women and between women would promote a guilt-free personality and harmonious community. One of a number of such communal experiments triggered by the anti-individualistic, antitraditional thinking of the counterculture of the 1960s, it had been founded by an engineer named John Williamson with the help of his wife. He quit his job and bought an isolated hilltop fifteen-acre property in Topanga Canyon, in the San Fernando Valley. There they and four other couples built a house which they lived in and to which they invited others who paid dues to belong to the club. One member who was to become well known was Daniel Ellsberg, then a policy analyst at RAND, who would leak the "Pentagon Papers" to the *New York Times*. The house contained a large room on the lower level which was called the "ball room" and was the scene of free-wheeling sexual activities. A central founding belief of the club was that it was time to eliminate the double-standard that had allowed men to have extramarital liaisons while women were expected to be monogamous. One woman in the group, Betty Dodson, an artist who specialized in genital imagery and called herself "Phallic Woman," went even further. "To love only one person," she said, "is anti-social." [31]

Between 1970 and 1972, Sandstone received considerable publicity and attracted hundreds of members, though it was still losing money. In 1972, it was improved and advertised, and special services were added. Members and guests could receive "everything from sessions in Rolfing and the Esalen massage to bioenergetic and hatha-yoga." For the price of $250, including room and board, guests could spend the weekend using the facilities and attending gestalt therapy sessions. The retreat received favorable notices from writers, even a mention by the actor Orson Bean, who had been a guest on the Johnny Carson show. The hope and expectation was that more chapters or similar clubs would be opened elsewhere and one similar club, called Plato's Retreat, opened in Manhattan. As Topanga Canyon became more built-up, the Williamsons explored the possibility of opening another branch in the even more isolated setting of Montana.

Although the Williamsons usually required that new members be couples, exceptions were allowed for people who might enhance the club's reputation. Among these "honorary members" were Lerner, as well as Alex Comfort, the British scientist who devoted a chapter on the experiment in his phenomenally successful book, *The Joy of Sex,* observing that "one could go quite frankly to get laid—but having got that out of the way, participants were surprised to find that "sensitivity," "encounter," and a good deal of genuine self-education quite often followed.[32] Lerner mentioned Sandstone in a column but took pains to record that contrary to Comfort he did not believe "that the privacy with which we continue to invest the sexual act is the expression of our hostile fear of strangers. I should myself have thought that it is our way of keeping our sense of uniqueness, even as we strain to break our loneliness by reaching out sexually for another person."[33] By 1977, the tide had begun to turn against sexual experimentation, and Sandstone was closed for lack of support. In a column entitled "Ebb Tide for *Eros*" Lerner noted that "even in California, the fount and origin of the erotic revolutions during the last two decades, there is a waning of the flamboyance of past years in the public airing of new attitudes on sexuality and the public display of new behavior." He was confident, however, that the underlying quest for freedom and gender equality that this revolution had involved would be maintained, but wondered whether, like the labor movement, this revolution would simply keep asking for more or make some qualitative difference in American life.[34]

A Final Affair

While teaching at USIU Lerner attracted a coterie of women friends, including some who worked with him as teaching assistants and were awed by his extraordinary classroom abilities, and another, Mary Duncan, who taught at San Diego State University. As one of the teaching assistants said, he was the only professor she knew who could make a lecture course with two hundred students seem like an intimate seminar, one in which everyone would speak honestly about his or her innermost thoughts and feelings. Lerner had affairs with several of the women and became especially attached to one graduate student who was not one of the teaching assistants.

Mary Ellen was a tall, strikingly beautiful twenty-seven-year-old graduate student in sociology at USIU who may well have reminded him of the women he had so admired at Sarah Lawrence. She had

come to California some years earlier from a Main Line Philadel-
phia upbringing to work for Jonas Salk, the celebrated developer of
the first polio vaccine, and had begun to edit his journals. Salk became a second father to her and encouraged her to go to graduate
school. There she heard about Lerner and asked him to read an essay she had written on the painter Andrew Wyeth that was ultimately published in *The Virginia Woolf Quarterly.* She was thrilled
when Lerner told her, "It's very good; I think you're a writer." He
asked her to have dinner with him and she agreed. Afterward he invited her to "a friend's" birthday party. She asked what she should
wear. He replied that the party was "at Hef's." She did not realize
at first who "Hef" was and was startled to learn that she was being
invited to the Playboy Mansion, but went along out of curiosity.
Later, she enrolled in one of Lerner's classes on politics, then in another entitled "Marriage, Family, and *Eros*"—which the students
jokingly said was about Marriage, Family, and *Eros,* minus the
marriage and family.

She came to admire him, especially his gift for teaching: "not just
his style; it was extraordinary the way his mind worked, the way he
could take disparate elements and put them into an integrated
scheme." Although she came from a conservative Republican background, she found herself nodding in agreement at what he would
say, recognizing only afterward that what he was saying was at odds
with the beliefs in which she had been raised. He had the talents
of a southern evangelist, she thought. They would go to Hefner's on
alternate weekends when he was in California. As they saw more
of each other, she marveled at his physical energy. He would work
around the clock, taking a twenty minute catnap now and then. At
the base of all that energy, she thought, was a passion for life. Even
after bouts with illness, he would joke that he almost had gotten
back to believing he would live forever. She was infuriated when
the Hollywood agent, Irving "Swifty" Lazar, told him bluntly that
there was no longer a market for his work because he was "yester-
day's news" and that no one would care to read anything he wrote
because most people thought he was already dead. She thought
that what he had already done was worthy of respect and tried to
persuade him to take Lazar's message to mean only that he could
not expect to rest on his laurels. He replied that he was ready to
reinvent himself and renew his celebrity by writing the great book
about *Eros* in America, but she felt that his heart was not in it.

Lerner told her that he had always been attracted to bright and beautiful women. He had felt great sympathy for Marilyn Monroe because she was desperately lonely, and he had been enthralled by Elizabeth Taylor's beauty. And now, he told her, he was just as much drawn to her. "You are very special to me," he assured her. She was not sure that she wanted to become deeply involved with him but found him wonderful to be with. "I loved him for the person he was. Jonas was in the clouds; the oxygen was so thin, he was so abstract and ivory-towerish; Max was of this world." But although he was a caring person, she felt, love was something he experienced by himself and for himself. He seemed to her to be living out an ideal of romantic love, and she was merely the latest version of the Norma Shearer dream he had fantasized about as a boy absorbed in the films he had seen in Poli's Theater in New Haven.

In his classes and with Mary Ellen, Lerner emphasized that he saw his own insistence on living life to the full as a way of resisting the force of the death instinct. The best way to fight against death, he said, was to embrace life in all its forms. In one seminar he talked of his rage at the death of his daughter Pamela from cancer, something that tore at the roots of his sense of justice in the universe. "In his own fantasy world," Mary Ellen reflected, "Max could almost imagine being the first human to evade death and live eternally." Hefner, anxious over his own prospects, encouraged the fantasy, and applauded him for enjoying life's pleasures to the full. But she knew it was a charade aimed at keeping up appearances:

> What Hef did not know, and Max would never disclose, was that by the spring of 1977 (when Max and I first met), Max was suffering the effects of a prostate disorder which had rendered him impotent. Months earlier, Max had sought medical help for the problem, and in an effort to rule out cancer as the cause for the enlarged prostate, Max's physician had ordered testing (a biopsy, I believe). Although the test results did not lead to a cancer diagnosis at that time, Max himself was not confident that the results were accurate. He continued to worry over the possibility of cancer, the prostate condition did not improve, and his problems with impotence persisted throughout the time I knew him.

She entered into the fantasy out of affection for him:

> Given his understandable anxieties about cancer and his failing sexual capacity, Max found it all the more important to keep up the appearance of sexual prowess. He knew that to admit openly to having a sexual problem would only aggravate the problem, and since his

style of coping was typically denial, he was most comfortable be-
having as if all were well behind the closed door. It was *not*, but I saw
no reason then to dispel the myth.

Neither Lerner nor Mary Ellen anticipated, when they first became acquainted, how intensely involved with each other they
would become for almost two years. But as much as he importuned
Mary Ellen, in the early months with her he was not ready to break
up his marriage and start over again. He wanted to have the best
of both his worlds. Mary Ellen realized that his early pursuit of her
had been more a reflection of his determination to deny the inti-
mations of mortality in his failing sexual prowess than of any feelings he may have had toward her:

> The kind of idealism Max brought to his politics he brought to his
> unending pursuit of women, and as he did in the face of other ob-
> stacles, he confronted his failing health and sexual capacity by be-
> coming all the more intensely idealistic and romantic. In me he saw
> one last chance to find his ideal love with one of the daughters of the
> conquerors. At first he was in love with being in love; later he ap-
> parently did feel something substantial for me. Unfortunately, by
> that point in his life it was really too late for him to start over. The
> dying process was underway; he knew it and I knew it months be-
> fore the first cancer, the lymphoma, was diagnosed.

To her the question was where he belonged during that final phase
of his life. She had experienced the illness of her father from mul-
tiple sclerosis and the death from Parkinson's and Alzheimer's dis-
eases of a grandfather who lived with them. She thought Lerner
would be best cared for at home by his family, and told him so. "If
Max wanted to have one last chance at love, I thought it should be
with the woman he'd been married to all those years." Lerner tried
for weeks to persuade her to change her mind, frantically asking advice on tactics from one of the members of his coterie of teaching assistants. Finally, he asked Mary Ellen whether she would marry him
if he would leave Edna and move to California, but she persisted in
refusing him. Reluctantly, he gave up his California dream. Illness
soon struck, and he had to rely on Edna, who cared for him, stoically
and lovingly, through years of intermittent illness and remission. He
never did write a book on *Eros* in America. If he glimpsed utopia at
all in these years, it was only as a poignant fantasy, an imaginary
working out of the ancient human yearning for sustained ecstasy
and eternal life.

NINE ෨ ෨ ෨

Thanatos in New York

Myself, when young. The likeness
becomes a memory of what became
a book   and that fades into
a palimpsest of my buried lives.
Can I live now
with what I knew—and was—
without diminishing what I am?
How can I not? To reconcile the likeness
With my spavined bones is to compound
the ultimate antinomy. I am the pale horse
and rider too. I am both
lovers, wandering the forest path,
coming upon themselves returning. Turn
the page. Another portrait, another
book, another corpse to be covered up, lest
it dazzle the eyes as I contemplate
myself when old.
—Max Lerner (September 15/16, 1988; Southampton)

As the decade of the 1980s began,
a newly elected Republican president, Ronald Reagan, electrified
his supporters by declaring it was "morning in America." Max Lerner—to the horror of his liberal friends and admirers—welcomed

the dawn of the new day as an opportunity for vigorous national renewal. But whatever rejuvenation may have been in store for the
country could not help Lerner fend off indefinitely the twilight of
his own life. Although he continued to write and teach, he entered
a period of declining health from 1980 onward in which he would
"wrestle with the angel" of his own mortality, manfully and at first
successfully, until he met inexorable defeat and succumbed to a
stroke in 1992. Until the very end he lived life to the full, thinking
and writing and enjoying the company of family and friends and
of the new friends he made in his classes and lectures. Throughout
this period, whenever he was able, he continued to teach university
courses—for two successive and especially enjoyable years at Notre
Dame. He also kept up his column, less frequently as illness inca-
pacitated him. In 1990, he published one last defiant book—a bit-
tersweet valedictory celebrating his victory over illness and extol-
ling whatever blessings for life old age conferred.

Welcoming the "Reagan Revolution"

"No greater political upheaval in American politics has occurred
for a half century," Lerner wrote the day after election day in 1979,
when Reagan overwhelmed the incumbent president, Jimmy Carter. Lerner had sensed it would come during the presidential pri-
maries. Carter struck him, as he did many voters, as a "nice man" too
weak-willed for the post. The liberal media elite, quartered in the
Northeast, simply did not appreciate what was happening in the
rest of the country. Well before election day Lerner felt sure that,
"unthinkable as it may seem," Reagan would carry not only California but New York as well, and, with his "massive strength in the
Sun Belt, from Florida to Texas to Arizona," gain an electoral land-
slide.[1] His impending victory was not just a protest against Carter's
failures, Lerner was convinced, but the beginning of a veritable social revolution, comparable to that of the New Deal. This too, he
thought, would be a class revolution, though one tinged with religious overtones and a reassertion of national pride. This time,
however, the revolution was being propelled not by a coalition of
working people and immigrant groups, held together by urban political machines, but by a growing suburban middle class seething
with resentments over economic breakdown and runaway cultural
change.[2] Lerner sympathized with their frustration and welcomed
the change in direction, thinking of it not as a radical departure

from traditional American values but as a reaffirmation of those values and a righting of the balance.

The revolution had been brought on, he thought, by the success of the New Left in influencing the character of American liberalism. Rather than being allowed to adapt to changing circumstances, New Deal liberalism had become a rigid, outworn creed, cut off from domestic and international realities and from the people it was supposed to benefit. The pendulum of American politics had swung too far to the Left, producing a hand-wringing sense of guilt over every compromise in foreign policy and a paralyzing "post-Vietnam syndrome." Especially among the young adherents of the counterculture, left-wing radicalism had promoted disrespect for the conventions of political civility, for parental authority, and for established social institutions.

What had happened to liberalism, he thought, was reflected in what had happened to the Democratic Party. The rise of the McGovernite wing of the party brought enough of the New Left agenda into the party to convince Lerner that it was time for a change of allegiance. He had sided with the Democrats when they had aimed, as James Wechsler liked to say, "to comfort the afflicted and afflict the comfortable," but he thought the party had lost its focus on the needs of the nation as a whole and become a collection of interest groups, demanding job set-asides and ethnic and gender quotas—fragmenting rather than uniting the country. "The result has been," he wrote, "to alienate the Americans at their grass roots, to rouse group passions against group passions, and cut the Democratic Party off from the sources of America's inner strength."[3]

Lerner was no less critical of the impact of the New Left on academic life. He cherished the Western tradition in literature into which he had been so well initiated at Yale, and he thought of colleges and universities as vital repositories of learning and academic freedom. He agreed wholeheartedly with those academics offended by demands for a non-"Eurocentric" curriculum, and he deplored the "trashing" of the universities for their supposed complicity in all manner of social evil. He denounced academic surrender to the dogmas of "political correctness"—especially those claiming that the American political system is an instrument of injustice, that independent scholarship is a hoax, that teachers should be chosen to represent groups, that the heterosexual white male is an oppressive villain, and that Western culture is a yoke forced upon his victims. To all such bogus claims and mischievous demands, he declared,

"[I]t is time for us to say, as we did to the betrayal of our traditional values in the 1960s, 'enough is enough.'"[4] Invited to contribute to a symposium in *Commentary*, he warmly agreed with the magazine's neoconservative hostility toward the New Left. Attacking the new radicals' sympathy for all Third World guerrilla movements (including the Palestine Liberation Organization) as well as their support for "welfare statism" and ethnic preferences, he called for a "new centrism" that would combine the best elements of liberalism and conservatism and move away from "the guilt-ridden self-hatred of the traditional liberals."[5]

Lerner saw the "Reagan revolution" as a response to the failures of this traditional liberalism that would purge the social system of at least some of its pathologies. Reagan's popularity, he thought, showed that most Americans, especially those in the relatively affluent middle class, were fed up with rebellions against traditional values and determined to restore a sense of authority and order. They wanted neither "a New Left nor a revamped traditional liberalism, but a more tough-minded liberalism and a more humanist conservatism."[6] Lerner's own wish to be "tough-minded" made him increasingly unsympathetic toward "doctrinaire liberalism," with its naive expectation that politics required saintliness rather than Machiavellian realism. To blame middle-class voters for not wanting to transfer yet more of their income to support the idle was "eyewash." To ask that Washington abandon authoritarian allies who were fighting communism and building free-market economies was to play into the hands of America's enemies. The conservatives were right, he thought, to contend that the country was suffering from a social breakdown with many immediate causes: a rejection of the work ethic in favor of a culture of entitlements, declining productivity due in part to overregulation by officious bureaucrats, and moral decay stemming from "the beliefs that 'anything goes' and that 'nothing is sacred,' resulting in runaway crime, drugs, and mental disease statistics."[7]

As Reagan took control, Lerner continued to be impressed. The president-elect's inaugural address was "a crisp, forceful statement of his philosophy by an effective and credible personality." It promised an "era of renewal" in which actions would show "a resurgent America confident enough of itself so that America's global allies and adversaries will respect its strength." Reagan's own confidence in the future embodied a national self-confidence that Lerner sensed would now reassert itself.[8] "He has purpose, conviction, doggedness, drama, and, most surprisingly, a largeness of view that no one gave him credit for." Lerner recognized fully that Reagan's determination to set aside Keynesian theory in favor of a return to competitive free-market economics, complete with tax cuts to stimulate investment and consumption, was a bold move. Like Roosevelt's New Deal, he thought, its success would ultimately depend less on the validity of its economic theory than on the psychological impact of the program. If it revived confidence—and if Reagan was lucky— "his program can work."[9] Lerner even had a good word to say about the advocates of supply-side economics. They might seem eccentric, he observed, in arguing that capitalism is the best answer for all that ails a society, but they were at least right to point out that entrepreneurs "do produce wealth—not just their individual richness but social wealth," and therefore that "we had better pay more attention to the incentives which will help, not hamper, the productive energies of these enterprisers." That was what the Reagan program was all about, he argued.[10] The criticism that "the Reagan budget will bear harshly on the poor, that the Reagan tax cuts will favor the rich, and that the increase in arms costs will threaten the whole economy" had some merit, but the time had come to try something new: "[T]he welfare economy has had its chance and failed . . . it is not part of the solution but of the prob lem." The "real point is not to make the rich richer but to increase the total pool of production and income from which both rich and poor grow—to increase the incentive to save, invest, produce." Supply-side economics was a gamble, but one "worth taking."[11] Lerner also endorsed Reagan's campaign for the Strategic Defense Initiative, not because he thought it would replace reliance on nuclear deterrence but because it could enhance it. As to the liberal argument that the Anti-Ballistic Missile Treaty, considered the cornerstone of deterrence, precluded testing and deployment of space-based systems, Lerner found it strange that those in favor of a broad interpretation of the Constitution should insist on a narrow interpretation of a treaty.[12]

In coming to these views, Lerner found himself very much in agreement with the neoconservative intellectuals who were for Reagan what the New Deal braintrusters had been for Franklin Roosevelt. They had produced a powerful synthesis of ideas, he thought, in reaction to such excesses of the 1960s as protests against American resistance to communism, calls for "black power" instead of racial integration, the nihilism of the drug culture, and self-indulgent narcissism masquerading as "flower power." These developments had been the watershed, he thought, the nadir of American liberalism, and the product of the "febrile mind" of an intellectual class spawned by the Welfare State. At its heart was an implacable hostility both to capitalism and to America itself. The "neocons" were right, too, to be offended by a judicial opinion that went into contortions to justify even forms of protest that desecrated the flag, the very symbol of national unity. "What in the name of intellectual integrity is happening here?" he asked of the opinion written in 1989 by Justice William Brennan for a 5−4 majority. How could Brennan have transformed "the deepest symbolism of a country and its consciousness" into "a juggling feat of semiotics?" It was time, he thought, for a constitutional amendment "to outlaw flag-burning" and "nonsense" to claim that such an amendment would erode the Bill of Rights.[13] And by what logic could the Democrats claim a right to block the appointment of Robert Bork to the Supreme Court on the ground that he was ideologically biased when Democratic presidents had created courts "top-heavy with result-oriented liberal activists?"[14] New Left liberalism had made a caricature out of the traditional American belief in liberty and equality. Liberty had been made a synonym for feckless anarchy, and equality "had become a quota system." The growing middle class was upset with programs like school busing and affirmative action and offended by pornography and the casual resort to abortion, but these concerns were simply not on the liberal agenda. Nor, for that matter, was a strong national defense or an economy that would not be shackled by a pessimistic fear that the world had entered "the era of limits." Too many liberals were wallowing in guilt over every social imperfection and were so paralyzed by fear, whether of nuclear weapons or dependency on fossil fuels, that they were ready to repeat the folly of appeasement rather than face down aggressors and blackmailers. The neoconservatives "simply confronted, met and answered this array of attitudes."[15]

In 1989, when Reagan left office, Lerner summed up the president's record and concluded that the credits outweighed the debits. True, he had blundered into the Iran-Contra scandal, had done nothing to alleviate the debt crisis of the developing countries, had allowed the savings-and-loan industry to escape regulation and cause massive losses for investors, and had encouraged an ethos of greed among businessmen. But in the major areas of domestic and foreign policy he had presided over a welcome turnaround. Reagan would be remembered, Lerner thought,

> as the president of a prospering economy, with little inflation and unemployment, of a business entrepreneurial system that has released the open-market energies around the world, of reform that has lowered the tax level and closed many loopholes.
>
> He will be remembered as the president who rearmed America with a clout adequate to its commitments abroad, gave its people a sense of confidence about their world role, strengthened the nation as "first among equals" in the Western community, and—wonder of wonders—established a post–Cold War relation to the Soviet Union.[16]

Thanks to these epoch-making achievements, Lerner thought, the nation was defying the gloomy prophecies of those who predicted it would decline just as other great empires had in the past. Instead, America had become a model for efforts to establish democracy and free markets around the world, "a command post at the center of a tornado of world change, as historic as any in our century." [17] Nothing could have better vindicated his confidence in America's adaptive genius.

Lerner would have stoutly denied that his endorsement of the Reagan revolution was a symptom of the conservatism that is often said to come with age. He certainly thought of the social and economic policies that Reagan represented as an agenda for rejuvenation that would revitalize a social system showing serious symptoms of breakdown. He tried to distinguish that form of conservatism from the "cultural populism" of "Radical Right zealots" like Jesse Helms and the fundamentalist religious dogmatism of the "Moral Majority." Nor would he have anything to do with Pat Buchanan's isolationist conservatism, which, with its appeal to paranoid nativism and possibly to anti-Semitism, reminded him of Lindbergh and the America First movement of the 1930s.[18] He compared the ex-Klansman David Duke to the "populist fascists" who had threatened the New Deal.[19] These faces of extremism recalled the hatred and repressiveness of European fascism. He could hardly think of himself as a conservative if that term extended to these elements of the political Right, for he remained strongly in favor of the toleration essential to a pluralist democracy.[20]

But neither could he still think of himself as a liberal. On a television program in 1989, he and his friend and former Williams student James MacGregor Burns were asked whom they would favor for president as Reagan's successor. Burns opted for the governor of New York, Mario Cuomo, or for Senator Ted Kennedy. Lerner replied that he was sorry that he could not go along with his former student. He found himself drawn to Jeane Kirkpatrick, who had been appointed by Reagan to serve as ambassador to the United Nations and whom he admired for her militant anticommunism and staunch support of Israel.[21] On a second program, they were asked how their political views had changed. Burns harked back to the Lerner he had known in the 1930s, saying he still favored something more militant than wishy-washy and pragmatic liberalism, perhaps a new form of progressivism. Lerner was asked pointedly if over the years he himself had not become more conservative. He answered that none of the conventional labels adequately described his progress on his "intellectual pilgrim's journey." He preferred to think of himself as a "centrist" who cared most about "the cohesion of our society, its resistance to extremisms and its equilibrium in the midst of a changing world that is responding to our ideas of free markets and open societies." [22] If this was not exactly a doctrinal creed of any sort, let alone one that could be passionately championed, it came closest to describing the position in which he found himself.

Living and Aging

Lerner was by no means the only one to move toward the political right in the 1970s and 1980s. Other liberals and Democrats were also becoming centrists, if not outright conservatives or neoconservatives, in response to the same forces that were repelling Lerner from the political Left. He may well have been "feeling his age," however, if only in wanting to play the contrarian curmudgeon among those in his own camp, or perhaps to make clear by supporting Reagan that he was still an independent thinker who followed no party line. But aging was certainly very much on his mind in these years. The subject had not escaped his notice, even before he entered the period Americans are supposed to think of as their "golden age." Now it forced itself more and more on his thinking. He wrote about it frequently, as he also did about the subject of death.

Already in *America as a Civilization,* he noted the American discomfort with thoughts of death and dying:

> Whether through fear of the emotional depths or because of a drying up of the sluices of religious intensity, the American avoids dwelling on death or even coming to terms with it: he finds it morbid and recoils from it, surrounding it with word avoidance (Americans never die, but "pass away") and various taboos of speech and practice. A "funeral parlor" is decorated to look like a bank; everything in a funeral ceremony is done in hushed tones, as if it were something furtive, to be concealed from the world: there is so much emphasis on being dignified that the ceremony often loses its quality of dignity.[23]

As he grew older, he often wrote about aging, sometimes with a sense of bravado, but usually in order to assert the will to live and to reflect on the opportunities of life in the years of maturity. He saw aging as a challenge—an opportunity to defy the inevitability of death by continuing to be creative—and as a time to profit from the wisdom that presumably comes with the experience of life. He did not think that aging brought profound changes in character or personality. When he reached the age of fifty, he remarked in a column that "the real sadness of fifty is not that you change so much but that you change so little." Agreeing with Dostoevsky, he added that "the last half of your life is lived with the habits contracted in the first half."[24]

This was certainly true of him. The way of life and even the pace of life he had established for himself in his younger years continued unchanged. He continued to write his column almost until the very end, dictating from his sickbed when he could no longer type. He remained a working professor almost as long. He wrote books, started new writing projects, and lectured and traveled around the country almost as much as ever. He felt that he was in the grip of a "can't help" attitude toward work. He could struggle best against illness by refusing to let it stop him from working. He was especially proud that in 1981, when he recovered from a serious illness and went back to USIU to lecture, the entire graduate school turned out, anxious that he manage to get through the three-hour session. He was moved by their concern and thankful that he did get through it.

Earlier, when he had turned sixty-five, he devoted a column to the question of aging and reiterated his previously stated view that the only answer to the aging process is to insist on living as if it were not happening: "Time starts eating at you terribly early; you begin to die from the moment you are born, even as you begin to grow, until somewhere at the midpoint the dying wins the upper hand and you die more than you grow." The only answer is "the continued renewal of outlook, attitude and vigor even when your basic cellular structure is no longer being renewed . . . to live more expressively and joyfully the years that we have, right to the hilt." [25] A few years later, in a column on the death of Bertrand Russell at the age of ninety-seven, Lerner mused that if he could create a perfect world, "I should arrange death to come when a man was finally ready for it—no sooner, no later—when he felt that his work was reasonably finished, and it made more sense to cease than to go on. I agree with Ionesco that death under our present arrangement is a scandal. It cuts life short just when the gathered sheaves can be of some use." [26] The worst death, he thought, was one that came prematurely, "anywhere from childhood through the fifties." "Men fear death," he quoted Francis Bacon, "as they fear to go in the dark," adding, "Perhaps. But my own feeling about death is based not on the fear of the unknown but on the sense of injustice at seeing a flowering functioning life struck down—so much mastered, so much to come, all erased." [27] In 1973, at the fiftieth reunion of his class at Yale, he reflected that while it is impossible to escape a feeling of foreboding at the impending end of life, "we also know that our little ship is borne along on vast changing tides of recurrent life, in the procession of the generations." [28] In a notebook entry dated 1987, he wrote that he wanted his epitaph to read: "He died young, joyful, in his stirrups, riding life, at an advanced age."

Because he was busy living life to the hilt, Lerner's thoughts about death did not make him morbid. He enjoyed living too much to dwell upon death. Ever since they had settled in Manhattan in 1943, the Lerners had been happily active New Yorkers. They made many friends, especially in literary and academic circles, took advantage of the city's vibrant cultural life, and built an active and full family life. They amused each other by quoting lines of poetry both enjoyed and conjuring up memorable characters in novels and plays they both knew. Lerner knew many poems by heart and loved to recite them. Mary Ellin Barrett, the novelist daughter of Irving Berlin and a close friend of the Lerners for many years, remarked that he "would break into poetry like other people would break into song." The Lerners often gave dinner parties at which many of New York's literary lions rubbed shoulders with academics, publishers, Broadway and television producers, and actors and actresses. At family gatherings Lerner played his old violin in trios and quartets. On car trips, he would lead the children in singing labor songs. And all the while, he liked to say, he kept up an interior dialogue, after the manner of Machiavelli, who said that every evening he would dress himself in white and enter the hall of the ancients to converse with them.

Until they moved to a smaller apartment in 1978, and had to dispose of much of his library, their Manhattan home on East 84th Street was crammed with books of all sorts. Max and Edna were voracious readers who were drawn both to favorite classics and to provocative new writing. In the evenings they would each read separately and then break off to discuss what they had learned and enjoyed. Puzzled sometimes about how to focus a column, he would ask Edna to talk about what was on her mind so that he could get a better idea of how to express things. She was sometimes startled to pick up the newspaper and find her thoughts in his column. He took pride in being able to learn from her, particularly about her findings as a clinical psychologist. She read his book manuscripts and called his attention to repetitions and structural problems. She admired him for working so hard and was proud simply of being his wife.

Although he had no head for practical matters, and was disorganized and untidy in other respects, when it came to work he was a model of self-discipline. He read until late at night, sometimes into the early morning hours, constantly making notes for lectures, columns, and books he intended to write, often jotting down ideas on a blank page of paper, circling them, and linking the circles by crisscrossing lines and arrows. In the early years, he typed his newspaper pieces and sent them to his secretary; in later years he wrote them out in longhand and read them to his secretary. He would scan the morning papers over breakfast. On the days when he wrote his columns, he would sometimes talk to his family about possible topics and then disappear into his study to read and write.

If there was a single axiom by which Lerner lived, it was that work and love were all important. He liked to work late at night because he felt he was then in a "hypnogogic state" in which his mind could elude the self-censor that might have banned an original thought during waking hours. But he did not try to shut out the life around him in order to concentrate on his work. In Manhattan, even as he retired into his study to concentrate on his work, he kept his door open to the family. He made it clear to his children that he never minded being interrupted by them. Steve would sometimes drop in after returning home from a date in the early hours of the morning. His father would look up over the tops of his reading glasses from his old Royal typewriter and greet him warmly. Steve remembers the typical scene vividly:

> His chair had a piece of plywood on the seat to give him support. He sat straight up in it, not leaning back. There was nothing "laid back" about his work habits. He said that he had grown accustomed to getting by without much sleep from his early years delivering milk in the wee hours of the morning. There is a scooped out grapefruit rind on a plate, a scattering of cracker crumbs on the desk along with piles of newspapers, books, and notes. He is on deadline but not overly worried about it. I sit in the red leather armchair, the one other piece of furniture in the study. We talk about what I am up to and what he is writing about. He has found a quote from a book about mythology that fits neatly with the column. He starts talking about the myth and we lose sight of the current affairs topic to which he is directing the column. Some of my best talks and most intimate moments with him came in these early hour encounters while he was hard at work.[29]

He was in fact, as Edna has remarked, a "wonderful father" to all his children. Although he traveled a great deal, he made sure to be with each of them as they graduated from school and college, and he often visited them and took them on his trips. She thought he had conveyed his energy to the children, especially the boys, genetically and by upbringing, who had his characteristically effervescent temperament. All the children were well educated. After private schooling in New York and Vermont, Connie was sent to Smith College and Sarah Lawrence, Pamela to Brandeis, and Joanna to Sarah Lawrence. Connie married and subsequently divorced the financial analyst Richard Russell. Pamela married, had two children, and died tragically of cancer at the age of twenty-eight. Joanna married Peter Townsend, an executive with Exxon. All the boys were sent to prep school, either Andover or Exeter. Michael and Steve went on to Harvard while Adam enrolled at Amherst. Michael earned a Ph.D. at Yale in political science and seemed to be following in his father's footsteps when he was appointed to the faculty. After taking a leave to spend a year in California, however, he

decided not to return to Yale. Instead, he went on to found an innovative center for alternative healing, was married, divorced, and
remarried. In 1983, in recognition of his achievements, he was
awarded a coveted five-year MacArthur Foundation Prize Fellowship and wrote a book about supplementary care for cancer patients.[30] Steve became a writer with a special concern for the environment[31] and wed the daughter of the Lerner family friends
Marvin and Mary Ellin Barrett. Adam earned an M.D. at Yale, became a research oncologist, and married. Lerner was particularly
pleased to have grandchildren, partly because he had the view
common among parents that he would live on through his progeny.
At the birth of Michael's son Joshua, he was moved to reflect in his
column on the cycle of life:

> I hold him over my shoulder, and burp him, much as I did when I
> paced the floor with his father some thirty years ago. This is the con-
> tinuity of the generations, the eternal recurrence which gives life
> its endearing quality, despite all the ephemeral headline happen-
> ings I have been writing about. You hold the tiny creature in your
> arms, and you think about what he has become part of—a life web
> at once enduring and fragile—and you get a lump in your throat.

Summers on Long Island were especially happy times. The girls
would descend on them, relieving his guilt feelings at having abandoned them, but they sometimes subjected Edna to the subtle tor-
tures children of divorced parents can inflict on the woman who re
places their mother. The Lerners were part of the social whirl in
the Hamptons and enjoyed dinner parties with friends and family
outings at the beach. Friends remember the dinners around a big
oval table, with Lerner presiding like a professor at a seminar, encouraging everyone to take part. Lerner would take long walks with
the children. He taught the boys to ride a bike, intent on making
up with them for his own father's lack of physical activity in raising him. As they grew older, he taught them how to drive, seating
them at first on his lap. In the evenings, they would gather drift-
wood, build a fire, and picnic at Flying Point Beach. He would write
his columns earlier than in Manhattan and take the boys with him
at eleven o'clock in the evening to the telegraph office, where he
would dictate the piece to the clerk, complete with semi-colons and
full stops. He had time to think about the doings of the family
dogs, which he described in a column about the summer's ease:

Even our big Bouviers—Shadow and Aquarius—lead a bi-polar
life. For part of the week they hibernate in the warmth of the city
house, barking at anything that moves inside or out, but sleeping the
rest of the unreturning time, dreaming doubtless of the dog heaven
in the country. Then they reach the sun and wind of that heaven,
with its delights of chasing rabbits and running through the fields
and digging in the marshes, and they come to life again. But in both
places they go back to their centuries-old role of pacing the turf they
are protecting, warily standing guard over what has been entrusted
to them. They too have their rituals of meaning.[32]

But although Lerner continued to enjoy life and found some aspects of aging acceptable and even gratifying, in one important respect he found what was happening to him deeply disappointing.
He had always enjoyed celebrity, not only because it gave him recognition but because it meant that his opinions were taken seriously.
With the passage of time and the appearance of younger pundits,
he was losing prominence. Already in 1972, he noted in a diary that
he was sometimes experiencing depression and a "fear of declining
powers" when he found that his chief outlets were not running his
column as frequently as in the past. Against his will, he found himself becoming less a public figure and more an introspective "self,"
even as he continued to think of himself as a kind of American
everyman. In his column he continued to chronicle the great events
in the nation's history, agonizing over Watergate in the '70s and endorsing the swing toward conservatism in the '80s. He went through
the sexual revolution with the younger generation, although the
drug culture remained utterly beyond his ken. In his struggle against
illness he saw himself asserting the universal principle of autonomy. He rejected the idea of retirement; it meant, he said, retiring
from life.

He was especially happy when he was able to continue teaching.
In 1982, he was invited to inaugurate the newly established W. Harold and Martha Welch Chair in American Studies at Notre Dame,
at the initiative of Professor Donald P. Costello, then chairman of
the university's departments of American Studies and Communi-
cation Arts. Teaching two three-hour evening classes each week
with a hundred students in each did not exhaust him. On the contrary, they left him glowing with excitement, pleased with having
enthralled another audience, excited by the play of ideas and by
the recognition of some new thought that had emerged in his dialogue with students. Continued contact with young people made

him feel that he was imparting the wisdom of age to them and that they were rejuvenating him by keeping him sensitive to the novelties of the rising generation. To his surprise and pleasure, the university provost, Timothy O'Meara, invited him to occupy the chair a second year. He was especially pleased to be so warmly welcomed at Notre Dame, he wrote for the university magazine, because it made it so clear that the animosities of the past "between a conservative Catholic hierarchy and my liberal Jewish culture" were over:

> All that American Catholics and Jews have ever wanted from one another—given their built-in theological and cultural differences—has been a sympathetic acceptance of their diversity, an understanding of their common biblical tradition, and a creative effort to work together within the common frame of our American civilization. I found that sympathy and understanding at Notre Dame.[33]

He was also delighted to be writing his column because it enabled him to remain a commentator on the events of the day. He sought new and wider audiences by writing for mass-circulation magazines. He tried his hand at a documentary film script for the Hollywood producer Otto Preminger on the career of Justice Black, but the result was wooden and didactic, and Preminger turned it down. In these late years, however, he also had a nagging sense that he had not done enough important work, having put too much into newspaper journalism and not enough into more enduring forms of writing. He had left too many books uncompleted, including a study of the presidency he wanted very much to finish. When he was asked, after many years away from studying the Supreme Court, to give a talk on the Court at a scholarly conference, he felt challenged and pleased, and worked hard to produce something they would find worthwhile. He knew, though, that others had taken up where he had left off. He came to feel that he had spread his talents thin and that as a result his reputation as a serious thinker had suffered. To compound the problem, his personal behavior had opened him to scandal and to Edna's rebuke. In a dream he recorded in a journal in 1976, he saw both anxieties symbolized. He dreamed that he was with the president of Brandeis, Abram Sachar, looking at a book Sachar had presumably written in the 1920s on medieval history (like his *A History of the Jews*) but about which he had done nothing more since:

> I . . . comment on how it looks like a Knopf book—the design of outside, the title page with a long eighteenth-century description.

He says testily *no*. I say "Perhaps they copied it from a Knopf book?" No. I examine it—published by a small local firm when he was teaching in the provinces (Actually he was at Urbana), having come over from Germany(?). It has a dedication, added later, to a faculty friend who died . . . Dream shifts . . . I am at his house, with students. He says stay for dinner. I finally agree. It takes long to prepare. Finally we sit down. I find him later(?), looking tragic. Why? He shows me slips of paper—mine—I read them. One is about him—his Napoleonic pose, etc—also about myself, + my being handsome(!). He seems more shocked by the second than first. I say well, not in conventional way, but I *am*, sort of. How did he get these? J had sent them as a gift for some occasion—had picked them herself, sent them with a student, to show the better side of me?

Then he added a parenthetical decoding of the dream:

I think the failure to write more books is my own . . . The dedication to a dead professor is to myself. The "handsome" part my feeling that I am attractive to women, which is why they cluster around me. The notes I have left behind after death, like Paul Tillich, and J is Hannah [Tillich] going through them, unwittingly exposing me "naked to my enemies," thus betraying and punishing me . . .[34]

Coping with Illness

In 1990, in *Wrestling with the Angel,* he set down an often- poignant memoir of his struggle with illness. The first time in his adult life he experienced the symptoms of an illness was in 1977, when at the age of seventy-three he experienced prostate-related difficulties. The first of several biopsies, which he found "ravaging," showed that he was suffering from benign enlargement of the gland, not cancer. That news at least was something to celebrate. Then, from 1979 through 1981, he felt an intermittent sense of cramp and pain unrelated to the prostate that bought him discomfort and an anxiety. At first he tried to deny that there was anything wrong. During this period, there was "an episode of intense emotional distress," clearly a reference to the breakup with Mary Ellen in San Diego. Despite his pains, he agreed to do a piece for a magazine celebrating "The Delights of Aging," something he felt afterward had been an "idiotic" thing to do. In the third week of January 1981, the pain became more intense and he lost five pounds. He felt that he must have developed a cancer "somewhere in my gut." Tests showed that he had a greatly enlarged spleen, "probably a carcinoma," which would require hospitalization. There he began to receive chemotherapy. A year later, he was examined by a specialist, who informed him that he had large-cell lymphoma in an advanced state. He would need more aggressive chemotherapy as well as radiation, and his age, seventy-nine, made it unlikely that the cancer could be eliminated. Pressed to estimate survival time, the doctor said, as kindly as he could, that it probably would not be much more than six months.

Lerner was determined to remain the captain of his fate so long as he possibly could. He made up his mind to find out what he could about his disease so that he would be sure that every possible measure was being taken to defeat it. "I decided to fight back," he wrote in his memoir, "if only to show that, however ravaged by the divided cell, I was not a statistic but a sovereign person." [35] In New York Hospital he discovered to his dismay that no matter how sovereign a person may consider himself, once he becomes a patient he inevitably becomes subject to the health care system, ruled by the routines and requirements of the professional practice of medicine. Lerner's stubborn ego asserted itself; he bent every effort toward putting himself, not the doctor and the hospital staff, at the center of decision making. But it was they who determined that the spleen should be removed, and he who had no other choice but to give his consent; they who found the organ impossible to remove because it was too entangled with others; they who began administering the chemotherapy. Because he gave his consent at every step, he could at least console himself with the thought, however illusory, that he was in charge. Later, he learned that they had not told him that evidence of cancer on the pancreas had been found and removed for analysis. He had to inveigle that information out of a young medical intern. They did not tell him the news, he learned afterward, because pancreatic cancer is so implacable that, if they had told him, the news might have weakened his will to live, and with it his body's ability to resist disease. They informed him only when the tests showed he was suffering from a much less threatening form of cancer—lymphoma of the spleen that had attached itself to the pancreas. Through all the treatment, despite the pain and drowsiness, he insisted on writing his column regularly, dictating it to his secretary at the *Post,* Evelyn Irsay.

Thinking about his illness, Lerner pondered the relationship of mind and body, *psyche* and *soma,* and was drawn closer to his family. In their different ways, each member of the family circle tried to help him. Edna, as a practicing clinical psychologist, was dubious about the "will therapies" he had learned about in California. Adam, a medical student, took a technical interest in the disease and helped him understand it as a cellular dysfunction. Steve offered a sympathetic ear. Joanna was supportive from the distance of London, where her husband was posted. Connie was involved in a religious-psychological support group, and she and her father had been estranged. Both he and Edna thought her beliefs and way of life beyond the pale. But they tried to overcome the estrangement with some success.

In discussions with Michael, Lerner considered whether to try an alternative to medical therapy rather than go through what he knew would be the ravages of medical treatment. He finally opted for chemotherapy. In the hospital, he looked on what was happening to him through his old literary eyes:

> I had been much taken by Tennyson's *Idylls of the King*. I now half expected Merlin, maguslike, to enter with the cup. If I was to drink the healing potion I should have liked it in a silver chalice, preceded by a flourish of trumpets. Instead there came a very business-like nurse pushing a trolley mounted with a large inverted bottle. I didn't drink the potion, which was fed into my system intravenously through a needle inserted in my wrist. Lying in bed I used to watch the clockwork drip-drip of the liquid which slowly, efficiently—along with my other drugs—was transforming my interior into a chemical vat.[36]

The therapy worked. He was able to travel to California to resume his teaching in the early months of the year and then to give his fall course at the New School as usual. His sleep was good, as was his weight and energy. Then came a series of new difficulties. He suffered from shingles, he was operated on for a hernia, a nosebleed hemorrhaged. But he hung on and felt confident enough to accept the invitation to teach at Notre Dame. In 1982, he taught the winter semester at USIU and then went to South Bend. He was seized by an impulse to write his autobiography and began to do so, though he left it uncompleted. He did a rough draft of the first volume and planned to call it *Delight of Battle*, drawing from a favorite stanza of Tennyson's "Ulyssses":

> Much have I seen and known; cities of men
> And manners, climates, councils, governments,
> Myself not least, but honour'd of them all;

And drunk delight of battle with my peers,
Far on the ringing plains of windy Troy.

As his illnesses persisted, he saw a renowned cancer specialist, Dr. James Holland, characteristically investing the physician with literary adornments:

> I could have wished for a Picasso to draw him, with all the lines and angles intersecting to express the rich contradictions of the man. The face was at once open, sympathetic, engaged, dispassionate, quizzical, absorbed, amused. Always (as I was to discover) it carried authority, always it conveyed an image of total immersion. At that moment, I felt, I was the only person who counted, because for that moment I represented the particular of the larger issue Holland cared about most. For me he had—and has retained—the charisma that goes with earned authority. No Dante about to be inducted into the circles of the Inferno welcomed his Virgil as fervently as I welcomed this guide through the Hell, Purgatory, and Paradise of my illness and health.[37]

Holland initially thought that the lymphoma had spread to the lungs and that more chemotherapy would be required. But a month later, he examined new X-rays and decided a biopsy was advisable to determine whether the spots on the lung were indeed cancerous. Lerner was told the operation involved would be minimal, but he found to his dismay that it would involve sawing through one rib. The procedure was successful, however, and he came though well. The results showed that the cancer was probably not lymphoma but rather a low-grade malignancy of another sort that could probably be dealt with by chemotherapy. Since Lerner wanted very much to take up the post at Notre Dame, he arranged to commute every two weeks between New York and South Bend, allowing his doctors to see him at regular intervals. Holland consulted the head of surgical pathology who determined that the cancer probably originated from the prostate and was therefore a slower-developing, more manageable form of cancer. More tests removed all doubt.

Lerner then received the now standard choices most men who survive long enough must face about how to treat prostate cancer: whether to practice watchful waiting, to excise the cancer by castration, to take radiation therapy (with its risks of incontinence and impotence) or estrogen therapy, or, in his case, a then experimental drug called leuprolide, which was designed to reduce the secretion of a pituitary hormone necessary for the production of testosterone—the hormone necessary for the growth of the tumor. Although he was warned that as his testosterone level would be reduced virtually to zero—and with it his libido—he opted for the experimental therapy. In March 1983 the therapy began; he was able to inject himself in the thigh every day. As months passed, his symptoms diminished. He had been spitting blood but that stopped; the prostate became less swollen. In July X-rays revealed a dramatic change. The drug had been effective. Lerner thought that the result had been a compound of medical treatment and mental will. He came to believe that the healing process is both somatic and spiritual: "Along with the network of neural receptors and messengers it has as its base a spiritual reality which is grounded in survival but reaches to belief of some sort." [38]

The healing process left him with general weakness, skin rashes, edema in both legs, and at one point pneumonia—all indicating that his immune system had been compromised. Still, by December 1984, he could be presented at Grand Rounds as an example of a recovered cancer patient. He was kept on the hormone medication but weaned off others. By then, however, he had another medical complication: a sensation of discomfort and chest constriction that turned out to be a heart attack, fortunately a minor one. Warned that intrusive measures such as bypasses and angioplasty were too risky at his age, he adopted a new regimen of exercise and diet in the hope of clearing his arteries. In the East he walked; at Hefner's mansion he lifted weights and rode a stationary bicycle. The doctors were impressed by his renewed vigor.

Recovery from illness made him feel a greater kinship with his ancient forebears. Like the biblical patriarchs, he felt that he too had been "fecund, generative, intent on giving the children a strong family frame . . ." Watching his children grow brought back memories of his own youth and enabled him to enjoy the warmth of family life. "I love the occasions of the gathering of the clan," he exulted, "kin as well as kith, when the authority that family once had in America can be reclaimed, and the place of deference that aging parents had can be restored." [39] At the same time, he reflected, in a journal entry, on the contrast between the death that comes inexorably to the individual and the opportunity for a renewal of life that comes to a civilization in its senescence:

While the leaf on the tree and the early culture phase of a civilization may grow sere and die, the tree renews itself for another round,
as do many civilizations. "So careless of the single life, so careful of
the race," wrote Tennyson of evolution. Yet with all my vauntings
and passions and prides I am a leaf, not a tree. I am a single life, not
a race. The sheer facticity of it is that I am decaying to death, just
as the individual reed is. Yet though my strength is only that of the
reed I am, in Pascal's phrase, a "thinking reed." Hence both the
pathos and glory of it.[40]

He took some comfort from the fact that for many creative people
in the past old age had been the prime of life. Ulysses had returned
home to rule Syracuse after a lifetime of warring and wandering. We
now admire the wisdom of the older Ulysses, he remarked, more
than his youthful craftiness. He thought of the ripe work of Ho-
kusai and Tassai, of Michelangelo, Titian, and Rembrandt, Goya
and Cézanne, Monet and Turner, and in modern times Georgia
O'Keeffe and Louise Nevelson, Jacques Lipschitz, Alexander Cal-
der, and Frank Lloyd Wright. Not only were these artists working
hard and successfully in their later years, but each did so in a distinct
style. "In the large, the elder style moves away from the work of the
early and mid-years, sometimes into a lightness and freedom from
past forms, toward greater depth, intensity, imaginativeness." What
is true of artists is also true of playwrights, from Sophocles through
Goethe, to Hardy, Yeats, and O'Neill. Each time of life has its own
creativeness, some of which comes "from coping with the near presence of death and the preciousness of what time remains."[41] In a
journal entry dated January 7, 1986, he noted there were also intellectual benefits of aging:

If the young dream dreams, the old see visions of what can be . . .
There is a lightness of resolution in becoming old. Things that once
seemed impossibly knotty somehow get resolved. It is when you
have yourself been sternly tested in relation to events, family, and
friends—and they in relation to you—that you are surer of them
and yourself. Testing is all . . . At this point life acquires an economy, gets stripped of the inessential. You travel light, discard your
accumulated surplus anxiety and rage, get rid of the encumbering
baggage of life's heavy protocols. This becomes a new personal
polity, with power, rank, and status cut to the bone. You win a new
freedom from labels and slogans, even from those of your own intellectual gang . . . Thus equipped you are somewhat fitter to meet

the inevitable batterings that age inflicts on the body, fitter also to respond with a mind more seasoned by adversity. You might even learn to confront Death when he comes offering to be your fellow traveler.[42]

And he had second thoughts about Norman Brown's emphasis on the potential power of *Eros*. He was increasingly impressed by the countervailing weight of *Thanatos*, not in the morbid sense that death must triumph over life but rather in the dialectical sense that Freud had in mind, as the creative tension between negative and positive. *Thanatos* was just as important to life as *Eros*, he now appreciated, because it imposed limits, sharpened the sense of reality, compelled a vision of what was most important and most universal. In another journal entry he wrote in praise of a 1966 critique of Brown's *Love's Body* he had only recently discovered: "Death asserts the not to us. But if we have any spirit we assert it in turn to death. In dialectical terms, it spells the *negation of the negation* . . . That's what I've been doing to death, I suppose, through all these years—negating its negation . . . I prefer the Munch painting of the dialectical dance of life and death, with the pairs of lovers in embrace, and the new dancer entering the scene as the Dürer-like Death figure exits."[43] Hefner, struggling to recover from a stroke, looked to Lerner's battle with what initially appeared to be terminal cancer, compounded by a heart attack, as an inspiration:

> His remarkable strength of will and stubborn unwillingness to go into the dark night was, and is, a continuing source of inspiration for me . . . There was a point in time in which the chemotherapy had caused him to lose almost all of his hair, a white mane in which he had taken a lion's pride, and he became so weak that simply climbing the stairs to his room was a serious challenge . . . In the last few years, in this period of remarkable productivity, Max was so joyful that his wife would refer to his mood as "compulsive euphoria." He had walked to the edge of the abyss and refused to fall in. He was like a man reborn and this made him a special source of inspiration to me, especially after my stroke when I needed that optimism during my own period of recovery.[44]

Journey's End

A few years later cancer struck Lerner for the third time. At first his symptoms were misdiagnosed as a heart ailment, but when he turned yellow with jaundice he went back to Dr. Holland who immediately found that he was suffering from cancer of the bile duct. By surgically bypassing the duct, Holland extended Lerner's life for more than a year. When signs of cancer appeared elsewhere, Lerner urged the doctors to use the most aggressive therapies they had, and they prescribed both chemotherapy and radiation. Lerner became bedridden, a burden to himself and even more to his wife, who, with the help of nurses, devoted herself entirely to taking care of him. Finally, on June 5, 1992, two months after he had written his last column, he suffered a stroke, struggled in vain to speak, and died in the bosom of his family. At his funeral, Rachel Cowan, a convert to Judaism who had become a rabbi, recited the *Kaddish*, the Jewish prayer for the dead, in accordance with his wishes. In keeping with religious tradition, he was buried in a simple pine coffin.

The news of Lerner's death evoked warm tributes from many friends. Memorial meetings were held at the New School, Brandeis, and USIU. At the New School, where Lerner had given popular adult education classes for many years, Steve Lerner reminisced about his father and introduced Edward Albee, Mary Ellin Barrett, James MacGregor Burns, the sociologist Irving Louis Horowitz, Frank Manuel, Martin Peretz, and Jerry Talmer of the *New York Post*. Talmer remembered that the first time he heard Lerner lecture had been in his student days at Dartmouth in 1938. "This dynamic little Jewish guy would come into this very non-Jewish setting and explode it . . . He stirred us all up." At the *Post*, Talmer added, "he and Wechsler and Kempton were the guts of the paper." Horowitz discussed the significance of Lerner's work for the social sciences, emphasizing his "enduring faith in the law": "In this special concern with the just society Max was able to fuse with remarkable ease, in column after column, book after book, a Jewish faith, an American credo, and a European conscience." Burns said that he could think of no better tribute than to read a passage from the preface to *It Is Later than You Think*, the book that had inspired him as a young man. Barrett read a sixteenth-century poem about death at an early age that Lerner and Edna had admired. Albee said that he had befriended Lerner because he had always made friends with people who could teach him. "When you were with Max, he gave you the feeling that nobody in the world was more important to him . . . I never studied with Max, but he taught me all the time we knew each other . . . He constantly drove me toward

honesty, toward self-awareness, toward a kind of intellectual toughness and emotional softness." Manuel spoke of Lerner's symbolic
significance:

> If you cut a rough 200 mile swath across the isthmus of Europe from
> the Black Sea to the Baltic you will demarcate the area from which
> the ancestors of most American Jews migrated in the late nineteenth
> and twentieth centuries. Minsk is located in the heart of that band
> and it was the birthplace of Max Lerner. For me he remains a sym-
> bolic figure of that great migration. Though the immigrants passed
> through the gates of other major ports of the east, I think it was New
> York that became their new Jerusalem. They influenced its rhythms,
> its speech, its style and often its very words . . . For me he has al-
> ways been the spirit of this city in its heyday, when it was the scin-
> tillating light of this country and he was its official commentator.

Peretz gave an especially personal tribute, as he had already done
in *The New Republic,* in noting that Lerner had been more of father to him than his own father, reassuring him of his gifts, rebuk-
ing him for mistakes, but always encouraging him.[45] After the piece
appeared, he had been stunned, he remarked, to hear from so many
people of so many different backgrounds that they too thought of
Lerner as their teacher, even though most of them had never been
in a classroom of his. Lerner had that effect because he "was so restless, so exacting, so open, so skeptical . . . a mixture of gaiety with
gravitas, mischief with illumination." He was, Peretz added, "a dis-
coverer—of ideas, of people, of movements, and of America."

Steve Lerner concluded the ceremony by reading from a 1988
diary entry by his father, quoted at the end of *Wrestling with the
Angel,* about the sort of memorial service he would want:

> Yes, I want the *Yisgadal v'yiskadash shema rabbo* intoned, ritual
> fashion, as it was at my father's death. It's a great sound to die by . . .
> Yet I don't want a solemn, tear-filled service, or a memorial gather-
> ing to which people feel obligated to come, and a few offer eulogies
> from notes they have labored over. I would prefer some friends and
> family to gather under the pear tree where both Steve and Adam
> were married, and where my children and their children have gath-
> ered. Perhaps someone will read from stuff I have written, saying I
> lived for words. I shall die with some pleasure at leaving words be-
> hind, along with children and their children to recall them. When
> it's over, perhaps the young will go inside and dance the dance of
> love and life.[46]

Pilgrim in the Promised Land

These are my two giants, America and Russia, with whom my
life was intertwined. Russia was the one we got away from, with
rankling memories of persecution. America was the one we came
to, and it opened itself to us, made us work hard, yes, offered us
the challenge of hard ground, but gave us the chance to breathe
equal air.[1]

Frank Manuel's observation at the
New School memorial that Max Lerner had symbolized the Jewish
migration to America from Eastern Europe is especially apt, for Lerner was as much a pilgrim in the promised land as any Puritan child
transplanted from his native soil to some new haven of his own. The
first settlers too wanted to escape religious oppression, to live in
freedom, to make a home for their descendants, and to create a society where, as their leader John Winthrop wrote during an Atlantic
crossing in 1630, they might "be all knitt more nearly together
in the Bond of brotherly affeccion."[2] The European background
shaped Lerner's mind and character as it did theirs. The challenge
of the New World bred his ambition to succeed and his hopeful
vision of the future, as it did theirs. And the feeling of being part
of a great experiment in the building of a new community gave
him a commitment to social justice they also felt. In at least one

important respect, however, the experience of the early and later pilgrims was different. The first American settlers were colonists who reestablished the culture they brought with them. Driven, as Oliver Cromwell said, "to find their bread in a howling wilderness,"[3] the Puritans encountered incomparably more daunting physical hardships, but there was nothing problematic about their identity. They met no different way of life that defined them as outsiders. They did not have to choose whether to huddle together in their own separate community or try to gain acceptance in a more established society by shedding enough of their peculiarities to be granted membership. The experience of immigration was very different for those who came later. Most were in awe of the established culture they found and wanted desperately to merge with it. Lerner was acutely aware of being an immigrant, with an immigrant's sense of insecurity. Although at first he felt trapped between old and new, he soon found, like so many other newcomers, that education was the passport to acceptance. By taking advantage of the excellent schooling the society made available to him—both in the public schools and on a scholarship to a leading private university—he became as adept in the language of his adopted culture as anyone who could claim it as a birthright. But the warning that he could not hope to get a job teaching English literature was a harsh reminder that he was still regarded as an unwelcome intruder. This rejection at a critical time in his intellectual life may well have reinforced his youthful rebelliousness, though it was not the only stimulus that turned him toward social and political radicalism. For many immigrants, the experience of daily life was itself a socialization to radicalism. The Eastern European Jewish immigrants often became socialists, Irving Howe has pointed out,[4] mainly because of the poverty and injustice they experienced and witnessed in their ghettos and sweatshops. By the second decade of the century, their political spokesmen were Meyer London, elected to Congress from the East Side of Manhattan on the Socialist Party ticket, and Morris Hillquit, the lawyer and Socialist Labor Party mayoral candidate in 1917. Outside their own ranks, they and their offspring flocked, as Lerner did, to intellectuals like Walton Hamilton, Alvin Johnson, and the liberal politicians of the New Deal who denounced the injustices of an unregulated market economy and called for reform. More assimilated than those in the first generation, Lerner entered the mainstream of American life as a spokesmen not only for Jewish socialists but for a more diverse generation of Americans who identified with the labor movement and sought social and economic reforms, including especially an end to religious and racial discrimination. The success of the New Deal in curtailing corporate power and the general rise in living standards during the postwar economic boom mollified many Depression-era radicals, including Lerner, by reasserting the country's commitment to democratic inclusion. Many became liberals favoring active government which would regulate the economy and promote social welfare, rather than socialists demanding nationalization of industry and equalization of incomes. They campaigned for civil liberties for dissenters and civil rights for minority groups. As world events made America the "arsenal of democracy" in the struggle against fascism and totalitarian communism, Lerner came to appreciate the basic goodness of the country and its importance in the world as perhaps only an immigrant could. It is not hard to understand why someone of his background should have come up with the idea that America is a new civilization in its own right, one that had "slain the European father" and established itself as the "archetypical civilization of the West." More than those whose roots were already deep in the national soil, a newcomer who knew there was no going back to the old country was bound to want a new identity he could easily adopt as his own—a sense of nationhood he could claim as fully as any native.

For all his will to Americanize himself, however, Lerner remained acutely conscious of belonging to a minority within the larger society. For him, as for many others, the uneasiness associated with being considered a "foreigner" was not easily overcome by "naturalization" to a new nationality, even one to which he gave the exalted title of "civilization." Immigrants to an established society must choose whether to withdraw into their own ethnic or religious enclave or plunge into the larger culture by assimilating to it in one degree or another. In Lerner's case, this dilemma gave him an outsider's critical perspective and a sympathy for all those who suffered because of whatever set them apart—race, religion, ethnicity, gender or sexual preference. His own background stamped him with an Old World face and an Old World heritage, and not just any Old World face and heritage, but the inescapable burden of being a Jew in an overwhelmingly gentile society that did not value pluralism as much as it did assimilation. Though Jewishness was to become a source of pride to him, at first it was an incubus, a barrier to the full acceptance he craved and thought he could achieve only by complete cultural integration and intermarriage.

In some respects, *America as a Civilization* is a study not just of the country but of himself as a member of one of the country's hard-to-assimilate minorities, as is evident in his sensitive description of the plight of Jews and blacks:

> Like the other white ethnic groups, the Jew, to "pass," has only to become "assimilated," which is a matter of cultural conformity and absorption. Yet even the Jew who strives hardest for such absorption finds that it is not enough for him to wear his religion lightly or even discard it and break his ties of identification within his ethnic group. In many instances his offer of assimilation is not acknowledged: it is only his children and in turn their children who are finally accorded a substantial measure of acceptance. Even when the pride of Jacob has been discarded, the fear of Ahasuerus lingers.
>
> It is a hard thing for a member of such a minority group to hold the balance even between his sensitivities about status, his temptation to overreact toward hostility and either belittle himself or hate himself or flaunt in the face of the majority the very minority traits that have been called in question, his pride in his ethnic heritage, his ties with the victims and martyrs of his tradition, his hunger amidst it all to prove himself and fuse his experience into the larger cultural pattern. It is these crosscurrents of impulse and emotion that made the Negro or Jewish youth a stock figure in the problem novels of the 1940s and the 1950s. His quest for identity was a voyage that had to survive dangerous shoals and rapids. He had two cultures rather than one with which he somehow had to make his peace—identifying himself with segments of both as he grew up, sifting both of them through his fears and insecurities, his hopes and strengths, accepting and rejecting, and out of it having to discover who he was. The young Negro or the young Jew who managed to come through this experience was perhaps the sturdier personality for having been through it, and he carried with him a richer freightage of family and cultural memories. But in too many cases the experience warped or broke him.[5]

Because Lerner was so intent on becoming a part of the new society, the experience of America had a profound influence upon him, in some ways greater than that exerted by his Jewishness. His Jewish heritage was evident in his love of life and learning, and in the joy he felt as the patriarch of his own family, but the American influence was evident in his very attitude toward life. It transformed the feeling of tragic resignation imparted by his immigrant parents into the optimistic adventuresomeness of Tom Sawyer and Huckle-

berry Finn. It gave him a willingness to experiment and strike out
on his own like the pioneers who had set out in covered wagons to
settle new frontiers. It drew him to "realist" writers like Dreiser
and social theorists like Veblen who aimed to shock their countrymen into living up to the country's democratic promise. It gave him
compassion for all those denied the human rights Jefferson had declared to be the inalienable gift of nature and nature's God. It made
him sympathetic to the therapeutic innovators and sexual liberators
who wanted to lift the burdens of unwarranted guilt and unnecessary repression. And it also gave him a reverence both for the spirit
and political institutions that enabled people of diverse origins to
live together in harmony under just laws justly administered. The
Holocaust in Europe reinforced his sense of Jewish identity and
left him with a gnawing anxiety over the survival of Israel, but
paradoxically it did not make him a Zionist in the sense of someone who believes that Jews in the diaspora should return to their
ancestral homeland in Israel; instead, it made him a more intensely loyal American. It was not just that America—sometimes
alone in the world—had accepted a moral commitment to stand
by the new Jewish state, but that America was different from Europe especially because it was, as Whitman had said, a "nation of
nations," in which people of all races, all religions, all national origins, were striving to set an example for the world of harmony in
diversity. This was the America he felt so much a part of and
wanted to help preserve and keep influential in the world.

These American values found embodiment in his outlook on life
and his work as a teacher and writer. Like so many other immigrants, he too was remolded in the proverbial melting pot in which
America turned downtrodden peasants into factory workers and
craftsmen, independent farmers, middle-class entrepreneurs, and
professionals. The progeny of the immigrants, if not they themselves, came to believe that they could shape their own lives and
achieve virtually any goal they set for themselves. An upbeat American character ingrained itself in them, shadowed by reminders of
past oppressions and a lingering fear of the dark forces that mocked
but did not overcome the hopeful belief in "indefinite perfect-
ibility." For Lerner, as for Archibald MacLeish, "America was
promises." Lerner became convinced, as Peretz acutely observed at
the New School memorial, that "America itself was the decisive re-
pudiation, the ultimate denial, of pessimism."

The American outlook he took on was not just one of optimism but of a latter-day Promethean. In his graduate student years, Lerner was drawn to images of conquerors, and he thought that the peculiarly American conquerors were the "titans" of the business world. In them he saw the quintessence of the American outlook:

> . . . a daring vision and imagination and a reckless use of all resources to fulfill it; a continual restlessness, like that of a child, and a search for something new; a love of big things, and a joy in the mastery over them; the paradox of a savage exploitation of every resource, with the utmost economy of effort in attaining his ends; the ability to see his opportunity and to use his lucky chance; his intense arrogant individualism; his quick sense for estimating people and using them, and his blindness toward abstractions; his joy in the creation of means, and his ignorance of ends. This is by no means intended as a general formula; in every specific case the component qualities will be found different, often contradictory. But if ever America produces great biography it will have something of the character indicated. For that is also the American character.
>
> Above all things we must not make the mistake of judging these men from the point of view of the ascetic spirit. Their greatest quality is an insolent sense of life. See it on Wall Street during the day, and on Broadway at night. No renunciants they. They are as much at ease in the swift stream of events as healthy boys splashing in a pool. They are not "world-losers and world-forsakers." Rather is theirs the triumphant shrill of the conquerors, and the beatitude of the possessors.[6]

In some important respects, but not in all, Lerner himself acquired the same basic values he discerned in these heroic enterprisers. He too had "an insolent sense of life," a boldness of vision, and a restless desire for achievement. He wanted very much to make a name for himself and influence the course of events. He too was no ascetic. But here the parallel fades. He had no interest in acquiring wealth. Though he liked to live well and took every opportunity he could find to be well paid for his work, he gave no thought to accumulating wealth by savings or investment. He usually chose subjects to write about because they interested him and seemed important, not because he thought they would be remunerative. As a teacher, he gave of himself unstintingly and often amazed his friends by the care he took to send them newspaper clippings and books he thought might be of use to them.

When the Great Depression struck, his admiration for the heroes of industry was overwhelmed by contempt for the system of power that enabled the rich to survive and even thrive in the midst of great misery. He was never a sentimental or mainly moralistic critic of the economic system. That would have seemed to him "tender-minded." But he became a sharp critic of the productive and distributive efficiency of the unplanned economy and of the political institutions that protected it in America, especially the Supreme Court. He became a spokesman for the social underdog, not the titan. As capitalism was modified and regulated by the New Deal, however, he came to recognize that it was a much more efficient mode of production than socialism, and he was honest enough to admit that he had been wrong to suppose it was simply outmoded. He became a centrist liberal because he thought that the market economy had to be regulated by a democratic government if it was to serve the common good. The consistent thread in Lerner's thinking was his abiding faith in political liberalism and majoritarian democracy. He accepted the country's conservative turn in his later years because he agreed with the majority of Americans that it was time for the country to correct its course, so as to protect the liberty of the individual and the stability of the social and moral order from the overly leftward tendencies of the 1960s and 1970s.

The trajectory of Lerner's change of political views is an illuminating index to the shift in thinking among many public intellectuals in "the American century." In the 1920s and 1930s, he saw the country's economic institutions as systemically rigged against the working poor. Convinced by the Great Depression that buccaneer capitalism was on the way out, he embraced the cause of a militant democratic socialism and the tactic of the "popular front" as the most effective way to confront fascism. To his later regret, he did not denounce the misdeeds of the Soviet Union under Stalin as vigorously as others were doing in the 1930s, and he was among those who during the Second World War naively credited the heroic resistance of its people to their support for "the Soviet experiment." He thought that once the war was over, even those devoted to free enterprise would have to acknowledge the need for government regulation and planning. He also hoped that the wartime alliance between East and West could somehow be maintained, within the framework of the United Nations, both for the sake of world peace and so that anticommunism could not be used to thwart a transition to democratic socialism.

As a greatly modified capitalism survived the war, and as the internal repressiveness and external expansionism of the Stalinist system became all too obvious, Lerner realized that he had been wrong to suppose that political liberalism could survive without reinforcement from economic liberalism. He acquired a new respect for the virtues of liberalism as an integral social philosophy, especially in contrast to the Soviet Union's dictatorial brand of socialism. He was confident that the reforms of the New Deal and the civil rights movement were making the United States a more fully democratic society, and he now saw that a regulated market economy could become a great engine of universal prosperity. He also came to appreciate the need to protect the alliance of free nations. Convinced that the Truman Doctrine was a necessary defensive measure, he joined those other liberals who accepted the need for the United States to contain Soviet and Communist Chinese efforts to expand their power and influence.

In the process, he became a centrist liberal. Once Lerner experienced this intellectual climacteric, he reached a political plateau from which he could go no farther. The turmoil of the 1960s polarized the country in a way different from the polarization wrought by the Depression and the New Deal. Now the struggle was between those on the Left who saw America as an imperialistic force in the world, guided by an empty materialism, and those who saw America as the great champion of freedom in the world, but of a freedom guided by conventional Western values such as the belief in order, the work ethic, and the nuclear family. Lerner found himself a misfit, unable to move completely in either direction. He joined the Left in rejecting the narrowness of the traditional moral consensus, in favor of sexual openness and experimentalism, but he was a man of the Right now with respect to America's role in the world and even with respect to his strong belief in the need to maintain respect for the institutions of an orderly democracy. Once the goals of the civil rights movement—equal opportunity and the right to vote—were well on the way to being achieved, there was no longer in his view any justification for civil disobedience, let alone for conspiratorial subversion. He deplored the "black power" movement as a betrayal of the cause of integration. He believed in congressional debate and presidential leadership, not in demonstrations in the streets. Like other old-fashioned liberals of the 1940s and 1950s he was now caricatured as an arch conservative by the new radicals of the 1960s—some of whom, ironically, would soon become conservatives themselves.

In the 1960s and 1970s Lerner found neither extreme attractive.

On the one hand was the new conservatism, composed of a Radical Right linked to religious fundamentalism and of a neoconservative wing so anxious to save democracy from left-wing and countercultural subversion that it was prepared to sacrifice the achievements of the New Deal. On the other arose a New Left, led by youthful revolutionaries who professed to distrust everyone over thirty and who showed their contempt for academic and political liberalism by trashing universities, denying the right to free speech to anyone they disagreed with, and claiming that at its core America is racist and imperialist. He was simply unable and unwilling to move in either direction, and therefore remained fixed in a 1950s liberalism that could not provide a platform either for criticism or for advocacy. Politically, he had found a resting place; all that remained for him was to think about the meaning of life in more personal and psychological terms.

Finally, in the 1980s, he felt so frustrated by the willingness of liberal Democrats to embrace racial and gender quotas, to cling to welfare programs that worked only to promote dependency, to put so much stress on the rights of criminal defendants as to ignore the rights of the law-abiding citizens they preyed upon, and to weaken America's resolve to defend freedom abroad, that he announced his support for Reagan, dismaying his liberal friends and followers. Near the end of his life, he said that while he could no longer call himself a liberal, he did not think of himself as a conservative or as a neoliberal or neoconservative. None of these labels "would jibe with my progress on my intellectual pilgrim's journey": "What counts for me is the health of America as a social organism, in our own culture and society and in relation to others to sustain a viable world community." The critical question in American life, he thought, was "whether the center will hold" against fragmenting and polarizing divisions.[7]

Although these shifts of position left him open him to the charge of being a political chameleon, changing his views to suit the changing coloration of the prevailing political spectrum, he himself thought he was simply making his own objective judgments, and when necessary changing his mind, out of a continuing readiness to learn. He would have agreed with Emerson that "a foolish consistency is the hob-goblin of little minds." Throughout his adult life, Lerner often referred to himself both as a "possibilist" and a humanist. He explained what he meant by "possibilism" in reflecting on the impact of nuclear weapons:

As I look at man's calculable future I do not think in terms of either pessimism or optimism, but of possibilism. It is a stoic and tragic possibilism, yes, but there is no inherent doom discernible in the record of human history when you view it as the creative unfolding of human possibility. The Freudian conjectures, like those of Schopenhauer before him, are impressive and deeply moving, yet, until the last record is written, there is nothing certain about man's nature which shuts the door upon human possibility for contriving the resources of survival as well as for contriving the weapons of destruction. "Mankind," Romain Gary has said, "is born. Humanity must be created." [8]

By humanism he meant a commitment to reform in the light of what human beings were capable of achieving and of the constraints of human nature and circumstances. The idealistic poets and essayists he read as a young man—especially Tennyson, Coleridge, and Emerson—inspired him to think of worlds that might be, just as the realistic social theorists he studied in later years—Machiavelli, Veblen, and Marx—compelled him to think about the world that is. The question facing society, he thought, was how to find a middle way between creative imagination and harsh reality, how to keep open the possibilities for reform, how to make use of knowledge and its applications for the sake of personal and social betterment. In this respect, he was, like the country itself, a child of the Enlightenment, with its belief in progress and in liberalism, with its belief in the marketplace of ideas and equality of opportunity. "I lean to a radical humanism," he wrote, "which sees terror and apathy as only part of a bundle of human potentials, but sees in the same bundle compassion and fellow-feeling, with a dash of creativeness and a sprinkling of stoic endurance." [9] He also thought of himself as someone with a core character that did not change, even as he recognized, looking back upon his life, that his political views had mellowed considerably. He thought of America in the same way, as a society founded with certain ideals that shaped its character and were unchanging, but which had adapted its values to changing circumstances—as it had when it adopted a new constitution "in order to form a more perfect union." Veblen had seen society as an ever-adapting evolutionary system; Lerner saw American civilization in the same way, and in that respect he was himself an exemplary American. Tocqueville's notion that Americans had a "self-corrective capacity" struck him as right. Far from agreeing with those who thought America would be a declining civilization, he insisted, in an afterword to the anniversary edition of *America as a Civilization* that the opposite was more likely:

> Civilizations are more likely to die of rigidities, of absolutisms that become divisive and tear them apart, of loss of their psychic immune and support systems, of failure of nerve in the unwillingness or inability to face collective dangers, of failures of belief (especially among the young) in the viability and promise of the whole experience. Civilizations die, above all, of the impoverishment of the imagination and will that built and sustained them.[10]

Contrary to those who foresaw an American decline, Lerner was confident the country would not run out of energy precisely because its openness encouraged enterprise in generation after generation. He and his students at Notre Dame, he remarked in the 1980s, had seriously considered the notion that the country was a "dying civilization" and rejected it:

> We noted its critical elements of health and affirmation: its efforts to achieve consensus, its limits on the abuse of power, its growth and creativity, its promise and hope. The great American myth is that our children's lot will be better than our own. Our challenge is to carve out our future with coolness and courage.

The danger America faced was not a loss of creativity but the excesses of immaturity:

> Where it is lacking is in judgment and prudence, not in vitality. Its high arts as well as its popular culture revel in obsessions and excesses. The true dangers it runs, as a collective organism, are not of a spent senility but of the turmoils of adolescence. Compared with the historic civilizations which have lasted for millennia—China, India, Russia, Europe—America is still a stripling, with almost everything ahead of it to experience and suffer, but caught—as Alexander was—between the responsibilities of power and the dreams and excesses of youth.

He was sure that America would not go the way of Rome. Rome had been ruled by a patrician class that had exhausted its energies and kept outsiders from joining its ranks, he wrote, forcing them into opposition and making civil strife inevitable. By contrast, America's success had resulted from the openness of its elite structure. The secret to this success was not so much egalitarianism or even liberty in the sense of opportunity for a few to succeed, but the wholesale access it provided to all, the opportunity to participate fully in the economy, the power structure, and the culture of the entire society. When he was asked once in Warsaw to sum up in a single word what he had tried to say in his book on American civilization, Lerner thought and replied, "Access." His hosts said they had heard of Americans' interest in success but were surprised to hear him say "access." His explanation says a good deal about the way he thought about the country and his own experience of it:

> You see, we have a Declaration of Independence which says that all men are created free and equal. I hope they are born free and will remain free. But they are not born equal. They are born unequal, with very unequal abilities and potentials. Every teacher, every administrator, every businessman, every employer, every army commander, every parent knows it. I have five children of my own, and each of them was born unequal. But we have the notion in America that there ought to be equal access to equal opportunities and life chances, so that every one of these unequally born youngsters gets a chance to develop his unequal abilities to the full.

In recalling this to an audience of American educators he added:

> In this sense, access is the heart of the American experience. I was born in Russia. My parents brought their little brood of children to this country, back in 1907. Why did they come here, along with so many other immigrant families? Although there was a legend among immigrants that in America all the paving-stones were made of gold, they didn't come here to get rich. They came here so that their children could breathe freer air, could get a chance at a chance— an equal chance at life's chances. I have had it. My children are having it. To the best of my limited abilities I am determined that every other American youngster will have this kind of chance too.

Because he believed so strongly that the American ideal was to open opportunity to all individuals, he opposed the effort to make education "multi-cultural" and to substitute the goal of ethnic diversity for integration. Agreeing with Arthur Schlesinger, Jr. (*The Disuniting of America*, 1991), he thought that the new pedagogy might cause division and an imbalance between group identity and a sense of common nationality. America, Lerner wrote, was built "on fairness to all and privileges for none, on generosity, on a passion for the equality of all within the medley of races and religions, on the self-esteem that comes from individual and team effort." He thought it would be wrong to try to "dismember" this "good and caring America."[11] This confidence in America and its prospects did not come easily. It grew out of his experience of the basic decency of the American people and their willingness to reform when necessary and to defend the country and its values when threatened both by external and domestic dangers. Lerner's political pilgrimage—all the way from socialism to Reaganism—was made possible by his underlying conviction that what made America the very model of modernity was its inherent openness and constant ability to adapt to changing circumstances. In *America as a Civilization*, he rejected as incomplete all the formulaic explanations of America's success, such as the frontier, natural abundance, isolation, and ideology, both religious and secular. Instead, he argued that the key to understanding the civilization Americans had created is its special capacity for innovation and adaptation. It was this creative flexibility—"American dynamism"—which had enabled Americans to exploit the great resources of the continent, not the resources that inspired the character. Thanks to the contagion of this innovative spirit, the immigrants who were, like Lerner himself, the "wretched refuse" of the world's poorest regions, were able to achieve far more in the New World than they could possibly have in their native countries. Entrepreneurs, fortune-hunting explorers, inventors, scientists, and hard-working farmers, business men, and ordinary working people all found the country fertile ground for enterprise, creativity, and family building. Together, they had shown that poverty need not be the inevitable scourge of humanity and created an environment in which science and technology could be nurtured for human betterment. America had also encouraged a continuing quest for social reform. Inspired by the country's founding belief in individual liberty, those oppressed by traditional attitudes and institutions strove successfully to end slavery and religious bigotry and emancipate women from patriarchal servitude.

Lerner recognized that there was a dark side to American dynamism and reformism, but he was confident the problems they entailed would be surmounted. The very success of the country in unleashing entrepreneurial energies threatened to widen the gap between rich and poor and to create a permanent underclass. Liberation from old attitudes was bringing with it social instability. Revolutions in values engendered a host of social and cultural conflicts and pathologies. Despite the difficulties, he was buoyantly optimistic that the same capacity for adaptation that had empowered earlier generations of Americans would come to the rescue again. Well before others began to debate the "declinist thesis" Lerner ended *America as a Civilization* by raising and rejecting it.

The adaptive genius he thought so characteristically American helps explain the evolution of his own thinking. He was himself given to the pragmatic meliorism foreigners have often found so striking in America, Goethe's "land of unlimited possibilities." In the very eclecticism, openness, restlessness, and adaptability of his thinking and life, he was a specimen of the American character he discerned. To some extent, his changes of political viewpoint reflect an American enthusiasm for novelty and a fear of becoming outdated. As much as he deplored the worship of what William James had described as "the bitch goddess, success," a phrase he often quoted, he was himself drawn to the worship of that unholy goddess. As a teenager, he read and absorbed the message of the "rags to riches," "strive and succeed" novels of Horatio Alger. He wanted very much to be a success, not as an "economic royalist," for which career he had no gifts in any case, but as an intellectual conqueror who would gain control of the minds of his contemporaries rather as the titans of industry were gaining control of their material assets. He basked in his celebrity, even when it was tinged with mere notoriety, and was downcast when he had to admit to himself that his star was fading. He remained as cantankerously independent-minded as any of the frontiersman, robber barons, and cowboys celebrated in the American mythos. And although he was often very generous to others and concerned with their welfare, people who knew and admired him were sometimes shocked at how self-centered he could sometimes be when his own comfort was in question. "Sometimes," an intimate remarked, "he seemed to think the world could not exist without him." In his romantic escapades he was a kind of perpetual entrepreneur, a venture capitalist of the bedroom rather than the boardroom.

This is not to say that in his behavior or as a personality he was anything like the "average man" of his time, either in his public or private life. All who knew him agree that he had a prodigious degree of energy and vitality that sometimes seemed superhuman in its unflagging ambition and overflowing reach. Even late in life he would stay up nights, getting by on catnaps, writing his column, sketching new book projects, and preparing his lectures. Despite often debilitating illness, he prided himself on not missing a newspaper deadline until close to the end when pain killers made him too groggy to think or write. The same "life force" that enabled him to pursue his double career as a journalist and academic expressed itself in the amorous double life he led during both his marriages. To some extent the sexual adventurism was simply a deliberately open expression of the universal erotic impulse, no doubt reinforced by the Bohemian attitude of the avant-garde he acquired growing up in the 1920s, and of a masculine pride in sexual conquest, exacerbated by frustrations endured in adolescence and in his college years. Very likely it also reflected a keen desire to prove that he could make up by intellectual charisma what he lacked in matinee idol looks. And the fact that his amorous impulses were usually directed at non-Jewish women—the "daughters of the conquerors"—betrays a patent yearning to overcome the social handicap he felt as a cultural outsider. But even his adventurism became food for thought, an opportunity for self-analysis and social analysis aimed at deciphering the changing attitude toward the erotic in the 1960s and 1970s. Although he never completed the book he began to write on *Eros* in America, the hints about what he had come to think about the subject in fragmentary writings, interviews, and course notes indicate that he was drawn to a utopian belief in sexual liberation, even as he worried about its impact on the family and human dignity.

To appreciate Lerner at his best, he should be thought of as what he was most of all: a warm and passionate human being, a reflective commentator, a keen-eyed observer, an encyclopedic synthesizer, a gifted and prolific writer, and a captivating teacher—surely among the most inspiring of his time. In a life that stretched over almost the entire century, he was not only a witness to modern American history but an active participant in it, shaping and reflecting the attitudes of many of his fellow citizens. He was one of "the last intellectuals," as Russell Jacoby has described the relatively independent, broad-gauged mid-century thinkers who wrote for the general public.[12] With a few exceptions, they have been succeeded by narrower, university-based specialists who communicate more with each other than with a wider audience. Lerner wrote—in vivid, deliberately accessible prose—about politics and economics, history and constitutional law, international relations, education and culture, psychology and sexuality, moral values, and the family. In *Wrestling with the Angel,* he reflected upon aging, holistic healing, the struggle of the patient to maintain autonomy in the age of scientific medicine, and the state of his soul. He did not want to be confined to any one academic specialty, in the social sciences or history or philosophy, but, as he put it, to "smuggle ideas across the borders" of the disciplines.[13] He had great respect for the work of specialists and relied on their findings, but he saw his role to be that of a combiner and refiner, rather like the "interpreters of light" in Francis Bacon's *New Atlantis*. He was as concerned with the "hard realities" of economics and the medical approach to illness as he was with beliefs and mental states—realities that took shape in myths and symbols, in will rather than reason. He could be absorbed one minute in the study of the Supreme Court or the presidency, and the next in the "death dance of civilizations" or the "organismic character" of civilization.

This very eclecticism, which emboldened him to attempt a synoptic study of American life and thought, opened him to criticism. Especially in terms of academic standing, he paid a price for being a generalist. Had he pursued his early interest in judicial biography and constitutional law, he could easily have settled into a law school chair like his graduate mentor Walton Hamilton, who became a professor at the Yale Law School after the Brookings Graduate School closed. Lerner could have had a tenure-track appointment in political theory at Harvard when he decided instead to become political editor of *The Nation*. Other, more guild-oriented journalists sometimes saw him as an academic interloper—"the professor"—while some academics dismissed him as a mere journalist who wrote too glibly and about too many things to be taken seriously. But he was too restless to be satisfied either with a career as an academic specialist, devoted to what would have struck him as pedantic drudgery, or as a newspaper commentator so wholly absorbed in the daily flow of events as never to achieve perspective or depth. Like the romantic novelists and poets he read as an adolescent, he saw himself as an explorer of life determined to become one of its heroes of the intellect. He wanted to grasp the ideas and forces that controlled social interaction, to become an interpreter of great events, to experience passion in himself and others, to absorb all he could by reading widely and insatiably, and above all to make his mark upon the world by writing and teaching with originality and influence. What he conveyed most as a teacher was the sense that America remained "an unfinished country," open to what its energetic people could accomplish. Like other Americans he had a zest for all that was happening, he wanted to keep up with the times, not to fall behind. He also wanted to keep his balance, to be in favor of what was humane and against what seemed to be unruly, intolerant, and an appeal to violence. In his column and his other writings, he sought to take the measure, the pulse of his society, so as to praise its accomplishments and warn against its failings. Throughout he was on the side of ordinary people, wanting to see things done for their benefit, even as he admired the powerful, especially when they used their power for the common good.

His failings were the failings endemic to a political culture with a narrowly defined ideological spectrum and a pragmatic bent. His openness to all points of view could make him seem inconsistent, shifting with the electorate from left-of-center to right-of-center. Although, like other Americans, he prided himself on being autonomous, he was in some respects an example of the modern personality type identified by David Riesman as "other directed"— an actor anxious to please his audience, ready to take his cues from those he sought to reach. His early analysis of America suffered most from a failure—common among his Progressive mentors and peers—to appreciate the hold of the country's founding Lockian dogma and the strength of its free-market economy. When he finally recognized that American political ideology was too fervently individualist to change fundamentally, and that the free market remained a force to be reckoned with, he embraced the liberalism of the New Deal he had earlier seen as transitional. His interest in the psychology of the person in the later years did not reflect his belief that the transition to a postindustrial society had resolved old social issues so much as curiosity about what was happening to American society as economic issues became less salient. By focusing on the changes in lifestyle that so many seemed to be adopting, he thought he might discern some larger trend. In the 1960s and 1970s, America seemed to him to have become "a more hedonic society, less restrained by its Puritan origins and traditions than at any time before or since." By the 1980s, however, sexuality no longer held so central a place in the national psyche. Therapists reported a concern with the waning of desire. The society continued to be pleasure oriented, but pleasure was experienced as a staple of everyday life, much like work and recreation.[14] Lerner had second thoughts about the strength and durability of the sexual revolution, and he saw the country righting the balance with a new stress on family values and the need for a more cohesive civil society. He and his countrymen had come full cycle, longing for a return of the warmth and sense of community of their immigrant forebears. Lerner would not live to see the fin de siècle, but had he done so he would have had no doubt that American society would survive any inner malaise typical of such periods as it had the economic depression of his younger years. He would have been supremely confident that Americans would continue to exhibit a will to live vigorously, and to adapt, just as he had in his own life, and that their country would remain the world's promised land—for all who saw it, as he did, as the unfolding of a vision of liberty and equality and of joyful work and creativity. He would surely want to be remembered for sharing fervently the attitude toward life of his hero, Justice Holmes:

> Life is a roar of bargain and battle, but in the very heart of it there rises a mystic spiritual tone that gives meaning to the whole. It transmutes the dull details into romance. It reminds us that our only but wholly adequate significance is as parts of the unimaginable whole. It suggests that even while we think that we are egotists we are living to ends outside ourselves.[15]

ACKNOWLEDGMENTS

For help in preparing this book I am indebted most of all to Max Lerner's family—his widow, Edna, and the children, Connie Lerner Russell, Joanna Townsend, and Steve, Michael, and Adam Lerner. They all cheerfully submitted to interviews and made available letters, personal diaries, documents, and photographs. The documents include a memoir intended as the first volume of an autobiography. Along with a videotape kindly provided by Max Lerner's granddaughter, Daria Doering, it is the source for Chapter 1 and otherwise unattributed quotations. Adam Lerner's wife, Beth Warach, took the photograph of the portrait of Max Lerner by Marion Greenwood.

I am also grateful to various of Lerner's friends, associates, and former students. Evelyn Irsay, who was his reliable secretary at the *New York Post,* also came to my rescue by supplying copies of his *Post* columns. Martin Peretz was helpful and encouraging. Hugh Hefner generously provided the typescripts of interviews and other documents referred to in Chapter 8, as well as photographs and recollections. The Lerners' photographer friend Mary Morris Laurence delved into her collection and kindly gave me permission to use several of the photos. James MacGregor Burns shared his recollections. Others interviewed in the course of the research were

Edward Albee, Marvin and Mary Ellin Barrett, Arnold Beichman, Mary Ellen Brooks, Mary Duncan, Jody Fischer, Frank and Fritzie Manuel, and James Allen Smith.

I am also indebted to others for their generous help in other respects. Arthur Schlesinger, Jr., of the City University of New York and Jean Edward Smith of the University of Toronto made helpful comments on the penultimate version of the manuscript. Earlier draft chapters were read by Anita Safran, Sheila Tobias, Albert and Claire Harmon, and my wife Evelyn. Susan McGrath of the Brookings Institution located rare photos of Walton Hamilton. Hendrik Hertzberg was instrumental in arranging for the use of the *New Yorker* cartoon by F. B. Modell, who generously agreed to allow it to be reproduced. Erin Robertson served as my research assistant. Ginnah Saunders helped with secretarial chores. Robert Schmuhl of the University of Notre Dame shared tape recordings he had made of interviews with Max Lerner. My friend John de la Mothe of the University of Ottawa checked a research query.

Finally, I am especially grateful to the expert and imaginative editors at the University of Chicago Press—John Tryneski, Randy Petilos, and Lila Weinberg—who have brought this project to fruition.

I am indebted also to several institutions. The Max Lerner Papers are collected at Yale University. I thank the Manuscripts and Archives Division of the Sterling Library at Yale University for permission to use and quote from the Max Lerner Papers and for the staff's courtesy to a visitor. References to "YMA" are to this division; the numbers that follow are to series, box, and folder. I am grateful to the Brookings Institution for permitting me to see and make use of the Lerner files at the Robert Brookings Graduate School. This material is referred to as "Brookings file." The UCLA library kindly supplied microfilms. The Brandeis University library supplied photographs from its archives. As always I am especially indebted to the research, circulation, and interlibrary loan staffs of the Geisel Library at UCSD.

Preface

1. *Time Magazine,* April 25, 1960.

2. From a remarkably stirring Memorial Day speech by Holmes to an audience of Civil War veterans in New Hampshire in 1884, in Max Lerner, ed., *The Mind and Faith of Justice Holmes* (New York: Modern Library, 1943), pp. 9–16. Lerner drew upon Holmes's observation in entitling a volume of his columns *Actions and Passions.*

3. Preface to Lerner, *It Is Later than You Think* (New Brunswick, N.J.: Transaction Books, 1989), p. viii.

4. Letter, February 9, 1943, YMA, I, 1, 32.

5. John Gunther, *Inside USA* (New York: Harper and Brothers, 1947), p. 552.

6. Letter, December 20, 1951, YMA, I, 41, 195.

7. Reagan's comment was passed on to Lerner by Nixon's assistant John Taylor, according to Robert Schmuhl, "The Wit and Wisdom of Max Lerner," *The Quill* (November 1988): 35.

8. Letter, June 23, 1969, YMA, I, 9, 450.

9. *The Plain Dealer,* January 1, 1968.

10. Sanford Lakoff, "The Mind and Faith of Max Lerner," *Social Research* 61, no. 2 (Summer 1994): 245–268.

11. *New York Post,* December 11, 1961.

Chapter Two

1. George W. Pierson, *Yale: A Short History* (New Haven: Office of the Secretary, Yale University, 1979), p. 11.

2. Quoted in George W. Pierson, *Yale: College and University,* vol. 1: *Yale College: An Educational History, 1871–1921* (New Haven: Yale University Press, 1952), p. 8.

3. George W. Pierson, *Yale: College and University,* vol. 2: *Yale: The University College 1921–1937* (New Haven: Yale University Press, 1955), p. 523. Although political science had been taught at the college in one form or another for some time, the first two faculty members with degrees in political science were appointed in 1924.

4. President Angell, quoted in ibid., p. 23.

5. Pierson, *Yale: A Short History,* p. 41.

6. Ibid., p. 57.

7. Pierson, *Yale: College and University,* 1 : 19.

8. Ibid., 2 : 61.

9. Jacob Dinnerstein, *Anti-Semitism in America* (New York: Oxford University Press, 1994), pp. 80–81, 102.

10. Daniel Oren, *Joining the Club* (New Haven: Yale University Press, 1985), p. 116.

11. Dinnerstein, *Anti-Semitism in America,* pp. 40–41.

12. Ibid., pp. 84–85.

13. Oren, *Joining the Club,* p. 48.

14. Ibid., pp. 86–87.

15. Max Lerner, *Wrestling with the Angel* (New York: Norton, 1990), p. 165.

16. Max Lerner, "Veblen and the Wasteland," *Ideas Are Weapons* (New York: Viking Press, 1939), p. 123.

17. Lerner, "Recipe for an American Genius," *Ideas Are Weapons,* p. 120.

18. James Allen Smith, *Brookings at Seventy-Five* (Washington, D.C.: Brookings Institution, 1991), p. 21.

19. Brookings file.

20. Ibid.

21. Ibid.

22. Max Lerner, "The Economic Theories of Thorstein Veblen: An Analysis and Criticism," typescript, p. 102, YMA, III, 98, 2105.

23. Ibid., p. 111.

24. Max Lerner, editor's introduction to *The Portable Veblen* (New York: Viking Press, 1948), p. 16. See also Thorstein Veblen, *The Engineers and the Price System* (New York, 1921), pp. 138–169. For a comparison of Veblen's views with those of other theorists of industrial society see Sanford Lakoff, "The Third Culture: Science in Social Thought," in *Knowledge and Power: Essays in Science and Government,* ed. Lakoff (New York: Free Press, 1966), pp. 1–61.

25. Lerner, *The Portable Veblen,* p. 35. In an equally valuable but more critical commentary on Veblen, David Riesman describes Lerner's introductory essay

as "one of the best sympathetic statements on Veblen to be found" (David Riesman, *Thorstein Veblen: A Critical Interpretation* [New York: Charles Scribner's Sons, 1953]). For a perceptive analysis of Veblen's economic thinking from a later perspective see Douglas Dowd, *Thorstein Veblen* (New York: Washington Square Press, 1966).

26. Brookings file.

27. Ibid.

28. Donald T. Critchlow, *The Brookings Institution, 1916–1952* (DeKalb: Northern Illinois Press, 1985), pp. 41–42.

29. Ibid., pp. 57–58.

30. Ibid., p. 76.

31. Brookings file.

32. Critchlow, *The Brookings Institution, 1916–1952*, p. 77.

33. Brookings file.

34. Ibid.

35. Ibid.

36. Ibid.

37. Critchlow, *The Brookings Institution, 1916–1952*, p. 78.

38. Ibid., p. 77.

39. Ibid., pp. 75–76.

40. Ibid., p. 81.

41. For the later history see Smith, *Brookings at Seventy-Five.*

Chapter Three

1. Alvin Johnson, *Pioneer's Progress* (New York: Viking Press, 1952), p. 309.

2. Letter from Anita Lerner to Joanna Townsend (n.d.).

3. Ibid.

4. Ibid.

5. *New York Post*, April 26, 1965.

6. Letter from Anita Lerner to Joanna Townsend (n.d.).

7. Ronald Steel, *Walter Lippmann and the American Century*, pp. 291–292.

8. Elinor Langer, *Josephine Herbst* (Boston: Little, Brown, 1984), pp. 126–142.

9. Letter, July 27, 1937, YMA, I, 3, 120.

10. Letter, April 9, 1936, YMA, I, 3, 117.

11. Letter, April 10, 1936, YMA, I, 3, 117.

12. Letter, August 7, 1936, YMA, I, 3, 117.

13. Letter, April 25, 1945, YMA, I, 3, 128.

14. Letter, October 26, 1950, YMA, I, 33, 133.

15. *PM*, May 31, 1943.

16. After he was fired as political editor of *The Nation*, Lerner sharply attacked the "sickness" of Villard's "paleo-liberalism" in a review of Villard's memoirs in *The New Republic* in 1939, reprinted in Lerner's *Ideas Are Weapons* (1939). According to a diary entry by Lerner, Villard had his revenge when he warned

the History Department at Northwestern University, which was considering an appointment for Lerner, that he was not only unsound in his radicalism but corrupt in his morals—a reference to the breakup of Lerner's first marriage.

17. Letter, April 27, 1938, YMA, I, 3, 122. In the *Erie* decision, Justice Brandeis, writing for the Court, overthrew a long-standing precedent by declaring that the Supreme Court was bound by the rule of law established in a state where a cause of action had originated—thus effectively curbing the Court's discretionary authority.

18. Max Lerner, "The Great Constitutional War: A Perspective," draft typescript, pp. 3–8.

19. Ibid., p. 12.

20. Ibid., pp. 17–18.

21. Max Lerner, "The Supreme Court and American Capitalism," *Yale Law Journal* 42 (March 1933): 668–701; reprinted in Lerner's *Ideas Are Weapons* and elsewhere.

22. Max Lerner, "John Marshall's Long Shadow," *The New Republic*, September 18, 1935, pp. 148–152; reprinted in Lerner's *Ideas Are Weapons*.

23. Max Lerner, "Taney Redivivus," *American Historical Review* 42, no. 2 (January 1938): 415–418; reprinted in Lerner's *Ideas Are Weapons*.

Chapter Four

1. Lerner, "Introduction," *The Portable Veblen*, p. 39.

2. October 10, 1941, YMA, I, 5, 322.

3. Kirchwey paid $15,000 outright, using money her husband had inherited, and another $15,000 she borrowed interest free from a foundation set up by Wertheim. See Sara Alpern, *Freda Kirchwey: A Woman of the Nation* (Cambridge, Mass.: Harvard University Press, 1987), p. 112.

4. Letter, March 9, 1938, YMA, I, 1, 20.

5. Quoted by Lerner in his memoir.

6. Lerner, "Introduction" to Niccolò Machiavelli, *The Prince* and *The Discourses* (New York: Modern Library, 1940), p. xxv.

7. Letter from James M. Burns to the author.

8. Ibid.

9. Letter, June 20, 1944, YMA, I, 22, 45.

10. Sidney Hook, "On Ideas," *Partisan Review* 7 (March–April 1940): 52–60.

11. Lerner, review of Laski, *The Rise of Liberalism* (1936), reprinted in Lerner, *Ideas Are Weapons*, pp. 343–347.

12. Lerner, *It Is Later than You Think* (New York: Viking Press, 1943 [1938]), p. 77.

13. Ibid.

14. I. F. Stone, "Max Lerner's Capitalist Collectivism," *The Southern Review* 10, no. 4 (Spring 1939): 649.

15. Ibid., p. 662.

16. Sidney Hook, "The Anatomy of the Popular Front," *Partisan Review* 6 (Spring 1939): 29–45.

17. Max Lerner, "Can Communists and Non-Communists Unite? A Discussion by A. B. Magil and Max Lerner," *New Masses* 48, no. 2, July 13, 1943, p. 5.

18. Letter from Anita Lerner to Joanna Townsend (n.d.).

19. Possibly a reference to Alter Brody, *Behind the Polish-Soviet Break* (New York: Soviet Russia Today, 1940), to which Lamont had written an introduction.

20. Probably a reference to Stone's recently published review of *It Is Later than You Think*, "Max Lerner's Capitalist Collectivism," *Southern Review* 4 (Spring 1939), criticizing Lerner for advocating a "planned capitalism" more likely to lead to fascism than socialism. The review is cited in Robert C. Cottrell, *Izzy: A Biography of I. F. Stone* (New Brunswick, N.J.: Rutgers University Press), p. 74.

21. *Los Angeles Times*, February 11, 1975.

22. Samuel Sillen, "The Irrationals," *New Masses*, October 29, 1940, p. 22.

23. Sidney Hook, *Out of Step: An Unquiet Life in the 20th Century* (New York: Harper and Row, 1987), pp. 264–266.

24. Jacob Dinnerstein, *Anti-Semitism in America*, pp. 108–109.

25. Letter, October 24, 1936, YMA, I, 5, 221.

26. Dinnerstein, *Anti-Semitism in America*, p. 112.

27. Memorandum of a discussion at a conference called by Justice Felix Frankfurter in Washington, D.C., April 10, 1939, YMA, I, 3, 119.

28. Letter to Julian W. Mack, quoted in Dinnerstein, *Anti-Semitism in America*, p. 125.

29. September 10, 1941, YMA, I, 5, 392.

30. See David S. Wyman, *The Abandonment of the Jews: America and the Holocaust 1941–1945* (New York: Pantheon, 1984), pp. 13–15.

Chapter Five

1. A. J. Liebling, "The Wayward Press," *The New Yorker*, February 17, 1949, YMA, III, 97, 2092

2. Roy Hoopes, *Ralph Ingersoll: A Biography*, foreword by Max Lerner (New York: Atheneum, 1985), p. 188n.

3. Ibid., p. 216.

4. Paul Milkman, *PM: A New Deal in Journalism, 1940–1948* (New Brunswick, N.J.: Rutgers University Press, 1997), pp. 38–39.

5. Ibid., p. 217.

6. Milkman, *PM: A New Deal in Journalism, 1940–1948*, pp. 45–46.

7. *PM*, October 3, 1943.

8. Ingersoll, memo, December 21, 1940, YMA, III, 97, 2093.

9. Hoopes, *Ralph Ingersoll: A Biography*, pp. 220–221.

10. Ibid., pp. 241–242.

11. Ibid., p. 246.

12. Ibid., p. 254. Through Marshall Field III, *PM* may well have had a more lasting indirect effect in Chicago. At the same time as Field took on *PM*, he also became the publisher of the *Chicago Sun*, another liberal tabloid which sought to balance the pictorial and reportorial sides of journalism.

13. Ibid., p. 261.

14. Ibid., p. 272.

15. Liebling, "The Wayward Press," pp. 54–55, YMA, III, 97, 2092.

16. *PM*, November 11, 1943.

17. Along with the *New York Post, PM* was the only New York newspaper consistently supportive of FDR. It reported sympathetically on strikes and struggles over labor legislation. It was instrumental in publicizing a successful campaign to win jobs for blacks as city bus drivers. Its sports writers helped pressure baseball owners to break the color bar against black athletes and warmly supported the Brooklyn Dodgers owner, Branch Rickey, when he signed Jackie Robinson. Milkman, *PM: A New Deal in Journalism, 1940–1948,* provides a detailed, accurate, and properly appreciative account of *PM*'s efforts on behalf of these causes.

18. *PM*, May 16, 1944.

19. Robert C. Tucker, ed., *The Marx-Engels Reader* (New York: Norton, 1972), p. 436. The whole affair, Marx remarked famously, was a reminder of Hegel's aphorism that all great world-historical facts and personages appear twice: "the first time as tragedy, the second as farce."

20. *PM*, February 1, 1944.

21. See his *The Coming American Fascism* (New York: Harper, 1936).

22. *PM*, September 16, 1943.

23. *PM*, April 6, 1943.

24. *PM*, April 14, 1944.

25. *PM*, May 1, 1944.

26. *PM*, July 21, 1943.

27. *PM*, July 7, 1943.

28. Lerner, *It Is Later than You Think*, pp. xvii–xviii.

29. Ibid., p. xli

30. December 10, 1943, YMA, I, 1, 12.

31. Letter, January 6, 1945, YMA, I, 1, 11.

32. Letter, February 9, 1943, YMA, I, 1,32.

33. Letter, December 22, 1968, YMA, I, 1, 34.

34. Letter, June 23, 1944, YMA, I, 1, 45.

35. Letter, April 12, 1942, YMA, I, 5, 223.

36. *PM*, April 12, 1945.

37. *PM*, February 14, 1945.

38. Max Lerner, "Russia and the Future," *The Atlantic Monthly* (November 1942): 79–87.

39. *PM*, March 2, 1944.

40. *PM*, July 1, 1943.

41. Ibid.

42. *PM*, September 6, 1944.

43. *PM*, April 3, 1947.

44. Letter, April 7, 1947, YMA, I, 5, 224. The verdict in the trial had left Laski shaken and demoralized. See the detailed account in Isaac Kramnick and Barry Sheerman, *Harold Laski: A Life on the Left* (London: Allen Lane, 1993), pp. 516–543.

45. Letter, August 28, 1948, YMA, I, 3, 131.

46. Letter, January 23, 1947, YMA, I, 7, 360.

47. *PM*, February 1, 1948

48. *PM*, February 8, 1948.

49. Letter, January 18, 1948, YMA, I, 7, 362.

50. Letter, April 16, 1946, YMA, I, 1, 16.

51. Ibid.

52. Letter, November 15, 1948, YMA, I, 7, 360.

53. Letter, February 10, 1948, YMA, I, 1, 12.

54. Letter, August 16, 1948, YMA, I, 5, 224.

55. Letter, November 22, 1943, YMA, I, 3, 126.

56. Ronald Steel, *Walter Lippmann and the American Century,* pp. 391, 416.

57. Edwin M. Yoder, Jr., *Joe Alsop's Cold War* (Chapel Hill: University of North Carolina Press, 1993), p. 7.

58. William O'Neill, *A Better World: The Great Schism; Stalinism and the American Intellectuals* (New York: Simon and Schuster, 1992), pp. 30, 30.

59. Ibid., p. 49.

60. Ibid., p. 70n.

61. Lerner, *It Is Later than You Think,* p. 71.

62. Ibid., p. 44.

63. A. B. Magil, "Max Lerner's Credo," *New Masses* 30, no. 9, February 21, 1939, p. 25.

Chapter Six

1. Irving Howe, *World of Our Fathers* (New York: Harcourt Brace, 1976), p. 24.

2. Abram L. Sachar, *A Host at Last* (Boston: Little, Brown: 1976).

3. Ibid., pp. 197–200.

4. See Lawrence A. Fuchs, *The Political Behavior of American Jews* (Glencoe, Ill.: Free Press, 1956).

5. Howe, *World of Our Fathers,* p. 623.

6. *America and the Intellectuals: A Symposium* (*Partisan Review,* ser. no. 4, 1953): 64–67.

7. Ibid., p. 65

8. Max Lerner, *America as a Civilization: Life and Thought in the United States Today* (New York: Simon and Schuster, 1957), p. 958. (Reprinted with a new postscript chapter; New York: Henry Holt, 1987.)

9. New School memorial, tape recording.

10. Lerner, *America as a Civilization,* p. 715.

11. Ibid., p. 59.

12. Ibid., p. 61.

13. Ibid., p. 25.

14. Ibid., p. 27.

15. Ibid., pp. 23–25.

16. Ibid., p. 103

17. Ibid., p. 31.

18. Ibid., pp. 61-62.
19. Ibid., p. 62.
20. Ibid., p. 63.
21. Ibid., p. 68.
22. Ibid., pp. 71-73.
23. Ibid., pp. 525-537.
24. Ibid., p. 113.
25. Ibid., p. 611.
26. Ibid., pp. 516-521.
27. Ibid., p. 626.
28. Ibid., p. 102.
29. Ibid., p. 585.
30. Ibid., p. 725.
31. Ibid., pp. 317-322.
32. Ibid., pp. 324-325.
33. Ibid., p. 326.
34. Ibid., pp. 334-338.
35. Ibid., p. 451.
36. Ibid., p. 363.
37. Ibid., p. 536.
38. September 6, 1955, YMA, I, 9, 461.
39. Letter, January 25, 1955, YMA, I, 4, 207.
40. Ibid.
41. Letter, November 23, 1957, YMA, I, 2, 79.
42. Letter, December 5 [1957], YMA, I, 8, 415.
43. Letter, November 15, 1955, YMA, I, 4, 172.
44. [1955] YMA, I, 7, 361.
45. Lerner, *America as a Civilization*, p. 730.
46. Ibid., p. 950.

Chapter Seven

1. Letter, April 5, 1949, YMA, I, 2, 85.
2. Max Lerner, "Walter Lippmann," in *Ideas Are Weapons*, p. 187.
3. *New York Post*, April 9, 1973.
4. Ibid., May 8, 1967.
5. Letter, December 14, 1949, YMA, I, 16, 7.
6. *New York Post*, February 23, 1976
7. Max Lerner, *The Unfinished Country* (New York: Simon and Schuster, 1959), pp. xv-xvii.
8. Letter to Alfred E. Cohn, December 10, 1948, YMA, I, 2, 74.
9. Note [1968], YMA, I, 2, 53.
10. Letter, May 2, 1968, YMA, I, 2, 53.
11. Letter, May 16, 1968, YMA, I, 2, 53.
12. *New York Post*, February 9, 1960.
13. Ibid., March 8, 1960.

14. Ibid., January 11, 1960.

15. Ibid., August 20, 1965.

16. Ibid., March 18, 1968

17. Ibid., July 27, 1973.

18. Ibid., August 12, 1974.

19. Ibid., February 11, 1970.

20. Ibid., April 4, 1979.

21. Ibid., August 31, 1970.

22. Ibid., November 19, 1965.

23. Ibid., January 16, 1978.

24. Ibid., January 31, 1979.

25. Ibid., November 12, 1963.

26. Ibid., November 16, 1964.

27. [1962] YMA, III, 97, 2098.

28. Letter, September 28, 1966, YMA, I, 1, 3.

29. Letter [1956], YMA, I, 9, 455.

30. Letter, May 3, 1950, YMA, I, 2, 69.

31. [1945?] YMA, III, 96, 2091.

32. Norman Cousins, "View of a Columnist's Cosmos," *Saturday Review of Literature,* January 9, 1960, p. 21.

33. Letter, April 7, 1962.

34. Kitty Kelley, *Elizabeth Taylor, the Last Star* (New York: Simon and Schuster, 1981), pp. 182–187.

35. Ibid.

36. Ibid.

37. Max Lerner, "Return of the Femme Fatale," *Ladies' Home Journal* (June 1963): 80–81.

38. *New York Post,* May 31, 1961.

39. Letter, May 7, 1952, YMA I, 3, 35.

40. *New York Post,* July 25, 1961.

41. Max Lerner, *The Age of Overkill* (New York: Simon and Schuster, 1962), pp. 77.

42. Letter, February 24, 1956, YMA, I, 9, 422.

43. Letter, March 1, 1956, YMA, I, 9, 422. Thompson was undeterred and unrepentant; she continued to claim that all American political leaders were "in the pockets of the Zionists" and to cooperate with other American opponents of Israel. See Peter Kurth, *American Cassandra: The Life of Dorothy Thompson* (Boston: Little, Brown, 1990), pp. 422–430.

44. Lerner, *The Unfinished Country,* p. 395.

45. Ibid., pp. 425–426.

46. *New York Post,* January 4, 1960.

47. Ibid., June 1, 1960.

48. Ibid., June 12, 1960.

49. Ibid., January 11, 1961.

50. Ibid., April 21, 1961.

51. Ibid., May 10, 1961.

52. Ibid., February 20, 1962.

53. Ibid., November 5, 1963.

54. Ibid., March 4, 1964.

55. Ibid., May 22, 1964.

56. Harrison Salisbury, *Without Fear or Favor* (New York: Times Books, 1980), p. 42.

57. *New York Post*, May 7, 1965.

58. Ibid., April 19, 1965.

59. *Harvard Crimson*, March 9, 1965.

60. Letter, March 9, 1965.

61. Letter, March 12, 1965.

62. *New York Post*, August 1, 1966.

63. Ibid., July 24, 1967.

64. Ibid., August 18, 1967.

65. Ibid., November 20, 1967.

66. Ibid., November 28, 1969.

67. Ibid., September 8, 1967.

68. Ibid., November 7, 1970.

69. *New York Post*, December 29, 1969.

70. Ibid., January 26, 1970.

71. Ibid., January 28, 1970.

72. Ibid., November 12, 1969.

73. "Sorel's Bestiary," *Ramparts* (January 1967): 7.

74. Ibid. (February 1967): 6.

75. *New York Post*, November 7, 1970.

76. Ibid., October 10, 1977.

77. Ibid., June 16, 1961.

78. Ibid., February 13, 1961.

79. Ibid., October 5, 1970.

Chapter Eight

1. "Conversation with Hugh Hefner," October 25, 1988, typescript, p. 86.

2. *New York Post*, June 10, 1974.

3. Ibid., February 28, 1977.

4. Max Lerner, "The Years Are Not Such a Heavy Burden," *Next* (1981): 45.

5. *New York Post*, March 10, 1971.

6. Ibid., October 18, 1972.

7. Letter to Edna Lerner, June 8, 1971.

8. Max Lerner, *Wrestling with the Angel*, p. 22.

9. *New York Post*, January 10, 1979.

10. Interview with Larry Dubois, April 30, 1985, typescript, p. 24.

11. *New York Post*, January 10, 1979.

12. Interview with Dubois.

13. Ibid.

14. Interview with Lynch/Frost, April 19, 1991, typescript, p. 7.

15. "Conversation with Hugh Hefner."

16. See Gregory Bateson, *Steps to an Ecology of the Mind* (San Francisco: Chandler Publishing Co., 1972), 206–212.

17. *New York Post,* January 10, 1979

18. Interview with Lynch/Frost.

19. "Conversation with Hugh Hefner."

20. Interview with Murray Fisher, April 30, 1989, typescript, p. 55.

21. *New York Post,* February 5, 1975.

22. Peter Bogdanovich, *The Killing of the Unicorn: Dorothy Stratten (1960–1980)* (New York: W. W. Morrow, 1984).

23. Interview with Lynch/Frost.

24. *New York Post,* July 6, 1989.

25. Interview with Lynch/Frost.

26. Gay Talese, *Thy Neighbor's Wife* (Garden City, N.Y.: Doubleday, 1980), p. 28.

27. Lerner, *America as a Civilization,* p. 688.

28. Prospectus for *Eros in America,* typescript.

29. Max Lerner, "Desire and Power in the White House," ms., n.d.

30. Letter to the author from Hugh Hefner; Barbara Rowes, "Liberal Admirers, Don't Ask Where Max Lerner Is Coming From: It's Hefner's Hutch," *People,* March 12, 1979, pp. 49–56.

31. Talese, *Thy Neighbor's Wife,* p. 513.

32. Ibid., pp. 520–521.

33. *New York Post,* June 10, 1974.

34. Ibid., April 8, 1977.

Chapter Nine

1. *New York Post,* March 24, 1980.

2. Ibid., November 6, 1980.

3. Ibid., March 22, 1991.

4. Ibid., April 20, 1991.

5. Ibid., November 15, 1980.

6. Ibid., November 10, 1980.

7. Ibid., January 26, 1980.

8. Ibid., January 24, 1981.

9. Ibid., February 22, 1981.

10. Ibid., February 25, 1981.

11. Ibid., May 1, 1981.

12. Ibid., February 18, 1982. For a critical view of the SDI in general and the Reagan administration's reinterpretation of the ABM Treaty in particular, see Sanford Lakoff and Herbert F. York, *A Shield in Space? Technology, Politics, and the Strategic Defense Initiative* (Berkeley: University of California Press, 1989).

13. *New York Post,* June 15, 1990.

14. Ibid., September 15, 1987.

15. Ibid., March 25, 1981.

16. Ibid., January 9, 1989.

17. Ibid., January 17, 1989.

18. Ibid., December 21, 1991.

19. Ibid., November 23, 1991.

20. Ibid., September 13, 1982.

21. Ibid., March 25, 1985.

22. Ibid., March 25, 1989.

23. Lerner, *America as a Civilization*, p. 619. (Reprinted with a new post-script chapter; New York: Henry Holt, 1987.)

24. *New York Post*, December 18, 1952. Reprinted in *The Unfinished Country* (New York: Simon and Schuster, 1959), pp. 70–71.

25. Ibid., December 10, 1967.

26. Ibid., February 11, 1970.

27. Ibid., June 7, 1971.

28. Ibid., June 13, 1973.

29. Letter to the author from Steve D. Lerner.

30. Michael Lerner, *Choices in Healing: Integrating the Best of Conventional and Complementary Approaches to Cancer* (Cambridge, Mass: MIT Press, 1994).

31. He is the author of *Eco-Pioneers: Practical Visionaries Solving Today's Environmental Problems* (Cambridge, Mass.: MIT Press, 1997).

32. *New York Post*, December 4, 1972.

33. Max Lerner, "The Interplay of the Generations," *Notre Dame Magazine* (Spring 1985): 30.

34. Notebook entry dated January 4, 1976.

35. Max Lerner, *Wrestling with the Angel*, p. 25.

36. Ibid., p. 50.

37. Ibid., p. 82.

38. Ibid., p. 109.

39. Ibid., p. 156.

40. Ibid., p. 161.

41. Ibid., p. 164.

42. Ibid., p. 166.

43. Ibid., p. 178.

44. Letter to the author from Hugh Hefner.

45. Martin Peretz, "Sane Max: A Remembrance," *The New Republic*, June 29, 1992, pp. 9–11.

46. Lerner, *Wrestling with the Angel*, p. 195.

Chapter Ten

1. *New York Post*, May 31, 1972.

2. John Winthrop, "A Modell of Christian Charity," in Robert Isaak, ed., *American Political Thinking* (Fort Worth: Harcourt Brace, 1994), p. 35.

3. Quoted in Charles Firth, *Oliver Cromwell and the Rule of the Puritans in England* (London: Oxford University Press, 1953 [1900]), p. 36.

4. Irving Howe, *World of Our Fathers*, pp. 83, 287.

5. Lerner, *America as a Civilization,* pp. 510–511. (Reprinted with a new postscript chapter; New York: Henry Holt, 1987.)

6. Max Lerner, "The Titans," typescript.

7. *New York Post,* March 25, 1989.

8. Lerner, *The Age of Overkill,* p. 35.

9. *New York Post,* July 4, 1971.

10. Lerner, *America as a Civilization,* p. 1008.

11. *New York Post,* June 14, 1991.

12. Russell Jacoby, *The Last Intellectuals: American Culture in the Age of Academe* (New York: Basic Books, 1987).

13. Quoted in Robert Schmuhl, "A Man with Five Lives," *Notre Dame Magazine* (Autumn 1988): 34.

14. Lerner, *America as a Civilization,* pp. 989–990.

15. Speech for the fiftieth anniversary reunion of the Harvard class of 1861, June 28, 1911, *The Mind and Faith of Justice Holmes,* p. 27.

INDEX